East Hill Farm

East Hill Farm
SEASONS WITH ALLEN GINSBERG

Gordon Ball

COUNTERPOINT
BERKELEY

Candy O'Brien was Candy Mills in the author's *'66 Frames: A Memoir*. She now goes by the name Stella Jane. Some other names have been changed to protect identities.

Library of Congress Cataloging-in-Publication Data is available.

ISBN: 978-1-58243-776-7

Cover design by Silverander Communications
Interior design by meganjonesdesign.com

Printed in the United States of America

COUNTERPOINT
1919 Fifth Street
Berkeley, CA 94710
www.counterpointpress.com

Distributed by Publishers Group West

10 9 8 7 6 5 4 3 2 1

To Kathleen

East Hill Farm

THANK YOU

M UCH OF WHAT is good in these pages is due to the generosity of others. I
first drafted small sections of this book over a quarter century ago, feeling
fortunate to have retained cherished memories, movie footage, diaries, photographs,
taperecordings, correspondence, and artifacts from my three years (1968–1971) at
Allen Ginsberg's farm five miles from Cherry Valley, New York. But in time interven-
ing I've become even more fortunate to have the help of a great many people in a great
range of ways, and it is thanks to them that this book is now a reality.

My largest debt of all is to my wife Kathleen, who year-in and year-out read or
listened to countless drafts, rightly chastising me when my writing was below the
mark, yet finding every opportunity to encourage: when I despaired of my book ever
seeing print, she'd always assure me of its importance. My daughter Daisy must've
wondered at my long hours in the study, or return trips to New York and Cherry
Valley and beyond, or spates of long distance calls to people I'd not seen for decades,
but she seems to have taken it all with some measure of faith, tolerance, and humor.
Many years later during final stages of composition she made thoughtful comments.

At the office of the Allen Ginsberg Estate, Peter Hale has been ever helpful,
making available needed materials and offering pertinent counsel. Bob Rosenthal,
Allen's secretary of many years, was always responsive, extending himself by providing information and documents, translating Hebrew, and hosting me in his home and
on East Hill.

Among Ginsberg scholars, I offer great thanks to biographers Bill Morgan,
Michael Schumacher, and Barry Miles, all of whom have shared valuable material. Bill
read with enthusiasm the first long draft of the manuscript years ago, and has gone far
beyond friendship's call in offering every kind of advice and information ever since.
Michael studied a later draft, offered detailed suggestions, and patiently answered my
every query. Miles, whom I first befriended on East Hill in 1970, shared his journals
with me, and hosted Daisy and me for a week at his home in the south of France,
where he offered oral recollections as well. My presentation of several farm and farm-
related events would've been impossible without his allowing my use of his accounts.

Here at home in Lexington, Virginia, I'm especially indebted to two truly generous colleagues in the Department of English and Fine Arts at the Virginia Military

Institute: Alan Baragona and John Leland provided sound literary judgment and suggestions for a needy colleague who saw them much more frequently, I'm sure, than they ever wished. Alan, like Michael Brickler, Head of Media Services at VMI's Preston Library, was also extremely helpful technologically, including the conversion of photographic prints, some nearly a half-century old, to digital images. My department head Emily Miller was always supportive of my work, as was Peggy Herring. VMI's Research Committee, Faculty Development Committee, and Associate Dean Robert McDonald provided a great range of assistance, including faculty development leave and travel to Cherry Valley and Stanford University. At VMI's Preston Library I wish to thank especially Megan Newman, Cathy Wells, Janet Holly, Tonya Moore, Gwen Sichol, Accacia Flanagan, Brittany Robertson, and Susan Hastings.

A number of people whose lives intersected with mine on East Hill generously added to my store of memories, including Peter Orlovsky, Stephen Bornstein, Bonnie Bremser (Brenda Frazer), Gregory Corso, Edith Ginsberg, Robert Creeley, Carl La Salle, John Giorno, Stella Jane, Judy Cannon (who also hosted me on a return trip), Jon Sholle, Susan Brustman, Lawrence Ferlinghetti, Penny Rand, Nora Crain, Gary Snyder, Charles and Pamela Plymell, Lucien Carr, Wayne Graham, Charlene Graham Talbot, Michael Aldrich, Rosebud Pettet, Eugene and Connie Brooks, Ernie Whiteman, Sidney Goldfarb, Alan Brooks, Patti Ashley, Michael Morris, Drummond Hadley, Preston Faggart, Elsa Dorfman, Ann Charters, Peter Bornstein, Brett Aronowitz, Andy Clausen, Carolyn and Martin Karcher, and Kennett Love.

Film archivist Skip Elsheimer transformed tiny movie frames into digital images with generosity and expertise. I also thank Martee Umberger, John Sinclair, David Padwa, Pamela Badyk Mayo, Bruce Weigl, John Weston, Richard and Lois Shelton, Ed Sanders, Donald Hall, Devora O'Brien, Patrick Hinely, Chris Campbell, Itka Brill, Andrew Lampert, Jonas Mekas, Selma Katz, John Tytell, Fredricka Smith, Ellen Gordon, Heather Pawlak, Joyce Johnson, Adrienne and Charles Bodie, Danny Schechter, Michael Horowitz, Ben Schafer, Robert Greenfield, Andrew Schoenfeld, Robert H. Jackson, Toby Mussman, Rusty Ford, Steven Taylor; and the staff at Special Collections, Green Library, Stanford University. Finally, for generous help and guidance at Counterpoint, I thank Luke Gerwe, Julie Pinkerton, Jodi Hammerwold; and Jack Shoemaker, who a year and a half ago proposed that we "make a beautiful book together."

ONE

In the Beginning

Out of Mexico

"**D**AYPORTAY?" THE STEWARDESS asked the *federales*. They nodded, turned back down the ramp.

She led Joe and me inside, seated us. No other passengers had boarded the Delta jet. It was March 1968; we'd come from two weeks in jail, much of the time no running water or even a mirror for combing or shaving. The stewardess and captain following her were the first Americans we'd seen since our incarceration. When the captain reached our seats, he leaned over to tell us, "I want you to act like human beings while you're on this plane."

While living in the primitive, idyllic village of Yelapa where sea and mountains and jungle met, I'd gone to Puerto Vallarta on the motorized rowboat "ferry," along with Joe and others, for supplies to move deeper into the jungle. Just after setting foot in Vallarta, we'd been arrested without charge as part of a roundup of two dozen gringo hippies, and had then used all our money sending out for food from jail. Now, after a day of detention and interrogation in Mexico City, we were being deported to San Antonio, Texas.

We had $5 between us. I had no idea of the whereabouts of my lady friend Candy, who on learning I'd been busted had taken the ferry and sat in front of the jail all afternoon, waiting for my release or her own arrest—and was jailed herself. She'd been shipped out before me; I could only hope she was in New York.

Joe and I were apprehensive about our arrival in San Antonio and didn't know how we'd be treated, but as soon as we were conducted to an immigration officer I knew we'd be all right. He was a fiftyish slow-talking Southerner, and there wasn't a blink of malice about him.

"How were you treated in jail?"

"OK—better than some."

We were led to a side room divided into cubicles. Immigration officials scrutinized my backpack, sleeping bag, movie camera; they patted me down, told me to drop my pants, bend over, spread my cheeks.

Then I was led out, belongings in hand; Joe came through his door at the same time. We were free. Amplified weird human voices were calling out flights and names, people were moving quickly about us; counters were aglow under fluorescent lights with neat, identical-looking beings behind them. Electricity! We were far from the jungle.

I went to a phone and called a friend in New York. Candy was there, she was all right; she'd been deported the day after *federales* had escorted her and several others to Mexico City for extended interrogation.

"How'd you get there?" I asked.

Arthur Nelson, a shy straight fellow from Utah whose worldview underwent a sea change after his time in jail with us, had given her, and others in her group, the money to fly home. Just a gift, outright.

"I'm here with Joe," I reported. "He wants to get to New Orleans. But you know, neither of us has money."

"I'll round up enough for both of you." There were several friends she could ask, and funds could be cabled to the airport through Western Union.

So Joe and I spent the next eighteen hours there, exhausted, dirty, confused. We managed to sleep a little in molded upright plastic chairs under fluorescent light. I felt like I was speeding: another all-nighter. A hundred dollars came the next day.

We took the New York plane via New Orleans, embracing as Joe rose to get off. Three hours later, when I came through the door at LaGuardia, Candy, vivid as ever, long auburn hair and shapely energy, stood waiting. She had big news: "Barbara's going to marry Allen!" she exulted after we hugged and kissed.

She meant Allen Ginsberg. In the longstanding city-versus-country argument she'd had with her best friend, filmmaker Barbara Rubin, Candy had finally triumphed. Though Barbara had once called the country "boring," she was now helping Allen get a farm where we could all live together: Candy and I would be caretakers. Paradise was within reach.

Back in the City

M ANHATTAN: FAMILIAR TERRITORY. From October 1966 until leaving to hitchhike across the U.S. and Mexico in October 1967, Candy and I had shared a small apartment in what is now SoHo. Just one room, all mattresses—we couldn't get enough sex with each other, with friends, with strangers, or with people we met at "sex guru" Stanley Fisher's. But we hadn't solved the human problem of jealousy. . . .

We'd take acid regularly, once a week or so. I was searching for Absolute Reality, a white light manifestation of my soul—but gradually finding that "reality" wasn't fixed but fluid. Equally involved in avant-garde film, I worked for pioneer Jonas Mekas and his organizations for little money, much inspiration. I was a slow and young twenty-one, raised in the rarefied, elite (but repressed) foreign business community of postwar Tokyo, eager to burst into the utterly transforming American life and culture I now sensed all around me. At the same time, I was hesitant, unsure of who or what I might be, often passive and socially awkward, "un-Americanized." I hadn't held even a part-time job before returning to the states for college. I was good-looking, evidently, but not especially bright.

Candy, from New Jersey, rich brown eyes in a pretty face, large breasts, and enormous sexuality, had from her mid-teens shaken off her Catholic upbringing and committed herself to discovering the electric mystery of sexual bonding, vowing to sleep with a hundred men before ever marrying. She was strong, loud, a brassy know-it-all of motherly energy. She could be bossy—and I, compliant. Sociable and garrulous to a fault, she was far more level-headed and worldly than I.

When Candy and filmmaker Barbara Rubin first met in the fall of 1967, they quickly grew close. With great eagerness the two women shared ideas, energy, laughter. I too had been struck by Barbara's intense vitality and physical attractiveness: prominent cheekbones, broad dimpled smile, gleaming teeth, a doe-like softness of body. But I was relieved no sexual charge passed between us.

Instead we could talk about cinema!—most specifically, her ideas for Jonas's struggling showcase Cinematheque. Doing so, I found myself both wrestling with and intrigued by her deluge of ideas, her blasts of imagination: all things were possible—simultaneously. There was a quickness of temper, too, whenever she realized that she—like the rest of us—couldn't always keep up with her torrents of originality.

Though one friend called her "crazy," Barbara was a great bringer-together of people, often for her own projects: she gathered friends and other "flaming creatures" to shoot her landmark *Christmas on Earth* orgy film; she introduced Andy Warhol and the Velvet Underground, Andy and Dylan. Even the great international poetry reading at the Albert Hall, London 1965, was, according to Allen, "all Barbara's idea." And though she was half a year younger than I, there was already something of the mythic about her—as in the story, perhaps apocryphal, of her fleeing her middle-class Queens home at fourteen for California, taking acid there with Aldous Huxley. On return she was confined in asylum, then released via family connections—into Jonas's care. Whereby she blossomed.

□ □ □

WHILE CANDY AND I were first together in New York from the fall of 1966 through 1967, she worked as secretary, then photographer's model. As time passed and I grew disheartened with my workaday world as clerk at Filmmakers' Cooperative, she proposed Acapulco, where she'd visited when living in Mexico earlier. And so we'd left New York. . . .

Once back in the city, Candy and I moved into a four-room flat in a condemned building on East 8th between B and C, which Barbara and her friend Rosebud had recently taken: no electricity—just candles. Barbara and Rosebud had been two belles of the Lower East Side earlier in the 1960s, when Rose was friends with Lenny Bruce, in the "amphetamine days" when acid was just starting to come in.

Now a scarf covered Barbara's head. She was as becoming, as radiant with intellectual energy as ever, and seemed in good health—but something had caused her to lose some hair. Was it her recent single-minded vegetarianism? I wondered. She seemed to eat only spaghetti noodles with meatless tomato sauce and little cups of chocolate pudding from delis. And chocolate bars.

In the crook of her arm she carried the thick paperback she was reading, *The Autobiography of Malcolm X*, pronouncing its author "a great man." She had a mongrel black-and-white Persian cat whom she said Dylan had given her after its rescue from the jaws of hounding dogs; the animal was spaced-out, traumatized forever. Barbara called him Malcolm.

One afternoon Rachel Fleischman, erstwhile lover of Ginsberg's companion Peter Orlovsky, came by looking for Barbara—but only I was there. We'd never met, but she was pretty and sexy, dark hair, dark eyes, and we were alone in a bedroom. Within moments, between the sheets.

The day before I'd watched with interest when Candy made love with two male friends of ours, but when she learned of my afternoon with Rachel she was furious. "You *know* she has the clap!" she insisted. I *didn't* know, but when Candy demanded I get myself checked out immediately, I took the bus to Bellevue, where a Q-tip was stuck inside my cock, and results proved negative.

The next night Candy and I visited the Cornelia Street home of friends Bob and Diane Patterson. As we stretched out with Diane in their small dark room, shoeless on pillows and cushions, smoking cigarettes and grass, Bob suddenly burst in from the night's cold, his bright face vivid with joy: "Johnson's not gonna run! Johnson's not gonna run! People I passed on the way home looked *happy*!"

Candy and I had returned from Mexico with new eyes for the situation emerging here: America's predilection for violence, and the destructive polarization of youth and age, of black and white, had seemed worse than ever. Now, short of hearing our war had ended, this seemed, for a long moment, the best news possible.

□ □ □

AFTER A FEW days living with Barbara in the East 8th Street flat, I grew less sure about our future with Allen. Barbara hadn't discussed farm plans in detail other than saying we'd leave in a couple weeks for a secluded spot near the center of New York State: Cherry Valley. She didn't take kindly to questions either, especially if they seemed to doubt or challenge; and I, passive and quiet, was hardly a vigorous questioner. I tended to keep uncertainties within; even Candy, far more confident and assertive, could be diffident before her imposing best friend. Nonetheless, we pieced together some background.

Barbara had begun searching in earnest months earlier, driving Allen and Peter's Volkswagen camper bus, with Peter's catatonic schizophrenic brother Julius (whom she was then looking after) riding shotgun. She'd visited several areas upstate, but Cherry Valley held a special appeal because of the Hasidic presence in Sharon Springs, a mineral-springs resort town six miles away favored by Orthodox Jews. Rachel Fleischman had spent family summers there and recommended land nearby: it was beautiful and, at $100 an acre, inexpensive.

But was Allen going along with Barbara's plans? It seemed so, at least as far as the place upstate. And I felt I had to accept Barbara's version of things—it was she, after all, who had the close connection with Allen. I'd had only brief encounters.

Before coming to New York, my life had been spent worlds away. Growing up in Japan through the '50s, by age fifteen I was discontent enough with the specialized air of our Tokyo foreigners' home to search the streets of San Francisco for beatniks one afternoon on family furlough. Later, back in the U.S. for good, caught up in the tumult of a new era after four years at a Southern men's college, I'd come to view Allen Ginsberg as the one elder who understood youth, imagination, possibility.

I'd seen photographs of him—bathing in the Ganges, carrying a POT IS A REALITY KICK sign in snowy Manhattan. I'd read *Howl*; I knew of his heroic effort to inform a Senate subcommittee about LSD. Visiting New York my senior year, I'd stared into his eyes as we met briefly at patroness Panna Grady's. Moving to the city half a year later—September 1966—I looked for him on the street, saw him there once, then on stage, and, with Candy, was in his company New Year's Eve. After moving in with Candy, I'd scotchtaped to our wall a close-up news photo of him with my handwritten caption, "Mine eyes have seen the glory."

Of course I didn't really know him at all, but he was around, in our shared milieu, and I was gratified. Now, early spring 1968, Candy seemed charmed by the prospect of getting to know him, however unlikely his purported marriage to Barbara. And I, black sheep son of a dour and distant banker, searching for full engagement with a world of art and freedom, was profoundly excited. But we were hearing no further mention of a marriage-to-be. Barbara was given to wildly imagined undertakings, some of which—like *Christmas on Earth*—bore great fruit. But was the prospective union more imagination than reality? I couldn't ask her that.

But I *could* ask someone else. Filmmaker Shirley Clarke had loaned Candy the $100 that Joe and I had used to get back from San Antonio. I'd gotten work at the Elgin Theatre, projecting Warhol's *Chelsea Girls*, and when I'd saved a hundred bucks, I went to Shirley's Chelsea Hotel penthouse to repay her. She was particularly good friends with Barbara, and I took the opportunity to be direct: "Is Barbara's marriage to Allen for real?"

"No," Shirley answered immediately, looking me in the eyes, squinting a little behind a trail of cigarette smoke. She had a firm, warm voice and manner. "First Barbara wanted to marry Dylan, then the Beatles. Now it's Allen."

□ □ □

IT WASN'T THAT Barbara never spoke with us about Allen in those days. She once characterized two aspects of his personality—as she saw it. On the one hand, his will could be "like jello"; on the other, whenever he focused on a subject, it was so comprehensive, so complete—"like when he concentrates on China." In my mind I watched his head swell with the enormous dimensions of his thoughts, till it filled the very room in which he sat, till it was China-size.

Allen had been away some of the time on college reading tours. (Fees, after agent's cut, would be deposited in Committee on Poetry, Inc., the nonprofit foundation he set up for the benefit of other poets and artists.) Now he was back awhile in New York, and every few days Barbara would see him. Giggling with delight and a little mock consternation, she told us of a moment at lunch with editors of *Mademoiselle*: "We were seated next to each other, they were asking us big serious questions, and he stuck his finger up my ass as we spoke."

One day she asked if I'd pick up a couple of dollars Allen was loaning her. Wearing the oversized green-and-white sweater a friend had given me on hitching across the U.S. and Mexico, I went the few blocks to Allen's fourth-floor walk-up above a storefront at 408 East 10th, and knocked. I entered the narrow corridor next to the kitchen, and there was Allen: long dark hair and beard, large dark attentive eyes, the eyes I'd found myself looking into on our first encounter at Panna Grady's. But now as we spoke I was struck as much by the profound depth and humanity of his voice, so rich and gentle. I took the bills from his hand. Before stepping back through the door I told Allen I'd just gotten back from Mexico, where I'd been in jail. Reaching out to touch my sweater near the elbow, he asked, "Is this from Mexico?"

The next time we'd meet would be on the farm.

On to the Farm

I T WAS TIME to get to Cherry Valley: whether Barbara's marital dream would be realized, the farm itself—and our involvement in it—was taking shape. And while the notion of cutting urban ties and setting off for a rural retreat with vivid, dynamic young women and one of the great poets of the age was exciting, the circumstances that we eventually faced, including ten feet of snow, schizophrenia, paranoia, and dozens of separate egos all fighting for their moment in Allen's sun, were another matter.

Late one afternoon the second week of April, Barbara, Candy, Peter, Julius, and I piled into Allen's off-white Volkswagen camper. Allen had bought the bus, used, in 1965 when a Guggenheim Fellowship allowed him to travel cross-country, composing poetry "of These States." We drove first to Barbara's white frame family home in Jamaica, Queens.

Our two middle-aged hosts, Pauline and Lester Rubin, welcomed us generously, bedded us down, then served a full breakfast the next morning. Sharing her sense of anticipation, mother and father may have felt that their Barbara was making a new start in life.

We gathered a moment for farewells in morning sun on the front lawn, Peter at center. As energetic and animated as a cartoon character, he was tallish, big-boned, husky, but slender. And in constant motion. His brother Julius, shorter, phlegmatic, solemn, with a pot belly, remained to one side, stationary in catatonia. Peter—on amphetamine much of the time, he may not have eaten breakfast—set his black horn-rimmed glasses aside and performed a headstand. "Jack Kerouac called this 'scrambled eggs,'" he chuckled as he made a triangle of head and spread hands on the grass, releasing his legs from a crouch, arching them upward, toes to sky.

Soon we were heading north, through Westchester County into Duchess, past White Plains and Peekskill, beyond Poughkeepsie and Millbrook. At a diner where she and Allen once stopped, Barbara observed, "Allen's like a folk hero now. When we were here before, people came to our table asking for his autograph."

In Albany, we turned west toward Cherry Valley, a village of 800 a quarter-mile high. Sixteen miles from the more prosperous Cooperstown, it was tucked away a mile or two from Route 20, the modest Albany-to-Buffalo thoroughfare. Surrounding its one main intersection were hardware, liquor, and grocery stores; post office, butcher shop, bank, pharmacy, and service station. Our prospective land—no sales contract yet—lay east out Lancaster Street, five miles of rising, curving narrow road past open fields; groves of bare deciduous trees and new growths of the original hemlock; large single-family dairy farms; and a broad open bend high up—"the Beautiful View"— that unfolded a striking panorama of the Mohawk Valley. "When it's really clear, you can almost see Vermont," a neighbor would say.

As Barbara shifted into low, every now and then a woodchuck ran lumpety-lump across the asphalt between two sides of yellow-brown grass, putting his life at risk after winter's safety. Every now and then we'd see his cousins' sad remains. We were heading to East Hill; at length the road more or less straightened out, and a steep dirt lane emptied into it from the right.

We took that steep right to a crest and, turning left, entered a small forest of evergreens and leafless trees. Trees to the right soon disappeared and we could see westerly, where a plot of cleared land, with several wooden structures, began to reveal itself. As we curved gradually downhill and the dirt road—now a drive—began to straighten out, we could see the basic layout of East Hill Farm's seventy-some acres.

Woods to the left, uphill; woods at a distance straight ahead, beyond a broad meadow; dark green forest on an extended ridge lining the hundred yards of slop- ing meadow down to the right. At more or less the center of it all, a small, two-story house of grey asbestos shingles faced the untended front lawn rising gently above it with maples and a few boulders. Straight beyond the house, a dilapidated barn, two- story red and white, opened in our direction, with a small narrow building stretch- ing at right angle from its rear. Behind the house twenty paces lay a single-story green-and-white frame garage large enough to house a tractor. Fifty yards north of the house, just above the meadow fence line, stood the mid-nineteenth-century tomb- stones of first residents, the Milsons.

We could look inside the musty, cold house that had sat vacant for at least seven years, but legally we couldn't stay. (Few would've rushed to do so.) Even to my untrained eyes the stone foundation, though substantial, was cracking; rooms were small and low ceilinged; floors sloped; the short, steep stairway was narrow; and most inner walls were covered with faded, sometimes peeling floral paper. No running water, no electricity, and, with one big exception, no heat.

At the kitchen's eastern end, between two windows, nearly as large and com- manding as a baby grand piano, sat a grey-and-white, blacktopped four-burner Kalamazoo cooking stove, with two compartments above to keep just-cooked food warm. At right angle to stove and in front of what would become the bathroom stood an ancient kerosene refrigerator which, we'd discover, still worked. (We weren't the only ones to make use of it: for months Malcolm the bedraggled cat would cower behind it.) Beneath the kitchen lay an earthen-floor cellar space—coal for the stove could be stored there—and, two flights above, an unfinished attic.

The farm was to be bought by Committee on Poetry, Inc. (Allen was treasurer, Peter president, Ed Sanders vice president, Allen's lawyer brother Eugene secretary). Since Allen had seen many of his C.O.P. grants to fellow poets go up their arms, East Hill would be a refuge from such destructive urban habits, a haven for comrades in distress. Peter had been in the throes of amphetamine addiction a couple of years; and, Allen would tell me later, "I got the farm for Kerouac." But before long his reclusive friend would be finally settled in Florida with mother and wife and alcohol, and never lay eyes on East Hill Farm.

□ □ □

BARBARA, IN FREQUENT touch with Eugene (whom she called "YOO-gene"), reported that since negotiations for the land were under way, we could camp on the lawn. We had a four-person green tent and a portable Coleman white gas stove. Peter, if and when he slept, did so in the bus.

In those earliest days, we seemed to manage fine. Together or separately, we adapted: our first morning at East Hill, Candy reported seeing Peter, red-and-green tam-o'-shanter on dark blond head, horn-rimmed glasses on nose, set a styrofoam cup of coffee and an orange at the mouth of a woodchuck hole. On the Coleman we'd boil breakfast coffee and Wheatina. Lunch would be sandwiches; and Candy would often fry something up for dinner. I wrote a friend

> . . . land is beautiful, house semi-decrepit as it's not been lived in for 7 years. All our time's been spent cleaning it, trying to make it suitable for living. We've done nearly all we can do till Allen comes at the end of the month—then floors will be redone, heating, plumbing, electricity put in, etc.

Little did I realize all the effort and exasperation that would involve—or that electric power lines would never reach East Hill Farm.

We'd go on walks about the seventy acres, into the richly evergreened state forest surrounding it on three sides; then we'd board the VW again, explore countryside, visit town. There Barbara introduced us to Earl Watrous, our realtor, at Your Friendly Corner Store. He was a true extrovert with gold-capped teeth you always saw because he was always smiling; wife Beatrice, ever unfriendly, suffered from badly twisted arthritic fingers. We greeted others we passed on the street, doing our best to be congenial.

But could we make a go of it in such a setting? I wondered, I worried—we all did. A communal establishment not in New York City but at the state's heart, headed by one of the most notorious figures in American culture of the day: an outspoken opponent of the Vietnam War when to be such was considered "un-American" by many; a homosexual, a *celebrant* of homosexuality, of sexuality itself, when the very word "sex" was still uttered with a hush in homes across America; not merely a user but an advocate of marijuana and psychedelics, when prevailing opinion confused marijuana and heroin; a bearded, long-haired "grown-up" who unabashedly expressed sympathy for the emerging youth culture as police stepped up violence in the name of law enforcement. Would we survive?

Fortunately, we had a neighborly link to Cherry Valley. Edward Tyler Urich had been described by Barbara in pre-farm days as "an old Bohemian who knows Allen." When we got there, I discovered that Ed, who lived uphill across a meadow in a tar-paper shack near the small barn housing his bearded black Egyptian Nubian goats, had merely known *of* Allen. He wasn't "bohemian" in the sense of "beatnik" or aesthete—though certainly eccentric, he was more a *Popular Mechanics* sort of guy. But as to welcoming and looking out for us, he was all heart—and practical wisdom.

Ironically, Ed was born in Greenwich Village—on, as he'd fondly say, the day the city subway system was opened: December 2, 1904. Six feet tall, broad, with spreading paunch, he wore an old baseball cap above rimless glasses and overalls or jeans, and an old zip-up jacket. In his younger days radio operator work took him to the Amazon; later he was an electrical engineer for "Ma Bell" in Valhalla, New York. During World War II, he was again in South America, among Colorado Indians, gathering Cinchona bark to send to the U.S. for refining into quinine for the war effort.

He'd first set foot in Cherry Valley around the end of the 1930s, and ever since—I wouldn't learn why till much later—he'd been living essentially as now, apart from everyone else. He added to social security income by helping several women in town with gardens and flower beds. He was known—he himself encouraged the epithet—as "Ed the Hermit." And he loved to talk.

□ □ □

BARBARA REMAINED IN control of our little group. Our first evening there, having twisted a muscle in my back, I was about to take Darvon—a mild painkiller my friend Joe had given me—when Barbara intervened, "We're not having any drugs here." (I can still see her index finger pointed at me in the near darkness.) Later, after we'd moved into the house, I developed a boil on my hand that required daily soaking in hot water: Barbara instructed me to do the soaking outside. Of course we had some give-and-take; it's just that we knew—until Allen would arrive—that Barbara was the final authority.

Peter tended not to relate to the rest of us. He'd charge across meadow, uphill and down, shouting in his "leper's voice" what sounded like Turkish-Shakespearean soliloquies: "Ichtemehata bébé!" he'd gruffly call. Sometimes he wore a long-sleeved red corduroy shirt, tails out, under a large-linked chain wrapped several times around his waist.

After the first few days, Peter went back to the city—for more speed, we assumed. Just before his return, Eugene had signed a sales contract, giving us the go-ahead: we settled onto three bare mattresses on different parts of the small living room floor. Late one night after we'd blown out kerosene lamps and shut off flashlights, we found ourselves (all except Julius, who'd evidently gone out for a leak) suddenly awakened by clanging chains as Peter entered the front door, shouting at the shadowy speechless figure just in front of him, "Where're we goin', Julius, lead the way! Hrrmpf, Joolie Woolie! Show Petey where to lay his head!"

Allen Arrives

B ARBARA MADE A quick trip to the city. Then one mild grey afternoon at the start of May I watched the Volkswagen roll down the dirt drive, stop fifty feet above the house. Out from the driver's seat stepped Barbara; her passenger was Allen, in dark green long-sleeved work shirt, jeans, and little blue-grey all-cloth ("vegetarian," he'd call them) shoes.

Peter also saw their arrival. Still wearing a belt of chain with links as thick as index fingers, and swinging a machete over his head, he ran up the drive toward Allen. Trembling within, I watched Allen calmly stand there.

Without any display of feeling Allen began walking slowly toward him; as he drew abreast, Peter stopped his frantic motion, turned, and began to walk with him toward the house. Barbara, frozen in horror near the bus, now relaxed, came forward and introduced Allen and me. I breathed a sigh of relief—for a moment.

That first night Candy and Barbara and I sat at the kitchen table talking with Allen before we all went to bed. Much of the talk was Candy's: jail in Mexico, farm work she'd done, group sex, horseback riding. At one point just before we broke up, with Allen outside relieving himself, I told her, "You've talked a blue streak."

"Yes, that's all right," Barbara nodded.

On Allen's return, we made our way into the living room, kerosene lamp and flashlight in hand. Allen asked, "Where should I sleep?" Against the north wall Candy and I had a mattress; against another, Barbara; and against a third was one or more for Julius and Peter (when Peter slept, during those amphetamine days).

"Here," Barbara pointed to her bed.

Allen obeyed—after all, he'd asked. Subsequent nights he slept elsewhere. On the second or third night I called over to him, "Allen, are you feeling sexy?"

"Always," he answered, and came over to Candy and me.

□ □ □

THOSE EARLIEST DAYS could occasionally be pleasant for Barbara and Allen. That first night he caught her up on his life as they lay side by side on her mattress. "I had a big long dream of LeRoi Jones," I recall his saying, "and wrote him a description of it. He wrote back, 'Typical honky dream.'" I was amazed at Allen's amused equanimity.

He mentioned recent discussions with Abbie Hoffman, Jerry Rubin, and Timothy Leary of domestic and international problems, including protest plans at the Democratic convention in Chicago in August: "We got together to see what could be done to solve the biggest problems . . ."

Barbara challenged, teasing, "What makes you guys think *you* can run the world?!"

But pleasantry was often short-lived. "You're a great man," she once offered at the kitchen table—and he, a quiet "Thank you." "But, you know," she continued, as if about to make a major revelation, "uh, some people say you're not such a great poet." Allen remained silent; he seemed to have a capacity for letting Barbara and the rest of us speak without becoming emotionally involved. At the same time I wondered, What does he *really* feel? What was *he* making of this complex crazy scene that depended on him for support?

Early on I took a quick look inside his small black journal:

> *. . . slept & woke at dawn put on old fur coat went out to pee saluted Mr. Urich at daybreak walking in frosty grass to his car—lay down in bed ruminating—Peter scampering about in the grass apparently mad mooing like a cow—Julius trembling & indifferent to his medicine—Barbara up here on farm in design to transform my sex marry me have infants be Jewish Cinema mother—Candy & Gordon, young couple she invited up to be house-holder-caretakers more stable than the rest of us but held back by Barbara from displaying their own sexual imaginations—to ball everyone & leave for Amazon in November*—Who can do the work needed to clear the farm & supervise expense of money to rebuild house w/ furnaces & electrics & water & jack up sagging floors & install storm windows & tarpaper barn roof & seed field once plowed? If I'm away it'll all be so lackadaisical Julius will freeze to death in solitude 20 degrees below zero December?*

Meanwhile, Peter's behavior modified: chains disappeared; he'd crash a bit; relaxed, he sat in the dining room rocker reading *The New York Times*, twirling the moustache of his hearty dark blond beard, True Blue ciggyboo between big rough fingers.

We talked over farm plans. "Of course we have to be vegetarian," Barbara insisted. Candy was agreeable but without the fervor; Allen didn't argue. I'd avoided

---

* Though it was largely a fantasy, Candy had told Allen of our interest in a rumor from jail: Alan Watts's trip to the Amazon near the year's end. But now that Allen was at the farm we began to feel we could settle in, in earnest, and prospects of the Amazon dimmed forever.

meat since beholding myriad enormous carcasses hanging in the Acapulco *mercado central* late 1967. Then one bright June day in 1968, I'd pass a Cooperstown hot dog stand and could resist no longer. Later in the summer Barbara, index finger raised, would lecture her eight-year-old guest Joel Aronowitz: "If you take a knife and go out and kill an animal, then you can eat meat, Joel!"

Meantime how would the land, fallow many years, respond to our efforts at growing vegetables without the "boost" of synthetic fertilizers? Allen didn't feel the garden had to be wholly organic, which surprised me—yet I soon saw the virtue in his lack of doctrinaire attitudes. Could someone plow for us? What animals would we have? What would it cost for enough poultry to keep us in daily eggs?

"Just chicken feed," Allen answered. Shoulder ever to the wheel, he took out a hardbound marbled-cover notebook, labeled it "Farm Needs," and recorded a few necessities: a water pump—a hydraulic ram; tarpaper for the lean-to roof adjoining the barn; furring lathes; white gas lamps.

He made a drawing of first steps toward a water system: cleaning out the well fed by meadow spring, digging ditches for run-off; having a backhoe dig a trench, lay a new pipe to kitchen-sink hand pump. Ed Urich, source of much information for plumbing, carpentry, and more, came in helpfully on such discussions. I can hear him today, generous, crusty, droning, old man's voice just slightly loud: "Allen, what ya need to do is . . ." as his young acolyte bends his balding head at the oilclothed table, scrawling in earnest legibility with black ballpoint across white paper.

Peter would be at such discussions occasionally, but often he was out, scurrying across hills. Julius tended to stand by in the kitchen, silent, stiff, belly protruding, arching one shoulder up and the other one down, sipping tea or coffee or even hot water prepared on the Coleman stove.

We showed Allen around the area as we knew it; at the Beautiful View he exclaimed, "It's like Breughel!" We began making forays he loved—hunting in nearby towns for inexpensive antiques. And moving into individual rooms: a dresser here, a secretary there. Soon, he'd buy a pump organ for the living room, a large A.B. Chase pedal-action oak stop organ from the late nineteenth century. His room (which he'd give to others when away, and sometimes even when there) was on the north corner; over time various guests would take the one next to it. Across the hall from Allen slept Julius; next to Julius, Candy and I, in a nine-by-ten-foot space with one window overlooking barn and chicken house and Ed's meadow, another the front yard.

Some second floor rooms lacked doors that worked; all walls seemed paper-thin. Down on the first floor, Peter had an unfinished room just inside the front porch, facing the pantry, which adjoined the kitchen. Above everyone, Barbara took the unfinished attic, where you could stand up straight only directly beneath the peaked roof.

Neighbors, Uncertainties, Relationships

E D, ALWAYS EAGER to help, squired us around the area. His best friend was Myron Wiles, a smaller, thinner man of wispy white hair and ruddy complexion who—riding tractor, doing repairs, tending cows—favored blue denim: cap, jacket, shirt, overalls. His pretty blue eyes closed almost shut as he smiled; on occasion, a red bandana graced his neck. He lived in a white frame house close to the road, less than half a mile below the Beautiful View. Ed would stop in and chat, and we'd take an occasional cold shower in Myron's barn. His voice and manner were a little bit creakier than Ed's large sounds and spread-handed big galoot welcome, and he seemed a few years older. Myron had spent all his life in that same house, devoting many years to his ailing mother, who forbade his ever marrying. He was one of the most unsuspicious, good-hearted people I've met.

Living with him was Carl La Salle, who'd grown up in the house we'd just moved into. Now seventeen, blond hair in a vague ducktail, he looked like a smaller, subdued Jerry Lee Lewis. In salmon-colored shirt and denim vest he worked on his great love: cars. Several of them, some on cinder blocks, rested in Myron's front yard. As we chatted one cool spring day, he warned of weather to come, as if we expected refuge from the city's heat as well as its other woes. "Don't worry," he cautioned with a hapless grin, "it can get hot here!"

Carl's parents had divorced when he was ten. Ed gave me his take on Carl's father: he liked to keep a few horses (for trade or sale) and walk about his "estate" wearing belt and holsters with two toy pistols—fancying himself a cowboy hero, king of the hacienda. But Carl remembered his dad for the work he did: he put up all the outbuildings, tore down an earlier barn to build the present one.

And now in his mother's—Theresa's—hands lay our fate. Though we had a sales contract, we were months from closing, and if something displeased her, she could still back out. After our first couple of weeks, we received a handwritten letter of outrage from her, threatening to scrap the whole project because hippies were on her land. Let Eugene and Watrous the realtor take care of it, Barbara counseled, and so did Allen. In time, Mrs. La Salle would accept Allen's payment.

But meantime, would *we* take the farm? Allen wasn't sure, and argued with Barbara about going ahead with the deal. The question came up one evening at the kitchen table; Barbara's reaction to expressions of uncertainty was so strong that I can remember Allen saying calmly, "The problem is, you make everyone feel guilty for disagreeing with you." But at her emphatic "No, Allen, no one else can *make* you feel guilty. If you feel guilty, you feel guilty!" he was silent.

Allen seemed a victim of having encouraged—or just permitted?—Barbara to do the looking. So it appeared to me, more than ever, the next day. It was overcast and cool and the three of us set off on what I thought would be a pleasant afternoon ride in the countryside. Barbara, who liked to look at whomever she was speaking to while she drove, was behind the wheel of the Volkswagen bus, Allen next to her. I was in the back—and soon fearing for my life. Under best circumstances Barbara tended to drive in the center or even on the left side of these country roads—but now, where might heated words take her? Take all of us? "It's a *mystical* place!" Barbara insisted, letting the bus swerve at will on a narrow curve as she turned to spit her angry assertion at Allen. I shuddered silently in the backseat.

Allen was worried about committing to a deteriorating house so far from the city, so far from electric lines, with no plumbing. Since she'd looked at a few other places, why not look some more?

"And what do you mean, *mystical*!?" he shot back. "It's a *farm*! Am I sinking $7,000 into a white elephant?"

Finally, to her repeated insistence that now was the time and mystical the place, he asserted, fist-shaking mad, "I'm a Buddhist Jew!" As if driving itself, the Volkswagen bus stayed the course, edging away from sharp drop-offs and oncoming vehicles.

□ □ □

FARM OR NO farm, we—I—soon got a dog, vaguely resembling the black Labrador my family had in China before I was born, but smaller, long-haired. "God," I proposed calling him. "No," Allen said, "Godly." Candy agreed.

Down in Cherry Valley we continued getting to know people and places. A few doors from Watrous's Friendly Corner Store on Alden Street stood the post office and liquor store; out Genesee, the elegant redbrick high school on one side, Agway Farmers' Cooperative on the other; and across from Watrous's at the intersection of Alden and Montgomery, the Mobil Gas station run by Howie Fassett, in his early fifties, and Howie Jr., in his twenties. With the Volkswagen bus, a bright yellow 1957 jeep truck with snow plow and wooden bed which we'd soon purchase, a small Willys jeep loaned us for half a year, as well as a good number of guests driving our way in warmer months, we'd bring them lots of business.

A few steps up Lancaster Street, behind the Soldiers' and Sailors' Monument memorializing Cherry Valley men of the Civil War, sat Keller's Electric and Hardware. When once we entered with Julius in tow, permed and plump Mrs. Keller asked Candy, sub rosa, "Is he dangerous?" Nearby was Rury's Meats, a kind of classic Norman Rockwell butcher's with wooden floorboards and smiling, bald white-aproned Mr. Rury behind the counter. Then the tiny unpretentious Victory Market, the only "super market" in town.

On our antiques forays we might buy a used book or two—sometimes pretty, sometimes musty collections on plants and health. I began taking a few notes about flora of the area: musk mallow, buttercup, meadow rue, hawkeye. Allen told me of calamus ("sweet flag") and its importance to Whitman, showing me its phallic resemblance in printed illustration before I saw it growing in fields around us.

As I talked alone on occasion with Allen, some of what I said would later embarrass me. At Davidson College in the spring of 1966, I'd shot the breeze with friend Rob Fulmer in Duke Dormitory. Tall and gangly, Rob greeted the world with a big guffaw: he hated every inch of the pomp and posture he found at our school. On one occasion, he told me admiringly of the extensive May 27 *Life* magazine piece ("The Guru Comes to Kansas") by Barry Farrell that depicted Allen travelling cross-country with lover Peter Orlovsky, Julius, and other companions, making no secret of his homosexuality. As Rob put it, Allen was saying, "I'm homosexual and proud of it!"

But he also showed me a copy of Don Allen's landmark *The New American Poetry* anthology, with Ginsberg and Orlovsky poems among many others. Read aloud by Rob in dorm room boredom hilarity, lines by Peter ("I know if I could shave myself the bugs around my face would disappear forever. / The holes in my shoes are only temporary, I understand that. / My rug is dirty but whose that isent?"), and even some by Allen, seemed about as funny and ridiculous to me as they did to him.

Then one quiet evening two years and 800 miles distant from that dorm room, I sat with Allen at a small kitchen table, elbows on red plastic print oilcloth. I was jejune enough to volunteer, "You and Peter had some lousy lines in that Donald Allen anthology." Allen simply sat there quietly; he didn't argue or respond.

Another early occasion, I told him I thought Kerouac was a prophet who'd fizzled out. I embellished it by repeating my reflection on reading *On the Road* at the end of my freshman year: "I can write as good as that." Allen, having learned a little of my upbringing in a banker's household, responded calmly, amused, "See, that's an aristocratic attitude." He then explained, big eyes unfaltering in attention, large unexcited voice unfaltering in intent, that his friend bore a message of spirituality, of suffering, that was deeply pertinent.

Once—"Lady Madonna" had just come out—I asked him about the Beatles and their work. He admired the vivid concreteness of their lyrics, citing "Dragged a comb across my head." On a personal level, he volunteered, looking directly at me, "They're as smart as we are. They know it's all ashes."

And what of Peter? Allen's relationship with him seemed at times close, at times distant, but almost never sexual. In those early days, differences between the two seldom seemed to be over immediate issues at hand, but rather over something long-term—or speed. And, typically, they were given expression through something violent or upsetting on Peter's part.

And what of Barbara? Her present attachment to him—and her failing hopes—was by now evident to all. What was the basis of their relationship?

"I saw her movie [*Christmas on Earth*] at the Coop one evening, and we balled on the floor afterward. She was just this groovy girl who'd made this groovy film," Allen recounted.

Whatever she might've seemed when he first met her, Barbara continued to hope that Allen would "grow up" sexually (as she once put it), settle down, and have children—perhaps good Jewish children. She'd once written him in the mid-'60s:

What I'd really do?
Is marry you
And have lots of kids 24 in all
And see what that will do!

Even by mid-1968, with no sexual relationship with him, she hadn't given up her desire for marriage and children with Allen. He remained exquisitely aware of it.

Cleaning the Well,
Working with the World

O UR BACKYARD SLOPED gently some sixty feet to a meadow, just beyond the green and white garage. Another 250 feet, a small spring fed into an old well no higher than ground level: this was our house water supply, and in seven years of non-use the well had filled with mud and murk.

One mild day in early May, at Ed's suggestion, Allen, Peter, Julius, and I, in knee-high black rubber boots, made our way down there. Shoveling, we cleared the channel from spring to well. Then came the hard part: the only way to clean the small well was to get down inside. Allen removed boots and pants—leaving only yellow tee-shirt and glasses—and went first. Gingerly, without complaint, he lowered himself into ice-cold water rising above his knees. Bending down, he began scooping out potfuls of muddy gunk, avoiding as best he could any harm to newts and salamanders.

Standing around watching were Peter, in red and green tam-o'-shanter and glasses with dark horn-rims, smoking True Blues; Julius, in solemn silence; Candy in brown corduroy coat and jeans; me in grey long-sleeve work shirt, small notebook and pen in breast pocket; and Ed in usual cap and jacket. And there was Godly, amused, curious about the whole project.

When after some minutes in the wet and cold Allen climbed out, I replaced him, naked from waist down, as he and Peter in high rubber boots stood puffing True Blues on the marshland. It was cold and slimy in the well, but fun too, and gunk was coming out: progress was being made. Now we could drink clear water, haul buckets of it up to the house. Later we could lay that pipe to the ancient hand pump on kitchen counter.

Today, in decades-old 8-millimeter footage of the well-cleaning, Barbara's nowhere to be seen. Despite her devotion to caring for Julius, she sometimes seemed less involved in hands-on day-to-day housework. Like some strange Queens cousin of Gertrude Stein, she was an expositor, theoretician, wild imaginer, projector, director. When, seated in a chair in the dining room, she told a guest, "The first thing I have to do is get this house cleaned up," I was puzzled, since I seldom saw her do that kind of work. She was still pretty, smart, energetic, and, in her own way, saintly. But over time I watched her heart become sadder, her soft body even softer.

□ □ □

AND SO WE passed our earliest days. Allen would often stay up late into the night, writing letters by amber kerosene lamp or the stronger white-gas Aladdin. One to Ferlinghetti, regarding his next volume of verse, *Planet News*, included "final scraps and notes necessary for book." A key poem therein—"Wales Visitation"—was important to Allen in several ways. He was pleased, he told me, by its accuracy of detail—as in sheep "revolving their jaws." And part of its circumstance had directly to do with East Hill, as he told an interviewer:

> . . . I took an acid trip in Wales and got into a big plastic nature thing where the sky was like the breath of the earth and the earth was breathing and the movements of the trees and the grass were like filaments on the earth moving to the breath. I got very much involved with nature, ecology and the result of it all was that I got the farm.

Allen's vision in Wales helped set the course for a couple of his major preoccupations while he was living at East Hill: a deep involvement with ecology, and serious engagement with his nation's problematic, evolving criminalization of drugs.

Soon Allen had a couple of readings and public appearances, one on William F. Buckley's *Firing Line*. On return to the farm Allen told me about it. In introducing him Buckley volunteered, "In politics, he is sort of radical . . . In sex, he is homosexual."

In those days that last word was far more charged than today. "What did you do when he said that?" I asked.

"I made this *mudra*," Allen showed me, raising his left hand palm out to the side of his breast pocket, ring finger pointing down to thumb-tip, "for calm and pacification."

"I read a poem, 'Wales Visitation,' you know, which I wrote on acid," he added. "Afterwards Buckley said, 'That's beautiful.'"

The poem appeared in *The New Yorker* the same week. Beneath its last line came Allen's name, but as he showed me, something that should have appeared between last line and author's name had been removed: "July 29, 1967 (LSD)–August 3, 1967 (London)."

When I finally saw the show on tape, I realized it was to Buckley's credit that they could freely mention the influence of LSD in the writing of the poem, and that they could otherwise discuss drugs. Allen was clearly trying to appeal to Buckley's openness on the subject of marijuana legalization, reporting that over 30,000 people were in jail in the U.S. for mere possession of pot, with a great many more being arrested.

He argued with him about legalizing acid; the negative effects of criminalizing heroin addiction; and the brutality and waste of the war in Vietnam. When Buckley mentioned that many had mourned the death of his friend (and fellow hawk) Cardinal Spellman, Allen intoned an exorcism mantra, "Om Raksa Raksa Hum Hum Hum Phat Svaha!" Seeing the program thirty years later, I was impressed most of all by the direct, human way Allen related to his host: asking *him* if *he'd* ever turned on, asking William F. Buckley, Jr., if *he* had read Henry Miller, Jean Genet, and Louis-Ferdinand Céline.

"My Friend Al"

O NE AFTERNOON IN May I stood on the cracked kitchen linoleum looking through the window above the little three-legged telephone table, watching more rain wet the already soggy earth. Would it never dry enough to plow the garden?

The phone rang.

"Is Allen there?!" came the disembodied New York voice, abrupt, direct, demanding.

"Who may I say is calling?" I answered in semiformal chirp.

"CORSO!" the caller shouted.

The next day, rain letting up, we watched a long white convertible descend our muddy drive, then slide to one side, onto the plot we planned to garden, and get utterly stuck. Out came a short, squat, big-boned Italian in cloth hat, sunglasses, and loose open rain coat, with a beautiful, sophisticated-looking woman in dark jacket. In a moment Gregory Corso—dark-haired, a pudge of a nose, a poke of a chin—swaggered into the house, asking for "my friend Al." His face, a little like that of ballplayer Pete Rose, had a pugnacious, assertive cast; there was keenness and intensity there, too. He was big-mouthed, cheery, demonstrative, emotions to the fore.

Gregory had no license and couldn't really drive, but Belle Carpenter, lady friend and Du Pont heiress, let him take charge of her 1961 Lincoln Continental. He'd just made it up from Woodstock, where they'd been staying. Now within an hour Carl La Salle, responding to our call, was behind the wheel, deftly turning it this way and that, urging it a few inches one way and then another, until finally Belle's enormous and besplattered steamship of a car was freed from the embracing mud.

□ □ □

GIVEN THE WHOLE basis for the farm, the only rule that Allen—hardly a lawgiver or enforcer—asked anyone to abide by was, in his own words, "no needle drugs": for the sake of the entire effort, for the household, and for its relationship with town and larger community. He made it clear to all before they came, though he didn't always enforce it: he wasn't there all the time, and making Peter, for instance, surrender his amphetamine was another matter.

Gregory, many years committed to smack, was drinking on arrival that wet afternoon, and would spend much of his time kicking junk—sort of. He'd go away a day or two and evidently return with some. He'd nod and slur a bit, stay up in Allen's room, and be divinely oblivious to the general run of things. Knocked out, he wasn't a problem, but without heroin or with alcohol came big turns for the worse.

One day he found himself alone: everyone else, Belle included, had gone antique hunting. He knew that Julius, long ago identified as a catatonic schizophrenic and continuing under the treatment of a Central Park psychiatrist, was taking four medications a day: Benadryl, Permatil, Toffranil, Cogentin. ("Julius has been much better since he takes his medicine," Barbara had written Allen in the fall: ". . . his mind travels in such circles that he goes days unless told without eating or sleeping, and gets very depressed, but the medicine . . . will prevent this. . . .")

Most of Julie's pills had to be given more than once a day, and he tended to receive them with resignation. Since we were all there together, most of us except Peter (who once threatened to sue me for giving his brother medicine) took part in administering them, so Barbara wouldn't have to go it alone as she basically had for a number of months.

We all shared some uncertainty on the matter. In his nearly adamantine silence, Julius would on occasion become more tense, move more stiffly, and break out into small sweats as he nervously moved his limbs, shifting weight slightly from one side to the other, sternness fixing his face. Could the medicine have contributed to such symptoms, rather than relieving them? I was never sure, and over time it would be modified and eventually discontinued. But for now most of us went along with the regimen. Even Peter usually made no complaint.

Julie's pills were left out in the kitchen, within easy reach of everyone. Though as "drugs" they hardly appealed to us, on this day when he found himself alone, Gregory took a good sampling from each bottle.

As we later learned from the poet himself, Ed Urich came by that afternoon—to bring mail and visit as he often did—and was greeted by Gregory, who ran toward him screaming, "Ed, there are people in the closet of my room smoking hash, and they won't give me any!" Ed, doubtless a bit stunned, bent his ancient knees up the narrow wooden stairs, and faced the closet. "There's nobody here, Gregory," he called back down over his shoulder.

So Ed had taken it in stride, and Gregory eventually came down from the effects of the pharmaceuticals. He seemed amused by what he'd done, but I worried about our relationship with our closest neighbor. I wasn't alone: "Oh, shit!" Allen exclaimed when he heard. "That's exactly what I didn't want to happen!"

In the end, it didn't amount to much. But Gregory's endeavors ("The sleeping pills you gave me fell out of my pocket into the hole when I sat down in the outhouse," he told a doctor on an unscheduled second visit) often seemed at catastrophe's edge: relating to Corso could be harder than relating to neighbor and community.

□ □ □

EVENING SUPPERS USUALLY brought us all together, crowding seven or eight (Allen, Julius, Candy, Gregory, Belle, myself, Barbara, and often Peter) elbow-to-elbow and face-to-face at the small table in the tiny dining room. Candy often cooked; Allen sometimes cooked; Peter on occasion cooked; even Gregory once took over in the kitchen, complaining that others weren't making the noodles al dente nor the spaghetti sauce spicy hot enough: he left a legacy of red tomato paste over all the surfaces of the grey and white Kalamazoo.

One evening, I began to feel my way with Gregory and Belle at dinner. Allen had said grace, as he often would:

Blessed be this food, which is the product of the labor of other people and the suffering of other forms of life.

Shortly I began querying Gregory and Belle (seated opposite me) on their likes and dislikes, somewhat in the manner of group discussions with sex guru and psychologist Stanley Fisher in 1967. I was trying to figure them out as a couple, their psychodynamics; ultimately, of course, I wanted to sleep with Belle. But my queries were met with hesitation. Finally I said to her, "You're nervous or insecure about something." At that point, Allen offered, "That may be true, but I wouldn't make a federal case out of it."

"We're both high-strung people," Belle followed with a gasp. She often spoke in gasps, great influxes of air preceding each statement or phrase, her brow furrowed. She had dark hair and blue eyes and was slender and long-limbed.

Gregory dominated their relationship. Once when we'd been to town and were heading back up East Hill, Candy and I in front, he and Belle in back, Gregory called out of the blue, "You know what, Gordon, your girl friend has big tits. Mine has small ones, but they are very white and very fine!"

On another occasion, we pulled up for gas at Fassett's Mobil service station, Candy and I again in front, Belle and Gregory in back. In those days they really were service stations: instead of the driver pumping gas, a mechanic would come out and do so. We waited a brief moment; no one appeared. Suddenly Gregory was thrusting his face out the window, shouting mightily, *"SUUUHVICE!"*

Shocked, I turned round to him, in a loud whisper: "Gregory! Don't yell at them!"

And right away he shot back at me, "Don't tell *me* how to *speak*!" When Mr. Fassett—whom we were just getting to know—appeared moments later, I realized that slinking down out of sight, as I wished to, was futile. Weakly I greeted him, asked him to fill 'er up.

Myron Plows, Farm Thrives, Barbara Weeps

A s June approached, rains diminished, bright buttercups multiplied in meadow marshland and dotted hillsides, apple and lilac blooms embraced the Milsons' gravestones. Myron Wiles, in denim cap and jacket, with yellow leather gloves, soon drove his red tractor up and plowed the now drier half-acre plot near the house. Next day, he returned with a broad set of disks and harrowed all he'd plowed. Candy, in brown corduroy coat and jeans, knelt into the large broken furrows and pulled up an earthworm in delight. We were ready!

But it was June: just three months till first frost. Though tomatoes and other cold-sensitive plants couldn't be set till the end of May, radishes, peas, lettuce, and spinach could've been started a month earlier: we'd lost that much time. Nonetheless we now began from scratch, hoping to grow organic vegetables on land seven years fallow.

My father was raised on a farm near the banks of the Ohio, but I had only the Proustian memory of my maternal grandfather's backyard tomatoes to counter an upbringing in the world's biggest city. For several days running, from 8:00 AM till five or six in the evening, Candy, Barbara, Julius, and Peter and I—sometimes even Belle—were out in the field, first clearing a small fraction of the countless rocks, then planting.

Candy had gardened before; Peter had studied agriculture, but his work, for all his energy, could be erratic. But we persisted. Candy pushed little tomato transplants into the soft moist brown earth; with sticks and strings we made rows to seed with beans, lettuce, spinach, and radishes, as Peter and his family had done on Long Island. We hauled some of the horse manure from the side of the barn, where it was piled years ago by the La Salles, and made little hills into which we pushed the flat seeds for pumpkins, muskmelons, squash—even watermelons.

Several miles away in a large white rickety farmhouse outside tiny Pleasant Brook, near tiny Roseboom, lived the Hoose Brothers. One—300 pounds, dropsical—liked to rock on the front porch while all around the sloping earth many an animal, four-footed and fowl, sat or started and stirred. From the Hooses came our first farm animals: three goats for $25—one Brown Swiss nanny, two white Saanen nannies.

(By summer's end we'd give one Saanen to people in the next county.) We named the Brown Swiss Brahma, the one Saanen Shiva, the other Vishnu, after creator, destroyer, and preserver gods of Hinduism. Brahma was due to give birth in a month or so. We— Allen included—began milking Shiva and Vishnu.

Before long Barbara selected two large elegant African geese. Candy and I got a black-and-orange tortoise shell cat, Panda Manda, whom I'd soon come to love. And we picked up three ducks including "Papa," the male Muscovy; another dog, a mixed-breed blue tick lady with dark rings around her eyes, whom we called Sadeyes; five hens including two "long-haired" Polish ones who laid green eggs. We searched for a rooster.

□ □ □

IN THE FARM'S earliest days, Barbara and I, in our modest way, could have fun together. (We did have some things in common—as Candy noted years later, plaintively, "You and Barbara were artists—I was just a hippie.") Receiving a query from Filmmakers' Distribution Center on lecturing possibilities, we considered joint appearances, chuckling as we wrote back that we were living in the country, "raising organic film." But such light moments were now fewer, farther between. As Barbara began to realize Allen wasn't going to participate in her most personal plans, her attitude in general, and toward him in particular, began to change.

When she'd had Julius under wing, she observed that as he got better, Peter got worse; now, in her growing disappointment with Allen, she sometimes idealized Peter. She proposed we make a movie on him, and to that end borrowed Shirley Clarke's exquisite 16-millimeter Beaulieu. Telling me of the celebrated 1959 Chicago reading by Ginsberg, Orlovsky, and Corso, she claimed that not only did Peter "see through the poetry reading racket after that, man; he never read again."

Unfortunately, one afternoon when Peter saw me out in the field not with the Beaulieu but my own little 8-millimeter Camex, he promised, like a guard in the Mexican jail three months earlier, "If you point that camera at me I'll break it." And when Barbara—who typically discouraged my shooting her at all—handed me the Beaulieu, it was with an injunction: "Don't give it to Allen—he's not holy enough to use a movie camera."

David Savage, Allen's architect classmate from Columbia, drove up, examined the house, and concluded, "If it were up to me, I'd tear it down." When some of Allen's family heard of his judgment, they told Allen they, too, thought he should "throw it down"—but he seemed, they said, to be doing it for friends.

And so we continued at work on house and grounds, and Barbara remained in many ways actively involved—even, to some degree, still directing. She and Candy— and Allen, with his love of antique stores—continued filling the house with furnishings. Barbara's Aunt Selma and Uncle Morty sent up two handsome straight-backed chairs. A lionskin with head—it made some of us vaguely uneasy—from Belle's father's safari ended up in the attic; to the dining room Belle brought an exquisite Italian chair hundreds of years old; to the living room an oriental rug reportedly rescued from a room of cats and dogs at Dylan's house.

Outdoors, besides work in our huge garden, we repaired fences. Tugging a heavy roll of barbed wire, we followed Carl La Salle on his guided tour of fence lines as he showed how to use the special wire-tightening pliers and the long heavy posthole digger or "harpoon," as Peter and I called it. We cleaned out the garage, hauling waste to the dump every Saturday morning, added support to the nearly collapsing homes of goats and other barnyard animals, and started flower and herb beds.

We visited the Otsego County Agricultural Extension Service in Cooperstown, inquired about heating, lighting, sewage. We began researching ways to bring running water inside, and to get some sort of non-electric heating system in by winter. (It would cost $9,000 to bring in electric lines, we learned.) We got the old red cast-iron hand-pump at the kitchen sink hooked up with plastic pipe to the well, only to discover it was useless, then purchased a bright new green one that gave us water. Ed, as ever, was helpful with information and suggestions.

Much of this sounds matter-of-fact domestic or even relatively idyllic—and it was. But life at the farm was more complex than the "simple" problems of propping up dilapidated structures and bringing in water and heat. There was, continually, Gregory's shenanigans, Peter's amphetamine madness, and Barbara's broken heart.

Following private discussion with Allen late one afternoon, it finally became wholly, inescapably real to Barbara that there would be and could be no loving union. At dinner, we could see her through the windows. I got up and went outside. Against the golden light of the setting sun, she was standing in profile in front of the old green and white garage in her pink nightgown, weeping—to herself, by herself, beside herself. I stood there quietly a moment, at some distance; everyone else remained inside.

Guests Call

Warm weather brought visitors. One of the first, who came just before Myron plowed, was Mrs. La Salle. To our surprise, only a few weeks after her letter of outrage, we'd received another one telling us she wanted to visit May 25.

What had made the difference? Likely, something Allen had done. Not long after his argument with Barbara over committing to the farm, he'd decided to go ahead with it. I think he felt that given the givens—he couldn't or wouldn't undertake a wholehearted search himself at this point—East Hill might be the best he could do. It was remote, spacious, and quiet; we had the godsend of Ed Urich as neighbor, and we were already settling in.

And so Allen had answered Mrs. La Salle: a long letter showing respect for her concern about her land and giving some background:

I've lived in New York most of my adult life, but traveled a lot in Far East and done some wilderness-backpacking and mountain climbing so have developed more taste for mother nature that I had not known younger.

It was rich with appreciative references not only to land but to old familiar persons of the area, including, of course, her former neighbor Ed. It closed by offering to visit her in Buffalo, so ". . . you can look us over and see if we look fit to care for your land with the right attention it deserves . . ." It was masterly in its psychology, moving in its earnestness.

Of course we planned to welcome Mrs. La Salle, though I kept hoping she wouldn't show. That overcast afternoon found Barbara, Candy, and me seated around the kitchen table—Allen, unavoidably, was away. A car pulled up, and two men in their early thirties, one in raincoat and one in windbreaker, asked for Gregory. They came in and I went upstairs; he came down, roused from sleep or torpor, hair frazzled.

It turned out these unexpected guests were admirers rather than friends. "You're the best of all the Beat poets," one told him. They spoke with some knowledge of his life and work, but Gregory seemed almost utterly uninterested.

In the midst of their visit, Mrs. La Salle, a small blonde going grey, entered in raincoat and scarf. Candy and Barbara and I rose immediately, giving her the most comfortable chair. We introduced the others; Candy heated water for tea.

Gregory was eager to return upstairs, but not before one of his two visitors made a telling remark about his time in prison. Mrs. La Salle, teacup and saucer on coated knee, made no response, though she obviously heard it. I sat there thinking to myself, *Ohmygod! This poor woman! First hippies, now convicts! We'll never get this place.*

Yet the guests—and Gregory—left soon, and Mrs. La Salle remained outwardly unperturbed. We chatted about this and that—her years at East Hill Farm, her life in Buffalo. Gesturing toward us, Barbara characterized our group as "the creative type." Whatever we did or said, it must not have hurt. Allen visited Mrs. La Salle in mid-summer, and on October 25, through a $6,750 check, the seventy acres and all they contained became the property of Committee on Poetry, Inc. Eugene loaned Allen the bulk of the funds.

Though Barbara had spearheaded the farm search, the surrounding area was not wholly unfamiliar to Allen. That Buba—paternal grandmother Rebecca—had visited nearby Sharon Springs was part of family lore. The Hasidic presence there had encouraged Barbara to welcome the real estate opportunity in Cherry Valley, likely even to see East Hill Farm as "mystical." It was Rachel Fleischman, of course, who'd steered her in that direction to begin with, and now Rachel was due to join us for a few days.

She arrived in long purple silk scarf and black jacket with two silver buttons over a purple sweater. Drummond Hadley, a poet friend who summered in Cooperstown, had loaned us his father's vintage jeep, the small canvas-topped convertible sort that the armed forces used. Cooperstown was the site of the nearest movie theater, and one evening we—Candy, Barbara, Rachel, and I—drove the twenty-one miles there in the old Willys to see *In Cold Blood*. Our first night at the movies since moving into our electricity-less home was a big deal: we'd go again.

But not with Rachel. As we headed home, Candy driving, Barbara riding shot-gun, Rachel and I in the back, top down under the stars, soft summer breezes kissing our faces, we two began making out. After a few moments Candy lurched the jeep over to the side of the road, exclaiming in disgust, "I've had enough of this shit!"

Aside from her anger with me, Candy had picked up on Rachel's distaste for the life we were trying to build. Our guest seemed not at all sympathetic with our efforts at the farm; for her, they amounted to "people who aren't poor acting like they're poor." A day or so after our Cooperstown evening, she suddenly upturned the kitchen table; Candy's mother's tea pot crashed into a hundred pieces. Candy yelled at her in fury. Rachel had a supply of barbiturates which she began taking; Barbara seized them and threw them down the outhouse latrine. Rachel left almost immediately, but in time she'd return. In the meantime, I made amends with Candy.

One day, three friends drove up from Woodstock: Sally Grossman, Howard Alk, and Emmett Grogan. Sally was the wife of Dylan's manager Albert Grossman (once Dylan's lady, she'd graced the cover of *Bringing It All Back Home*); Howard, filmmaker, would later shoot Dylan's three-hour *Renaldo and Clara*; Emmett was a founder of the San Francisco–based Diggers. Sally was as attractive as she appeared in the Daniel Kramer cover photograph; Howard, large, black-bearded; Emmett, ruggedly good-looking as always: freckled, green-eyed, Irish.

Most of their visit was light and friendly, full of chitchat: at dinner Howard fantasized with Sally about publishing a community newspaper, and suggested with a laugh, "Bobby could write the social column!" But late that night Belle returned, shaken, from a long drive in her Lincoln with Emmett at the wheel. At suicidal speed he'd roared the big long white car up and down dark hills, 'round narrow curves. Later we learned that wheels had been loose on both axles: that they returned at all was miraculous.

Even Allen's parents came up a weekend: step-mother Edith ("my mother," Allen always called her) and father Louis. Louie, seventy-three, a couple inches shorter than Allen, squat (almost like a frog), balding and bespectacled, had a similarly deep voice but with some vestige of Old World tonalities—and attitudes, in spite of his assimilation, as first generation Russian Jew through high school and college teaching, home ownership, and poetry.

His commitment as poet was matched by his commitment as punster, humorist. "Gregory Corso is getting more so," Louie announced from the dining room rocker in the younger poet's presence. During his father's compulsive punning Allen would sit there pokerfaced and uncomplaining, though he must've heard the turned phrases hundreds of times:

I hear that in Greenwich Village the boys are making lasses of themselves.
Life? Depends on the liver.
A vacation is what you take when you can't take what you're taking.

Making sure I didn't escape the merriment, he called out twice, "Gordon, how do you like it here? If they're not treating you right, get your money back." Grey-haired Edith—a mere sixty-two in those days—was immensely agreeable and alert in all directions, and comfortable with her mate: "'A glass of wine, a loaf of bread, and thou,'" she characterized their early days together.

Our two elders seemed, in short, to enjoy their visit. Though they both were definitely "up" for the "outing" that the farm represented, I could sense that Louie, no outdoorsman, wanted to return to his desk, his poetry. Before long, adieus were made, with kisses, hugs, and well-wishing. Without puns.

Bard Out of New Jersey

A LLEN HAD TRAVEL plans of his own: a week in June in San Francisco; in July, to Mexico in the Volkswagen bus with brother and family; then a return to San Francisco. In late August he'd leave East Hill for the Democratic convention and Yippie Festival of Life in Chicago.

Meanwhile, I could visit with him, even share some intimate moments. Once I asked if he believed in reincarnation. "No," came the answer, immediately.

Then, a pause. I think it was nothing I heard, just something I could feel: as if he'd said, "Except—"

I asked, "What, Allen?"

"I just had a sense of Neal."

Once he volunteered to me of Gregory, "I think he may be a finer poet than I." And I asked him, "Of all you've written, what line do you think is most likely to last a century?"

He quoted from "The Change":

. . . so that I do
live I will die

I asked him another time what he thought of the Lobsang Rampa books. I was in part trying to get a better handle on our "sex guru" Stanley Fisher, who'd once held forth on the psychic experiences they presented. Allen answered in two words: "James Bond."

And I confessed to him, some weeks after the deed:

"Allen, I've taken a look at your diary."

"That's OK. I've looked at yours, too."

"Oh, really?"

"I didn't realize how sensitive you were."

□ □ □

I HADN'T FULLY understood *Howl* when I first read it, and my initial impression of Allen's work in the Don Allen anthology was wet behind the ears. But in the spring of 1968, both my understanding and attitude began to change. They did so most dramatically when I rode with Allen and Peter early on, just before the school year ended, to his reading at an Albany State University "Vietnam Commencement" program honoring draft resistance. There, for the first time, I beheld Allen's charged delivery, his riveting declamatory power.

More subtly, I was affected by his responses to student questions following the reading: "Christopher Smart, Ezra Pound, William Blake, and William Carlos Williams," he began, when asked his major poetic influences. "Hopeless," he responded—he was wearing a dark work shirt and jeans—when asked about the future. "Bellow?! C'mon!" he exclaimed in apparent disgust when asked if the novelist had influenced him.

Nearly as important as hearing Allen read and talk with students was what I witnessed that evening in a restaurant booth, when Allen and I sat across from Peter and a reporter from Albany's *Knickerbocker News*. Allen spoke on student movements, the war, the environment, the conflict between generations, the need for greater mass transit in America. He not only articulated but introduced some of the issues for the journalist. Such phrases as "the environment" and "ecology," for example, were heard far less than today; "mass transit," as Allen pointed out, was something many Americans, associating it with socialism, feared.

When I picked up the paper at Crain's Pharmacy on Main Street in Cherry Valley the next day, I read an article that accurately represented what Allen said, though it had him speaking "while gnawing on a slice of pizza and sipping a beer." (I don't think I ever saw Allen "gnaw" pizza.) Over time, as I continued to hear Allen's words and then see news accounts, I'd often note not only dismissiveness (e.g., "self-styled poet") but startling discrepancies between what I'd heard and what I saw in print.

His chanting of mantras learned in India 1962–63—"Hare Krishna," "Hare Om Namo Shivaye," and "Om Sri Maitreya"—moved me deeply. Seated on the grass near the front lawn, upper body rising and falling as sound burst from diaphragm past vocal chords through round open mouth, right hand vigorously pumping the bellows of his dark red Benares harmonium as fingers of his left held to a chord, his head and whole upper body shifted side to side, eyes sometimes open, sometimes shut, head tilting back and forth, his lips opened wide in powerful vibrating extended ancient syllables of worship.

This was the man whom one friend, so often at odds with me about the counterculture, had called "the saint" at the 1967 Central Park Be-In; this was the man whose first likeness I'd seen dripping with waters of the Ganges. This was the man who, as he would tell me, used to pitch "on my madhouse softball team."

This was Allen Ginsberg.

Captain Poetry

WITH WARMER WEATHER Peter had relinquished his belt of chains, but not necessarily his bizarre, even violent behavior. Some days he'd work hard in the huge garden area, swinging the big broad mattock or "clobber," as we called it; often he'd order Julius to help him. Or he'd relax, no longer scurry and shout up and down hill; perhaps as the farm grew increasingly "domestic" it helped focus, center him. But some midnights he'd scrub the kitchen floor, making strange loud sounds, going into Lear-like monologues, speaking to invisible entities, cleansing himself of germs.

One idyllic afternoon in the now fully green front yard, Gregory, Belle, Julius, Allen, and Ed (on the seat of honor, the large boulder) sat picnicking. Peter, energetically mowing the grass with our large power mower, came within six inches of Allen's protruding bare foot. Allen immediately turned and yelled at him, but Peter continued on his way. Another afternoon he threw the harmonium out Julius's second-story window. Allen ran outside and around the house, returning moments later, bearing the small red box between both hands, reporting that it had landed in the grass and was still working.

"I don't know where this violence comes from," sighed Gregory later, sitting upright on his bed. "Peter wasn't like that before."

At this time Allen would sometimes tell people who asked admiringly of Corso the poet that he'd retired. And Gregory himself would joke, "I'm a used poet," and East Hill was "a farm for used poets." But he too could become hostile and belligerent—violent—as time would tell. And though he wasn't expected to work in field, on house or in barn, he sometimes had expectations of those of us who did. When he and Belle first arrived, they brought with them a pretty tri-colored Persian cat named Earth. Almost immediately, Gregory looked into the pantry—"larder," Allen called it—and saw one or two cans of smoked oysters. Naturally, they went straight to kitty.

Second only to Belle, Earth was worshipped lavishly by Gregory. When after their first few days he and Belle went off, Gregory said to me, "Look after my cat." Since we were on a farm, unless I kept kitty tied up or enclosed, she was going to do some roaming. When Gregory returned, that's what the cat was doing, and immediately its upset owner exclaimed, inches from my face, "I thought I told you to look after my cat and now it's gone and may *nevah* return!" He wasn't just angry but miserable. And he was right: Earth, unheeding of Blake's imperative, did not return. Gregory was close to bawling.

He gave carte blanche to his emotions, and it was up to everyone else to adapt. Once, in midsummer, he went out to the garden for lettuce for his noon-day meal. All our early crops stretched up in brilliant light green tenderness, offering themselves to come who may. Entering the lettuce row, Gregory—rather than pick the leaves he needed—yanked a handful of plants up out of the earth, roots and all. Though the farm was hardly a preserve for finesse, I thought of him as a bull in a china shop. "Gregory needs a new personality," Allen had written ten years earlier: Allen, virtually his only friend for decades.

When Gregory wasn't badly indisposed, one could take him as court jester, a madcap fool. He sometimes played Tiny Tim on our small battery-operated player, chanting from under front yard shade to all who'd listen, "Tiny Tim is better than Dylan! Tiny Tim is better than Dylan!" He was a strange mixture of child idiot and child genius, crackerbarreling philosophies under the maple tree while goats romped and people worked around him: Chaplin and Falstaff.

"Shooting a movie is easy," Gregory once informed me when he saw me with my regular 8-millimeter Camex. "You just point the camera! Writing a poem, that's different."

"Hey, Allen," he once shouted, rolling out of the Lincoln after a return visit to Woodstock, "Dylan says you're a fascist! Ha! Ha!"

Early one afternoon on the grass above the drive, where we'd started a small herb garden, he recalled Anna Freud's telling him in Paris, "'You weren't yourself last night.' And I said, 'If I wasn't myself, who was I?' Ha! Ha! Ha!"

Once, standing on the wooden floor near the soda fountain, beneath the coffered ceiling of Crain's Pharmacy, "Captain Poetry," as he'd pronounced himself in 1966, held forth. Bert Crain, a quiet, white-haired, bespectacled pharmacist in his mid-fifties, seemed kindly disposed toward us, but I'd taken pains never to put him to a test. Now Gregory recited for anyone in distant earshot—besides Crain himself, there were a few patient, attentive customers—a complex and supposedly humorous narrative, the punch line of which, delivered in even louder voice, was, "He was a fuckin' *cavaleeah*!!" Silence—except for Gregory's hearty cackle—followed.

Several times that first summer we played softball, two or three to a team, using a wiffle ball; Allen eagerly joined in. Gregory, however, was steaming drunk on at least one such occasion. He favored a pair of white cotton pants in those days; this afternoon they were stuffed into a pair of our high black rubber boots and topped by a white sweatshirt. With our black bat he'd swing desperately at the evasive white plastic, then shout, "Hey, no *fayuh*! You cheated!"

One evening he was upstairs in their room as the rest of us, Belle included, sat down to dinner. The window at the end of the table just beneath theirs was open; there were no storm windows, no screens. Shortly someone looked up to see a stream of water running down the pane, and exclaimed, "Oh, my goodness, it's raining!" We then heard Gregory, upstairs at his window and not quite finished pissing, call out in distress, "Hey, Belle, it's raining! We bettah go out and close up the convertible!"

A Few Words About Me

A S I SKETCH everyday follies and worse on the part of others, readers may wonder if I consider myself undeserving of similar scrutiny. So let me offer a little
more background for Gordon Ball, this shadowy minor player who casts such an
intent eye upon others.

I'd come to the U.S. for college in 1962, from Tokyo. There I'd lived overly sheltered with houseboy-chauffeur and maids, in limited communication with my parents,
speaking an English language essentially detached from the much larger world and
culture all around me. Spending the next four years in an upper-class, white Southern
men's college, I remained grossly lacking not only in self-reliance but knowledge of the
quotidian physical world. I still didn't know many of the words for everyday items.

Visiting New York just after my freshman year, I spent a day in an apartment
with several young women. Late that afternoon I was asked to go to the store for spaghetti. Having seldom bought food in an American supermarket or corner store—or
cooked a real dinner—I quickly became confounded among aisles of material pleni-
tude: was "spaghetti" this can of Chef Boyardee that called itself so, or was it another
with clam sauce, or any of a half-dozen others which likewise shouted their identities
in reds and yellows from blue-papered cylinders? If I'd seen boxes of dry spaghetti
noodles, with those little plastic porthole glimpses of the humble yellowish brown
stalks themselves, they would've only confounded me further—but they, of course,
were what my hostess had in mind. I returned bearing cans.

By the end of my college career, I'd had only a little employment experience;
through frequent phone calls to girl friend Anna Marie in Charlotte, and repairs on
my used car (which I'd lent her) I'd run over $400 in debt at Harvard summer school
in 1965. Though I paid back my debts, my local bank shut down my checking account
before my senior year ended "to protect the community." And though I may have
rocked the staid Presbyterian world of Davidson College with an outrageously revealing first film inspired by Jonas's visit at the end of my senior year, I remained socially
and academically an "underachiever." My parents and other family members must
have despaired at their occasional glimpses of me in those days; even a friend from
Tokyo, seeing me at Harvard, declared me a "lost soul."

By the time I entered New York City in the fall of 1966, I was, as I reported in my memoir '66 *Frames*, "socially inept, shy, acutely self-conscious, and, on many occasions, almost mute." Surely, a year in New York in avant-garde film and psychedelics and group sex had some moderating influence on such a profile, as did hitching across the U.S. and much of Mexico, ending in jail in Mexico half a month. In any case, here I was, spring 1968, in a remote enclave where I was charged with "taking care" of house and grounds and animals and people, many of whom I'd never crossed paths with: I who'd grown up in the world's largest city, a privileged foreigner who could marginally take care of himself, who'd scarcely set foot on a farm in his life. In time, I'd come to be called "farm manager," a title I was never comfortable with.

So let these little historical and psychological bits make one thing clear: though I cast a large light on others, I too was part of the bizarre make-up of this funny farm, this ragtag group of urban castoffs, this lost battalion of pastoral conversationalists.

Constellations in Collision

E ARLY ON, ALLEN and I had walked out one night and lain awhile side-by-side in the night darkness, at the meadow's edge, under the stars. "Necking," he called it, and I was a little embarrassed when I heard him say it.

Of the heavenly bodies above I could recognize none. As we lay on the grass, Allen introduced to me a number of the constellations: Big Dipper, Cassiopeia's Chair; hunter Orion and his dog Sirius. Allen also gave me little thumbnail gists of his familiar human constellations below. Everyone, close and far, had a story, and he shared with me his versions. Before meeting Allen, Peter was eight months in the army. His 1953 discharge—he now received monthly veteran's checks of about $120—came after responding that "an army is an army against love" when an officer, finding him reading Erich Fromm's *Man For Himself*, and noting his Russian nameplate, asked if he were a Communist.

Within a year Allen found himself struck by the beautiful nude image of Peter on a painter friend's canvas; soon he was equally taken with the young man himself. A couple inches taller than Allen, slender and blue-eyed—that was the shy heterosexual Peter Orlovsky. Before long, they began sharing an apartment. But in those early days, Allen reported, Peter would sometimes withdraw, go on extended crying spells alone in his room.

They shared a sense of transcendental potential, as found in Allen's 1948 visionary experience of poet William Blake's voice, and in Peter's 1954 moment when the trees seemed to bow to him as he walked to classes at San Francisco Junior College. At a Foster's Cafeteria in San Francisco, 1955—in a visionary instant characterized by Allen as "celestial cold fire"—they vowed eternal commitment.

Julius Orlovsky, Allen told me, had grown up with elder brother Nicholas and younger brother Peter (twins Lafcadio and Marie came later) in sweat-shop conditions imposed on them by their father's necktie-making business. Oleg had been in the White Russian Army until fleeing the Revolution and making his way, eventually, to New York. Their mother, Kate, had come to Greenwich Village in the mid-'20s. An aspiring writer, she was encouraged in her short stories by Dorothy Parker. Then she met Oleg.

She was seventeen when they married. The next year she gave birth to Nicholas and was operated on for an ear infection. The drunken surgeon—she could smell his breath as he leaned over to wheel her into the operating room—severed a nerve, making one side of her face sag, leaving her permanently deaf in one ear.

As the family business began to fail, the children grew up in increasing poverty and Kate moved them to Long Island. In his late teens, Julius began to drop what interest he'd shown in girls, focusing on weightlifting instead; he then grew even more withdrawn. Not long after his mother told Peter he'd have to quit his senior year of high school and go to work, Julius was entering asylum. Years later, Allen told me, their mother, distraught and confused, stabbed Lafcadio in an altercation at a police station, desperately hoping it would keep him from being sent away too.

□ □ □

FOR BARBARA RUBIN, circumstances not only on East Hill but in the larger world were far from reassuring. Though her face already reflected her growing dejection over Allen, it showed a new bleakness early on the morning of June 6 when she and Candy and I stepped into the jeep for an appointment in Cooperstown. Perhaps the news had come from Ed (who had a short wave transistor radio, as well as a small TV run off golf cart batteries). Up before 6:00 and setting forth soon after letting his goats out, he might've stopped by if he'd seen someone up. In any case, the news was devastating: Robert Kennedy had been killed. I've seldom seen a human face as pale as Barbara's then—when tears finally freed it. The whole twenty-one miles to Cooperstown she sat there white and speechless in the olive green jeep.

She and Candy would still do things together, and would still argue with each other, but gradually, subtly, Barbara was growing more distant from us all. Kennedy's assassination came just a day after a journalist friend called Allen to verify that Andy Warhol had been shot—an event disturbing enough for each of us. But for Barbara, RFK's murder was apocalyptic: it spoke, loud and clear, like her relationship with Allen, of dreams unrealized. Candy and I, though shocked and distressed, saw it less as Apocalypse, more as further manifestation of fundamental conditions in a violent, corrupt nation. Candy, highly social but situating herself less in the center of things than Barbara, was in love with nature and animals, and had more points of contact for balance or support than her friend in anguish. And she was tougher physically, too.

I also think Candy's interest in open sex was starting to diminish. We were beginning to drift; her developing desire was to settle down into a more or less monogamous family scene and ultimately (though she didn't broach it with me then) to have children. And myself? I was interested in all that was around me, and I was intrigued—profoundly—by Allen.

In our nearly two years as a couple, Candy and I had had many great adventures and much great sex, together as well as with a large number of others, but I never knew if we really loved each other. Certainly, we were loving toward one another, I felt a great affection for her, and our ties seemed tight. But in the summer of 1968, that affection would begin to lessen.

We loved and respected Allen, and saw that with him came Peter. But there was something else: the extraordinary being that was Peter Orlovsky. There seemed no one like him in the universe—the breakfast offering to the woodchuck; his hyperbolic cartoon-character energy; the beauty of his hawknosed blue-eyed face and his incredible long thick hair; his cockeyed view of the world; the booming quality of his voice with its Long Island accent, its cadences rushed, then halted, nearly stuttered; its gruff, comic "AbbaDabbaDeDabbah!" and other phrases when words were too much—or too little; his rolling rapid funny paper talk—part Major Hoople, part Tweety Bird and Sylvester, part Katzenjammer, part who knows: the altogether magnificent, operatic absurdity of his character.

Not to mention his gift for poetry: William Carlos Williams, Allen told me, had made a survey of poets at the end of the '50s and proclaimed Peter the best lyric poet of his generation. And soon I would find myself admiring lines like

> I was born to remember a song about love—on a hill a butterfly
>   makes a cup that I drink from, walking over a bridge of
>   flowers.

One of the functions of the farm was as a stopping-off point for Allen's friends and colleagues. I'm sure part of what would become Candy's disappointment was that East Hill was a kind of rowdy bed-and-breakfast with the most raffish of guests and residents. Meantime, in these first few months, she "hung in" there, I think, grateful to be surrounded by animals, far from cities. And she and I basically got along. She seemed to love the area, the farm itself, and settling in; and after the rigors of Mexico and jail, she was putting on a few pounds. She was hoping, I imagine, in those early days, that East Hill Farm, even with all its psychic tumult, could be her site for nest-building.

Works and Days—and Stillbirth

L ATE JUNE: GEESE honked, goats knocked horns, and chickens scratched the warm surface of the earth. Life all around us, like the maples blessing our asbestos-sided house, had grown green and fat; corn reached knee-high; lettuce and radishes completed daily vegetarian dishes. Before summer was out, some cabbage family plants would make it to our table. Even Brussels sprouts, which I'd hated since childhood forced-feeding by my father: in the summer of 1968, they were the food of the gods.

Candy, who'd ridden since she was five at home in New Jersey, had made a request of Allen: could she get a horse? Yes, he answered, without hesitation, in characteristic generosity. She looked one place and another, then selected a spirited mare.

Our dairy farmer neighbor, Claude Graham, had a huge 635-acre spread: soon we'd help with the first haying of the season. And as long bright days charmed all growing things, more and more friends from the city would join us.

We resurrected the green tent, pitching it in the grass farther up along the drive. One clear moonlit night, a week after his return from California, Allen and I parted the green canvas flaps and went inside. I introduced him to Pertussin, an aerosol spray treatment for coughs; its effects—the sensation of expanding, spangling, spiraling universes—were like those of glue (which a girl friend and I, back at Davidson, had inhaled from the bottom of a paper bag). In the tent I sprayed the cough medication into a sack and passed it to Allen. In his journal, dated June 28, 1968, he wrote the poem published as "Pertussin," which ends

> the raw Aether
> shines with Brahmanic cool moonshine
> aftertaste, midnight Nostalgia.

Of course, everyday life, as we dealt with all it presented us in house, garden, and barn, was not usually so radiant. Already we were discovering problems with Brahma and Vishnu and Shiva: we couldn't let them roam free; the violated garden, flower bed, and herb plot testified to that. (But Ed's reassurance that they wouldn't eat everything was valid: they only nibbled clothing, and avoided tin cans.)

Near the end of the barn we'd readied some stalls for the goats, thick with straw bedding. On an inside wall near the front, before we had any animals, I'd tacked the cover of the "Changes" issue of the *San Francisco Oracle*, with its multiple color images of Allen, Gary Snyder, Alan Watts, and Timothy Leary. Now we began noticing the occasional disappearance of a smidgen here, a smidgen there, of the large sheet of paper.

Typically we'd let the goats out mornings with small chain leash and divot (a sort of long metal corkscrew attached to the other end of the leash, for twisting down into the earth) and situate them somewhere in the meadow above the house, just beyond the front yard—then return them to their stalls around 6:00 PM. Often they were visited by Ed's large ancient black Egyptian Nubians, especially his fifteen-year-old billy (named Billy), whose majestic curved and coiling horns spanned five feet. (Whenever he was let in and out of their barn, Billy automatically turned his head sideways so as to make it through the doorway.)

One afternoon several weeks after our goats had joined us we heard Brahma—we hadn't tied her up that day—bleating from her stall. Candy, Peter, and I hurried in. She was partly lying down, facing the wall, body twisted, throwing her head back toward us, bleating. The lower half of her body heaved rhythmically.

Now what to do? None of us knew about goat birthing, but someone gave a shout to Ed, who was nearby. He came right in, bending his denimed knees into soft yellow straw. With one quick motion he righted Brahma so her vagina faced him, then immediately stuck both hands in, one at each side. Gradually, slowly, carefully he pulled. A roundish dark wet thing began to emerge between his large enclosing hands: we could see ears, nose, front hoofs, then gradually the rest of the body. But its eyes were closed.

Ed got it all the way out and laid it in the straw near its bleating mama, who nudged at it unstoppingly with nose and tongue, urging, urging, urging its life. "He was too big and he got caught, you see," Ed said, squinting through his glasses, pointing to its umbilical cord tangled tight around its neck.

Though she was kidless, Brahma's udders were full. Ed had taught us how to milk: pressing your index finger and thumb around the very highest end of the nipple (where it meets the udder), you begin to squeeze, then gradually extend that squeeze all the six inches or so to nipple's end: the milk descends with the downward progress of your hand. Then you repeat, repeat, repeat—doing the same, simultaneously, with the other nipple.

Often I was the only one who drank the milk—thick, rich, luxuriant; others disliked its goaty smell and taste. There wouldn't be a whole lot of it, but leftovers went to dogs and cats: besides Barbara's Malcolm, still cringing behind the fridge, there was tortoise shell Panda Manda, who with a male tiger just moved in would soon have kitties. Death was momentary; life rolled on, vast and seemingly unstoppable.

The Fourth of July

Q UICKLY IT TURNED not just warm but, as Carl La Salle had promised, hot. Oppressively so. Independence Day, as it happened, was the hottest—and the worst—day yet.

The Fourth of July found Gregory, gifted at sketching and drawing, with brush in hand, at work on a canvas set upon an easel in the yard, just beyond the flagstones at the front of the house.

He was also at work on a bottle of whisky, and before long had made real progress. What began as difference of opinion between him and Belle now leapt into argument. I was standing nearby, next to a small stand of white peonies. On the large boulder, just beyond the center of the sloping yard and under shading maples, sat sixty-three-year-old Ed Urich, catching his breath in harsh heat. Often unstoppably talkative, our good neighbor was now totally quiet: he'd just learned of the death of an old friend.

Now Belle turned utterly livid; in fury she grabbed Gregory's painting with both hands and threw it at him—but hit me. Gregory reacted immediately: "Look what you've done! You've hurt my painting and my poor friend Gordon! Look what you've done!"

I wasn't hurt, of course, but no matter. He immediately turned to Ed, still sitting quietly on rock in hot shade, and challenged: "What kind of hermit are you?! You talk all the time! You're no hermit!" Ed sat there stoically, sweating, looking sternly back at Gregory, saying nothing.

Then out the front door came Barbara, in pink nightgown in mid-afternoon, stepping onto the first flagstone, heading for the backyard outhouse. Gregory saw her, ran after her, tackled her, cackling madly, delighted by how much fun it was to tackle her, rolling with her an instant on the grassy earth beyond the flagstones. Barbara pulled herself away, and picked herself up. In tears.

And anger: she bent over Gregory as he rose back up. "Since no one here's going to protect me, I'll call the police if you ever do that again." She didn't look my way. I felt bad, very bad.

□ □ □

DURING THE SCENE with Gregory, Allen had been inside, at work on details of acquiring the farm. Later, while I was still outside, Barbara spoke with him—about what, I don't know. Then speaking turned to disagreeing, then disagreeing to arguing. When I happened to walk into the house, Barbara began to shout uproariously at Allen, then at me as well. Her words are long gone from my memory; she is dead; Allen is dead. But the force of her anger and dejection remains inside me, all the screaming soul of her. And I hold in my hand the sad and comic effort she made to rebuild bridges hours later, on a hot Fourth of July forty-three years ago.

It's two pages of eight-and-a-half by eleven-inch white paper, stapled together bottom to top as a scroll, on which she'd ornately printed a message in purple magic marker. A "corporate seal" of lipsticked kisses appears opposite the signature.

Attention
Monsieur A. Ginsberg
Sir G. Ball

Sirs:

This document shall be its own evidence that I am attempting to close the communications gap (which has been opening for several years now).

That I, the undersigned, mea culpa, mea culpa, mea maxima culpa, raised my selfsame voice on the morning of our most honorable holiday, namely the 4th of July, year of our Lord, 1968.

I, the undersigned, do most humbly apologize for any eardrums that may have been desecrated by my excessive use of the decibel level.

Respectfully,
signed: Miss Barbara Rubin
witness: Miss Candy O'Brien

DATE: July 4, 1968

Such was Barbara's apology to Allen and me. I don't know that she received one from Gregory. Or that Ed did.

Allen Travels, Farm Grows

D ESPITE DIFFERENCES AND disappointments, Barbara and Candy remained active companions, filling days with furniture and equipment forays, house and barn with acquisitions. A pair of young carpenters from Cooperstown persuaded us that adding tongue-and-groove pine paneling to bedroom and attic walls would be as good as, and cheaper than, tearing walls out and stapling in insulation. They went to work in early July, putting in several hours a day at $2 an hour; by mid-August upstairs bedrooms were paneled and the attic finished, with a raised area for a bed (and extra space for altar) at the north end overlooking the drive. At Candy's request, each paneled bedroom was then equipped with a strong iron ring, screwed into the wall, to which fifteen feet of thick sisal were attached, for bailing out the window in case of fire.

We often worked with "the two Mikes" (one, Mike Morris, cheery, good-looking and bald; the other good-looking and long-haired); even Gregory joined in briefly once or twice (And Candy noted the surprising strength with which he swung his hammer.) We worked so hard indoors and out thinning plants and roofing the barn and at "a thousand chores a day," as I wrote a friend, there was "no time for anything at the end of day except SLEEP."

Downstairs, beyond the pantry and behind the narrow front porch, Peter was refurbishing his room. The attic, with just enough space to stand up straight under its peaked center, was not only the domain of Barbara, but soon, of her multiple guests.

Learning of their mother's terminal cancer, she invited the children of Ann and Al Aronowitz to come stay awhile. Journalist Al had written a series of *New York Post* articles on Kerouac and the Beats in 1959, and introduced Dylan and the Beatles in 1964. She invited Leigh Ziprin, son of mystical philosopher Lionel, and encouraged Belle to ask her ex-husband to send their daughter our way. There was additional sleeping space on living room sofa and floor, outdoors under the stars, and inside the Volkswagen camper. Allen's expressive young friend Stephen Bornstein and quiet girl friend Barbara Pionteck slept in the tent.

Before most of Barbara's guests arrived, Allen left for Mexico with Eugene and family. One afternoon at the end of the first week of July, a dusty green and white 1959 Ford Country Squire station wagon rolled down our dirt drive. Out stepped a

slender balding man in mid-forties with horn-rimmed glasses; a pretty, slender porce-
lain-doll-looking blonde with high cheekbones; and five children, ages five to twelve:
Eugene and Connie, his North Carolina–born wife and Alan, Neal, Ann, Peter, and
Lyle. They'd come to pick up Allen; they'd drive off with him in the bus all the way to
Mexico, D.F., leaving us with their station wagon and two gerbils, "Weasel" (whom
we later gave to captivated young friends) and "Joy."

None of us had heard of gerbils. Eugene took pains to introduce these two little
nervous creatures nestling among wood chips in a treadmill-equipped cage, explaining
how they differed from hamsters. Only later would he tell me that looking over what
struck him as rather flat and un-pretty land, he wondered why Allen had gotten it, and
assumed it was out of commitment to others.

Soon the gang of eight were off on a long leisurely trip south and west, spending
a week to reach the border at Nuevo Laredo. There, it would take Allen three hours
to be allowed to cross, only after winning special permission from the head of immigration. After his return, he told me of being detained before entering. Border officials
told him he had to shave and bathe: "'We don't like hippies and *existentialistas* in our
country; they make a bad impression for the tourists. We don't let hippies and com-
munists and Jews in.'" He had to get a lawyer.

With Allen gone, Candy began to assume more management of the farm: Barbara
was growing more erratic, and Candy had the responsibility of the checkbook. Six
months earlier, before there was a farm, Committee on Poetry, Inc., disbursements
had included grants-in-aid for LeRoi Jones (eight small checks in just over a month),
Andrei Codrescu, Charles Plymell, Herbert Huncke, and many others. Now there
were also entries such as $38 to John A. Morford, antique dealer; $100 to Carl La
Salle to build pasture fence; $30 to Lipe Feed Co. for tarpaper for woodshed and barn.

By mid-summer, the ranks of new arrivals, animal and human, became legion. A
pregnant Jersey cow, whom we named Bessie Smith, was delivered one day: she was
light brown like most Jerseys, much of her forehead was black, with a little white
diamond at top; the area around nose and mouth was white. And her mid-section was
huge: she was due to "freshen" in the next few weeks. Peter in tam-o'-shanter; Carl
La Salle in blue denim vest; Barbara in checkered smock, bell bottoms, red sweater on
shoulder; and I with movie camera, formed our welcoming committee. The startled
Jersey was led resignedly off the back of the truck. As she neared the barn, a bearded
Julius, head bent down, hair in eyes, joined Candy in petting her.

Joining Bessie were more chickens, swelling the ranks of barnyard poultry. But
from fellow fowl Barbara's two large, light grey and brown African geese remained

aloof: despite their long-necked elegance and dignity, they turned out to be nobody's friends. Sometimes they'd stand harmlessly on one leg, leaning forward, the other leg stretched out in the rear, or wiggle tail feathers as black beaks disappeared into a plastic bucket full of water. But they'd also follow you, broad wings flapping, trying to take a nip. They had the run of the place, especially in front of the house, where they dropped their little wet grey-green hillocks at will—even on the porch.

Soon after Bessie came the graceful, tall chestnut mare—part Arabian—that Candy had selected. Delighted, she began teaching several of us how to ride, how to handle tack, how to groom. At an auction we bought a used buggy and began training Penny to lead it. Allen had even agreed to the purchase of a Shetland pony for the summer, timed to arrive with visiting children. We hoped for—Candy dreamed of—a sleigh come winter.

In the meantime, our green beans and pumpkins flourished. When woodchucks or deer got 95% of the soybeans in two days, I placed a transistor radio in the main plot to protect all remaining crops. It worked—until batteries died.

Belle's five-year-old daughter Tasha joined her mother for a few weeks, and the Aronowitz kids were there a month or so. Al and Ann, thirty-eight, came up to visit their children, who were unaware of her cancer. Unfortunately Ann became ensnared with eight-year-old Joel, shouting at him again and again ("Joel! Joel!") for the impish delight he seemed to take in getting under her skin. They were like *The Simpsons'* Itchy and Scratchy, only given Ann's illness it was sad; it was a teaching.

Miles (twelve), Brett (ten), and Joel seemed to enjoy—some—the zaniness and fun of the farm, from using outhouse to jumping out of hayloft to defending themselves from geese. But a wicked bite on Brett's fanny sent the elegant aggressors back to the farm they came from—inelegantly stuffed into pillowcases inside a car trunk.

There was a darker side to the East Hill of these three siblings from West 93rd, who'd never gotten farther from the city than suburbs. Brett "never felt truly safe there"; it was ultimately a dangerous situation. One hot day a twenty-year-old friend from the Lower East Side was visiting and Barbara, against her better judgment, let him take the three children and Julius in the jeep to a nearby lake for a swim. But the jeep broke down five miles from the lake, and Jeff decided to lead them on foot. The children were too shy to complain effectively, Julius too silent. So they made their forced march under July sun, and finally got in a swim; Barbara was furious when Jeff called explaining at dusk, asking to be picked up.

Not having running water could be "painful" for the children. Sleeping in the attic of a lightless house, if they needed to pee they had to lay hands on a flashlight, go all the way down the steep attic ladder, then down the narrow stairs to the first floor, across the kitchen, and out the front door. Once Brett knew she had to go, but, scared of encountering the ghostly woman in white a grown-up had just told her about, she let herself fall back to sleep and peed in her sleeping bag.

Worse than any ghost was Gregory. One afternoon he returned from town with a large steak to grill outdoors on the Coleman stove. He held it up before the eyes of the three kids already confounded by no running water, no bathroom, and a meatless diet dominated by wheat pilaf. He taunted, "I'm not going to give you any!"

Brett and her brothers then watched as he proceeded to cook it and do just that. For good measure he added, "You think your father smokes Turkish tobacco. But it's not. It's marijuana!" Their dinner would once again feature the hated pilaf.

In this, as in most situations, individuals made a difference. Once Brett's younger brother Joel, full of energy and aspiration, was told by one of the big people he was simply too small to do something; in anguish he left the house, head down, for the barn. Allen, who'd overheard, ran out after him. "Are you hurt?" he asked, coming abreast. Joel paused, his face brightened, and he seemed fine after that. And for Brett herself, it was most of all Barbara who made a difference, Barbara who took an interest in her life. Barbara who, like their mother, would die prematurely.

□ □ □

LIFE WENT ON. And death, too. Candy had carefully run wire mesh around the front of the chicken coop to keep all other animals away: both chickens and ducks were setting. The ducks seemed to be taking inordinately long, but finally, five eggs hatched: we hadn't known that Muscovies took a week longer than most varieties.

Would that such had been the only problem. Candy, finding the baby ducklings, got down on hands and knees among them on the grey earth, exclaiming, "Oh my God, you're so precious!" Clasping him lightly, she raised to her face one little furry yellow ball with a beak, then set him down, reached for another. Then leaving the baby duck multitude in the doorway, and the chicken wire open, she ran in delight to our house, hoping for someone to join her in the new marvel. She called from the kitchen, stuck her head into the pantry toward Peter's room. She hurried upstairs, called up to the attic. But no one was home, so she returned to the chicken yard.

The grass in front of the chicken house was high; it was a moment or more before she discovered the first sign of what had happened in the interval of her absence: the two dogs, Godly and Sadeyes, had eaten or killed every baby but a crumpled one who lay dying in a corner.

Huncke

L ONG BEFORE HE left for Mexico and the West, Allen had told me he had someone
named Huncke in mind as long-term guest. A strange-sounding name, I thought,
imagining a short chunky guy, broad-shouldered, shirt-tails out. "Who's Huncke?" I
asked. Much later Allen with a chuckle would characterize several farm guests from
the old days as "archetypal dope fiends," but at that early point he answered simply,
"A writer."

Now, midsummer 1968, Huncke wrote Allen from San Francisco:

> I'm extremely anxious to get in touch with you. So far—I'm doing unusually well—
> holding out against getting hooked although I have gotten off several times since
> returning to the city. Nevertheless—all—at this point goes well—and there is an
> excellent chance if things work out per plans—I'll make it without too much
> difficulty. My hope is—something can be done about getting back east and upstate
> before I become involved in the scene here. Perhaps—it will sound phoney but I am
> more anxious than ever not to end up with a habit. Frankly—I simply am at my
> rope's end and if I crash this time—I'm afraid of the outcome. I'm sure it will mean
> nothing short of jail.

> Allen—please please don't delay getting in touch with me—any longer than is
> absolutely necessary.

> Meanwhile—I love you and need you.

Only days later, as it happened, just after his arrival in the Bay Area, Allen found
Huncke—broke and strung out on junk. He heard from others that Huncke had beaten
nearly everyone in town for money. He got him an airline ticket east and accompanied
him to the plane, lest ticket be cashed for junk. At the farm Huncke would kick.

At least momentarily, the prospect of Huncke's coming seemed to lift Barbara's
spirits. He was an old friend from the Lower East Side, and she seemed to like him
still. She and Candy joined Peter, who drove, and picked him up at the Albany airport, sixty miles east. When he stepped onto the worn linoleum of our kitchen later
that warm midsummer evening, he wore a tweedy overcoat, carried a small suitcase.
Sitting with me for coffee and tea under strips of sticky amber paper decked with

many a fly dead or dying, he was nothing but gracious: a warm deep voice and an eye-fastening look and attentiveness that put you at ease whenever he spoke. And whenever you spoke—at the center of his abiding calm lay his gift for making you feel that whatever problems or difficulties you had, they were familiar: from the perspective of those large regarding hazel eyes and that rich voice, they were his own.

He was now fifty-three. He had a big—grand—face, short black hair, small body. When I told him he resembled Humphrey Bogart, he chuckled. After Gregory's traumas and dramas and despoilations and debauches, and Peter's distress, Huncke was a swan gliding down a limpid stream. If I looked for anything to break, I quickly gave up.

The second day he was there he and Candy and I visited Myron Wiles. Huncke and I enjoyed a cool shower together in Myron's barn, talking much of the time, about this, about that. Later, Candy told me Huncke had confided to her after the shower that he thought I loved her very much.

The early part of Huncke's stay—it would be his first of several over the next few years—was uneventful. He'd generally remain in his room and make occasional appearances in the kitchen in his bathrobe, just to heat a bowl of soup from the can, and sit at the table. And snuggle and stroke the cowering Malcolm, who now began to truly rehabilitate, in his arms.

He didn't help much with chores, gardening or household, but wasn't really expected to. He was ten years younger than Ed, who left at 6:00 AM to tend other people's gardens. He told me I was doing a "wonderful job" managing the farm, which took me aback: I didn't think I was doing such, let alone doing it wonderfully. In one of many little talks I had with him at the time I confided, "You know, Huncke, I'm never sure if I'm on the same level as others." "I feel the same way," he answered immediately in rich, reassuring tones.

Stephen Bornstein had told me Huncke was a black magician. But one evening several of us were turning on to some good hash in the green tent; Candy talked excitedly at a rapid pace, only to suddenly interrupt herself and announce, "I feel like I'm dying." Huncke immediately moved right in, telling her calmly she was all right and we were all with her and cared for her, and it passed.

In those early days Huncke was given to putting people in a verbal situation and, based on their response, analyzing their personality. "You're walking down a road," he'd begin with any of us—Candy, Allen, myself—"and you see a house. What does it look like? Tell me what you see . . ." From the details of your response (Allen's was unbelievably detailed) he'd tell you your view of the world, whether you were generous toward others and trusting of them. And so forth.

A little later, Stephen Bornstein, who'd been to the city, brought up a small amount of amphetamine, crystal or sulfate, and Huncke, naturally, learned of it. I said I was of a mind to throw it away, but Huncke pulled a big pout, throwing his large lower lip out: "OK, then, throw it all away!"

He made it clear he'd help with work if he had some speed. To be able to store a long winter's worth of firewood for the Kalamazoo, we were starting to build a woodshed and needed help. It was the first time I felt at odds with Huncke; I felt bad; I gave in. We all snorted amphetamine, and did Huncke work! He not only helped carry flat boulders and lay the woodshed foundation; he swept the house as well as we all toiled like some "superhuman crew," cutting and laying 4 x 4s atop the boulders, cutting and nailing the plywood siding, the planks and tarpaper for the roof—all, or much of it, in a day's work.

Cherry Valley Days:
Main Street and East Hill

A N ANNUAL EVENT in Cherry Valley was the early August observation, in pageantry and floats, of "Yesteryear Day": the community paraded down Main Street in older clothing and trappings, celebrating a village whose history now covered 230 years.

Many of us went, dressed in old or frontier fashion—even Huncke, though he, like Barbara, stayed on the sidelines and watched the passing show. In movie footage glimpses, I see Barbara short-haired in white Nehru suit. She wears small round shades and leads Tasha, in cut-away red jacket and pants, by the hand. Candy, irrepressible as ever, had doubtless found her large lady's straw hat, decked with flowers and a blue ribbon, in an antique store. Barbara Pionteck, small, diffident, wears roses in her light brown hair. Joel's a cowboy, with hat and vest; Miles sports a kerchief at his neck, like Huncke sometimes favored; a brown sort of Hatfield-McCoy hat tops Stephen Bornstein's head.

The Main Street parade is bright and cheery in strong sun: two brown horses with blond manes pull a covered wagon; a single horse pulls a topless buggy bearing a couple in formal dress, white gloves, and parasols; a band follows, dark blue with gold braid, white shoes; several men march in Revolutionary War outfits, others in old-fashioned dress with derby hats. Candy and Barbara Pionteck walk among them, waving at the crowd; a large float carries three men in rocking chairs—one is Myron Wiles: in grey wig, black vest, and blue chambray shirt, he chugs from a jug.

Judging from the filmic record, we were integrated within the community; and in certain ways, mainly economically, we were. One Saturday night a few months later, one of the fellows at Howie Fassett's Mobil station, where we took so much business, would to general amusement answer my "See you later" with "See you in church!" Though at the time it unnerved me, I was pleased that enough familiarity had developed to joke about glaring differences.

Back on East Hill a week later it was raining, and Allen was to return in a few days—then leave in two weeks for Chicago. A soil test had shown deficiencies in each of the three basic elements (nitrogen, phosphorous, potassium), but much of our garden was thriving. Huge sprawling pumpkin vines now covered brown earth with deep

rich green; peas would be ready soon; we hoped for ripe potatoes, onions, beans, ruta-
bagas, parsnips, and much else before frost. I'd been taking a look at Euell Gibbons's
Stalking the Wild Asparagus, considering what food might be naturally rooted in the
earth all around us. Come Saturday it was raining again, and Peter—with typical
single-mindedness and enthusiasm—was cooking fish for dinner.

Given the givens, things seemed virtually idyllic, but the challenge of getting a
water system more sophisticated than the single pump at the kitchen sink was proving
complex. Since bringing in electricity would be prohibitively expensive, we turned to
other possibilities. We dug for a well in the meadow above the house, hoping to bring
ourselves water by gravity—but results were negative.

Ed said he'd heard—and old timers before him knew of—a well somewhere in the
front yard, long buried. Could we uncover it? And would it still be usable? No one
who'd claimed to know or hear of it could pinpoint where it might be. When someone
suggested trying a diviner, we did.

One afternoon, several of us watched a slight man in middle years walk back
and forth in our front yard and up toward the drive, holding a forked willow branch
straight out from his waist. Were there a significant underground stream, it would
begin to point downward, dramatically. But it wavered only slightly, inconclusively.
We paid him for his time—$10?—$15?—and figured what to do next.

A fellow with a backhoe dug a broad hole fifteen feet deep in the front yard. We
all, including Allen and the Aronowitz kids, stood and watched this sizable undertaking. But again, no soap. And the backhoe operator, squeezing us in between other jobs
on the same day, left before he could fill it back in.

Leaving it open for one of the lighter moments at the farm that summer. Over
the last few weeks, we'd given away all but one of the little kitties born to our Panda
Manda. Over the last few days, Ed Urich had been visited by an uninvited guest who
seemed to want to stay: a baby raccoon, whom he named "Any." With his tiny dark
paws which he'd wash beforehand, he'd eat anything.

Now Any—he soon became our daily visitor—and the multi-colored kitty played
the livelong day in the torn-up area. He'd run through a pipe; kitty, waiting at the
other end, would strike his face lightly with her paw. Any would chase kitty over the
planks covering the big hole; kitty would suddenly stop and turn and bat Any right on
his little pointed nose. Kitty would retreat to a higher prospect, and when Any at last
came abreast of her she'd jump right over him. . . . Would that humans—at the farm,
in Chicago, in Vietnam, across the planet—could chase and fall and swivel and play
with such light, such affection, such mercy!

Barbara and the Hasidim

O NE NIGHT CANDY, Barbara, and I drove to Cooperstown to see Roman Polanski's *Rosemary's Baby*. Barbara had befriended Polanski in 1963 at age eighteen when she went with Jonas to the Knokke-Le-Zoute Third International Experimental Film Festival. Polanski later drew a cartoon of her sucking a popsicle which was an erect cock.

Now we entered the darkness of a cinema together for what proved the last time. Was Barbara, who'd so wanted a baby with Allen, now testing the waters of the past in "reconnecting" with Polanski and even the Barbara Rubin of yesteryear, the maker of the orgiastic *Christmas on Earth*? Was there any such tension in her mind as we watched the dark fable of a young woman in congress with the Devil? I'll never know. But her life's direction was about to be clarified more sharply than ever before, thanks to a visit from a sometimes troublesome friend.

Shortly after we saw the Polanski film, Rachel Fleischman took the bus up from the city. This time, I kept my distance.

One afternoon, in our World War II vintage jeep, Barbara drove Rachel to visit Rachel's grandmother and other relatives at their family home in Sharon Springs. The Fleischmans fell madly in love with Barbara and her many questions about their family roots. Then, starting back, turning a corner on the way out of town, Barbara screeched to a stop before a large Victorian wooden frame building of several stories. It was the Meshiach Orach Ohayim, a Yeshiva and home for troubled Hasidic youths. Quickly she turned to Rachel: "Do you feel those vibes?" In an instant she was out of the jeep, rushing up the broad flight of steps, across the front porch, toward the door; children clamored about her. Rachel waited in the Willys a good fifteen minutes; Barbara returned singing.

Thus began Barbara's visits to the Satmar Hasidic community in Sharon Springs. Such a complex creature was Barbara! One moment revisiting her "transgressive" past, another following her yearning and love for children, exploring mystic roots. And forever gathering diverse people together: all of it was only characteristic.

One afternoon she brought—unexpectedly—several young women from the Yeshiva to the farm for a visit. They huddled above the drive near the Volkswagen bus from which they'd just emerged, in long plain body-covering dresses, insecurely

clutching arms across chests, scarves covering heads, gazing the short distance downhill toward the farmhouse, the human center of our seventy acres. They may have seen
Candy, long auburn hair flowing freely, large breasts unrestrained; they may have
seen Peter, walking or stomping about, clothed only in dungaree shorts; they may
have seen me, bare from waist up. They came no closer; one started to slump over, as
if in a faint, until she was held up by her companions. They left soon.

Allen Returns, a Calf Is Born

NEAR THE END of his California visit, Allen had gone to the Los Gatos home of widow Carolyn Cassady. In the hands of Neal's oldest son John Allen he'd beheld a silk bag containing the remains of his erstwhile love and inspiration. "On Neal's Ashes" soon followed:

> Delicate eyes that blinked blue Rockies all ash
> nipples, Ribs I touched w/ my thumb are ash
> mouth my tongue touched once or twice all ash
> bony cheeks soft on my belly are cinder, ash
> earlobes & eyelids, youthful cock tip, curly pubis
> breast warmth, man palm, high school thigh,
> baseball bicept arm, asshole anneal'd to silken skin
>   all ashes, all ashes again.

When I saw it I asked, "Allen, you kissed Neal just a couple of times?"

"Oh, that's a charming understatement," he answered.

Allen's period back "home" after intensive travel—9,000 miles in just over a month—could scarcely have been restful for him, for it was marked by argument.

A week or two before his return, Bessie had given birth to a little tan and white calf, wet with wombly fluid, wobbly on uncertain legs, an uncertain expression on her broad face as she greeted this variegated world. A marvel!

But what now to do with her, amidst a burgeoning animal population, some of it pregnant? With winter and all its Snow Belt problems and preparations now on the horizon for a remote, electricity-less household? Another large and growing animal, with the possibility of offspring, in our verge-of-collapse barn? Yet a marvel she was.

As we discussed it, Rachel joined in: we ought to keep it, she said, but if we couldn't, give it to a kosher butcher. (We'd found no one in the area who wanted to raise a calf.) Barbara's thoughts ran along similar lines, but more passionately: the horror of slaughter was unthinkable and unspeakable, but were there truly no choice, as a dire last resort it should be carried out by a kosher butcher. Peter, in rare agreement with Barbara, felt the calf should be kept in the field.

Allen joined Ed, Stephen, Barbara Pionteck, and me in arguing that if we kept her, the calf would be taking milk Bessie was here to give. The most vehement opposition to Barbara came from Candy, who saw Barbara's position as just another effort on her part to control Allen: "This whole thing is ridiculous! It's not the calf, it's Barbara!"

The dispute lasted over a week. What were we to do with such an impasse? A solution came one afternoon when we were haying with Claude Graham, our friendly dairy farmer neighbor. Dust and chaff exploded all about us in radiant golden light as we heaved heavy bales of alfalfa onto the conveyor belt feeding into the dark upper loft of his barn. Pausing a moment, I mentioned the problem. "You ought to," Claude said, catching his breath and turning our way, "just call the butcher we use around here, the one over to Albany. He'll take 'er away for you."

That evening Stephen and I told Allen, seated at the dining room table with Barbara, what Claude had said—and that we agreed. Allen also agreed. "At least let it have a kosher butcher!" Barbara shouted in desperation. She stormed out, calling us heretics.

After several more days, Claude's butcher—a quiet man in Can't Bust 'Em overalls and floppy canvas hat—showed up. But by now Bessie had taken the calf far down into the pasture, which was overgrown with countless scrub bushes—and we couldn't find her. We looked and looked over the course of two days, while the fellow from Albany stayed on call. Finally, we found Bessie deep in the meadow, beyond the well, amidst myriad goldenrod and hawkeye and milkweed, her pink-nosed and still slightly spraddle-legged little girl at her side. We managed to get the calf away, and hauled her into the back of the butcher's big truck. Then, just before the butcher drove off, Stephen took him aside and asked the question that none of us—we'd all grown to love the calf—had wanted to ask.

"And so what will happen to her, now?" Stephen asked him.

"Oh, I don't know," he answered. "I'll keep it in Albany 'til the kosher butcher comes around."

Chicago Looms

TIME BEGAN RUNNING out before the Chicago Democratic Convention and Yippie Festival of Life. Allen had committed to going, and would join Burroughs, Jean Genet, and Terry Southern, who were to write for *Esquire*, as well as Yippie friends and associates. But should he really go ahead, some of us wondered. He might be killed! And, wasn't he needed at the farm?

Around Columbia University in the mid-forties, Allen, Kerouac, and Lucien Carr had discussed what they called a "New Vision," with its idealistic Rimbaudian projection of "Christmas on earth." The problem was, how to realize ecstatic or sacred vision not merely in the profane but the political world. What *was* the relation between poetry and politics—if any? In that breakthrough moment in "Wichita Vortex Sutra" (1966), Allen had declared the war over—but it had raged on, even escalated, ever since.

That same poem invoked a Whitmanic sense of humanity in America, but against such hopeful projections, reality now looked grimmer and grimmer. Allen's arrest with the kindly Dr. Spock and others at New York's draft board headquarters at the end of 1967; the ominous Grand Central Yip-In with its poor planning and police violence the following spring; the assassinations of King (a year after calling "my own government" "the greatest purveyor of violence in the world today") and Robert Kennedy: all testified to crisis conditions nationwide. And on Memorial Day 1968, the village of Cherry Valley had learned of its first son lost to America's Vietnam War: the mother of Clarence Baldwin was notified by Marines minutes before the annual parade began.

In June, Jerry Rubin's tailbone was broken when police entered his apartment without warrant, ransacked it, and beat him. In mid-July, the Yippies, following months of Mayor Daley's unresponsiveness to their requests for park space for thousands of youths in Chicago late August, asked yet again; Attorney General Ramsey Clark even sent an assistant to Daley's office asking for permits.

And at the beginning of August, Allen articulated his own uncertainties about Chicago:

. . . I'm confused about the Youth International Party plans to hold a be-in during political convention time in Chicago; as above so below—confusion of assassinations, resignations, changes of terminology, police violence, make the purpose of me or younger people going to Chicago unclear and I worry about it at night. I don't want to go or attract anyone else to go and get their heads busted. . . . As it is, there are giant verbal plans for assemblage of youths in Chicago—plans in which I'm sentimentally involved not really knowing what I'm doing. . . .

Meantime at the farm, Gregory had returned, as rowdy as before. Peter's behavior was even more bizarre, and no one seemed to know what to do about it. He'd recently broken the portable yellow record player by dashing it to the floor. He wasn't speaking to anyone but himself. He'd cut himself handling tools; people were afraid to work near him. Poor Julius took a greater share of his brother's abuse.

Everyone knew Peter was on speed (though he denied it), but no one could wrest it from him. One afternoon, when Peter seemed calm, Allen tried talking with him about his amphetamine problem. Several of us were gathered in the dining room; Peter remained in profile to the rest of us, standing at the Kalamazoo, stringing laces into an old pair of sneakers. "I'm sorry I ever met any of you," he said after Allen tried to start a dialogue. He put the sneakers on, walked away, and was gone until nightfall.

And so came one sunny afternoon the third week of August, a day before Allen was to leave for Chicago. Having discussed among ourselves problems connected with Peter, difficulties brought by Gregory, and other critical issues at East Hill Farm, we asked Allen if we might talk with him. Barbara, Candy, and I walked together up the sloping lawn just above the front of the house, and sat down with Allen on the grass under the maples. Through the green leaves golden light darted softly upon us, here and there, as the breeze picked up. From the lower meadow Bessie mooed; above us a hawk glided through blue sky.

I looked Allen directly in his dark eyes, and began.

"We're worried about you—and about things here: look at Gregory; look at Peter; look at how things are.

"Instead of going off to deal with national problems, maybe you should think about staying here. It would be like a great existential act if you chose to stay here."

"I'm not an existentialist," he returned, immediately, dispassionately. My effort at persuasion had fallen flat.

Above our heads I could hear cicadas drone. Then the breeze picked up again through the maples; I watched the sun mottle patterns across Allen's green work shirt. Now Barbara began, bending from her waist, earnestly, toward him. Her mouth seemed to widen as it sometimes did when she tried to explain things to people who couldn't understand. From the start, she was point-blank.

"Allen, look! The whole source of our problems here is Peter—don't you see?!" Her voice began to rise. I looked quickly at Candy's worried face, then back at Allen. Barbara's voice held sway.

"Peter's schizophrenic, don't you see it, Allen?! He should be locked up in an asylum!"

"The problem is, with all the amphetamine—" Allen's voice was quick, but still thoughtful.

"Allen!" Barbara shouted back, face starting to redden, head turning slightly side to side in disbelief that he couldn't see what was so elementary. "It's not a matter of a drug! It's not the amphetamine!"

Allen sat there quietly facing her, as if calm for a final time.

"He's naturally crazy to begin with! It's not the amphetamine! It's Peter! He's schizophrenic! Can't you see it?! He needs serious medical attention!"

Now Allen let go. "Well, *you're* schizophrenic!" he shouted back.

Barbara gasped; Allen looked down, catching himself from saying more. Up over in Ed's meadow I could see his mighty Nubians move through high grass. No one said anything; finally each of us got up and left. Separately.

And so, our session on the sloping lawn under the shade of the maples came to an end. Inevitably, chore time came; we had goats and a cow to milk. Candy put dinner together. Night came.

And then the sun rose once more, lighting the tops of large-leafed maples just above East Hill farmhouse. Inside, in his small second-story room overlooking green garden and fading cemetery, Allen Ginsberg packed for Chicago.

A Break Is Made

A ND SO ALLEN was gone to the Apocalypse that was Chicago.
On return, he spoke again and again of violent confrontations. The first was "the gassing of the cross." Police lobbed tear gas in the direction of a large crucifix erected in Lincoln Park by ministers of several faiths. The clergymen were gathered 'round, leading several hundred others in "We Shall Overcome" and Christian hymns when canisters began landing in their midst. "They gassed the cross!" Allen repeatedly exclaimed to me. "They gassed the cross!" That surreal image of the authoritarian police state run so wild it attacked its own most sacred image was for him an enduring emblem of Chicago's horror.

The most vicious battle of all took place the night of Humphrey's nomination, when many hundreds of people—demonstrators and non-demonstrators alike—found themselves bottlenecked and suddenly attacked in utter recklessness by police. The cops pushed their victims through the ground floor plate glass of the Hilton—and continued to charge after them, clubs flailing.

I first learned of such events in brief gists on the small black and white, golf cart-batteried TV at Ed's. Back home later in the evening, I was overjoyed hearing Abraham Ribicoff from the convention floor on our little transistor radio: "With George McGovern as president of the United States, we wouldn't have those Gestapo tactics in the streets of Chicago!"

While Allen was away, nine of us were on East Hill: Peter, Julius, Barbara, Huncke, Barbara Pionteck and Stephen, Candy and myself, and fourteen-year-old Leigh Ziprin, son of Barbara's friend Lionel. Leigh was up for a week, kicking junk; Gregory had suddenly gone. For all the mayhem at the height of summer, the farm was now—compared to Chicago—an American utopia. We had our workaday life, our accidents and close calls, our own strangeness and differences. But in contrast to the streets of Chicago, our green bowers offered sanctuary and harmony.

As we unloaded the heavy snowplow from our jeep truck one afternoon, one sharp edge landed on Julius's foot, cutting into it. We rushed Julie to Cooperstown's Bassett Hospital, where—no bones broken—a doctor's bandage took care of the wound. Julie scarcely made a peep, except for an "Uohh" on impact.

Peter stayed up most of that night, cleaning the floor of his room and stapling in insulation—all in darkness except for a Coleman lantern. And except for the click of the stapler and persistent nose-blowing, it was quiet.

The next few days Peter maintained this strange, intense state, going into sniffing routines, avoiding others—but he did join us for dinner two nights in a row. And everyone else? After baling at Graham's Friday, August 30, I noted in my diary:

> Candy—tired from fighting with Barbara.
>
> Barbara—gone to Yeshiva.
>
> Julius—went to hospital, got bandage off, walking around & drinking a lot
>   [of liquids].
>
> Huncke—self-pitying on phone to Emmett Grogan, planning "getaway."

□ □ □

SUNDAY MORNING I slept unusually late, waking to the news that Allen had called: he hadn't taken the morning bus as expected. I also learned that Barbara, just back from the Yeshiva, would move there.

I hiked the short distance upmeadow to Ed's, tarpaper nails and hammer in hand, to help him on his barn roof. While we worked, his magnificent horned goats roamed in the distance. Back down at our place after lunch, blacksmith Carruthers and wife pulled up in their blue pick-up, to shoe our Penny. Candy led the large elegant chestnut-colored creature up to the lower edge of our drive. The short-haired big-armed smith, in smudged white tee-shirt and long dark leather apron, set up gear and began work, taking the lower part of one powerful leg, then another, under his arm. His wife at his side watched and helped; Candy held Penny at the halter, pressing small handfuls of grain to her mouth to keep her distracted.

No one, not even the smith when he'd look up, could fail to notice the strange activity taking place in full view in the backyard. Peter, naked except for white terrycloth towel at midsection, bent and stooped before two buckets of water which he'd splash into, raising arms and hands back up and twisting them around each other in brisk staccato motions, turning his whole body away and then back, assuming split-second Egyptian frieze-like poses, seeming to hold up invisible entities just before his eyes, as if searching for germ universes. He was at the height of amphetamine mania.

Carruthers and wife remained quiet; they survived their visit. Even starting to leave they allowed not a word about the phenomenon they'd beheld some ten yards away. But would we survive such an occasion, all the new gossip and scrutiny it might generate about this wayward little "city on a hill"?

Peter *did* seem to be growing increasingly loco. What would the next event be? How long before police checked out such interesting occurrences? Steeling ourselves, Stephen and I decided to try the impossible: looking up to the heavens where we saw a huge thundercloud close to bursting, we crossed the backyard to Peter. "Peter, you can't go on and on like this on speed!" we chimed.

"What speed," he muttered underneath his breath, not looking up, continuing his movement, talking to himself, grunting softly.

We didn't accept his denial—or his act. "We know you've got it, Peter! Give it here! You've had enough! You know it!" we chanted, my heart rising to my throat. He was big and strong enough to maybe handle both of us.

But he didn't. Instead, without speaking he turned away, walked up into the woodshed. Moments later, to our surprise, he returned, studiedly looking away, but extending his large crusty hand, opening it slightly to reveal a little black-capped vial he gave us. Then he turned his back.

Near disbelief, the two of us headed for the lower meadow as Stephen told me, "Allen once saw him store it up his ass, you know." He raised the barbed wire for me, I for him, and we pushed through goldenrod and milkweed. Beyond the well we stopped and unscrewed the small top, emptied the vial thinly on the ground, and covered the area with rocks. The massive thundercloud began to crack.

□ □ □

INDOORS THE REST of the day, Barbara was distant to everyone, as if in a trance.

The closeness she knew four years earlier with Stephen (and Allen) was now utterly gone. Stephen had first met Barbara and Rosebud when he was sixteen; he and Rose were staying at Kerista, a free love commune on Suffolk Street. When Kerista was busted, he went with the two young women to Allen's on East 5th. He had easy access to DMT, which he shared generously, giving Allen his first taste. Soon he moved in down the hall.

To gratify the amorous Barbara, Allen would get Stephen (who was attracted to her) into bed with them so he could get it up. Now—Sunday, September 1, 1968—Stephen and Barbara were like ice and fire. Barbara scarcely mixed with anyone; instead, she trudged about the house, arranging her things, with a long pale face, in long pale dress and wooden clogs. She appeared at dinner only on the way to washing up, just as bubbly little Stephen, fork in hand and food on plate, was having a high old time telling of past adventures with other old friends. In grim pallor she inter-rupted him: "Stephen," she called, scarcely breaking her step, "the worst sin is of the mouth."

Before the day was over, Allen telephoned: he'd return in two days, following an interview for *Playboy* with poet Paul Carroll. But Tuesday evening would find him in the audience of William F. Buckley's *Firing Line*, for its host had called him to attend. In case guest Jack Kerouac showed up drunk, Buckley asked, would Allen be there to hold his hand—or, if needed, take his place on stage? Jack did come drunk, but his disarming directness was a relief from Buckley's nasal stiffness. Allen remained in the audience.

On Monday Stephen left with Barbara Pionteck in the morning. Leigh Ziprin, who'd successfully kicked junk in a week at the farm, also left, wearing a handsome sport coat Gregory left behind—only to find a glassine bag of heroin in the pocket. Except for a little skirmish with Leigh and Huncke, Barbara was in a very good mood now that her departure was imminent, dealing with last details and giving us little keepsakes.

Then, in the middle of the day, as she had many times before, she stepped up into the off-white Volkswagen bus. It was hers now. The night before, Peter, crashing after the surrender of his amphetamine, had writhed on a mattress while Barbara soothed him. And signed the VW over to her for a dollar.

And so the once dynamic Barbara Rubin, she who'd first been excited by the idea of a farm, who'd persisted in it, who'd searched and found East Hill, who'd coaxed Allen into getting it, who'd centered its first seasons, now left it all behind. Left it to a crashing speed freak, a speechless schizophrenic long in her care, a dreamy youth and his heads-up lady friend—once her best friend. And the man she'd loved. She drove a final time from East Hill Farm to Sharon Springs.

Two

After Barbara

After Barbara

TIMOTHY LEARY, ALLEN told me, believed that communal living required a place where everyone could be alone. For Allen, such a refuge was necessarily spiritual. Returning a couple days after Barbara's departure, he climbed the ladder steps to the space she'd vacated. There he made a shrine of the raised bed-platform area next to the dormer window on the north end:

> Today prepared a meditation room & altar in attic . . . on a mirrored tray set on board shelf under eaves, I put Kamakura Buddha model bought last month in S.F. Chinatown, symmetric hands set in Dhyana Mudra, thumbtips touching on lap. Wooden Beads Phil Whalen brought from Japan, with a 4 pointed Lightningbolt Vajra-Dorje, Vajra handled Shingon prayer bell, and Yamabushi conch shell on the shelf opposite a Shigetsu Noise-Wand. Also . . . winged & beaked-masked god of Teotihuacan, a transparent Commanche stone, an iron incense plate. . . . and an imitation Tibetan Tantric prayer bell. Also a red wooden Fish.
>
> Above that shelf, incense, the skeleton of a cactus picked up in New Mexico, a shell-fossil found on the farm, rose scented candles, a Roman household god with bowl & broom, and the painted wooden spoon Lili Brik gave me 3 years ago in Moscow, souvenir of Poetry & her friendship with Mayakovsky & Vosnesensky.
>
> On the wall, Vishnu four armed poster set with tacks, and a medal of the Sacred heart aflame behind Buddha's head. . . .
>
> On Mexican cloth before the altar, flowers, a bowl of fruit store bought and cucumbers & corn grown on this farm, a tiny colored glass lamp, and harmonium for chanting.
>
> Nearby on shelves, sacred texts from Mormon to Essene to Gita to Tantra, a bowl of cut glass beads & chandelier droplets, a toy sparkler, flutes, mandoline & tamboura, ashtray & matches, fine cloths, silk & synthetic weaves; on the bed a single colored eagle-sewn blanket from Saltillo—and a grey serape gift of Margaret Randall on the floor for rug by the platform edge where the mattress is set at the storm window facing East.

And so the character of the long narrow room was changed. In time many different people—drunken poets, mindful poets, lexicographers, mothers and children, saddhus, an ecologist with the flu, musicians, lawyers, and artists would occupy that space, but it was from now on infused with Allen's spirituality. I don't know if any of us appreciated the irony that it had been vacated by Barbara, pregnant with desire for children with Allen, as she left for a hermitage of her own.

Blake in Chicago,
Police at the Farm

O F COURSE, WITH Allen, things were fundamentally spiritual. As he said at Albany in May, when questioned about the possibility of an imminent American revolution, "If the revolution's not spiritual, it's not worth it." Most recently, his approach to the debacle that was Chicago had combined two of his most basic recognitions: mortality as universal condition, and wariness of political—especially violent—solutions to human problems.

The former had been catalyzed at various points in his life, including his 1948 Blake visions; his study of Buddhism, which began before the composition of *Howl*; and the death of his mother Naomi in 1956. The latter had been in his psyche at least as long—from the collision of his youthful commitment to save mankind with schoolmate Lucien Carr's challenge that he didn't know the working class, to the hostile conditions he found firsthand in workers' paradises Havana and Prague in 1965.

Such recognitions were renewed in 1968. The death of Neal Cassady in February, followed by Allen's beholding Neal's ashes that summer—just two weeks before Chicago—reactivated the central poetic role of William Blake in his life. Though in his 1963 poem "The Change" Allen had forsaken fifteen years of Blakean vision-seeking for a Zen Buddhist Ordinary Mind centered in everyday reality, the English poet's prophetic legacy seemed realized tenfold when Allen faced an apocalyptic Chicago.

This extraordinary renewal expressed itself in original music he began creating for Blake's lyrics. In his mind political conditions during the French Revolution (depicted in "The Grey Monk," the first Blake poem he set to music) and in America 1968 were linked. In his own "Going to Chicago," written "in mid Heaven" after leaving Cherry Valley, he proclaimed, "Democratic Anger is an Illusion, Democratic Joy is God." He worried that not all youthful minds trained on Chicago were pacific: karate classes, confrontational tactics, and Jerry Rubin's aggressiveness proved his point. And he objected aesthetically as well: the epithet "Pig" for police wasn't "good poetry."

Allen's point, simple and profound, was that political change through violence would merely bring more violence—as "The Grey Monk" argues:

But vain the Sword & vain the Bow,
They never can work War's overthrow.
The Hermit's Prayer & the Widow's tear
Alone can free the World from fear.

Allen carried in his head his melody for "The Grey Monk" as he flew into Chicago, where he first sang it publicly in Lincoln Park. He'd later write that his Blake music was "first composed on tape recorder, improvised on pump organ in farmhouse upstate NY in two nights after returning from Democratic Convention 1968 Tear Gas Chicago." When he came back, he wrote,

> . . . in a state of shock from seeing the bare skull of a Police State to preserve the war. After all the teargas police riot, the only thing I could think of that made any sense was transcending all that war horror and snakepit of politics with Blake's "Vain the sword and vain the bow."

Allen's Blake compositions as reaction to the enormity of Chicago/Vietnam constitute an extraordinary example of creative response to political crisis. He didn't know musical notation, and couldn't read music, but his Blake creations so thoroughly absorbed him that Brett Aronowitz remembers hearing the "'I die, I die!' the Mother said" of "The Grey Monk" even as Allen walked down the stairs, pumping his little hand-held Benares harmonium as he went. In those first nights back he sketched melodies for over two dozen of Blake's Songs.

In the process, Allen's poetic voice was renewed with stunning force. As summer neared its end, whether inside our lantern-lit farmhouse or outside amongst grass and maples, one could hear his baritone tremolo intone the "Introduction" to *Songs of Experience*. I'd be shaken by the recognition that "Bard" was equally Blake and Ginsberg:

Hear the voice of the Bard!
Who Present, Past, & Future, sees;
Whose ears have heard
The Holy Word
That walk'd among the ancient trees.

Calling the lapsed Soul,
And weeping in the evening dew . . .

For Allen, poetry and music were linked; one of their meeting grounds was the charged psychic seed syllables of the East. In Chicago, he'd used Om to startling effect: the first night police suddenly appeared, driving young people from Lincoln Park half an hour before curfew. Facing a fully armed mass of advancing men in blue, everyone was startled, frightened, seized by adrenaline. Allen, walking with Ed Sanders, began chanting Om, and as others joined them, they slowly made their way from the park.

The following afternoon Allen chanted "Hare Krishna" and sang "The Grey Monk." After rock musicians performed, police surrounded the concert area. Allen in response began chanting Om, and many others joined in. This continued for seven hours, even as an Indian man passed him a note telling him the correct way of pronouncing Om. The enormous universal vibration that was created left Allen and perhaps many others in a state of extended ecstasy—and out of harm's way.

Back on East Hill, Allen offered his accounts not only to myself and others there, but also to a stranger. One afternoon when he was out of the house, and I was upstairs, I heard something outside. I looked out the window. In the dirt driveway, not far from the used Mercury station wagon we'd just bought to replace the Volkswagen bus, sat a blue police car, large unlit red bulb on its roof. We'd thought—even fantasized— that police could come at any moment, day or night, for any or no legitimate reason: it was part of why we were so anxious not to disturb the larger community. Now thought and fantasy were reality.

But this was just one state police car, and as I watched from my second-story redoubt, just one trooper appeared, joining Allen—who seemed to manifest from nowhere—near the driver's door. I breathed slightly more easily—but only slightly. Side-by-side, trooper in blue and poet in dark work shirt and jeans, the two men walked toward the house.

I decided to join them. "This is Officer Ray Daniels, this is Gordon Ball," Allen said as I neared them at the dining room table. Allen was just getting his guest a cup of instant coffee.

Officer Daniels was blond and blue-eyed and his tan trooper's hat sat in the lap of the chair next to him. "I just thought I'd drop by to say hello," he was saying. Of course that might or might not have been his motive. It did seem like we might've had some previous casual contact, however fleeting, with our guest—perhaps in Cherry Valley, perhaps during "Yesteryear Day."

In any case, once the two men had coffee in hand, Allen mentioned having recently returned from Chicago.

"Oh, what was it like, Allen?" asked our guest, eager to hear.

"Well, basically, the police had been given unreasonable orders and so behaved unreasonably. There was a riot."

"Is that right? Is that right?" Officer Daniels repeated then and at intervals, musing upon Allen's elaborations. A few more details from Allen, one or two more topics, some concluding sips of coffee, and then that basically was that: Allen remained calm, thoughtful, low-key and inviting throughout; our guest, polite, interested. We rose and shook hands as he left.

Social Calls at Harvesttime

ROM NEAR AND far, other guests came too, late summer and autumn 1968. Charlene Graham, a petite blonde with glasses, was a daughter of neighbor Claude; her older sister Claudia was the 1968 Otsego County Dairy Princess. Occasionally she'd hike up and visit Candy and me. She was congenial; we, a curiosity from the larger world. On her first visit with Allen (of whom she'd heard so much as public speaker) they sat for tea at the dining room table. She was impressed, she said, by his quietness—for all his public persona.

With Gregory in San Francisco, Peter temporarily off speed, Barbara gone for good, and Huncke having made that "getaway," things seemed stable. From our bountiful garden we harvested green beans, zucchinis, cucumbers—even some corn— and respectable-sized pumpkins. First frost was due soon. We pickled cukes, spread out pumpkins and winter squash in makeshift cellar space. We wrapped green tomatoes in newspaper one by one, setting others on window sills to slowly ripen.

Louie and Edie Ginsberg returned for a weekend, this time with her young granddaughters, Jane and Lynne. It was mid-September and mild: the sun lingered golden beyond the lower meadow as Candy and I sat with some of the family at the dining room table. Along with board games (Monopoly, Clue) that had come into the house that summer of children was a Ouija board: we brought it down from the attic, set it on the tablecloth before us. I'd never used one before, and my curiosity was roused. I wasn't content to see it as pure parlor play; I hoped we could contact a true "spirit" for answers to life's fundamental questions. After all, I was then a reader of *Cheiro's Book of Numbers* ("The Complete Science of Numerology"), and a follower (through farmer's almanacs) of the waxings and wanings of the moon, the positions of the planets. As multiple fingertips—eight-year-old Jane's, sixty-two-year-old Edith's—began to lightly touch the small board's plastic surface, giggles diminished and concentration rose. We seemed to make contact: the little black pointer began moving, indicating letters to spell out words, answer questions. Soon after others asked the spirit to tell more about himself and predict the future—and before Candy shut me up—I allowed my own obsessions to come to the fore: "Will I die?" I asked repeatedly. "Will I die?"

□ □ □

POET DRUMMOND HADLEY, who'd lent us his father's vintage jeep, summered with wife and children in Cooperstown, a host of relatives near. His well-connected Aunt Alice lived in a large home on spacious grounds not far from Lake Otsego ("Glimmerglass" in Cooper's novels). Planning a big gathering one warm September night, she put Allen on the guest list. Cooperstown society then—in this outsider's view—seemed dominated by Old Money and old ways; prominent members included the wealthy right-wing family of Stephen Clark, Singer Sewing Machine heir. An Episcopal priest's wife, learning of Allen's intentions to settle nearby, had circulated a petition aimed at blocking his move.

At Aunt Alice's, Candy and I mixed with some well-heeled, well-suited guests; sociable and vivacious Allen immersed himself with nearly all of them. Neatly bearded Drum and wife Diana, a blonde with classical good looks, added youth and levity to an evening not without tense moments. "I just think that for someone who's tried so hard to tear down our country it's an outrage to even have him around," I heard from one middle-aged dyed blonde, iced drink in ringed and braceleted hand. Off in the distance the moon rose over old Glimmerglass; somewhere in forest or churchyard or prairie slept Natty Bumppo and Chingachgook and Judge Templeton and Cooper himself. . . .

Whether he heard what I heard, Allen of course was unfazed—and, as far as I could tell, won the evening. At its midpoint I saw him in a small separate room, eager listeners pressing close; after its end, I learned, Dr. John Minhoffer, a fifty-year-old cardiac physician, confided to Drum, "You know, your friend Allen kissed me good-bye, and I liked it."

All the Bones Are Mashed Potatoes

N EITHER ALLEN NOR I ever quite understood how Penny—the part Arabian chestnut mare and former polo pony Candy had gotten—was right for the farm.

Candy had begun teaching me to ride on this large powerful sophisticated contraption of muscle and speed—then I took her out alone. She started galloping fast, then faster, faster—as the road began a slight upward incline. Soon we came to a tee (the intersection of Kniskern and Wilson roads) whereupon she herself brought an end to her stirring rush and vigor. It had been thrilling, like charging full speed on a motorcycle, wind pounding my face—only with the mighty thump-diddy-thum of her driving gallop, metal-rimmed feet striking hard dirt. I managed, more or less, to keep posting in the saddle, as I'd been taught on far slower outings.

So that worked out OK. But early one sunny afternoon when Charlene Graham had walked up to visit Candy, I took Penny out a second time. As we began heading back the long stretch from that intersection toward the house (a distance of six-tenths of a mile) she began a gallop at breakneck speed. And all—the barn her ultimate goal—was at a downhill slant, with curves.

After the first rushing thrill of it my boots began to lose their grip in the stirrups; I tried wedging them back in but the stirrups would fly loose, then swing back, hitting my boot tips, hitting Penny's side. I pulled on the reins but Penny wouldn't alter her breakneck pace. I began slipping a little in the saddle, and knew I'd fall: I couldn't right myself, I could no longer post.

In an expanded second I studied the vanishing earth ahead and alongside, hoping for a soft spot in roadside grass. We'd just rounded the bend where Ed kept his large Oldsmobile, near where we parked our own vehicles. Just after that spot I went flying out from the saddle. Remembering a judo teaching from first days in Tokyo—to let an arm absorb a fall's impact—I extended my right one.

But rather than positioning the entire length of my forearm beneath me, it was as if I were trying to straightarm the green earth that suddenly rose to me: the heel and palm of my outstretched hand took the full velocity of my fall. I lay in fresh green and brown; I looked at my right forearm. Just below the wrist its inner bone was trying to break out of my flesh, which had turned from suntanned-brown to white from the pressure. My hand had been shoved in the opposite direction, to the right. The pain was severe.

I got myself up and began walking down the drive to the house. Then I saw Charlene walking up. As we neared each other I saw her face suddenly pale as her eyes took in my hand.

"Are you OK?" she asked—though I knew she could see otherwise. "We saw Penny come back without you. Candy's in the barn."

Momentarily everyone else emptied from the house. Then Candy came out the barn door, shouted, "Oh no!" when she drew close, and together we turned to walk up to the Mercury station wagon. I got in back; Peter sat next to me, helping to hold my hand and forearm erect so as to keep the swelling from worsening. Allen came running up. "What should I do? Should I come?" he asked, peering in. "No," said Candy, twisting the key, igniting the engine, backing into the drive.

In the emergency room at Bassett Hospital half an hour later, I was X-rayed—then X-rayed again. ("Don't tell anyone you're having these additional X-rays," the young M.D. bent near to whisper as he wheeled me a second time into Radiology.) Minutes later, darkhaired Dr. Kenneth Singer, not a whole lot older than myself, told me my wrist was dislocated; all the bones within it as well as those in the main lower part of my hand (carpals and metacarpals) had "turned to mashed potatoes." One of the two main nerves running through wrist and hand had been severed—but would, he said, grow back in time. "Your hand should be usable again," he added, "but we can't restructure it to make the hand and wrist anatomically perfect. It's the worst break we've seen here."

I was right-handed, and from early years had loved to draw. Now, I wondered, in pain grown even greater, would I be able to take pencil between thumb and index finger and shade and limn the human body again? Make cartoons, even? Hold a movie camera easily? Several hours later, coming out of what felt like shock, wrist in excruciating pain but set in protective white plaster from elbow to fingertip, I was given Darvon for pain, and more to take at home, along with Seconal to help me sleep.

The nappy and by now slightly ratty Danish modern sofa from Jonas's 3rd Avenue loft had made its way to the farm, just inside the living room. It was there that I headed when we got back in the early evening, light still bright outdoors. I lay on my back with my arm and hand propped up on pillows as the doctor had ordered. Allen came in and I raised myself up and opened both arms as he came over and bent into my embrace.

"I love you," I said.

"You're high," he returned.
It was true, just as he said.
And it was true, just as I said.

Allen Leaves, Billy Comes

B ACK IN AUGUST, with the calf's departure, we'd all learned how to milk Bessie. It was different from goats: instead of beginning the squeeze at the top of your hand and extending it through the bottom, you simply squeezed with your whole hand all at once, moving it down the length of the nipple, then started at the base of the udder again. But now, with arm and hand in cast and sling, I couldn't milk at all, and could join in the harvest remaining with just one hand.

Several days after my fall Allen left to read in Oneonta, forty miles south, then bussed to the city. "Be good to Candy and Gordon," he called to Peter as he stepped out onto the flagstones. Up the drive, engine idling, young kids from the state university waited.

Peter—who'd kindly helped me prop up my arm as we rode to the hospital—was back, unfortunately, in a familiar mode. He returned, "Ah, they're just a couple of accident-prone maniacs!"

Now there were five of us, with Julius and Huncke, as winter loomed in the distance. Brilliant maple leaves kissed green and brown earth, frost threatened East Hill and our porous asbestos-shingled house. Until Candy arranged for propane gas heating and lighting a few weeks later, our only source of warmth was the Kalamazoo.

Peter continued stomping his separate way, often threatening when he came into contact. Once after I did something I *could* do one-handed—bring the mail up, and separate it on the dining room table into small individual piles for each of us— he yelled, "Don't get my mail, Mr. Ball!" That form of address was the same he sometimes used when angry with Allen, who suddenly became "Mr. Ginsberg." On another occasion, he informed me, bending close to inspect the area around the dining room table where I'd just eaten breakfast, "Gordon, you dropped five Rice Krispies on the floor!"

Candy, perhaps nearing her wits' end with Peter and a now semi-invalid partner, picked up the phone and called my old friend Billy Trotter from college—a gifted writer, one of my main correspondents, and, on many aspects of the 1960s, my chief antagonist. I'd invited him up repeatedly; now Candy put it to him directly: Gordon's broken his wrist in a bad way—could he spare a day or two to visit his friend in his

misery? Perhaps he might appreciate a brief break from his dank 27th Street apartment and the gnomic, daemonic intensity of his work on a big novel and a biography
of conductor Leopold Stokowski.

Very generously, Billy took the bus—you had to be at Port Authority before 6:00
AM, get a $9 one-way ticket, ride several hours to Albany, change, then get off at
Crain's in Cherry Valley over five hours later.

"You've really become a gentleman farmer, Ballox," he offered as we returned to
the garden after a long walk. He was short, broad-shouldered, handsome, with enormous energy emanating from his upper body. As he spoke we surveyed the immediate
landscape of skeletal corn stalks, green turning brown.

"Whaddaya mean, 'gentleman'?" I thought but didn't say.

In the distance Peter harrumphed and strutted across a hillside in brisk giant
steps, swinging large arms and hands high and far, sticking his ass out behind him.
Billy reported waking to see Peter "stark naked except for a sort of jock strap" chas-
ing goats; he'd also seen him fondling the machete indoors and out. Whatever shock
he must've felt, Billy seemed to accept it, as he'd later say with a shudder, as "crazy
Peter Orlovsky."

Inside our house on East Hill, there were no screens on windows; to Billy's disgust, flies by the hundreds came in from the cold, joining Billy in the attic where he
slept. But he seemed otherwise to enjoy his visit. Ed's large Egyptian Nubians, led
by fifteen-year-old Billy in all the majesty of his matted black hair, long wattles, and
triumphant looping horns, came down to visit our smaller nannies: sometimes on
the way, with a reverberating, repeating "Crack!" like giant beasts upon savannahs,
they'd butt horns on the grassy hillside.

I took Billy up to Ed's one evening, to introduce the two of them and watch the
evening news. Outside Ed's shack Any the raccoon, whom I hadn't seen in weeks, was
washing his paws prior to eating. Inside, Ed welcomed us into his musty dark main
room amidst small canyons of *National Geographic*s (a "complete set," he said) and
Sears Roebuck catalogs. Decades-old mason jars of beets and beans lined the corridor
just beyond, leading to his tiny bedroom.

While guests took a straight-back chair, or stump, or stand of newspapers, Ed
loved to sit in his creaky wooden rocker and talk and watch TV. Everything he needed
was at arm's length. His small wood stove was ready and waiting for further install-
ments of kindling or hardwood; his nine-inch black-and-white set rested on a small
dining room table; on an even smaller table, closer to the door than where guests
would sit, Ed propped his broganed foot; unless you remained standing in the door,

on the other side of your genial, garrulous host, you found yourself in his company for an extended visit.

We watched Walter Cronkite report on Biafra's request for help from the People's Republic of China; Humphrey's plan to end the bombing of North Vietnam; and the withdrawal of the military from the university in Mexico City, after over a hundred people had been shot.

News over, Ed asked us to wait with him for his favorite program, Rowan and Martin's *Laugh-In*. That relatively new, fast-paced collage of silly skits and biting satire had captivated Ed and many thousands of others. It pushed the envelope not only in sexual mores but, I thought, even in subtle (for TV) suggestions that our war was wrong. Waiting for it, Ed filled Billy in on radio operator days in the Amazon four decades earlier. His guest got in a few words about observing Stokowski conduct rehearsals, and I—Ed liked to call me "Pogo," after the Walt Kelly comic strip character—sat and listened.

Outside after Rowan and Martin, a three-quarters moon was climbing over Ed's maples and elms and firs, clouds were fleeing, stars were breaking through as our feet brushed downhill meadow grass toward unheated house. With hermit and madman and goats, Billy and I were a long way from college days and going out for girls, even from New York City when we argued over LSD and the counterculture and other weighty issues of the day.

Julius on Trial

N OT LONG AFTER Allen returned, Julius's behavior became an issue. His actions and attitudes could be consternating, even obstreperous—but to what extent was he responsible? Did he remain speechless or even motionless because of mental anguish?—or was it only a perverse desire to put the busy world in its place? Aside from the medication question, should we expect Julius to act as independently as the rest of us? Judge this stern Bartleby as freely as we might each other?

The grounds of the problem, of course, lay in history: a past whose fuller detail, beyond the sketch Allen had given me, was touched upon only decades later by a grey-haired Peter. Fattened and partially lame, but free of amphetamine, legs crossed on a park bench as we overlooked the Hudson a few blocks from the halfway house where he resided, he spoke to me softly. It was just before the spring equinox, 2000; Allen had been dead nearly three years.

In the early and mid-1940s, a young Julius was at odds with Oleg, their former Russian cavalry officer father from Tbilisi. In a wooden building on Manhattan's Washington Street, the family sweatshop, with eight black helpers and a bookkeeper, made neckties; the children's duties involved needlework as well as silk screening. The needlework required methodical care, but Julius, as his younger brother told it, was sloppy, lazy.

When fourteen, Julius had hair styling equipment in the basement of their house. But Oleg, thinking such things swishy, chased Julius out. Now he had to provide for himself—and, he may have thought, prove himself. He began hanging around with a gang that robbed. They'd take a Marine who was looking for sex—it was shortly after the end of the war—to a hotel, get him undressed, lock him in the bathroom, leave with his wallet.

Julius worked briefly for a bakery in East Northport; then in 1951, when he was twenty, Peter found him a job in the old men's center at Creedmore Mental Hospital, where Peter was working. But once on the job, Julie refused to make way for M.D.'s when they came down the narrow corridors from the opposite direction. He was let go. Finally, he started a fire in front of the chicken coop house in which the poverty-stricken Orlovskys then lived. His mother, thinking he was going crazy and being unable to put up with further mayhem, committed him to Central Islip.

Released in Allen and Peter's care after over a dozen years, Julius became their silent tag-along—except for occasional periods of disappearance. I first saw him New Year's Eve 1966:

> . . . a silent, sullen fellow with something of a scowl on his face, just slightly short, lips glued together in a downward slant. Socially, he seemed to absorb—or reflect—nothing. He simply stood there in his crewcut: a white T-shirt stretched its bottom half over a pot belly. Was he retarded? A juvenile delinquent?

□ □ □

ON THE FARM in 1968, he was Peter's lackey, subject to all the vagaries of his will. Fortunately, there were occasions when Peter seemed to forget him: ripe stretches of time when Julius could rest his silent head on his own pillow on his own bed in his own room, or pace the kitchen floor gulping from a cup of hot liquid, or walk up the drive in morning light, cigarette joining fingers.

But what, in his quietude, did he know? We all wondered. Was he Buddha? Was he Krishna? Was he, as actor Joseph Chaiken proposes in the film Robert Frank would soon release, a saint? Allen, discussing the arbitrariness of European aristocratic systems one night at dinner, used him as an example—"Julius might be appointed the Duke of Marlborough"—and Julie's molars kept grinding away at his wheat pilaf, without a glimmer of recognition. On another occasion, we heard of a rape in Cherry Valley, and a rumor that one of us had done it. "Who?" someone asked. "Julius?!" someone else responded, and everyone chuckled. An effort at a smile crossed Julie's face.

In recent weeks, Julius had grown more resistant to what was expected of him. On a visit to Cooperstown, Candy had become particularly upset. Every so often some of us went to Mike Morris's or others' for the rare treat of a warm shower. One Saturday night, Candy and I took Julius to Mike's. Amidst the socializing—friends came for drinks and food and movies—Candy went into the small bathroom to shower. Julius followed, emerging with hair slicked back, blowing smoke rings from pursed lips, belly sticking out unashamedly under a beige sweater. The shower had obviously done him good; he was strutting his stuff, lacking only spats and a twirled walking stick.

The problem was, the sweater he sported was Candy's: after the invigorating warmth of her shower, she'd left it in the bathroom, rather than put it back on over her blouse. Now it stretched itself tight over Julius's midsection, beneath two large loose areas once filled by sizable breasts. And now in fury she flew at him: "Julius! What are you doing! That's *my* sweater!!!" She shoved him back into the bathroom and into his own shirt.

By mid-October, many of us worked outside in chill autumn air that told us winter wasn't far. There were more tasks than people: leaves accumulated on front steps, a pile of wood in the chicken yard awaited the saw. But Julius remained inside, virtually making a show of lazing about the house. After Allen had tried to persuade Julie to get to work, I saw him, arms extended full length, fingers upright and thumbs out in classic style, push Julius angrily from the center of the kitchen floor all the way out the door. "I'm not supporting you!" he shouted.

On another occasion, as we were all about to leave to meet some people in Cooperstown, Allen looked Julius up and down and barked, "You look like a bum! Go comb your hair! I'm not taking you out looking like that!" Wordless, chin tucked in, Julius turned heel and complied.

Such events led to a talk at the dining room table: what to do about Julius? It included Julius, except he didn't talk. The difficulty stayed unresolved, though perhaps discussion made an impression on its silent subject. "I've always wondered if he's a metaphysical conman," I said; Allen took that up, repeating that phrase, trying to bring Julius in. "I don't wanna live with him," Candy concluded.

Peter and Candy and Penny

HER STATEMENT BOTHERED Allen—and me too: Julius was part of Allen's territory, and we were all free to take it or leave it, not the other way around. Candy undoubtedly was frustrated, one-time best friend gone, and now the only woman in a small group of males, one of whom was hostile and one a slob. And, like her relationship with Peter, that situation would only worsen.

After one of several emotional exchanges with Peter, she shouted at him as he stomped away, "And don't stick your ass out at me!" The first time I'd encountered him was at Panna Grady's in the spring of 1966: high cheek bones, horn-rimmed glasses, skinny and animated, he introduced me to one young woman after another ("And this is Miss Beverly Johnson, and this is Miss Benedict, and—") in comic rapid-fire amphetamine velocity like a hyped-up Groucho Marx—his attitude toward women was hard to figure. There was a definite antifeminist streak; I never saw him friendly toward Candy or Barbara. Patti Benson, an attractive Cooperstown friend, once said, "He always ignores me." One of his favorite everyday expressions was "Don't bust a tit."

Of course, one might wonder about insensitive attitudes toward women among most of us males at the farm in those days. In any case Peter and Candy continued at loggerheads; a climax came one afternoon as Allen and I were at the dining room table. Coming from the barn, Peter burst into the house, reporting in a loud voice, "Allen, she's mistreating that horse! She's cussing at it!"

Candy, following him, and hot in the face, answered immediately, "That's how you talk to horses! You don't know what you're talking about!"

"I do *too*!" he shouted back in fury.

Allen looked up, calmly. "It's normal, Peter—"

"It is *not*!"

"—or it's average," he continued slowly, thoughtfully. He pronounced each of the three syllables of "average" slowly, carefully.

Peter stormed off, Candy returned to the barn. The issue wasn't resolved. There was more to it than how to talk to horses, but that was at its center—for this extended moment. Candy felt Peter was ruining Penny by giving her too much grain: he'd feed her whenever he took a notion to. According to Candy, "sweet mix"—a combination of corn, oats, barley, and molasses—was a powerful stimulant, and should be given out sparingly.

Especially for horses not being worked and only occasionally ridden, she said. They'd gladly overeat such grain, and Peter, Candy claimed, always fed Penny little handfuls when she wasn't looking, after she'd asked him not to. That, Candy said, was what made Penny more and more "insane," and caused my fall.

Eventually, after further mishaps, Penny would be sold at an auction for horse meat. But in the fall of 1968, Peter insisted, "This horse is hungry! Just look at this horse! It needs to be fed!"

Both Candy and Peter were animal lovers—of very different sorts. Candy, a rider of horses from childhood, once called animals "my wonderful companions and helpers in this life." Back at Newtown Agricultural Annex High School in 1950, Peter had used a team of horses to pull a transplanting machine over some of the school's twenty-two acres set aside for tomatoes. On East Hill Farm, Peter's apparent attitude toward animals could be amusing, charming, and perplexing. He seemed to love them—and then some. I have a photograph of Peter, in red felt hat, kissing Bessie in the snow, and movie footage of him rubbing her under the chin and feeding her corn shucks (even taking shucks into his own mouth at one point). A friend remembers him lying down in the meadow with Bessie, grazing with her. In a letter to Philip Whalen in the fall of 1968, Allen reported, ". . . cow & Peter are lovers. . . . Peter's . . . kissing the sacred animal on the nose & rump all the time, feeling her up. Milk production soared to astounding gallons."

And I recall his rubbing the balls of Tiger Cat, at the windowsill and on the dining room table, as he exclaimed in delight; and reaching under Godly dog, between his legs. But the growing hostility between Peter and Candy would not be resolved until, come December, Candy left the farm. In the meantime, the status of Penny the horse was clarified after we hit upon the idea of having Judy Cannon try her out.

Judy, of an old Cherry Valley family, lived in their eighteenth-century house at the Glensfoot estate and dairy farm on the western edge of town. She'd ridden horses much more than Candy had, and would be only too happy to help us evaluate Penny by trying her out. Was Penny a manageable horse for us? Was my fall from her an anomaly? Penny's performance with Judy would shape the future of these 600 pounds of sentient grace and speed and power.

Arm in cast and sling, I watched from just inside the kitchen as Judy saddled up the large handsome chestnut near the front of the house and took her off a dozen paces at a slow trot . . . and as Penny suddenly lurched and rose on her hind feet, and Judy, jodhpurs, boots, and spurs, went tumbling to the earth. She luckily was unharmed, but there was no future for Penny the polo pony on East Hill Farm.

The Mail, and All It Brings

O NE OF THOSE August days when I baled hay at Graham's, Candy and I got a call from a close friend, Enrique Benvenutti, who'd just crossed the border into California. Soon, we heard again—and, to our joy, he seemed determined to come our way:

Dear Gordon & Candy,

I'm very happy to think that I'll see you soon . . . as soon as I get the money. . . . Always I think about you like if Gordon and Candy were only one person, you know that I'm olso part of you and you part of me, remember our trip in Yelapa I always do, I see it again in my trips . . . the night I coll you I was feeling kind of sorry because I didnt ask what time it was in new York and maybee you were sleeping as I hear your voice, if so scuse me, anyway remember that no matter time cicunstances or distans I love you in name of the universal laws of brotherhood, I ned you

Love
Enrique

Several months before the farm, when Candy and I lived with half a dozen others in a *palapa* (wall-less house, palm-leaf roof) in tiny, primitive Yelapa, Enrique became part of our group. He was my size but broad-shouldered, with Clark Gable good looks, and very quiet. He kept mostly to himself, did his share of work. To the two admiring little gringo kids in our midst, he was "Henry K."

I never began to really know him until one afternoon when we all took LSD. Suddenly I became aware of a new and very strong psychic energy as I turned and saw him facing me, his hands a powerful triangle, thumb to thumb, fingertip to fingertip, radiating a vibrant rainbow of energy. I looked into his eyes; I saw his face become mine; I felt myself merge and exchange with him; I saw his beauty. I was overjoyed. Our energies exchanged; I saw his lips and hands tremble.

Thereafter, we were fast friends; we three formed a solid core. When storms commenced in early March, Candy and I invited Enrique, who'd been sleeping under the stars, into bed with us. We three huddled together, rain swooped down on jungle, mountain, and sea.

Eventually we decided to move deeper into the jungle, forsaking virtually all ties to "civilization," minimal as our involvement in it already was. Enrique and I went for supplies to Puerto Vallarta—where we were arrested together, moments after we stepped out of the tiny *barca*, or ferry: it was the day *federales* had scheduled one of their periodic "round-ups." The morning after our first night in jail he was told to get out of town, never come back—and I hadn't seen him since. Now, after he'd hitched over 1,000 miles, his arrival on East Hill was imminent.

Meantime, cards and letters continued descending upon Allen. His father, confessing to guilt at the prospect, proposed they collect all Allen had written him, for Louie to sell. In elegant hand Phil Whalen wrote chatty, idiosyncratic letters, wishing Allen and his farm well: "I suppose that Huncke is now bronzed & robust & heavily muscled." From *Playboy* had come the editors' version of Allen's interview, which enraged him: I heard him on the phone at length to Paul Carroll, complaining of distorting words put into his mouth by editors. Now, at his insistence, the original transcript arrived; he'd work on and off over a month toward a publishable version. Five months later, Allen would appear between the covers with Vladimir Nabokov and Brigitte Bardot.

□ □ □

JOY DELIGHT WAS a tall, attractive young woman who first caught my eye when I saw her amble across Main Street in serape and jeans one spring morning—an extraordinary sight for Cherry Valley 1968. Daughter of the Reverend Maxfield Delight and wife, she and Candy and I and her husband Dennis met once or twice in the summer—before Dennis was drafted to San Diego.

In November Joy wrote, "Den and I are deserting the Navy . . ." and heading for Canada—did we know anyone who could help? Allen immediately volunteered Douglas Featherling and his House of Anansi publishing company, which had brought out Allen's *Airplane Dreams* (whose sales would help draft resisters across the border).

And Allen heard from Louis Cartwright, a young friend of his and Huncke's. One day, riding in the jeep, Allen asked Peter, "Louis Cartwright wants to come up. Is that OK with you?"

"Sure, Allen." Peter's eyes stayed on the road, hands on wheel.

Years later I saw a letter from Louie that may have prompted Allen's query:

Dear Allen,

Thank you for writing me, things in New York are really becoming a drag, want to get out soon as possible. When things are secure at the farm please write me there is nothing I'd rather do this winter than work on your farm. And fuck.

I send my greetings to Huncke, Peter & Julius.

And to our surprise, just before October's end—nearly two months after she left—we heard from Barbara:

> *Dear Candy Gordon Peter Hunkey Julius*
>   *Allen farm animals, Ed, Myron*
>   *Cherry Valley, earth sky all*
>   *around you—*

—to say that the clandestineing of where I am & how why for what when where how in relationship to the proximity of Sharon Springs versus Cherry Valley & why it must be so is obviously because where close, in all the dimensions obviously

I cannot be here near with both since you all are close to me in the time emotions of living together through what we've been through to understand . . . I wish you all well & graciousness to your live's & care that it be long and good and that I must keep here & do what I want to do...be well & good. Care for each other.

>   *love*
>   *Barbara*

Candy had once visited Barbara during the fall. Barbara's parents, concerned about their daughter, had called, asking if she might check on her.

They went together into the hot springs, the old Imperial Baths near the Yeshiva. In an enclosed warm pool smelling of sulfur, women relaxed quietly. They were people Candy wasn't used to—it wasn't a problem of nudity, for they were "dressed" for their baths. Candy wanted to stare—as some of them seemed inclined to do at her. Everyone was basically covered up; Barbara and Candy wore tee-shirts over swimsuits. Did Barbara seem at ease? Happy? "I'm the happiest I've ever been," she said softly, letting one hand drift across the warm water. "Now I live in a state of purity."

The Farm at Work

E NRIQUE ARRIVED, LOOKING well after 5,000 miles of travel. I'd known him less than a year, but he was perhaps my truest friend; seeing him again exhilarated Candy and me alike. He took the altar bed that was once Barbara's, and in character-istic quiet contributed generously to unending chores.

Although closing on the farm (plus other expenses) had put Allen $12,000 in debt, in a letter to Philip Whalen he declared himself gratified to have the deed for East Hill—and, characteristically, since he expected a spring reading tour to get him out of debt, he offered to help Phil reach Japan within the year.

My hand and arm would stay in a cast a while longer. It was uncomfortable, awkward, and, at times, still painful. I had to keep my forearm elevated as much as possible, but did as I could indoors and out. Candy continued with a lion's share of household chores: our car insurance was suddenly canceled, and she confronted that paper headache. Weekly she'd gather dirty laundry, haul it to the Landmark Village Laundromat next to Crain's Pharmacy, get the right change, wash and dry, haul it back into the car, drive home, carry it into the house, sort it, fold it, distribute it: Julie's blue flowered white pillow case, Huncke's three pillowcases, gold fitted bottom sheet, gold-striped top . . . She assembled a standard shopping list for foodstuffs and supplies in bulk, including, among much else, thirty-five rolls of toilet paper as well as fifteen cans of Snow's Minced Clams for Allen's clam sauce spaghetti—a household favorite whose recipe he'd gotten from the manager of the San Remo in the West Village.

Peter was active again after a subdued period following his last crash from speed. On a warm Halloween night, he chopped wood long after dark under bright white Coleman Lantern light. Allen, pleased by his return to productiveness, came out to exclaim, "Great! Pete's really workin'!"

Even Huncke carried in a box of firewood from shed to stove. While the weather was still good, we'd wash outdoors, hauling galvanized pails of water from the well, splashing the shocking cold on our warm skin in front of the house. Julius in plaid sportcoat, striped black-and-purple sweater stretched over belly, paced back and forth in the morning sun.

Just before real cold set in, Suburban Propane would install a heating system, with storage tank near garden, large heater in living room and attic, smaller one in each bedroom; a small kitchen range; several gaslights; and, though we hadn't yet the plumbing for it, a water heater in bathroom. With LP gas we wouldn't have to spend the long severe winter huddled around the Kalamazoo; with a range there'd be much more cooking versatility; and though the amber gaslight was far from brilliant, we'd have a little added light for long nights. We hadn't solved electric or water problems, but Allen kept his shoulder to the wheel, typing out an extraordinarily detailed letter to the "Baker Mfg. Co." in Evansville, Wisconsin, inquiring about windmills and windchargers and asking for literature, describing our circumstance in several precise paragraphs, adding a tiny diagram, enclosing 30¢ in airmail stamps for their response.

Nixon's the One

I N THE AFTERMATH of Chicago and amidst escalating war, a national election loomed. The race between Nixon and Humphrey seemed close, particularly as George Wallace, running with General Curtis Le May as an Independent, threatened to take a significant share of votes from Nixon; and as Eugene McCarthy, with only a week left before election day, had yet to endorse Humphrey.

On Halloween night, Ed Urich tromped down the meadow under a partly starry sky. He often stopped in to talk during the day, but now came our way after dark. Catching his breath, he told us his short wave had picked up a report that the Seventh Fleet was being recalled: a let-up in war was now possible. The next day we learned Johnson had halted the bombing of Vietnam; expanded peace talks would begin in Paris.

The timing, of course, was political. Nonetheless, a halt in bombing was a halt in bombing. How could one argue? Still, I couldn't bring myself to vote for Humphrey, because of his involvement with Johnson's war. On November 5, my first presidential election, I chose Dick Gregory.

But Allen could bring himself to vote for Humphrey, and told me, dispassionately, he'd done so. Though Nixon's electoral college margin was more decisive (with 301 to 191 for Humphrey, 46 for Wallace), he won by just over half a million votes. He took only 43% of the popular vote.

Candy and I watched the depressing returns at Mike Morris's in Cooperstown. Not only would Nixon be in office, with our war likely becoming even more aggressive, more murderous; Spiro T. Agnew, who claimed, "When you have seen one slum, you have seen them all," would be waiting behind him. Was it, in part, my own fault?

I didn't think in such terms then; nor did any of us know what *Ramparts* magazine would later reveal: simultaneous with Johnson's eleventh-hour peace move, Nixon sent Madame Chennault to President Thieu to tell him not to make any deals now—Nixon would likely be elected, and he intended to continue the war. A little over four years later, the re-elected Nixon officially brought his war to an end.

Seven years after Ed's message that Halloween night, I argued with Allen about the peace movement one evening in Boulder, Colorado. "Didn't our peace effort," I asked him, "help end the war?"

"I think the movement—its anger—made it last four more years," Allen answered. "As Jerry Rubin boasted, 'I got Nixon elected.'"

□ □ □

THE DAY AFTER the election I returned to Cooperstown, and Dr. Singer removed my cast. Before it was wrapped in an ace bandage and placed in a sling, I stared at my whole forearm and the greater portion of my hand, immobile and protected from light and air for six weeks. The suddenly exposed flesh had that eerie look of some almost half-dead creature, shrunken, as if it had been underwater. But my wrist had been basically "righted" on my forearm; that one bone beneath it was no longer about to burst through skin.

Yet it was excruciatingly stiff. Very gradually, with daily exercises squeezing and unsqueezing in warm water, it began to loosen a little. But as Singer reminded me, even when completely healed, it wouldn't be "anatomically perfect."

Allen was in and out of East Hill in mid-November, reading at Manhattanville College, City College, and Albany. While he was away the sky darkened as snow fell, swirling and buffeting in fierce northeast winds. Going out to the barn, I struggled to see twenty feet beyond. When it was over late the next day, we had two feet of snow, cow and goats were bedded down in ample layers of straw, and we were snowbound.

How fortunate to have just gotten gas heat! Ed, in layer upon layer of clothing beneath a parka lined with synthetic fur—went out on snowshoes all the way down to our mailbox, and brought us the daily post. Seating himself at our dining room table, he unwound for some gab and a cup of tea, as usual. A blizzard like this was uncommon before February, he said, as snow on his boots turned liquid and sweat grew on his brow. Fortunately, we had plenty of food, and Candy was kneading dough, making bread. We stoked up the Kalamazoo, and with nice new propane heaters felt warm and cozy.

Musical Notation & Social Relations

R ETURNING TO THE farm, Allen resumed work on melodies for some of Blake's *Songs of Innocence* and *Songs of Experience*: "The Grey Monk" (again), "The Chimney Sweeper," "Holy Thursday," "London." As delicate white mantles of gas light made their almost silent amber whish, he'd be perched on the small bench mid-morning through afternoon or night, "vegetarian" shoes to the pedals, notes and chords vibrating, swirling, stopping and starting, the old A.B. Chase organ wheezing as he pumped. Often he sang in his rich baritone, occasionally with Peter stopping by his side to join him. From time to time he'd reach for a True Blue—an ashtray sat on the organ's projecting ledge.

Knowing nothing formally of music, Allen arranged for pianist Lee Crabtree, who'd been with the Fugs, to teach him arranging, notating, and composing, for which Lee would receive room, board, and $50 a week. Tall and slender, with a narrow face, he was bright and gifted, but could be temperamental—as we'd see in the confinement of an East Hill winter.

He and Allen worked hour upon hour together, intensely but irregularly and erratically, over the next several months. They weren't always compatible. Allen, with his loyalty to the imagination, may have been (as Lee seemed to think) at loggerheads with the strictures of musical systems, but sometimes seemed at odds with Lee's personality as well. In one dispute, Lee rose from the organ bench in petulance, and climbed the stairs to his room. Allen hurried after him: "Aw, c'mon, Lee, I'll suck your cock, I'll lick your asshole, I'll . . ." he called merrily from the foot of the stairs, hamming it up, hoping for reconciliation. The response—utter silence.

Once, when Lee saw a note left by Allen, I watched him analyze its handwriting: "It shows that this person likes to find things difficult, make problems." I wondered, of course, if he was reflecting his own experience working with Allen.

But in these late autumn days at the farm, we all more or less got along: perhaps the newness of the experience, and Allen's benign influence, ensured as much. Except for Candy: by the time Thanksgiving came and went, the charm of East Hill had vanished like her friend Barbara. She was fed up with us all, and none of us, I think, understood that.

Thanksgiving Disaster

T HE DAYS LEADING up to the holiday seemed pleasant enough. Prompted by the early November blizzard, we had seven storm windows put in, making our drafty old house a little less vulnerable to inevitable icy blasts. And a week before Thanksgiving, my right hand and arm were freed at last, ace bandage and sling removed.

Louis Cartwright arrived a day early. Thanksgiving morning Lawrence Ferlinghetti bussed up from Port Authority; Barbara Pionteck and Stephen drove up from the city. Candy had spent all Wednesday keeping the Kalamazoo woodstove going, baking pies from our own pumpkins, housecleaning, organizing. Early Thanksgiving morning, she asked me to sweep kitchen and dining room, then complained I was too slow. It bothered her that Peter and others kept going to the stove, spoon in hand, dipping into saucepans for a taste. On his way in the door and up the stairs, Lee tossed his coat on a dining room chair; that too disturbed her.

Rain was falling—it had snowed a little earlier, and would snow a little more, later in the day. Allen was up in his room finishing his edit of the *Playboy* interview; at 10:30, he and Peter and I took our 1963 Mercury station wagon to meet Ferlinghetti, who was on his way to Taormina, Sicily, to receive the Premio di Taormina for *A Coney Island of the Mind*. We'd drive him to Albany late the following afternoon for flights to JFK and Italy.

Down at Crain's the big Greyhound pulled in and caught its pistoned breath. Out stepped a tallish, ruddy man whose mottled grey-and-black fur cap rhymed with his short trimmed beard. Moments later, taking Lawrence on a drive around the area, we headed for Sharon Springs. Going uphill as white flakes descended, the station wagon skidded a second on ice. We managed a brief, cautious tour of the town and returned carefully up East Hill.

The snow was pretty, but the weather much of Thanksgiving Day and Friday was dismal—cold and wet. Many guests remained indoors, which I'm sure didn't sit well with Candy's nerves as she applied finishing touches to ham and turkey and much else. The house was dark, with modest illumination through windows while there was still light outdoors, and then from the even more modest gas lights. Peter, good-spirited—not on amphetamine—continued dipping into this pot and that.

A dozen people sat down for dinner that afternoon, everyone barely squeezing in at the "big" table in the small dining room. Stephen, now a technical illustrator while studying at the School of the Visual Arts in New York, drank too much wine and had to rush outside. But not before engaging quiet Ferlinghetti in conversation: yes, Lawrence knew at the time that Allen's Six Gallery reading of *Howl* would change American literature.

Even Candy, before the day was over, got to have some fun—a spirited game of chess with one guest—but fun wasn't the order of her day. During dinner she'd heard no one acknowledge her two days of preparation, no one so much as thank her for her cooking. Someone said to Allen: "Oh, Allen, it's really wonderful that you provide all this."

Thursday evening, we—Allen, Candy, several others, and I—beheld distant arcing rays of green, red, blue, orange in the northern sky: the first aurora borealis most of us had ever seen. Friday there was some debate about who'd go to the Albany airport. I was unsure myself—what about chores? I'd do them early. Though I still couldn't milk, Stephen could, and was always willing.

The weather had continued miserable, very cold, dark, rainy, with some wet flakes among the drops. But we expected to be back by 6:30, avoiding worse weather that could come with night.

I grew anxious about time, and tried to get everyone out: "We're going to be late, we won't make it, it's a long drive!" Peter putzed about, Ferlinghetti seemed low key, not roused even though his long journey hung in the balance. Allen sealed the manila envelope holding his revised *Playboy* manuscript and slipped it inside his red-and-white Greek cloth shoulder bag, all ready for a stop at the Cherry Valley post office on the way out of town.

Eventually Allen, Peter (with a small flask of wine), Julius, Lawrence, and I hit the road, making the sixty-some miles to the airport in time for Ferlinghetti's flight. After seeing him safely off, the four of us—Peter driving, Allen next to him, Julius shotgun, me in the rear—started out of the parking lot. It was dusk; more rain was falling. Cars coming at us had their lights on. The road exiting the airport led into a major artery just as it swooped by in a curve. In the dark and rain, it wasn't clear if oncoming traffic would feed into our road or go past us, just beyond the stop sign to our right.

It wasn't, certainly, clear to Peter, who entered the artery in front of oncoming forty-five-mile-an-hour traffic. Immediately we collided with another car, and in one expanded instant:

Peter says, "Uh-oh!"

Allen hurtles forward, hitting his head against the windshield.

I'm thrust against the back of the front seat, hitting it hard with the same forearm that had been freed at last.

I could sense Allen was really hurt (Julius was quiet, so seemingly more or less OK; Peter seemed the same). I thought selfishly, "Oh, it's just Allen!" but worried out loud an instant later, "Allen, are you OK?"

"I don't know, I think so. My glasses are broken." His head seemed pushed down, as if he were preoccupied; he seemed enclosed in his body. I could sense he'd gotten the worst of it, even as I worried my arm was broken again.

Peter and I got out in the rain. Our Mercury's front was completely mashed in; the side of the other car, ten feet away, was dramatically dented. There was that familiar car-wreck smell of anti-freeze from a broken radiator.

In the sedan sat a young woman and her mother. As Peter and I approached to check on them, both began screaming, and kept screaming, as within minutes the whirling bright red top of the ambulance appeared and attendants hurried out to lay them on stretchers, *"Those beards! Those beards! Those beards!"* They continued screaming as they caught sight of Julius and Allen.

Police sirens added to the uproar. Cops slowed and redirected traffic. Allen was carried on a stretcher into the rear of the ambulance where the two women were, Peter stepped up into the front, and Julius and I followed in the back of a police car. At Albany Memorial Hospital Allen was rushed to Emergency. Peter and Julie and I were X-rayed. Pete and I endured long waits in an empty room; he told me that on the questionnaire we both were given, he identified himself as "unemployed."

"Oh, you should've put 'poet,' or 'farmer,'" I said.

Julius, in a room just across the hall, door open, engaged in extended and inexplicably animated conversation with a couple of doctors: I could see and hear much of it. With curious M.D.'s he examined the nature of the universe as well as his own philosophies. In his chair he relaxed with a doctor's cigarette: it was his moment. Apparently one of the physicians had recognized Allen, for soon Julius was responding to a question, brow wrinkled behind smoke rising from a Lucky, "No, I don't like poetry a whole lot. I like philosophy more." He was relaxed, demonstrative, expansive, holding forth in his deep voice. Much later in the evening, as Lee Crabtree, come from the farm, drove us back in his new Datsun, Julius would allow, "It was a pretty good accident."

Word spread through parts of the hospital that poet Allen Ginsberg had been injured in a car wreck; one reporter was already present in the hallway when we saw Allen wheeled out on a stretcher. Allen had been informed of all our X-Ray results, for he told me, "I have four broken ribs and a broken hip," then immediately shifted to concern for our condition: "Peter and Julius are OK, but you may have a forearm fracture, Gordon."

I later learned that my arm, although swollen around point of contact, was not broken; and the two women had escaped serious injury. I found a pay phone and called the farm. Candy answered, telling me she'd feared we had a wreck. When I mentioned that Peter had been driving, she immediately said, "I knew it! He shouldn't have!" Then Stephen came on, urging that I make sure the doctors knew who Allen was, "So they know he's not just an ordinary bum!" Later I learned that Huncke too had claimed to know "something has happened," and had seemed pleased his prophetic sense was confirmed.

Next day we saw a brief article in the Albany paper, a photo of Allen against a hospital pillow. Soon the *Village Voice* reported on its front page: "Ginsberg in Crash; Condition 'Good.'"

When Peter and I returned to the hospital, Allen told us the story of what happened during his first night's effort to deal with severe pain. Though it was recognized that his body was in shock, both doctors and nurses turned deaf ears when he asked for morphine; they seemed to think they were hearing the pleadings of some sort of beatnik dope addict.

"I wanted to die from the pain," he reported. "I had to yell most of the night for morphine. I told them over and over I'd been treated with it for kidney stones since 1947, that Demerol wasn't effective—but they freaked out every time.

"Finally I exploded," he continued: "'I'm giving you the information and you won't accept it!'" The nurses turned hysterical; Allen began shouting, "Give me morphine!" A doctor at last returned—only to argue with him. Finally Allen said, "I'm trying to give you information. Do you want the information?!" and repeated his case history with kidney stones. At last—it was around 3:00 AM—the doctor complied, and Allen Ginsberg got some relief.

In the Aftermath

W E RETURNED TO see Allen in slightly better condition over the next few days, left foot raised in five pounds of traction, voice and breath soft above cracked ribs and hip. A photo of Rimbaud was at his bed. We handed him a letter Ed had written:

Dear Allen,

I've just finished having Lee and Enrico up here . . . to watch you over TV Channel 10 during your bedside interview. What you said about the world and what's going to happen to it, in near future, is so very true that its too bad that everybody, everywhere, didn't hear and see you tonite and really take heed, 'ere its too late!

Everything is going along OK up here. . . . I thoroly enjoyed the nice big birthday cake that Candy bought for me. . . . I hear that all of you have bought me a keroscene mantel lantern (it hasn't come along yet) and I really appreciate such a nice gift. . . .

Several folks in CV village have asked me how you are getting on in the hospital and everyone wants you to get well soon!! Every morning when I go down to Graham's farm the first thing Charlene always asks me is "How is Allen doing?" So you see, fellow, we are all rooting for you—so don't fail us—get well soon!!

Take care now, keep smiling and your spirits up and may

God bless you!

As always just
Eddie—the hermit

□ □ □

A FEW DAYS later I left the farm for a North Carolina family visit, with a whole other set of concerns. Once in early days on East Hill I'd called my parents. My mother answered, her speech halting, confused. Yet she made it clear that my father had been ill—mononucleosis—but was now starting to recover. The source of her confusion may have been not only my father's illness (strange for a man of sixty-seven) but the onset, at sixty-two, of her Alzheimer's Disease: it hadn't been diagnosed yet (and wasn't widely known in those days), but every now and then I'd learn from my sister of lapses of speech, action, memory. . . .

Hearing in the summer that my father was virtually normal, I'd written that Candy and I hoped to bus down to Winston-Salem in October, stay a few days nearby with my sister and her husband. A lot of outdoor work on East Hill would be done by then; we'd be free to travel some.

I heard back not from my parents but my brother-in-law Harold. He was many years my sister's senior, with a stern Blue Ridge upbringing that seemed a foil to Maylee's emotions, idealism. He and I had somewhat gotten along, but he tended to be short of speech. Now he reported that with Maylee expecting their fourth child, it wouldn't "be a suitable time for house guests." But he went on "in confidence":

> . . . you may consider this none of my business but since it does involve me indirectly I think I should mention it in case you are not fully aware . . . your folks do not approve of the relationship in which you are living. While they may be able to tolerate it at a distance, your visiting here together tends to rub it in their faces. I would not presume to tell you how to handle this since you know your business better than I. I trust that you will not think that I am meddling but at the same time feel that you should be aware that this places some people in a very difficult position.

Candy and I had visited in 1967. Candy had been Candy, garrulous and irrepressible: she'd volunteered to my sedate parents that she was once married: "I think they think of me as a Fallen Woman," she later confided. And I in my ineptitude had made no secret of our living together. Now, with Harold's letter, I was hurt, angry.

But in time I resolved the matter, rightly or wrongly: seeing my aging parents, my father having had mono and my mother beginning to suffer from Alzheimer's, was the most important thing. I'd visit—by myself.

At Thanksgiving I'd written again, planning to come the first week of December. Then came the car wreck—and two days later, a call from my worried mother. She'd just seen the brief article on the wreck, naming everyone in the station wagon, in the Winston-Salem paper.

In his hospital room I talked with Allen about going ahead, back on East Hill, with Candy. I arranged for Mr. Keller to come up with a bulldozer, bury the plastic pipe we'd connected from well to kitchen sink: submerging it four and a half feet—beneath the frost line—-should ensure water at the kitchen-counter hand pump throughout winter. And soon after I left, Lee Crabtree would sell us a fine old car, his grandfather's grey-and-white 1955 Oldsmobile, replacing the totaled Mercury. So the farm seemed in basic working order, in Candy's hands, more or less.

Meantime, Allen remained in room 208, Albany Memorial. The Cooperstown newspaper—*The Freeman's Journal*—ran a small article:

ALLEN GINSBERG SAYS IT'S A ROUGH WORLD

His bushy beard threatened by a "straight" roommate, yippie poet Allen Ginsberg let the world in on his latest hang-up.

Specifically, the elder state-man guru of the hippie-yippie world, who lives on a farm near Cherry Valley, is hung up in a traction apparatus. . . .

The balding Ginsberg promised his roommate that the man might get a chance at the whiskers . . . in another world.

Ginsberg . . . described his feelings during the accident as a "physical nightmare."

. . . Ginsberg warned that, at the rate the earth is poisoning its air and water, there are, perhaps, only 30 years left.

Although his home is listed as Paterson, N.J., Ginsberg seemed more attracted to his farm near Cherry Valley, where, he said, he grows vegetables without any sprays or other chemicals.

He clutched a yellow rose in one hand and, in the other, a copy of the works of 18th Century mystical poet William Blake. . . .

Nurses peeked into the chamber, patients walked by the door repeatedly and reporters waited their turn to hear the bearded bard discuss the spiritual aspects of a car crash.

Meanwhile, Down South

F OR MONTHS HUNCKE had been waiting for a check from Harvey Brown, who intended to publish a book he'd written. At last it came: $200. The wait had clearly irritated the storyteller.

Now, of course, he was in fine spirits. And, cash in pocket, he wasn't about to stay on East Hill Farm. In early December we set out together—he for the Splendid City and its crucial substance, I for Southland and family. On the way to the Cooperstown bus—Candy drove the Oldsmobile—Huncke asked to stop a minute at the liquor store. He returned with a quart of whisky "for the boys back there."

In Winston my mother seemed largely the same as before, her self-expression perhaps more hesitant. My sister had grown concerned when Mother—after decades of being driven by Chinese and then Japanese chauffeurs as she lived the foreigner's life dictated by her husband's social status—prepared for her first driver's license in many years. She couldn't understand the information booklet: she began copying it, but having trouble, she showed booklet and notes to Maylee, saying, "I'm trying to learn this": my sister saw that some words were copied twice, others left out.

And my mother worried, "I can't remember things, Maylee. Well, what am I going to do?"

"You're still beautiful," my sister answered, "and you're still our mother and we're going to look after you."

But any difference I might've seen in my mother's condition just before Christmas was subtle. As Harold later said, "If she'd been more expressive, it might've shown sooner." Though my mother was always warm to me, my conversations with my parents were as usual dominated by a high degree of formality.

We were a guarded, unconversant family—torn apart before I was born, when my father was in prison camp in China, and perhaps never fully mended. When I was growing up in Tokyo, it wasn't just that we knew little of the language all around us. The Cold War'd 1950s, in our rarefied foreign culture, was even more an era of reticence, denial.

And now, back in the U.S.A. in the late 1960s, social and sexual values were in upheaval, and a war—though undeclared!—was raging. I hoped that my being on a farm could serve as a bridge with my father (who'd been raised on one by the Ohio

River) and end decades of minimal communication. But one morning I realized that such was only a hope. As I stood on the wall-to-wall carpeted landing of the house to which he and my mother had returned from Tokyo, he came abreast of me:

"Why are you there with Ginsberg?"

"Why not? What do you mean?"

"Isn't he a homo?"

"What's wrong with that?"

"Has he touched you?"

"No," I lied. "So, what's the matter?"

"Well, what if everyone was one?"

"Well, what if everyone was a banker?"

At such a time I never imagined that in 1977, on my sister's living room couch, Allen and my father, a month before his death, would sit side-by-side holding hands, singing Allen's Blake.

Before leaving Carolina I made a quick trip east to Chapel Hill, where I dropped in on journalism professor Walter Spearman and Davidson friend Bill Wiseman. Then from a pay phone in front of Kemp's Record Shop I called my brother, who drove the thirty miles from Raleigh and took me back for an overnight visit with him and wife Paula. It was the first time I'd seen them in several years.

We had drinks in the living room of their comfortable split-level home and talked. Then later, in their softly carpeted hallway (not unlike the site of my talk with my father about Allen), I told Edgar, "I was in jail in Mexico—arrested and held half a month without charge." He eyed me silently and I took his expression—or lack of it—as disapproval.

Returning to the city a twelve-hour bus ride later, I stayed overnight with friend and former employer Leslie Trumbull, who'd run Filmmakers' Cooperative since 1964. The Coop, Jonas's brainchild and the main distributor of independent, avant-garde films in New York, was naturally a center of information, news, gossip: filmmakers, renters, other artists, and friends (even, on occasion, lawmen) came in and out. And now Leslie had some news for me.

"Barbara Rubin," he calmly reported, "slipped on the ice here in the city a week or two ago. She broke her ankle badly."

"What was she doing here?"

"Visiting with a group of Hasids. She had to stay in the hospital for the physician to insert a steel pin. She was there a few days, at least."

I thought of the irony of her and Allen being under hospital sheets simultaneously—but separately. I didn't know Barbara's parents' number, but later in the evening, I called Allen's step-mother Edith on Leslie's kitchen phone. Being near the city, as well as in touch with the farm, she might know more. She knew, as it turned out, far more than I expected.

"Oh, I'm fine, and Louie's well, except for just a little trouble with his kidneys," she returned my opening, chipper as ever. "How were your folks down South?"

I sketched an answer, then she said something that fairly pulled Leslie's linoleum out from under my feet.

"I hear Candy is going to California."

Back on East Hill

O F COURSE, THERE were dozens of ways I might've guessed—but I simply hadn't, any more than most of us at Thanksgiving had realized they should help or get out of the kitchen. (And I'd called Candy once or twice while away; all seemed fine.) Yet in that suddenly extended moment at the receiver I pretended to know all about it and told Edith "Yes." I asked how she'd heard, and she said from Barbara, who'd heard from Huncke, who'd kept in touch with the farm while away.

I asked Leslie if I could stay on the line a little longer, and called the farm. Candy answered. We spoke of this and that and this; she made no mention of leaving—and I was too chicken to ask. Leslie was comforting before we had to go to bed—he to rise for work, I for the 6:00 AM bus.

Perhaps if I'd seen circumstances on East Hill as Candy did I would've expected her move, but surely there were plenty of clues. And though I didn't read it till decades later, she made at least some of them clear in a letter she wrote Allen just after my departure:

Dearest Allen—

Glad to hear you're feeling better. . . . Today the backhoe buried the pipe and although Mr. Keller had the pump going previous to our disconnecting it, it's not going now. But I'm sure we can get it going shortly. Gave Huncke his $200 and he went to the city. I think Peter thinks it was COP's money 'cause he made some kind of a crack to Huncke about it. Maybe you can straighten Peter out about it? He's not speaking to any of us . . . since the night . . . he & Lee got in at 2:30 AM after visiting you. Neither he or Lee would say where they'd been but wherever it was it really brought Peter's guilt problems to a hurting head again and he's working like mad and not wearing much clothing (bare feet in cold mud helping backhoe man) also mopping floors again & other A trips of his. Huncke is sure P & Lee split to city to cop but I don't know or care only that whatever they did, it did Peter no good. Lee is very uppity & doesn't quite really understand Peter's problem (not that anyone really does) and is very above-it-all with me. Also he's really a slob & everyone notices it even Gordon—never makes his (your) bed, etc etc. I think it puts a lot of strain on this household having people in it who are neither temporary *guests . . . nor permanent residents. Reason being that they do not consider the effects of their words and actions on a long-term basis but only as it might affect them. . . . Louie Cartwright has had a very bad effect on all of our Cooperstown friends. . . . After we asked him not to speak of drugs & violence etc. the first week he was here & we went to the Bensons', he proceeded to scare the hell out of Paul Benson on just those subjects & Michael Morris told me yesterday that Louie was like Gregory and bound to ruin us as he was uncool & very bigmouthed—Mike had heard via Cooperstown grapevine how Louie had told the dentist that COP supported him & charge the bill to them. . . . I can't stand him as he's a pain in the ass & never lets me say anything to anyone that he doesn't approve of—and he doesn't approve of anything but sex, violence, big talk, more violence & the "glorification of Louie." Don't see how you can stand him either but I'll put up with him if you can get him to shut up around town etc & cool himself. God help us if he talks too much this Sat. when he takes Charleen to the high school dance or tries to get her into bed or, worse, succeeds. . . .*

Love to you. Try to get better quickly, don't work too hard. Sorry I don't have much good news but everyone else can tell you that so I get stuck with being the bearer of ill tidings.

Much love
Candy

□ □ □

I LEFT LESLIE's before dawn the next morning. Long before the Greyhound pulled in at Crain's over six hours later, I was furious—not so much with Candy's reported plans but how I learned of them: Otis Redding's "Heard It Through the Grapevine" played over and over in my head, with a fiery resonance I'd never known. But when I saw Candy at the bus, waiting inside the Oldsmobile, I contained myself.

I tossed my duffel bag in the rear and settled into the front seat, waiting to see how she'd say it. She didn't wait long; and she was direct. "Why, um," she began as her eyes followed the hill up Lancaster Street, the big engine of the '55 Olds thrumming strongly, "Enrique and I are leaving the farm for California."

I said nothing. Then a few moments later she added, "I don't think the farm is a good place to be right now." I could see she had a point.

Back in our room, I slammed several dresser drawers closed; she seemed to tense up—but held her ground. Enrique, hearing the commotion from the attic, appeared in our doorway. Though I loved him too I continued my fit. He watched, turning glassy-eyed on the verge of tears. "Gordon," he said unreprovingly, looking into my eyes, "you are not the same person I knew before." There wasn't judgment in his look and voice; it was the whole emotional press of him: love, sadness, anguish. Now I'd hurt two people. I stopped.

Some moments later, Enrique back in the attic, Candy and I sat side-by-side on the bed, talking quietly. Then we closed the door and undressed each other and I knelt down on the floor and brought my face between her legs and then we made love, long and strong. I did it as richly as I could.

We had, I knew, a deteriorating sex life, and looking back I wonder if my crimped appreciation of Candy's disaffection was in part willful. A week or so before Thanksgiving I was alone in our room when Julius, stern-faced and pot-bellied as ever, suddenly appeared in the doorway. This time instead of remaining silent he burst into speech, his voice deep and alarmed despite its characteristic monotone: "Gordon, Candy's fuckin' Enrique in the attic!"

Then he turned heel for his own room next door. The messenger was as stunning as, perhaps more than, the message: here was not the self-encased Julius. (Did he even know Enrique's name? One might've wondered.) Here was a speaking Julius, a friend Julius, even a spy Julius.

But what was I to do? Candy and Enrique and I were so close; and what was all our talk (historical, at least) of free love, open relationship, if I couldn't accept the consequences? For the two years Candy and I had been together, our shared ethos had been largely centered on sexual honesty. After she came down from the attic, we sat together in our room and talked. When she told me it was the first time in a long while she felt she was really being made love to, I knew it was true.

□ □ □

THE AFTERNOON OF December 23, three American men hurtled through thousands of miles of space, en route to their orbit of the moon. Far below, beneath cumulus clouds above East Hill, Peter Orlovsky slid behind the wheel of a thirteen-year-old used car, Candy between him and me, gazing straight ahead. Huncke (back from the city, coming for the ride) and Enrique took the rear.

Candy and I had spoken little during the day, and when we did it was almost nonchalant—as if we were about to go to a ball game, or visit friends. Now, as Peter drove toward Cooperstown and the bus, we spoke even less. I sat there feeling tight and heavy inside, like I enclosed a block of ice that wouldn't thaw. I wondered what was going on inside Candy, how she might be facing the uncertainties—and the freedom—she'd brought into her life. I turned to look at her, studying her pale profile a moment as she continued gazing straight down the snow-lined road, then lightly bit her lip.

Enrique sat in the rear looking dazed. Huncke, across from him, tilted and stretched his chin up from his neck. A fuzzy red-and-white synthetic angora cap crowned his head.

In Cooperstown—the bus stopped at a restaurant on Main Street—we visited a few minutes, Huncke made a purchase at the liquor store, then as the bus pulled in we started our goodbyes. It was short, it was simple; once their bags were checked we turned back to the Olds. I didn't wait to watch them board.

□ □ □

ON OUR RETURN trip Huncke—once more in the back—asked, "And so what are you going to do, Gordon?"

"I'll stay at the farm—it's my home," I answered. Peter said "Uh-huh"; Huncke was silent. In my near-constant insecurity toward virtually everything, I felt unwelcome—but I didn't see at that moment, as I would after Christmas Eve, why Huncke—or Huncke and Peter—might prefer I not be there.

But I didn't feel unwelcome with Allen, who'd returned to East Hill some days earlier. He'd repaired a good bit since I'd last seen him in the hospital, when just breathing easily—with four broken ribs—was difficult. He wasn't in particular pain, it seemed, and was still not smoking again (that was the crash's silver lining), though he'd be on crutches another three months.

Left leg wrapped in plaster toes to hip, crutches propped against kitchen wall, he spent most of the next night—Christmas Eve—talking with me, reviewing my visit South, soothing me over Candy's departure. I mentioned my exchange with my father; at my line about bankers he laughed, but when I repeated some things my father said, he stopped me, stunned me. "You see," he pointed out, "your father's opening the door there, he's giving you an opportunity to communicate." And when I reported one of several instances of my mother's difficulty speaking, of her grasping for words—she could remember some people, but not their names, and she struggled to describe them—he offered, "Oh—so it may be a problem of articulation rather than memory."

On my relationship with Candy, history ancient and recent, he was again sympathetic, and seemed to want to hear but not intrude. Starting to offer a comment of his own, he cut himself off.

□ □ □

A RELATIONSHIP I knew much less about, naturally, was Huncke and Peter's. Only decades later did I learn that in 1960, with Allen away in South America, there'd been a romance—at least in Huncke's mind: "I have never really loved before nor will I again," he protested in one of several ardent letters.

Late in the afternoon on Christmas Eve, just before Allen and I began talking together much of the evening, Peter and Huncke had suddenly announced to Allen their eagerness to drive to Albany for last-minute Christmas items. We had a small tree, with a few decorations; it needed more, "plus a few surprises," Huncke explained: "We need to get into the spirit of things." The few Cherry Valley stores would be closing, and Cooperstown's wouldn't be open any later; they might as well go all the way to Albany. "And we'll get some more groceries too," Peter volunteered. Allen nodded phlegmatically, and they took off just as dusk fell. For many hours they didn't return. Allen and I continued at the kitchen table.

We didn't see them again till late Christmas morning.

"I got stopped by a cop," Peter said in consternation, brandishing his ticket. He was harrumphing about the house in overalls and brogans. "He saw we had an open wine bottle in the car."

An hour later, we were at the dining room table finishing lunch, when Ed, bundled in padded parka over several layers of clothing, entered the kitchen, wishing everyone Merry Christmas. Peter (whose moping had made him late for the meal) was still sighing over his ticket, moving energetically up and down from the table, to and from the kitchen. Huncke remained seated—and silent.

Peter told Ed of the ticket. "Let me take a look at it, Pete," he said, extending his hand. Parka hood down, cap still on his head, Ed squinted through small Santa glasses at the rectangle of flimsy manila paper. Then as surprise crept across his face he looked up at Peter, then the rest of us. "This cop was working out of his vicinity," he exclaimed, emphatic. "This is from the interstate between Albany and New York!"

Allen instantly put it all together, face brightening as he laughed: "Oh, you went to New York to score!" General silence followed. On the floor, Godly dog stirred as if in curiosity; at the windowsill tortoise shell Panda Manda paused in attention.

Ed stood there just a moment, puzzled, ticket in generous hand. Then he returned it to Peter. Huncke sat silently. I watched. Julius continued, speechless. Then Peter, eyes to the floor, admitted it: "Yeah, we went to the city."

So, we didn't see any last-minute Christmas decorations, or get into the spirit— though there was a surprise. Upstairs a little later, I sat with Huncke in his room. "Oh,

I feel so guilty," he confided in apparent anguish, shaking his head, eyes downcast. Still later, he and Allen fell into terrific argument as he accused Allen of hypocrisy in banning needle drugs. Meanwhile, outside there was over two feet of snow, more was about to come down, and the temperature the next night reached seventeen below. Peter shot speed a few days and then handed the rest of it over to Allen and became raving mad for a week thereafter, cutting—shaving—every centimeter of long blond hair from his head.

A Correspondence in Bed

D URING HIS TWO weeks at the hospital, Allen had received a number of visitors, and when he returned to the farm for six weeks' convalescence, he continued a correspondence even more vigorous than when on his feet and healthy.

"I never did get back to the farm from the airport," he'd told Ferlinghetti while still in traction. "I've been in Albany hospital . . . a sort of pleasure to go thru—I never had a broken bone before in 42 years. Nobody else was hurt bad except for a few scratches. . . . My bowels were paralyzed . . . for almost a week. . . ."

To Charles Olson, who'd cabled "HOPE ITS NO MORE THAN A BRUISE," he replied:

> No more than a bruise on my soul—Ugh thud—nausea hip to rib for a day and night realizing the body's a collapsible pain trap—& couldnt get past that, "How'd I get into this body-stump? and how do I get out, except by worse mortification?" . . . So I've been setting Blake's songs to music.

He heard from others, as well. Gary Snyder's sister Thea called from the West Coast, reporting that her brother, back from years in Japan, would soon be staying with her. Updating Louis and Edith, Allen characterized his situation as a "sort of kindly vacation with occasional stabs of rib pain from leftover bronchial cough. Anyway, not smoking."

And to East Hill came a Christmas card, its printed message "Hope your Christmas is just HEAVENLY." A feminine hand inscribed the following:

> Dear Allen—
>
> As you can see we are back Down South—Mémère ['s] health required it.
>   We have heard that you had a serious accident & would appreciate details as to your progress—
>   In any or other case we send you our prayers—
>
> Regards
> Jack & Stella

The City Again

THIRTY YEARS EARLIER, a classmate of Jack Kerouac's at Horace Mann Preparatory School was a tall, slender youth named Julian Beck. A decade later, Beck and Judith Malina started the Living Theatre, an experimental repertory group motivated by radical dissatisfaction with the drama of the day. Drawing from Brecht, Artaud, and other forebears, it was galvanized with hope and vision for a theater so revolutionary as to change the world.

In 1950–51, Allen had first met the Becks (married in 1948) and other "subterraneans" at the San Remo. He, Judith, and Julian remained friends thereafter and he vigorously supported their cause in various ways, on numerous occasions. (In 1971 he'd labor mightily to wrest the whole company from Brazilian jail.)

Late in 1968, after returning to the U.S. from a spring and summer involved in uprisings in France, they performed again in the New York area. *Paradise Now* was a series of tableaux designed to liberate the audience from conventional thought, politics, and mores so it might spontaneously join with the Theatre on stage, en masse, stripping and embracing: its ultimate purpose, as Beck would write, was "nonviolent anarchist revolution." On occasion, the production ended with Theatre and audience exiting the hall together to reclaim the streets. "It changed my life," Robert La Vigne, the painter who'd introduced Allen and Peter in San Francisco, told me.

On New Year's Day 1969, Allen, resting upright in bed against tongue-in-groove pine paneling, made me an offering: "They're holding two tickets for me for January 4th, but I can't get in. Would you like them? Take a date!"

A few days and I was boarding that Greyhound with a note from Allen to the Living Theatre, signed and stamped with his red Tibetan seal, and plans to take a young woman friend. Andrea Zimmer, whom I'd first seen a couple of years earlier, was exquisitely cute, but we didn't develop a "relationship"—she seemed too young, and I never pushed it as far as I would've liked—even though I found her, in her dark rounded shapelessness, a Hindu relief come to life.

The evening began with Judith, Julian, and others striding up and down the aisles. I was struck by Julian's look: intense blue eyes envisioning a future which already possessed him. He and his colleagues in dramatic urgency confronted the audience as a whole, as well as individual members at random, with "personal" problems made universal by their cultural and political base.

"I'm not allowed to smoke marijuana!"

"I'm not allowed to travel without a passport!"

"I don't know how to stop the war!"

The evening's climax was a mass "orgy" of nakedness and affection on stage. Andrea and I joined the many dozens of others there, Theatre and audience alike, but she was too shy to even begin to remove light blouse, heavy sweater, and tight jeans. We milled about, surrounded by upright moving bodies varyingly naked, Theatre members in loincloths (ever since being busted in New Haven they had to wear g-strings), audience members totally nude (the distinction between the two roles now irrelevant). Many were sweating, in harsh light and dark, flesh and face beaming in the general exaltation. I would join them totally—but there was Andrea, my guest, my companion, shy, clothed, lovely, a college girl now, but virginal. I stripped—down to my underwear.

"What?!" a stunned Allen exclaimed when I gave him the details of our evening. "You didn't get naked?!"

At Winter's Heart

E D HAD TOLD us our average winter temperature was zero; by the end of January's first week his words proved true. The usual lowest, he'd said, was twenty to twenty-four below—and already we were close.

The pine paneling installed upstairs didn't really take the place of insulation. And the wind—especially north and west—would whistle and tear through open slits of space around the upstairs propane heaters, sometimes with such strength it blew out the pilots.

Having more than one heat source made our leaky old house inhabitable, providing relative comfort to most of its parts. We had too the grand Kalamazoo: wood or coal by day, always coal at night. Come nine o'clock Peter or I would "bank" it, piling into its deep heating bed as much dark shiny anthracite as we could while letting some air circulate through vents at the side. Checking on it several hours later we'd see the thick black iron-stove surface glow a rich orange red: a small wonder to behold, a wondrous heat to feel. I even loved, almost, the smell—that carbon and sulfur that could turn nauseating, I suppose, if pushed: it signaled warmth, security, stability; it told me I could go back to sleep.

We lived at the end of a private dirt road connecting to two state dirt roads, a mile later to a state paved road. Although they didn't have to, the road crew would sometimes plow through heavy snow to the top of our drive, a hundred feet from our house. But often we'd end up parking at Schoolhouse Corners, the nondescript dirt road intersection at the top of the hill above our mailbox and walking the distance, sometimes through heavy snow. By late winter plowed piles of white on either side of Kniskern Road—that last stretch before our drive—made canyon-like walls the height of a man.

Our yellow jeep truck had four-wheel drive and a small snow plow at front, but it scarcely matched the town's huge orange snow plow truck, and was far less effective—when it wasn't rendered immobile by frequent mechanical problems. We had snow tires put on the Olds, then soon saw we needed chains as well. Peter and I lay on hard flat whiteness, mouths gasping steam in the cold, and nudged and pushed and pulled the heavy metal links around the tires, stubbing and pinching icy fingers as we did so, grunting and cursing in the chill and clank. Into the trunk of the old Olds we heaved a couple of hundred-pound bags of fittin' ration for added weight, better traction.

Allen, broken-bodied still, remained as generous and providing as ever. We'd already gotten a range of winter clothing supplies: from L.L. Bean (not then a "status" item, it was recommended by Ed the Hermit) had come a couple of "featherweight" rain parkas; from Watrous's Friendly Corner Store, insulated Ball Brand rubber snow boots; from the mail-order catalog for Montgomery Ward ("Monky Ward," Ed called it), thermal long underwear, work gloves and horsehide mittens with liners, and one or two pairs of coveralls. From J.C. Penney's in Oneonta, nylon and wool boot socks. Outdoors I wore a dull greyish-green nylon parka from Monky Ward.

Julius typically chose a corduroy coat, often buttoning only half of it as if in defiance of the cold, even as we tackled daily tasks: hauling several times from the well two buckets of drinking and washing water, a hundred yards through the snow (in spite of our having laid the pipe to the kitchen sink, the hand pump still didn't work); footing it up to our vehicles, trying to get them started (once it was so cold the Oldsmobile's emergency brake froze); shoveling a path through snow in front of the house and around to the barn; feeding the animals and letting them out on relatively good days—Bessie and Lash (an older, slow-footed horse we'd gotten to replace Penny, as restful as Penny was restive); Brahma and Shiva; the chickens and Papa Duck and his Muscovy brood; as well as Godly and Sadeyes and other dogs who were now showing up along with Panda Manda, Tiger, and other cats; shoveling manure (when not wholly frozen) in horse and cow and goat stalls; adding fresh straw to the stalls; hauling down hay from the loft above; carrying boiling water to all the animals' water buckets; milking; making barn and chicken house repairs; emptying our night soil from the white porcelain potty enclosed in the little wooden toilet in the bathroom space beyond the kitchen.

Even Huncke helped out, as Allen wrote Burroughs:

Huncke here in healthy country mood, goes into NY every month & comes back sallow, skin-ruptured & stomach sour'd & recovers after 4 days & goes out with mittens in 3 feet of snow to carry waterpail with red ears, & purple wool skullcap.... I'm a nervous wreck dictator waving my crutches ordering everyone to work in the snow half the time.

Now, with spring on the horizon, it was apparent that we who were ablebodied would before long have to be outdoors, meeting the new season's demands. Why not have someone properly skilled come to work now on the many repairs needed indoors? Whenever he wanted a hand, we could join in.

Carl La Salle's older brother Erroll was, as Ed told us, a reliable carpenter. We drew up lists of needed work (by the end of December, I could make legible scrawls, a little slowly) and called quiet sturdy Erroll. On and off, January into February, he came with tool box and t-square and the rest of his arsenal, and took on a range of tasks—making doors windproof and closeable; installing a new door for Peter's room; adding insulation in several rooms; finishing attic moulding . . .

In the bathroom, we helped Erroll tear up surface flooring, lay down plywood, brush glue across its surface, then spread tarpaper, then glue new plastic tile to the tarpaper. But even with his good work, would our hundred-year-old house—which architect David Savage recommended we tear down—hold its own through the north wind's blast, the Snow Belt's blizzards? As Allen asked a year and a half later in verse, would "the mortician come and look us over"?

A dozen years later my wife Kathleen and I bought our first little home down South, a wall-to-wall carpeted brick bungalow; on entering, Allen gazed out the living room picture window and exclaimed, "This is what we should've bought instead of that farm! A tidy little place where everything works!"

The Gang Grows Again;
Peter Turns Enforcer

AFTER THE HOLIDAYS our house filled up. Through much of January, besides Allen, Peter, Julius, Huncke, and myself, there was Louie Cartwright, Lee Crabtree, Michael Braddocks, and Sophie Clark.

"Huncke's grooming him," Allen would say of Louie.

"To be what?" I asked.

"Another Huncke."

Louie grew up in Ashtabula, Ohio, adopted by a rather poor, rural family—but seemed like an orphan from the streets. He hadn't felt well-treated in Ohio. Dropping out of high school, he went to California, where he met Rosebud, who brought him to New York. Now, a year or so later, he still had some contact with his adoptive family. I once overheard him tell his father on the phone that he was here with Allen, adding with emphasis, "Yeah, he's a pretty big deal."

Bucktoothed but good-looking with broad nose, brown eyes, wide sideburns, rose-bud lips, and black Italianate hair, a junky and not very effective conman, Louie was just a couple of years younger than I. He came on "dumb" like Marlon Brando's Stanley Kowalski in *A Streetcar Named Desire*—but without Kowalski's physical power. Yet Stephen Bornstein's lady friend Barbara Pionteck found him sexy, and Allen, seated at the dining room table, crutches to wall, remarked to Peter, "He's intelligent."

I always thought Allen went out of his way for people, sometimes seeing more in them than was there. But later I read a good story Louie had written about himself and his friend Andy stealing a TV for junk. Louie had read it to a small group of older people one evening in the city and, he reported, was acclaimed "a great naturalistic writer." He was very pleased.

Allen and Lee were now recording some of Allen's singing and playing on the Uher, and at Lee's suggestion another musician joined us. Michael Braddocks played guitar and other instruments, and seemed overall quite a capable fellow. He and Lee soon persuaded Allen to get a piano, an old upright which we all (except invalid Allen) lifted and pushed and tugged and maneuvered from the truck down the snow-packed path in front of the house, up onto the porch, across the kitchen linoleum and the dining room and into the living room.

Michael brought with him his girl friend, fifteen-year-old Sophie Clark. She was beautiful, with thick lips, large blue eyes, puffy round blushing cheeks, long straight blonde hair. She was still baby-fatted, tender—not half through her teens.

After dinner their first night there she spent a little time up in my room: we sat together on my bed, talking—just talking. After twenty minutes we suddenly heard Michael's voice, calling up to her from the floor below. She had, it seemed, used up her permitted length of time away.

She was in awe of Michael. He was versatile not just musically but practically and mechanically (in the middle of January he brought back to life Ed's old abandoned tractor), as well as socially. I recall one moment in town with Sophie, sitting in the Olds, waiting on Michael. We continued to wait because Michael had become engaged in conversation with one person after another in store, on street. "He can talk to anyone!" Sophie exclaimed, admiring.

In those days, of course, a dramatic polarity of cultural difference and escalating war divided many of the young from the old, long-hairs from straights. (Allen, far more than anyone else I knew, was gifted at speaking across the divide.) Though Cherry Valley was basically friendly, it was after all "in the provinces" and tradition-bound: Michael's sociability was notable.

With two musicians and now piano and guitar as well as organ, wintry days and nights were livelier—if not harmonious in every sense. I really liked hearing Michael and Lee talk about music, punctuating their words with improvisations on key and string. They seemed to get along like the chums they were.

But now a new challenge loomed: Huncke and Louie were bringing in heroin and shooting up. Peter (an ardent convert to abstinence now that he'd thrown out the last of his Christmas speed) and Allen suspected as much, and a major scene took place one afternoon in late January, with Lee and Michael in and out of the dining room, alternately tinkling the ivories or pumping the A.B. Chase or sitting around the table. Immediately next to the dining room—there was no dividing wall—was the kitchen, with the Kalamazoo and the range, and a sink with a tub of dishwater, pots and plates and pans nearby.

I set a five-inch reel onto the Uher, turned it on. It took in all sounds, all clunks of coffee mugs on oilclothed wood, all coughs and scrapings of chairs, mutterings and shoutings. At beginning as at end, Huncke—who could be quite domestic (sometimes donning an apron) puttered about table, sink, and stove, keeping house.

The first words we hear are Huncke's, with a little mock consternation: "Michael, I'm moving your things on top of the . . . Who do I hear giggling? . . . trying to get things neat here so people can relax. . . ." Turning to the Kalamazoo, he peers inside a pot: "Now just who left this in here? Burning till it's all fucked up!?"

Meanwhile, Allen reviews some of his Blake for Michael, explaining that in "The Shepherd," "Piping is a symbol of the imagination. The piper is the imagination." With tunes for fourteen of them already on tape, he intends to make a record of the whole *Songs of Innocence* and *Songs of Experience*. Sitting at the organ, Louie imitates Allen's words and music, singing "Blah blah blah" in parody of his Blake.

Peter begins bantering with Huncke. When they discuss the evening's dinner, Peter reminds him it's meatless lasagna, warning, "You'd better behave yourself, Herbie!" The text is vegetarianism, but the subtext is needle drugs. That's the current bee in Peter's bonnet, and it's a big and busy one.

Within moments Orlovsky turns to Ginsberg: "Now, both these guys got needles. So you both [Huncke and Louie] have to keep your needles out of the house, you understand?" Allen asks the two of them directly if they have needles—no response. He warns that his friend Maretta Greer, due to arrive the next day, may have a "sentimental drug problem" and be "constantly chattering" about drugs. Peter, meanwhile, won't be deterred, and his exchange with Huncke is a study in bluster:

PETER: You guys got needles outside the house?
HUNCKE: What needles?
PETER: Have you got your needles outside the house?
HUNCKE: Have you got your needles outside the house?
PETER: I have no needle. I have no needle.
HUNCKE: I have no needle.
PETER: You've got no needle at all?
HUNCKE: No needle.
PETER: Is it outside the house? [general laughter]
HUNCKE: Where's *your* needle?
PETER: It's outside the house [general laughter] . . . is your needle outside the house?
HUNCKE: If your needle's outside the house, *my* needle's outside the house.

. . . .

PETER: Have you two guys got your spikes out of the house?
HUNCKE: Yes.

PETER: You do?

HUNCKE: I don't have anything to get out of the house.

LOUIE: I don't shoot up anyway.

But Inspector Orlovsky remains undeterred: "Get the spikes, put 'em on the table, and take 'em outside the house," he orders, without response. Michael tells of having walked into Keller's Hardware recently: plump Mrs. Keller called him over and handed him six tablespoons, saying, "I'm putting these on Herbie's bill—make sure he gets 'em." Huncke responds, "On *Herbie's* bill? It's a bitch."

Then Peter devises a plan to answer the question once and for all—but no one, including Allen, supports it. At once earnest and antic, Peter becomes increasingly consternated, his voice Daffy Duckish:

PETER: The only way to test is to see when you say "Go!" whether they're
    going upstairs or downstairs or in the cellar or around the back of the
    house, to put 'em on the table, and then go outside. . . . When you say
    the word "Go," you see where they go. If they go upstairs, downstairs,
    or in the cellar, you know it's in the house.

ALLEN: What if they just sit here?

PETER: Huh?

ALLEN: What if they just sit here?

As he exclaims in comic mumble and stutter, Peter sees the two confreres as wholly guilty, with "their dicks hangin' down to their goddamn toenails, and they got dirty toenails!" But the problem, Michael puts in, is that the state police can appear en masse in an instant. And if they can't find anything, "They bring their own." Allen, to my surprise, says, "It's all right if they bring their own—we can defend against that." But adds:

. . . they've had massive raids in all the nearby counties, you know. Our
presence is obvious here and it's just automatically logical that if they're going
to do any kind of raiding activity in this area around Cooperstown and all,
they'll simply add our names to the list of places to be raided, just as . . . an
administrative check-up. So—be prepared. . . . I don't have enough money to
pay lawyers.

Therefore, he urges, anything coming into the house must be stashed. Maretta, for instance, might bring pot. He worries she might freak out downtown, like she did once over a boy friend in Ceylon. Allen will leave for readings the day after she arrives; to Huncke he adds, ". . . she's a little crazier than you to take care of."

Peter stays his course. Making himself an example, he goes outside, to return with his own stash. As we sit waiting, an offended Huncke urges Julius not to brush his teeth in the dishwater.

Peter returns with two syringes (no needles), which he says he'll throw in the stove. Huncke, disgusted by now with the whole business, proposes doing the dishes. Allen's amused: "Peter's just a little small-time penny-ante needle head, and you're an old-time big one, so if *he's* got a spike, you must have a whole collection!"

When Peter resumes his interrogation, Huncke tries to protect his young companion: "Louie is not involved!" But Louie joins in, admitting to "the little brown spike" that Peter said he'd seen: it's in the house.

Yet Huncke holds his ground: "I don't know what you're talkin' about." Peter returns to near-hysterical comic book exasperation, exclaiming of Huncke, "What a tough dick, Allen!" He goes to the sink to start on the dishes; Huncke offers to help. The scene begins breaking up. Sophie appears, speaking personally to Huncke about her period. He counsels, "I wouldn't worry if I were you. You're probably just upset. . . . your menstruation. It's when you stop . . ." Michael reports that he once "ran into a coil" [an I.U.D.]: "Those things are dangerous. They ought to be outlawed. Pills too!" Peter complains that Allen didn't support his effort to rid the house of needle drugs just now, and asks Huncke to keep quiet about an earlier conversation they had, as Huncke joins him at the sink.

We hear the rattling of pans and other utensils as Huncke exclaims to himself, "Oh my gosh, oh my gosh, oh my gosh. Oh by golly, oh by gum."

More Paper

ALLEN CONTINUED HIS prolific correspondence. It was a chronic burden; later in the year he answered a friend: ". . . I am not able to walk into the woods w/ notebook watch dragonflies zip over iron-rust leaf'd creek beds & sigh with the frog's sposh."

Ed or Peter or I would bring to the dining room table, or up to his pine-paneled bedroom, bills, personal letters, manila envelopes bearing manuscripts, even telegrams. He wrote Dave Haselwood in San Francisco about designing Huncke's "long delayed mss.," now that it seemed Harvey Brown would publish it. Haselwood and City Lights were preparing Allen's *Indian Journals*, but—typical of Allen—he urged, "Huncke's book should be put out more swiftly than mine . . . he's waited so long."

Gary Snyder, viewing his homeland anew after over a decade in Japan, checked in with his old friend from mid-'50s Berkeley on one of the crucial questions of the day: ". . . for me, *no violence*. He [activist Keith Lampe] says you are holding firm on that too. I think Good must work . . . as Gandhi insisted. . . ."

Indeed Allen agreed; recently he'd written Burroughs in favor of "Non violent upaya (skillful means)," rejecting Jerry Rubin's "creepy symbols (toy gun & live ammo necklace)" which "just increases stereotype."

Harrison Salisbury at *The Times* answered Allen's letter about the recent Cleveland, Ohio, suicide of the young poet named d.a. levy: he'd "get our correspondent in Cleveland to see what he can do. . . ." To Ferlinghetti, who'd expressed interest in publishing his Blake compositions, Allen reported on his "transcribing Blake songs & taping them," complained of correspondence swallowing time, and asked:

> I am broke again and need another $500.00 if you can afford that much more advance. . . .
>
>   . . . I have huge reading tour again—wipe out debts & finish C.O.P. farm house & retire.

Writing his father just as he set out for readings from south Florida to Notre Dame, Minneapolis, and the West inside of two weeks, he told of present predicament and joy—and future hope:

Happy news your kidneys are in Running order—It's lovely good luck you are still here for company and I feel sad I'm not more near your side—I hope what I'm doing is worth while—which is, privately, setting up a refuge for people who need refuge—and the need for Balance here has kept me tied down (as well as the hip) more than I'd wanted or anticipated. I'd like to be able to leave this place running independently, or at least independent of my presence. . . .

I got a lot of work done on music—have actually learned elementary notation and harmony & so have a new language & have written out some lovely tunes for Blake—which will last a long time & give pleasure & probably also make some $ to take care of farm.

Maretta—and Cheri

L ATE IN THE fall of 1968, Allen had received an aerogramme from Dacca, East
Pakistan (now Bangladesh):

> *Allen*
>
> *I love you*
>
> *3 months no money yr. 3 letters received but no $.*
>
> *Please help*
>
> *c/o U.S. Consul Dacca.*
>
> *Maretta*

I hadn't met Maretta Greer, but two years earlier I'd seen her in Allen's company
at Jonas's subterranean Cinematheque on 41st Street. I wrote in '66 *Frames*:

> *She was silent, slim, blond, and high-cheekboned, a small wool cap on her head,*
> *a big dark heavy coat from neck down. Lips tightly closed, head and back erect,*
> *she moved slowly, deliberately, quietly, sternly, a crane among ostriches. She was*
> *Maretta Greer, back from many months among saddhus in India, Pakistan, Tibet.*
> *Someone in the crowded linoleum-floored lobby whispered, "She knows Tibetan!"*

She'd appeared on the Golden Gate Park dais at the San Francisco Be-In, January
1967, with Allen, Snyder, Leary, and others. She was twenty-four then. Now, her
arrival on East Hill imminent, Allen told me she'd left home to become a saddhu at
age fifteen and confided, "Her problem is she thinks wherever she is is her own private
garden." But I was unprepared for what I saw.

The day before Allen and Peter's departure on February 1, Maretta, whom Ed
Sanders had encountered unfed and shoeless and "having visions" at his Peace Eye
Bookstore, was driven up from Manhattan. One cold grey afternoon I was out near
the front of the house, when a small car rolled down our drive: the huge orange snow
plow had paid a recent visit, coming, unusually, all the way down that narrow channel bordered each side by hillocks of snow.

From out the passenger's seat stepped a pale young woman who held herself with
consummate bearing, clutching the blanket that embraced her. Lips sealed, eyes fixed
on the front of our little house, she walked proudly, deliberately yet quickly, over the

hardpacked snow. Barefoot. I stood nearby in amazement, parka and long underwear, lined boots and thermal socks, my eyes following her all the way to the front door.

□ □ □

ONE SPRING DAY back in 1967 when I was working at Filmmakers' Cooperative, the phone rang; my friend Andrew answered. "That woman has the sexiest voice I've ever heard," he offered as he came for me.

My caller was Cheri Eve, whom I was often seeing then, when Candy and I visited Stanley Fisher's for group sex. She was smart and funny, skinny and flat-chested and sexy and I liked her. Her face was pretty and her voice—well, her voice was every bit as my friend said. Candy's voice, in its whiskyish tones, could sound inviting; Cheri's had already taken you in.

I hadn't been in touch with her since well before Candy and I had left for Mexico in late 1967. But over a year later—December 5, 1968—she wrote me a note, enclosing the short front-page notice of our car wreck from *The Village Voice*. As for an address, she had only the news report information to go on. Her envelope was addressed to me in Allen's care at Memorial Hospital, Albany, and thanks to him I got it after my return from Carolina: doubtless it helped me deal with Candy's departure. Her typewritten note accompanying *The Voice* piece was even shorter than that front-page blurb:

> *Saw this thursday night in the newspaper and was glad to know you weren't hurt.*
> *of course I hope mr. ginsberg will soon be better say hello to candy for me.*
>
> *Cheri*

Now, nearly two months later, as Allen was about to leave, Cheri was coming for a brief visit, arriving just after barefoot Maretta. I was looking forward.

Me and My Brother and a Blizzard

ALLEN'S READINGS MADE Committee on Poetry, Inc., and the farm possible: his royalties, though good for a poet's income in those days, wouldn't nearly have met our needs. Of course, anyone in Allen's position would've had serious second thoughts about the farm—not to mention preferring recuperation to strenuous travel and performance. The day before leaving he complained in a letter to Whalen, "... I didn't even want to leave home but this giant White Elephant Poesy Household Farm!" (To Burroughs he'd confided, "I've sunk over $20,000 into it ...")

Our poet on crutches—Peter his nurse—left for several days in Miami before key-noting a Pornography Conference at Notre Dame. They'd be gone a fortnight, return briefly, and be off again. The farm was now in my hands: house, Julius, animals, guests, checkbook, snow, vehicles.

Michael Braddocks drove them to the Albany airport, but before they set off in the Olds, Huncke entered my room.

"Say, Gordon, I'm going with them to Albany, just for the ride."

"Oh."

"I don't want Allen to know it, but after we leave them at the airport, I'll ask Michael to drop me at the bus station so I can get into the city. Can you give me just a little check, say $25?"

I knew he'd score with it, and possibly return to the farm with his purchase. Here we go again with the no-needle-drugs issue, I thought to myself. But I also thought $25 wasn't worth hassling. I reached onto the top shelf of my secretary for the large black checkbook binder and wrote one on the C.O.P. account. "Square business," Huncke replied, with typically old-fashioned phrasing.

Me and My Brother, Robert Frank's film about Julius and Peter, was premiering in the city the next day at the New Yorker Theatre. Knowing that several of us might make a quick trip in for it—but not planning to attend himself—Huncke wrote the filmmaker and his sculptor wife:

Robert—

Regards.

Everyone excited by—'Me and My Brother' and will in all probability—fall in to see
the film.

Personally had hoped you would fall by here. Since apparently you wont be out
this way soon—perhaps you could duke Gordon a small surprise to bring me.

Hello—Mary Frank—and the rest of the family.

Huncke

In the meantime Cheri had arrived. Even though her visit was short and dominated by unexpected stress, seeing Cheri again was special. Bright and communica-
tive, she was entering law school, and spoke once or twice about the future. But in
those days I always drew back from talk of what might come.

The day after Allen and Peter set off, I did afternoon chores early, made sure all
barn and chicken house animals were locked in, fed and hayed and watered. (Wrist
now two months out of sling, I was milking again, both Bessie and one of the goats.
Shiva would soon give birth.) Then most of the rest of us piled into the Olds: Michael
(driving), Sophie, Julius, Maretta in Irish cap and London Fog coat, Cheri, and myself.
I looked forward to the film and its subject's—its star's—reaction.

Me and My Brother was Frank's first feature. Its genesis dated back to 1963, after
Allen's return from India, when the two of them discussed making a film of *Kaddish*.
Allen was broke; Robert paid him a small daily sum to work on a script. But he didn't
have enough funds, and began filming casually around Allen's apartment. Julius soon
entered after a dozen years in the mental hospital; his "otherness" intrigued the filmmaker, and he became Frank's focus. It was shot over three years, East Coast to West,
as Julius lived with, traveled with—and ran away from—Allen and Peter.

Michael drove fast and we entered Manhattan with just enough time to make
it to the theater. En route, I pointed out a large sign for ORANGE JULIUS (a kind of
orange smoothie chain in those days) to Julius, but he responded no more than he had
to anything else the whole trip: stoical, nearly stern, lips closed or occasionally pursed,
he simply sat there, unblinking behind serious horn-rims.

At the New Yorker, we saw *Me and My Brother* in big black block lettering on
its white marquee; a brightly lit display case proclaimed U.S. PREMIERE. I took out my
movie camera for a quick shot of some of us, including the laconic star, immediately
underneath the glowing sign.

The film was interesting, jagged, elliptical. Given Julius's basic nonspeaking persona (though he did speak at certain key points in the film, including its beautiful
ending), and his disappearances, Robert had hired actor Joe Chaiken to play him

part of the time. This perhaps introduced some confusion but also gave complexity to some of Frank's central questions about the nature of identity. And I was struck by the sort of Dickensian anger and madness Peter displayed in speaking to, threatening Julius. But as in most of the scenes on the large screen, Julie remained speechless inside the theater, and unacknowledging of our queries as we filed out at movie's end.

Re-entering upper Broadway, we saw it was snowing. I didn't like that a bit—if it was doing so moderately in the city, what might it be doing a few hours later as we tried to approach our home in the Snow Belt? I was quiet at first, but as we took a quick bite at a diner, I could see through the plate glass window that it was coming down thicker than before. The Olds had snow tires, and 200-pound bags of feed in the trunk, but if snow accumulated quickly I didn't know if we'd make it through hours and hours of upstate driving. On the other hand, could I entrust Lee or Louie or Louie's visiting friend David with morning chores? They'd never taken on barn and chicken house tasks, but they weren't incapable, and Ed might check in. . . .

Tense, I sat on my stool, deliberating. Finally I leaned over the counter and said to Michael, "I don't know if we ought to drive back tonight. Maybe we could stay with friends here, get an early start in the morning when we can see—"

"No, we'll make it," Michael said immediately, without further consideration. He wasn't only a talker but a doer, and now his mind was fixed. And I regretted it. If I was tense on the counter stool, I was profoundly distressed as we began making our way up the turnpike. It *was* a blizzard, as I feared—and before long we could see only a couple feet ahead through illuminated raging atomic whiteness.

Yet Michael persisted, and fortunately there was virtually no other traffic, since most drivers had had the good sense to turn back. Cheri and I held each other tight—nothing to complain about there!—while the applied stoicism of Julius, also in the rear, doubtless stood him in good stead. In front, Sophie was next to Michael as they chatted on and on; next to her a closed-lipped Maretta, Irish cap on head.

We skidded twice, but Michael persisted through the white darkness. At this point—half or more of the distance covered—what could I do? If there were places to pull over and stop, I couldn't see them.

To Michael's credit, and with considerable luck, we made it. More than six hours after leaving Manhattan—at times, we scarcely managed twenty miles an hour—we were pulling up near our mailbox alongside Claude Graham's spread. The blizzard continued to rage—and it would take how long to make it on foot, one flashlight between the six of us, that last uphill mile?

An hour, surely. We lost our way more than once, and the dim amber from a gaslight in the house became visible only near the very end of our bitter journey. Breathless, wet in layer upon layer of clothes, bodies soaked with sweat, yet cold on the outside, we shook the snow from our boots and pants at the front porch. No one seemed to have frostbite from the long hike, and all I had to do in the house was bank the fire in the good old Kalamazoo. Morning chores would come soon.

Chores & a Slap

A ND THOSE CHORES, morning and evening, were once outlined as follows. Leaving the farm six weeks later for Manhattan and (briefly) Carolina, I typed up a detailed listing. I don't remember who remained to carry them out—of course Julius was there, perhaps Michael and Sophie, others. Allen, with Peter, had just returned from another series of readings. Shiva, the white Saanen, had had kids.

SCHEDULE OF CHORES

A.M.

- Feed cats & dogs

- Feed animules—Bessie 2 scoops fittin ration in bucket
    Lash (horse) 1 scoop
    goats 1/2 scoop each

- Milk Bessie & goats & feed little uns (goats)

- If decent weather, let Bessie & Lash out & put 4-5 leaves hay out for them & 3 buckets water in tub outside. If weather not decent (i.e. overcast, storm threatening or snow falling, or below 20°), 2 buckets in Bessie's tub, one for hoss, & 3 leaves hay for Lash & 2 for Bessie. 1/2 leaf @ for goats. *Offer* water to goats.

- Feed chickens & ducks—2-3 scoops scratch feed. Fill laying mash trough. Gather eggs. Resupply floors & nests w/ straw or hay when needed. Leave open door about 1 ft. (unless blizzard), put chair against it so Bessie & Lash cannot enter if they are out. 1 bucket of water; rinse dish first.

[At all times]
- Keep snow around barn & chicken house doors shoveled so they open & close freely. Keep barn door locked at all times unless you're inside. Make sure Bess & Lash are properly tucked in at nite. Lock chicken house door tight at nite.

P.M.

- Feed, milk & water as above. If animals are out during day, they should go in no later than 5:30....

- Feed birds as needed

- Make sure all feed cans are tightly covered after feeding.

- Make sure gerbil & turtles have food & water.

□ □ □

HUNCKE RETURNED FROM the city soon after the film premiere; I picked him up at Crain's. That afternoon I went by his room, which he now shared with Louie. The door was so warped he'd simply hung a curtain, only partly covering the doorway. I poked my head in.

"You shoulda knocked," said Louie, about to insert a needle connected to a brown eyedropper into his vein.

Of course I was complicit—even though Huncke could hardly have bought more than five bags with the $25. When he picked up on it Lee was uptight that they were shooting smack, but I figured let them shoot and be done with it.

With almost daily snowfalls and vehicles parked at some distance, we felt even farther from the city than the 200 miles: we were cozy in our Mohawk Valley redoubt. Nonetheless, midway during Allen and Peter's fortnight away, one visitor made it up: Rachel Fleischman. Why she returned, I don't know; she knew Peter was gone, presumably—and their relationship had ended sometime earlier, anyway. She didn't seem interested in me now—just as well!—and she was in as bad shape as ever: she slurred about, like waves lapping over a dock, but without their rhythm.

One morning she hung around Cherry Valley's Landmark Village Laundromat with her blouse mostly open, breasts mostly visible in her bra. Back on East Hill, she and Louie got together. But then she became so restless and aggravated she threatened to call the cops on us. Huncke slapped her. Instantaneously. It shut her up, stopped her cold.

"Oh, I hated doing that," he told me later in the afternoon, lower lip out, head down and shaking just slightly back and forth.

"Many would say she deserved it, Huncke."

Rachel left soon; and Allen and Peter returned—for a night and a day.

Allen Takes the Bull by the Horns

I N TWO WEEKS Allen had travelled over 9,000 miles, lost his voice at least once, given a dozen poetry readings, sung Blake, and delivered that keynote at Notre Dame's pornography conference. Though he now seemed on the verge of exhaustion if not illness, he dealt with the situation at the farm as soon as he set his crutches down. He had precious little time—just the one day—to do otherwise, before heading for the city and more engagements.

I talked with Allen in my room, told him of my writing the check for Huncke. I didn't say anything else about it.

"Thank you for keeping the farm together," he offered.

I felt especially gratified hearing this, for a good while before his departure I'd asked him, "Tell me what you think—am I stupid or smart? Sometimes I feel like I'm really sharp, other times really dumb—"

"Well, I've thought that administratively you were extraordinarily dumb," he'd answered, "but I guess everybody has their own strengths and weaknesses."

Now he added that he'd run into Candy in San Francisco. "I told her you were competent as farm manager, and that seemed to surprise her."

I then mentioned the card I'd recently received from her, its face bearing the question, "Would you care to drift aimlessly in my direction?" She'd written:

> . . . *Enrique split without ever saying goodbye one day. Nice cat. He is more egotistical than just about anyone I ever met. . . . Tell Allen I am under the guidance of Vajrabodi. . . . been climbing mountains w. Mountain Yogis.*
> . . . *I'm quite happy now—better than ever.*

> *Lots of Love*
> *Candy*

I spoke with Allen about Maretta: for two weeks I'd had virtually no communication with her; she'd been typically close-lipped, unto herself except when I heard her crying one day in the attic, near the south window.

"America is so horrible!" she'd exclaimed, sitting near the window ledge. "Pakistan was so beautiful. I'm so unhappy here!" Wanting to give her sympathy—and curious besides—I sat down near her, stayed, listened. I tried, probably not very successfully, to make her feel better. Her voice was high, Bostonian, almost English.

I didn't particularly care that Maretta was otherwise uncommunicative, except she never helped with the slightest daily task: aside from all the outdoor work, the porcelain potty (which we all used at least at night, rather than trudge through snow to outhouse) needed emptying every morning; floors downstairs always needed sweeping; wood and coal—and water, for that matter—could always be gotten; dishes could always be washed. I was growing tired of emptying her shit.

"Would you mind asking Maretta if she could help with just a few household chores every day?" I asked Allen. He agreed, but when I saw the result, I wished I'd never brought it up.

The next afternoon, an hour or two before he and Peter set off again, Allen, on crutches, in dark green work shirt and Can't Bust'em overalls, approached Maretta as she was starting up to the attic.

"Say, Maretta," he called softly from the foot of the stairs. She stopped and turned toward him, a few steps above. "While I'm gone can you pitch in and do a little work around the place?"

Maretta immediately began screaming, striking out several times at Allen's face and upper body, knocking off his glasses, sending one crutch tumbling to the floor. Allen remained in place, the other crutch and a wall of the narrow stairway providing support.

"I'll never tell you the seven secret mysteries! You're not holy any more!" She shouted in high-pitched Bostonian English. "How I regret I taught you any mantras!" She swung again, missing.

Allen remained calm, looking up at her. "Keep on," he said at one point, inviting her to continue her harangue. "What else will you do?"

Strangely, Maretta then interrupted herself: "I need a cigarette!" Her eyes darted sharply about the dining room full of frozen onlookers just beneath her—Lee and myself, Peter and Julius, possibly Michael and Sophie, even Ed—as she insisted, "Can no one give me one fuckin' lousy cigarette?!"

No one did.

She disappeared into the attic; we helped Allen with his crutch and glasses.

□ □ □

OF COURSE, EVERY bull has two horns. The other had to do with Huncke, who'd chosen to leave just before Allen's return. Stamping it at the end with his red Tibetan seal, Allen typed a letter:

Dear Herbert:

. . . Louis left this afternoon, to get job in NY; David went with him, unable to sleep most of last night, still sick, saying he was going into city to work music & stay clean. I tried persuading David to stay, but as I was leaving today myself it lacked force. I told him he was welcome to rest/cure/, but NOT welcome to wobble back & forth between here & NY scoring weekly which he you & Louis have been doing.

As you remember this place was set up as refuge from chemical city conditions, & it worked with difficulty reasonably well for you the first months. Since Louis & then David been here & since you've been adamantly guarding yr spike the last month, that original condition has degenerated more & more till the issue's muddy.

So I'm taking it on myself to clarify the original proposition to which you originally agreed, & repeat it clearly: you're welcome to home here, but no needle drugs and no needles on the premises. If there are no needle drugs here there's also no function for needles. Their presence is not sentimentality, it's practical. If this condition doesn't meet with your approval, then the whole house is not a viable situation for you and I suggest you make some other arrangement, & go back to the city.

This is nothing new, just repeat of the old conditions. If you don't think it's suitable that's up to you, & you're free to choose another household elsewhere.

I mean this seriously enough, once for all, to be understood. As you do have a tendency to deceive & burn yourself and others I will have to insist on your following the ground rules already agreed to. If I have any suspicion that you are creating illusions, speaking false words on the subject, I will not hesitate to search your room and your person.

As you may remember the last time round your words did not mean what they said and were meant to confuse me.

My own words above mean what they say: you're welcome here without needle without needle drugs. You are not welcome here with needle & needle drugs. You're welcome here to kick & lay out. The house-social and town social situation won't support the strain of needle drugs.

I'm leaving this explicit here, including the flat statement that I won't hesitate to search if I'm being doublecrossed on the matter. It's not very pleasant but there

seems to be no other way of definitively, actually, clearly & straightforwardly
ending a problem which has been too long prolonged by my hesitancy and your
insistancy on having needle & drugs here. OKOKOK.

as ever Allen

I'm showing this note to all concerned and leaving it to be given to you on yr
return if I'm not here, so there will be no ambiguity.

When Huncke returned and read the letter, he left it on the dining room table—
and went back to New York soon thereafter. Later, in cleaning up, I realized that
if left out any longer the letter would go the way of all unneeded paper—into the
Kalamazoo. I put it away in my room for safekeeping. Nearly a decade later, opening
a cardboard box in my small rental cottage in Carrboro, North Carolina, I found this
extraordinary artifact.

Allen's on *Merv Griffin*

I N THE SPACE of a few days Allen was reading at the New School, meeting accountant Don Wilen, going on Merv Griffin, and returning to the New School to teach mantra chanting—"Om Raksha Raksha Hum Hum Hum Phat Svaha," "Om A Ra Ba Tsa Na De De De De," "Aum," "La Illaha Ill' Allah Who," and others, including the Prajna Paramita (Highest Perfect Wisdom) Sutra. He'd mimeographed a four-page handout of texts and comments, stamped with his Tibetan seal.

Michael and Sophie and Lee went with him and Peter to the city. Huncke remained away and considered going to San Francisco, hoping to stay with Candy there. That left just Julius, Maretta, and myself on East Hill. And I got a surprise visit from a friend from jail in Mexico.

Like Candy and me and nearly two dozen others, Bernie Mayo had been arrested and held at Puerto Vallarta. Following deportation, he'd settled forty miles south of us in Oneonta, where he and lady friend Mary Hopkins had opened a boutique that was the town's first store for "hippie" products. Now their landlord was evicting them because of their store's orientation.

Early one evening, Bernie, Mary, Julius, and I hiked up through the snow to Ed's to look at Allen on *Merv Griffin*. Intent on recording, I'd slung Allen's Uher over my shoulder.

We sat—pressed so close together we touched—on chair, stump, newspapers, *National Geographics*—and waited. Griffin's show began with Genevieve, a heavily accented fluffy frou-frou Zsa Zsa Gabor sort of French woman clutching her poodle in her lap. Her discussion centered on her pet, how he liked to play with a ball, and other likes and dislikes. Joining them were singer Enzo Stuarti and comedian and former TV host Garry Moore. Arthur Treacher, Griffin's English-accented cohort and bandleader, was part of the discussion as well.

But would Allen ever appear? We waited and waited. Then late in the show, after a commercial break, there he was, seated on a chair center stage, harmonium on his blue-jeaned lap, announcing, "'Introduction' to *Songs of Experience* by the seventeenth [*sic*] century prophet William Blake, poet."

After the Blake, Allen reached for his crutches, rose from his seat, and began making his way to host and other guests—whereupon the little poodle jumped from

Genevieve's lap and briskly approached him, barking. Perhaps the crutches made Allen seem some sort of strange beast; in any case this event was greeted with laughter by some of the audience, and a male guest offered, "Some kinda comment . . ."

AG: It was a cry, from the animal soul . . . the alternative to what we were talking about is, something charming and cheerful, would be if you realized that all the kids that are now ten, fifteen years old, or younger, when they are Arthur Treacher's age—

AT: They'll never live that long, old man!

AG: If we destroy the planet they won't live that long—

AT: . . . But I really believe that in twenty years all the things that they're saying will probably happen . . .

AG: This is the difficulty—

AT: I'm still going to talk for a second. I'm *all* for the young taking over, you know [applause] . . . I'm all for it—but thank God I won't be here when they do it! [laughter, applause]

AG: . . . they are presented with a task by their elders, like ourselves—we have presented the young with a task that we ourselves say is almost insuperable: to save the planet.

AT: I don't think when the young get in they'll clean the sewers any quicker . . .

AG: On the other hand, if you realize, if the young do get to be your age, there'll be fifty more years of medicine, or more, say, which means a half century of medicine, which means that they're gonna live to be 150. And if they live to be 150, they're gonna be up to *300*, 'cause that means 150 years of medicine. Which means that . . . I'm just saying we are in a science fiction situation where people who are on this planet, young now, may wind up living to be as old as Methuselah in a Garden of Eden, or may be living on a destroyed planet if they survive. And that's what's confronting all middle class people—

MG: Are you a peaceful man, Allen?

AG: Aum [pronounced fully, with the two vowels and one consonant distinct and drawn out]

MG: Hm?

AG: Aum. Classically speaking, it's a Tibetan or Hindu mantra or magic syllable—"Ah," which opens the Gates of Heaven as you open the back

of your throat to pronounce it—"Uh," you traverse the phenomenal
stations of the palette on the bottom of the skull, the mouth—Close the
Gates of Hell when you say "A-u-*m*."

GENEVIEVE: What does eet mean?

AG: The sound of creation, of the universe. Physiologically, it's like phys.
ed.: as you say it—"Aah"—it's like a sigh, you get a vibration in the
middle of your body, and it's very relaxing.

MG: You're a man of peace, and yet you show a lot of anger, Allen. Or a
lack of respect if someone doesn't absolutely agree with your ideas.

AG: It's all right, on this program everybody's agreeing with each other.
. . . a little reality . . .

MG: We're very agreeable people—I've known Garry a long time, respect
him enormously, and Genevieve is a charming, talented—needless to
say, Enzo sings beautifully, Arthur—are you awake?

AT: Aum! [laughter and a little applause]

MG: It's not necessary in a meeting of people to be fiery—sometimes it's
just kinda fun to relax and enjoy and laugh—

AG: Except I been *teargassed* over the situation—I'm not going to sit here
and say, 'Oh yes, it's all very nice and we're all doing the right things.
. . . People I know are in jail, 30,000 people in California every year for
pot, even—

MG: What would you rather have us do than sit here and talk and relax?

AG: I would rather have us talk to the point—which is like what *shall* we
do with the situation we're in now?

SOMEONE: What to do?

AG: . . . Yeah, I have a few ideas about what to do. *Lots* of people do—
nobody's listening to them—and they rarely get a chance to pronounce
them—But, one, I would say, first thing you gotta do is end police state
in America. Which means limit power of the police—

MG: That's before the war?

AG: That's a main problem—what I would say is like all police should
be negroes or ladies, blacks or ladies, in America . . . and we'll have a
little calm in the streets. End the police state on marijuana, so that several hundred thousand people now in jail get out of jail—that's a *lot* of
political prisoners—and send all the junkies to doctors, thus eliminating

. . . [His words are obliterated by sudden, and suddenly rising, upbeat
theme music which signals show's end.] . . . in New York—

MG: We have to go! Our thanks to everybody—thank you, Allen, thank
you, Garry Moore . . . thank you, Genevieve . . . by Delta Air Lines, the
best thing that ever happened to air traffic! Border to border, coast to
coast! Fly Delta's big jets!

A week later, when Allen told me of his appearance, he said that one of Griffin's
assistants asked him afterward how he could submit to such a thing—whereupon he
quoted the Bodhisattva's Vow:

Sentient beings are numberless; I vow to enlighten them all.
Passions are numberless; I vow to extinguish them all.
The gates of the dharma are endless; I vow to enter them all.
The Buddha path is endless; I vow to follow it through.

Old Winter, New Worlds

F OR STRETCHES OF February as well as March, only Julius, Maretta, and I remained on East Hill. February alone brought three feet of snow; as I recall that month, vast repeating snowscapes and drifts haunt my mind.

Shoveling out the path to the barn and clearing the area in front of the chicken house—which created even higher snowbanks—was only the prelude to everyday chores. Luckily barn animals seemed warm enough—we'd added insulation—and when it was really mild (I remember one day it reached thirty-three degrees, the sun shone, and snow fell from trees) I'd let all the animals out, throwing cow and goat and horse sheafs of hay. Ducks wagged tail feathers and arched necks in brisk bold light; aging Lash seemed to meditate on the stunning change.

Julius would help, whenever asked. Several times I shot him with my Camex, lugubriously doing his share like a Volga boatman, hauling water from the well a hundred yards below the house, galvanized pail in each hand, hair hanging across face, chin tucked in, corduroy coat nearly half unbuttoned, or, occasionally, Sophie's big black fur coat not fully buttoned. Sometimes we'd get into town, then make the long hike back from mailbox, or Schoolhouse Corners, in thermal boots, bearing *The New York Times* and Victory Market paper bags, Julius as silent and stoical as ever confronting snowbank, snow drift, and the occasional plot of ice. With my Camex I'd shoot the blue-shadowed lines of trees across snow, the spiring peaks of evergreens under clearing blue sky . . .

One night I broiled a fish dinner (turbot, from Victory Market), called upstairs to Maretta and Julius, and waited. Neither of them left room or attic, so I ate the delicate flesh alone. Next day at lunch, I was eating it still.

We changed clothes even less than ever, wore the same underwear over and over. I worried about the snow plow getting all the way down the drive so the Suburban Propane truck could bring us another several weeks of moderate light and heat: if it didn't, we'd almost certainly have to camp around the Kalamazoo.

At February's end Allen was at a conference at the State University of New York at Buffalo: "New Worlds of Our Making," the first international drug policy conference open to the public. It was sponsored by graduate student Michael Aldrich's Buffalo chapter of LEMAR, the group founded in 1964 by Allen, Ed Sanders, and others, for the legalization of marijuana. It was chartered as a student organization at the University, with English professor Leslie Fiedler faculty advisor. Fiedler, an abstainer from pot, had already been illegally busted for his noble efforts by city cops.

Over the course of three days, the Symposium featured many guests, including Dr. Tod Mikuriya, *Realist* editor Paul Krassner, Timothy Leary, psychedelics expert Peter Stafford, Abbie Hoffman, and writer-organizer John Sinclair (who in five months would be sentenced to nine and a half to ten years for two joints), and his band the MC5. And, of course, Allen, still on crutches, in Peter's company.

A Symposium highlight was to be a "Drugs and the Arts" panel the second evening, featuring Allen, Sinclair, Fiedler, Krassner, and poet John Wieners. But it was scheduled to precede an MC5 concert in the same spot (the gym), and some of the young crowd of 1,500 were from the beginning impatient for live music. Though Aldrich later characterized the audience as "not angry, but celebrating," a small group of them—the Up Against the Wall Motherfuckers commune from the city—attempted to disrupt Allen and other speakers. Allen had begun the evening with Om, Hare Krishna, and Blake; when it came time for Wieners to read, he was simply not allowed to do so by the unhappy throng—in spite of a plea from Allen. When the MC5 at last appeared—to the delight of many—chairs were cleared from the floor, young people danced, and the band played on.

□ □ □

AFTER WRITING CANDY one night on mescaline, I got back a whale of a letter—two of them, really.

As usual, Candy offered more than asked. In her first she was typically enthusiastic, expressing concern for me as she reveled in her situation:

Dearest Gordon—

Sorry I'm such an awful letter writer—you aren't so hot yourself actually—I understood a lot of what you wrote me on mescaline but not all. How come if Cheri's so crazy about you you didn't get together on a more permanent basis? . . .

. . . I'm amazed at the difference between East Coast & West coast people. People here are much more confident, self-assured and capable. I've got a half dozen (literally) young men between 20-27 coming to see me. . . . all over 6' tall, extremely masculine, heterosexual & aggressive. . . . I've never had so many reasonable intelligent men around me, nor have I ever felt so beautiful & so young. . . .

My love to all. Now that I'm away from there I can safely love you all again but it's incredible *how much better I feel. High* all the time *with color floods et al on* nothing *but health food. . . .*

In her second she encouraged me, rightly, to continue efforts for help building a pond at the farm: we'd visited the Extension Service together, and now I ought to return. She also offered, gratuitously, a psychological critique of her correspondent:

How come you still don't have any other female there?

Get yourself together—you're really starting to sound wishy-washy . . . God Gordon! You can be more together than that for Christ sake—And I'm willing to bet you're balling Allen—Give it up for Lent man—where's it going to get you? Ball Maretta instead—hopefully you are already. Well—none of my business anyhow.

Goats Are Born; Ed Talks: A Long Night

O NE COLD AFTERNOON while Allen and Peter were away I did chores as usual, finished milking Bessie by dusk. Then I happened to return to the barn just a little later and by flashlight saw something dark and shiny emerging from Shiva, our white Saanen many months pregnant: she was giving birth. Since the stillbirth back in July had been disastrous, and this evening's would undoubtedly be complicated by cold, I fairly charged up the white hill to Ed, who hurried down and stood by as several of us watched three little soft-boned black-and-white kids make their slow wet way out their mommy, steaming in the air above the straw bedding as she licked their heads, breaking their placentas and allowing them to breathe.

One seemed strong and able, but two were weak, and we carried them into the house. With Ed directing, supervising, we—guests Bernie and Mary, Lee, and I— spread hay in a large cardboard box, heated a hot water bottle which we placed just underneath the hay, added a pillow or towel or two, and placed the little kids in the box. One was especially frail, unable to hold its head up; "I don't think it's gonna make it," Bernie said.

I banked the mighty Kalamazoo, then got out Allen's Uher and started recording, capturing the early stages of the evening in its range of sounds. (Lee, I could sense, was disapproving of such frivolity on my part.) The conversation centered on Goatmeister Ed, the Hermit who loved to talk. Punctuated by occasional "Maa!"s from the box as we bent down to drop warmed mother's milk into their mouths, adjust their positions on the hay, slip in a reheated hot water bottle wrapped in a towel, Ed regaled us with tales from the Amazon in the 1920s, when he was a nineteen-year-old radio operator for a United Fruit Company expedition.

He was first stationed where Venezuela, Colombia, and Brazil meet, near the River Japurá, which flows into the Rio Negro, then the Amazon. He was 800 miles from the Caribbean, 700 from the Pacific. "Even the birds brought their lunch when they visited," he told us.

He spoke of the candiru (man-eating fish of Burroughs's *Naked Lunch*) and how with his bamboo tweezers and Malacca sword he removed one from within a young woman. And of slavery in Maldonado state, Peru, that turned young women into whores: their tongues cut in infancy, they were speechless and servile the rest of their lives. And of other young women, not yet so ruined, whom he and his group employed as housekeepers:

When these girls come over they were mourning their dead [Maaa!] an' they had painted themselves from here on up—red—and they were stark naked. And of course I'd never seen anything like that before, an' I sort of went into shock. And then...it wasn't a matter of eenie meenie minie mo who gets which girl. This guy thought of the bright idea of drawing straws. An' who should I get? The only pregnant one, ten years older than I was.

Now in radio you have a coded sequence, duh duh ditt ditt ditt, which means WAIT—in other words, you've dropped your pencil, or you've done some damn thing, so you go duh duh ditt ditt ditt. An' I was sittin' there, an' I knew this woman was gonna have a baby. An' she was sittin' over in one corner on a mat [Maaa!] an' I wasn't payin' much attention to her.

All of a sudden she let out a little screech—out come the kid, slow but sure. An' I was talkin', tappin' out to New Orleans at the time, an' I subconsciously just tapped out I'm havin' a baby duh duh ditt ditt ditt!

Bernie: She handle it well?

Oh yeah—I didn't know till afterwards that it was her sixth kid. No, she wasn't calm, if that's what you wanna know. 'Cause I did somethin' I shouldn't, but I had sense enough to quit. I thought it'd be a kinda nice thing, you know, to wash up baby an' Mama, but that was the wrong thing to do.... [Maaa!]

So I stopped just in time. Her notion was that I was gonna boil the baby, I guess. It was quite an experience....

And the girls built their own little club house an' their own little idol, which was—as best as they could—an image of a Papa rebus monkey. And once every full moon they would put on their little show for themselves. It was strictly a female club.

While I was in Lima I went into a five-and-ten to buy lipstick, knowin' they'd never seen it. But they used it to make hex signs—swastikas—under their breasts, to ward off evil spirits that could make them infertile. Alicia came over to me—she didn't have any clothes on, or anything like that—an' she had this goddam swastika painted on an' I asked her what the hell she did that for an' she come out an' says "I want a baby!"

[Maaa!]

Though he kept saying he had to get back to watch the Smothers Brothers at 9:00 PM on his little TV, Ed stayed with us—talking and talking, as was his wont. And guiding and helping—as was his wont.

□ □ □

IT WAS A long night, and Bernie was proven right—the frail kid died. In the morning Lee told me it was my fault, claiming I hadn't gotten up in the middle of the night to feed him when I was supposed to. I'd spent much of the night caring for the babies; I was stunned.

A few years later, learning that Lee had taken his own life, I talked with Allen about him and some of our farm experiences. "So maybe that was Lee's mystery," he offered. "He identified with the baby goat."

Snow and Greenery

D ISABLED THOUGH HE was, Allen was off again after a brief return, for coast-to-coast readings to support farm and Committee on Poetry. Peter was at his side. After Baltimore and a week in Vancouver, he'd spend several days in Manhattan, reading at NYU, meeting with *Look* magazine editors: "I've been working on Look magazine people," he later wrote Gary Snyder, "feeding them suggestions for ecology crisis issue, and a poem too . . . & Smokey Bear Sutra."

In the meantime, I enjoyed two visitors. Heidi Randall was a beautiful young woman—pure white skin, shiny long black hair—with whom I'd spent part of an evening once at Stanley Fisher's. She loved the two baby goats, who were now milking Shiva dry, with vigor. We brought them from the red-and-white barn through the passageway of snow in front of the house, into the kitchen. There, on the daisy-patterned red oilcloth of the kitchen table, they became dancers with prancing little hoofs, flapping ears, wiggling black-and-white tails.

Heidi snuggled them close and we enjoyed each other, too, without the kids. But though she was lovely and we had good times in bed, I don't know that we had much communication otherwise. Yet that, in those days, was often sufficient for me . . .

□ □ □

STEPHEN BORNSTEIN WAS up, energetic as ever, weekend pack on his back. But by the time he reached our door, he had a changed view of himself in the natural world. A big winter storm had ended just the day before he drove up. He called from Cherry Valley; I told him to wait for me at Schoolhouse Corners. I'd go up to Ed's and borrow a pair of snowshoes—they looked like huge tennis rackets strapped to your boots—to go with the pair we had. "Wait for me there," I repeated.

City boy Stephen had never been upstate, let alone Cherry Valley, in real winter. At Schoolhouse Corners, he parked near our Olds, steering clear of the enormous snowbank bordering both cars. Then instead of waiting he told himself "What the hell" and stepped out into the snow. Inserting his arms through the shoulder straps of his pack, he started walking.

Soon he began sinking down within enormous drifts. Then he was waist deep, and every next step became unpredictable. Snow isn't heavy, but when you're in three feet or more of it, it is. Stephen kept on, out of breath, whiteness in three directions. But how could he turn back, now? Hadn't he gone half the distance to the house? Where *was* the house? Was he still on the road? He pushed forward, he plunged, he lunged. His mouth was snow.

A white hillock loomed above him beneath grey sky. He was hot and panting, surrounded by frozen white, the beat of his heart loud, relentless. Then suddenly, peering over a rim of white, was a dark, friendly face, brown eyes gazing intently into his—it was our dog Godly. Now Stephen knew I wasn't far behind. Within moments, I was pulling him aside, up, and around—and then these large, strange, utterly awkward-looking waxed and webbed white-and-orange flat things were being slipped and tied onto his shoes. He took a step. Then another. It was walking on air.

□ □ □

I WAS USING my wrist fully now, but with some stiffness, some limitation of movement. A friend recommended a Manhattan orthopedic specialist, Dr. Leo Mayer. Should I, I wondered—then asked Allen on his return to East Hill. Allen favored second opinions: Why not? I could go while there was still snow on the ground—maybe, time and East Hill conditions permitting, make a quick trip South to family. But Allen had come back worn out, chilled, feverish—and Peter was hyper. Shouldn't I stay? No, Michael and Sophie were here too, Maretta had just left for the East again, and Allen's ills would pass. I called Mayer's office, got an appointment.

During the third week of March 1969, I took my 8-millimeter Camex, with which I'd shot "Mexican Jail Footage," as well as an impressionistic record of the farm to date, and left it for repair with Karl Heitz on 3rd Avenue. Allen's Uher had broken down, too; I took it to Martel on West 22nd. I delivered books to Gotham Book Mart, bought organic vitamin C and comfrey at Kiehl's Pharmacy, got a laundry bag and waterproof matchholder at Hudson's, a few pounds of tobacco and a roller at the Tobacco Center. From Ted Wilentz I picked up books for Allen at the 8th Street Bookshop.

Soon I received a note from Allen, with a $25 check, encouraging me to go South but revealing disturbing conditions at home.

"No need return April one, so take yr time & enjoy yrself," he wrote. "Peter back to normal tho I was flipping (fever & anger) for a day or so." A pattern was being established: Allen returning exhausted and ill from readings; Peter, having been in the city once more, shooting amphetamine till it ran out and he returned to "normal."

My visit to Dr. Mayer went well. An elfish white-haired man, he greeted me with enthusiasm and a hearty handshake. Following X-rays, he was encouraging, allowing for the imperfection Dr. Singer had indicated. I'd return in June.

Soon I was on the big Greyhound for twelve hours, changing in Washington and Richmond before hauling into the Cherry Street station, Winston-Salem. Here grass grew green; daffodils, camellias, and cherry trees pushed into bloom.

My mother seemed no worse than at Christmas, but she continued to show some difficulty recalling and articulating. My brief visit was in general low-key, subdued. Just before I left, Maylee and I argued about the war. Not that she was in favor of it, but I think her closeness to our family's Republican orientation made her bridle when I criticized Nixon. Though he was beginning to develop his gradual withdrawal policy, our troop strength was nearing its greatest: 543,400. I remained stupefied that Americans—who'd never experienced a foreign power's massive bombing of their own land—could accept even a day of hundreds of tons of bombs eliminating hundreds or thousands of sisters and brothers, mothers and fathers.

Many of us, I think, had begun to sense that Nixon would do nothing to jeopardize re-election by a people who, polls reported, approved of him: power and its extension came before the sanctity of human life. And though I was righteous on the subject it made me sad—and almost sadder today as I look back: it took a toll on my relationship with my sister, so long the person in my family I felt closest to. But the war had that effect across America, its cruel chauvinism dividing families as it destroyed animal and plant and land and water and human and home in Asia.

□ □ □

RETURNING TO NEW York with an extra day, I looked up Cheri, whom I'd failed to reach earlier. Here was a relationship, I may have thought, that I could expect to grow—but that potential turned out to be much greater than I'd realized. She was house-sitting for a psychiatrist friend; she greeted me at the door of the wall-to-wall red-carpeted apartment saying, "Let's make love," pulled me down to the floor, climbed on top, and fucked me flat. I loved that greeting and its follow-up and our whole night together in her Central Park West sanctuary. But before I left the next day she said something that scared me.

We were at a small table in the kitchen, enjoying toast and eggs. Our eyes met.

"Marry me," she said.

I tended, of course, to be shy of speech. Now I spoke not a whispered syllable. She was so pretty and sexy and held her fork delicately and I could be happy just drawing breath and watching her move. Eventually, someone said something.

Allen, Oh Allen! But It's Spring

WHILE I WAS away from East Hill, Allen felt worse than he'd let on. Ill and depressed, he wrote his brother Eugene, ". . . I'll do another trip during April May & then I think I'll quit forever."

But on my return he seemed much improved; Julie and Peter and I could now prepare for spring planting. Once the remaining snow (eight inches the first of April) melted and the land began to dry, we could plow and harrow with Ed's small, ancient red tractor.

Though we'd hold off on fruit trees another year, I was giving some thought to them as well as vegetable crops. In a little red-and-black hardbound, I began entering information from winter reading. (We subscribed to Rodale's *Organic Gardening* magazine, had a copy of his large organic gardening book.) For apple trees I noted:

Place 18" collar hardware cloth around trunk to protect against mice & rabbits.
Spread 3 bu. rotted manure round tree in six ft. circle, & mulch same area w/ 8–10"
of hay or straw, leaving bare a circle 1' diam. around trunk.

Through a regional salesman we arranged for deliveries of organic fertilizers in 50- and 100-pound bags, including Se-Bo-phos (phosphorous with bone meal) and K-Mag (potassium). That, in addition to the manure we hauled from barn and chicken house, would begin to build up our soil and make this second season—our first full one—much more productive.

Ed was always on hand to help, advise, demonstrate. From him, more than anyone or anything else, I learned the basics of gardening, including his own phraseology: "Tamp it down," he'd say, pushing with the broad heel of his hand against the upturned earth when we transplanted tomatoes or peppers or the flowering clematis he brought for the little white trellis near the front of our house.

And in that same little red-and-black book I also noted bits of information about names and places: Canajoharie meant "the pot that washes itself"; highways out of Utica still followed old Iroquois trails (north to Canada, south to the Susquehanna Valley, east and west between the Hudson and the Great Lakes); Schenectady meant "the place beyond the plains"; "Iroquois," a French corruption of "Onk-we-on-we ke," were "the only real men."

So: a year after Candy, Barbara, Peter, Julius, and I had left the Lower East Side in the Volkswagen camper, after seasons of unrequited love and needle drugs, of fights and tears and broken bones, we who remained were settled in at East Hill Farm. In greater earnest.

Back in late January, recuperating from our car crash and thinking of his slowly repairing physical self, Allen had written Ferlinghetti, "I gotta get a new metaphysics. Body's too unreliable." Now, a mild bright Easter Sunday in 1969, he was able to use a cane in place of crutches. In a poem he described what he saw in and around the front of our humble home:

Slope woods' snows melt
Streams gush, ducks stand one foot
beak eye buried in backfeathers,
Jerusalem pillars' gold sunlight
yellow in window-shine . . .
coo coo ripples thru maple branch,
horse limps head down, pale grass shoots
green winter's brown vegetable
hair—washed by transparent trickling
ice water freshets . . . .

Goat bells move, black kids bounce,
butting mother's hairy side tender tit
one maa'ing child hangs under Bessie's udder
ducks waggle yellow beaks, new grass flooded,
tiger cat maeows on barn straw,
herb patch by stone wall's a shiny marsh,
. . . birds whistle
from icecrystal beds under bare bushes,
breeze blows rooster crow thru chill light. . . .

A sunny day, snow melts in streams, animals rejoice in bright light, and Allen has his Blake: what could be more idyllic? But only days before, he awoke with the left side of his face—eye and jaw particularly—paralyzed. Puzzled, he told me of it. I could see the strange, slight droop as he spoke.

Soon, at a Cooperstown doctor's office he learned it was a neurological disorder, cause unknown—Bell's Palsy—and should go away in several weeks or months. But it would take over a decade to begin to ease away, bringing him not only discomfort but pain and embarrassment, causing one eye to tear, his mouth to salivate uncontrollably. Now, developing this affliction out of the blue, he canceled a speaking engagement in the city, hoping for a moment's rest at his rural redoubt.

Others in his condition might've canceled far more than one appearance, but Allen, still unsteady on his feet and facing a serious neurological problem, met all remaining commitments. And before an extended reading tour, he spent an active six days back in the city.

As he joined a Mobilization Against the War in New Jersey and a second gathering in Manhattan, America's Vietnam War under Nixon continued to escalate. In March, Nixon had begun "Operation Menu," his secret, illegal fifteen-month bombing of Cambodia with more than 3,600 B-52 raids and 100,000 tons of bombs.

The day Nixon began his "Menu," Defense Secretary Melvin Laird announced Nixon's strategy of Vietnamization. Easter weekend saw antiwar protests coast-to-coast, as thousands marched in New York under a heavy downpour. Some banners proclaimed G.I.'S AGAINST THE WAR IN VIETNAM; some armbands displayed the number 33,000, referring to U.S. dead.

Around mid-April, Allen noted that 52% of Americans recently polled by Gallup felt their war "always had been a mistake." Yet by the end of the month, American troop strength in Vietnam would reach its height.

In April's third week, a light covering of fresh snow graced our land. Then the weather turned benign, the ground began to warm and dry. Now we could spread rich manure and straw we'd piled up cleaning animal stalls over winter—all but the small heap I kept in back of the barn to see if I could grow plants without plowing. I began breaking up the garden area with Ed's tractor and plow. Ed, of course, was always there to help whenever needed—from showing me how to crank the tractor ("Lay yer whole hand on the crank, don't have yer thumb on the other side or ya might break some bones!") to figuring it wouldn't turn one day because of water in the gas line. It worked in fits and starts—for the time being. Between that and the fact that we were planting nearly twice as much as before, it took me several days. And good old Myron came up to finish off a little strip I couldn't handle.

One mild sunny afternoon, having just detached our small plow to put on Ed's ancient cultivator in order to harrow, I stopped and went inside for lunch. The phone rang.

I'd recently learned there was a Cherry Valley softball team, and had asked Watrous to give them my name. On the line was Dick Russo, son of Sal, a politically conservative plumber I'd met in exploring water system possibilities: would I like to come to practice that afternoon?

"I'm going to do some harrowing, but I'd really like to come next time," I answered, hoping I'd still be welcome. I would be—which was surprising since next time I learned what he thought I'd said: "I'm going to do some heroin . . ."

Such activities may, for all I know, have been on the mind of every Cherry Valley person thinking of East Hill Farm. And for good reason: Huncke—with Louie in tow—had returned, usual practices unabated, then left just before Allen came back to rest a night or two. As he'd done when home briefly in midwinter, Allen had taken pen to paper to warn one of his oldest friends:

Huncke—

Last time you burned place down (i.e. total reversal of original ground rules & agreement no needles, etc.) If you visit & want rest here OK but absolute Prohibition reigns, and please come alone.

I don't want Louis here when I'm not here, please don't invite him (or anyone) without checking with me in advance.

Allen

That done, he reached for a second sheet of paper:

Cher Lee:

If you visit please make your bed keep your area neat & help with your share of chores created by everyone's mutual presence (intake and output) like cleaning dishes, disposing garbage & nightsoil, providing water etc.

OK—
Allen

I'll be back late May, probably record soon after—early June—

I've left my room clean if you stay in it please leave it as neat as you enter. I don't want to exhaust my time reconstructing the clarity I've left behind.

Face partly paralyzed, unable to walk unaided, Allen left the next day for eighteen spring readings in four weeks—to raise money for the nonprofit Committee on Poetry, Inc., and its East Hill Farm, a retreat for needy poets and artists less fortunate than he.

Sadness and Happiness on East Hill

MICHAEL BRADDOCKS AND Sophie Clark had a falling out at East Hill in the spring: she told me he'd gotten her pregnant and refused to do anything about it. In their final argument, she said, he walked off, turning back toward her just to shoot her the bird.

Now the problem was entirely Sophie's—at age fifteen. And in those days before *Roe v. Wade,* only proof of the very direst circumstance could secure a legal abortion. She left East Hill, went into the city. Perhaps Allen helped her financially. A month later I'd hear:

Dear Gordon,

I've been in the City so long. I went to the Doctor Krassner recommended. [Realist editor Paul Krassner was then an underground abortion referral service, connecting with a Dr. Spencer in Pennsylvania.] *He told me I was too late—for him to do it. So he said I would have to go to a hospital in England. I went to Beth Israel the other day. I got one psychiatrist's OK. Today I have to get the other one's OK. If things go positive I'll be in the hospital by next Thursday. I really miss the farm & Bessie & Shiva & Brahma & everyone. The sunrise & birds in the morning at the attic window. As soon as I get things done I'll be back—to bake more bread. Give much love to Ed for me. Hope to see him soon. I hope the garden is growing.*

Om Shanti
Sophie

Evidently the second psychiatrist approved and the abortion went through, and she was all right, for when I heard from her next it seemed all a matter of the past.

New guests came while Allen was away. Rosebud's younger sister Denise was seventeen, had a strong musical background, was keen on rock 'n' roll, and played guitar. She was no bigger than Rose—let's say five-three—but had a large head and considerable energy. She wasn't quite as pretty as her older sister, but her vitality and geniality made her as appealing. She reminded me of Lenore Goldfarb in R. Crumb's comics, one of his tough gals who strut their stuff. But she was young and tender, too.

Rose's boy friend in those days was Andy, a handsome, well-built Dane. He had younger, identical twin brothers who were involved in smack. Denise was very fond of Carsten, and when he overdosed she was devastated.

And therein lay an impetus for Rose to send Denise to East Hill for a few days. She came with her friend Penny, an attractive woman a couple years older with long dark hair who liked to draw and design with bright magic markers. Denise, like her sisters, had grown up in Queens; she and Penny were city girls to the core. Hitchhiking to Cherry Valley one starry evening, Penny found herself looking up and reflecting, "This looks just like the Planetarium!"

Only Peter and Julius and I were at the farm when they came. Denise and I seemed to hit it off the first day, and we got together. But it wasn't good, and it was my fault. The next evening Penny and I were a couple. From my room late that night, she and I could hear Peter energetically scrubbing the kitchen floor with his familiar range of grunts, groans, and Shakespearean-Turkish exclamations as the white Coleman lantern gave out its steady hiss.

But now there was something unfamiliar, something new: persistent efforts at conversation made by Denise, standing near him—as we could see on trips down to the potty, or outdoors to pee—while he was on his hands and knees on worn linoleum. She asked what he was doing, about his life, his brother, another brother, his sister, the farm. . . . She wouldn't give up, and by the time Peter turned down its wick and the Coleman gave its last hiss, they were heading to his room together.

At some point the next day, when I joined Penny after chores, she eyed me and held up four fingers beside her grinning face, whispering, "Four times!" In a couple of days, she and Denise would be gone, but now, for the extended moments of their visit, four out of five people at East Hill Farm were happy. It must've been some kind of record. Only Julius, solemn in company and solemn—I assume—in his bed next door to mine—wasn't. Or was he?

Allen Is Punched in the Mouth

His name-calling days are probably not over, but in future Poet Allen Ginsberg may be more selective about his targets. In Tucson to give a poetry reading at the University of Arizona, Ginsberg held a typically empurpled news conference; then he began berating Arizona Republic *Correspondent Bob Thomas about a story that had appeared in the Tucson* Daily Citizen *criticizing the poet for his self-proclaimed sexual aberrations. When Thomas finally walked away, the guru followed and shouted a string of obscenities at him. Mother, whose day is celebrated this week, seemed to have a prominent place in the epithets. Whereupon Thomas wheeled and clouted Ginsberg twice on his shrub-bordered mouth. "Ah, those were only words I was speaking!" cried Ginsberg. Replied Thomas in a hard, code-of-the-West drawl: "They may have been only words to you, Mr. Ginsberg, but out here they are fighting words."*

S TUNNED, I READ this account in the "People" section of *Time* in early May. What was this, I wondered—and what really happened? The smug righteousness of the prose only added to my discontent—and to my doubt of the article's accuracy. What was the basis for such ugliness?

The day after I saw the piece in *Time*, I was walking down Main Street in Cherry Valley, and encountered vet William Schaer and wife Susan. I'd last seen him a month or two earlier when Godly had run into a porcupine, returning home with a pitiful nose full of quills. It looked not only sad but comical—and what could we do? Every time we tried pulling them out, Godly winced or yelped. "Call the vet," Ed had said, and Doc Schaer, taking a look at suffering Godly, counseled simply leaving him alone. Over a period of days, with extra food, treats, pats, and hugs, Godly's black nose was free of projectiles and he was full of bounding energy again.

Now, this bright day in May, no sooner were the Schaers and I stopping to greet each other near the bank parking lot, across from Crain's Pharmacy and the Village Landmark laundromat, than the vet—to my surprise—brought up *Time* magazine. I took it as foreboding: stereotyping a bit, I thought smalltowners would take the report at face value. Further, I knew the Schaers' son was a cadet at a military academy.

But quickly I saw I was mistaken.

"Everybody gets bad press," Schaer volunteered with a chuckle. "This was Allen's turn." Though I may have wondered if he really took it with such a grain of salt, I was gratified. But moments later our talk turned to Vietnam. "I think we have a job to do there," offered Susan, who was in charge of Cherry Valley's Red Cross funding drive: "We should just go ahead and do it." How I wished I could have remained at ease with them, that there weren't this immoral and divisive war, that it didn't have to again assert itself in everyone's life.

□ □ □

A COUPLE WEEKS later Allen gave me his own account of the Arizona incident. The piece in *Time* was written or drafted, he understood, by Bob Thomas himself. The reporter had challenged him, Allen said, on homosexuality. The *Tucson Citizen* had not criticized his sexual preference, but mentioned it as part of his public persona; Thomas disapproved of Allen's highlighting his sexual preference.

Responding to Thomas, Allen defended homosexuality, drawing on recent reading in Van Der Pizl and Dodson's *Orchid Flowers: Their Pollination and Evolution*. The *Ophrys*, a genus of orchid with thirty species, mimics stinging insects in odor, shape, color, and tactility, and engages in pseudocopulation with them. And, as Allen said he pointed out in Tucson and as I read when later looking it up, "Simultaneous visits by two bees have a strange consequence. The stimulated second visitor tries to copulate with the first male."

So, Allen proposed to Thomas, there's some evidence of homosexuality in nature—so it can't be said to be "unnatural." This bit of biology seemed to amuse Allen, but evidently charmed Mr. Thomas not at all. Allen tried another tack. Since Thomas seemed bent on characterizing homosexuality as not just immoral but utterly alien, the poet would demonstrate otherwise by using the language which he sensed, through friend Lucien Carr and others, that journalists were especially familiar with on an everyday basis.

"Aw, c'mon, you cocksucker! It ain't nothin' new!" he tried.

Shortly thereafter, the journalist hit him.

"What?" I asked Allen. "And he saw you were limping?"

"Yes."

"And did you say anything once he hit you?"

"'You should learn to control your temper, sir.'"

While Allen's account seemed convincing, I found myself curious about other versions. Had Allen really begun the contretemps by attacking Thomas? Why was it reported he'd shouted "a string" of curse words? Had he in fact engaged in persistent pursuit, walking his way into a cracked lip? Did he, afterward, attempt to minimize his comments? Did Thomas truly get in his cowboyish final words, as with *Time*'s melodramatic account? What were the real details?

Over three decades after the event, I contacted some who were on hand in the Ruth Stephan Poetry Center at the University of Arizona. I heard from Richard Shelton, Professor of English and former director of the Center; his wife, Lois; and John Weston, director of the Center at the time. The account I most rely on is Richard's, for it's generally supported by Lois's.

At the small Poetry Center cottage, Weston had arranged for a late-morning press conference. (Allen had made no friend in John; the director told me "I still wish I had slugged him myself—not for the homosexual context but because he was so impossibly self-centered and demanding.") Lights and microphones were directed at Allen; members of the press as well as students—some sixty people—packed into the small space for the hour-long session.

Most questions concerned Allen's poetry; then as the hour reached its end, "This man said something in a very hostile tone about Allen's homosexuality," Shelton recalled. It was "something to do with Allen not being a very good example, or something. . . . He resented the fact that a celebrity was homosexual." According to Weston, "He asked about an earlier remark that had been circulated in the media, to the effect that Allen believed young men of college age should be happy to have sex with him because he was America's foremost poet (after Whitman). Thomas's tone was antagonistic and Allen's was disputatious."

Perhaps there were one or two more exchanges, whereupon Allen replied, "What gives you the right to judge me, you cocksucker?" Richard recalled Allen's tone as

> . . . very friendly, non-threatening . . . sort of half-joking. I mean he was serious about the fact that the man should not judge him, but he was not using that term in a threatening way—very gentle. And sort of bantering . . .

The session ending, Thomas hurried outside in an evident huff, disturbed by Allen's last words; there may have been one or two further exchanges as he did so. Allen, with Richard, followed—onto the small porch, down a few steps, onto a short ramp, into the small graveled parking lot. Not in pursuit of Thomas—they were headed for the guest house just beyond the lot, where Allen was staying, and would have lunch. (Though, Shelton told me, he sensed Allen may have recognized he'd overstepped, and sought to apologize if he saw the man.)

"We got about a third of the way across the parking lot," Richard recalled, "and out of nowhere—perhaps he was in his car, I don't know . . . this man just rushed at him and hit him in the mouth off center, on the side of the mouth—and knocked him into my arms. And I caught him—

"I sort of held him and got him up. In the meantime the man jumped in his car and spun out—it was a gravel driveway, so there was a great throwing of gravel as he left.

"And John came rushing out, and we took Allen to the guest house and checked him out, and he was bleeding. I don't recall that we took him to the infirmary—I don't think he would let us—the injury wasn't that bad. He was bleeding, a cut lip, and he said it was nothing. And he said immediately, 'I shouldn't have used language like that, it was my own fault,' and we sort of doctored him and he said he'd be able to read that night, although his mouth was swollen. And he did read, and he did very well.

"Everybody was very solicitous, but he was very self-effacing about it, and never seemed to feel that he was a victim.

"He seemed to think it was his own fault—that he shouldn't have used that kind of language. Certainly, he was aware of the power of language. He had violated it."

Allen apologized to director John Weston, and Weston wrote, as he put it, "a scathing note to Thomas's editor, asking that he never be allowed near us again."

Everything Happens at Once

MAY: BUTTERCUPS YELLOWED hillsides in luminous dots; marsh grass came alive again down near the spring; robins and finches flew back to branch and stem; and if you looked close you could see tiny buds hinting green life on the mighty maples near the old asbestos-shingled house.

Light came early and I'd get chores done, let animals out, stake the goats, then bend my head to garden rows. When I wasn't trying to better last year's production, I was starting on arrangements for a water system. We—with Ed's input and Allen's decisiveness—had decided on a hydraulic ram.

A small machine invented late in the eighteenth century, the ram works like the human heart. Using the force of gravity, it takes water flowing from above and pumps a fraction of it back—and up. We would order one.

It sounds simple, but installing the entire water system was a grand undertaking, one that several of us would be physically involved in over many weeks. And it would cost over $2,000 (not counting subsequent amenities like toilet, tub, shower). We'd decided on a contractor, a Mr. Ed Smith in Sharon Springs, who'd already come to look over the lay of the land and given us one or two assignments before beginning work.

In mid-July he'd return with backhoe and bulldozer, dig out the lower meadow's spring area and re-do the old well by stacking three large 500-pound ceramic pipes one on top of the other. A pipe one inch across would connect this new housing to a larger excavation task ten yards farther downhill: there the ram would be located, at the bottom of a cinder block "house" we'd construct, eight feet deep. The ram would then pump that fraction of incoming water through underground pipes (to be laid four and a half feet deep) running back uphill far beyond well and house to a reservoir to be buried fifty feet above our house. From there water would again flow downhill by gravity any time a faucet—in kitchen or bathroom, or a special one with an anti-freezing lock in front of the barn—was turned on.

The development of such plans coincided with another major event: Allen's recording many of his Blake songs in a professional studio, using amateur and professional musicians to produce an album for release. In certain ways the two projects were equally complex, and though the main work on the water system didn't begin till after recording and editing ended in early July, at one point the two overlapped.

Around mid-May, no one was at the farm but Julius and I, and I'd invited a friend to visit. Jon Sholle, whom I'd worked with at Filmmakers' Cooperative summer 1967, was a gifted guitarist from Great Neck, already a winner of prizes at prestigious competitions down South. The last time I'd seen him was during my brief stint at the Elgin Theatre in the spring of 1968, projecting *The Chelsea Girls*. Jon would come in for the later shift with a couple of quarts of beer and it was always good to see him.

He was modest and unpretentious, especially considering his gifts. When he arrived at the farm he offered to help with a task that was glaringly at hand. Ed Smith (or "Smitty," as Peter called him) had just delivered one of those three 500-pound ceramic pipes. It was my job to hammer and chisel a hole of a certain size in a certain part of it, all the way through its two-inch-thick wall. (Through that hole, the pipe would extend from well to ram house.) Jon had never undertaken anything like this, but immediately rolled up his sleeves to help.

That made it simple and we completed this delicate yet forceful task in surprising time. When Allen returned a day or two later I introduced middle-aged adept to young master, and the two began jamming right away, on the grass and boulders just above the front of the house. Jon took out his Martin steel-string; Allen set his Benares harmonium on his knees. He showed the young visitor some rudimentary notations: groups of five lines with notes and a clef, but no time signatures.

They performed song after song of Blake, later moving into the living room, Allen at the eighty-year-old organ. Jon told me later he was impressed: though some were written down (after a fashion), Allen had all the melodies in his head. They were strong; his conception of them was definite, confident; they bore his personality.

When about to head for the city, Allen asked if he'd play in his Blake sessions. Jon wasn't free at the beginning, but arrived soon after and contributed significantly to arranging, rehearsing, recording.

But Jon wasn't a producer. And Allen, of course, was no music business professional. How, then, to arrange for sessions with a variety of musicians in a high quality, expensive recording studio? Deal with the gamut of major logistical headaches involved in producing an album?

Taking on that monster full-face was Barry Miles (he never went by his first name, which he despised), a young Englishman a couple years older than I. In 1964–65, with help from Paul McCartney and others, he'd founded Indica Books, the Indica Gallery, and the *International Times*, and had hosted Allen when he arrived for the international reading of poets at the Albert Hall, 1965. Proficient in a wide range of recording equipment and methods, he'd already been to the U.S. to preserve the words of contemporary poets on acetate. Most recently, he'd been appointed label chief of Zapple, a new experimental branch of the Beatles' Apple Records.

And so, near the end of May 1969, Miles returned to New York to arrange and supervise Allen's studio recordings—by now music for over half of *Songs of Innocence* and *Songs of Experience* was complete—and its release on Zapple. Miles had heard some of the songs on tape, and looked forward to the production. But from the beginning, both he and Allen were beset by problems, and the entire effort extended over a month.

Allen had invited Lee Crabtree, then in Iowa, to join him for further rehearsals and recording. He'd offered to cover airfare, and in what he hoped was final negotiation, he telegrammed:

> . . . *O.K. Union scale rehearsal & recording from 1st of month please do come as Miles arrives from London expressly to record the Blake. Please phone me collect.*

Lee wrote, "If you really think we are ready to record, you are off your rocker. In the first place you need to find out what *part* of your voice to sing with. . . ." Allen went ahead, with old friend jazz pianist Bob Dorough.

Allen approached other musicians. Visiting friend Charles Mingus between his sets at the Village Vanguard, Allen and Miles were invited to Mingus's home to discuss recording together. The next day, a hot one, found them sitting in Mingus's East 5th Street living room as their host, in boxer shorts, his body marked with operation scars, talked affably. But he didn't join their effort—perhaps it seemed too amateurish. Instead, he recommended bassist Herman Wright.

Trumpeter Don Cherry came in on several numbers, with finger cymbals, sleigh bells, beaded gourd, bass tom, trumpet. French-hornist Julius Watkins signed up, and, for one special number, drummer Elvin Jones came aboard. Allen told me later of how Jones performed his part of "The Grey Monk" with great flourish, including an extraordinary solo that ends the whole four-minute piece—and the album. At the end Jones asked if that was OK, and then, Allen indicating his approval, declared, "That'll be $500." Allen, taken aback, reached for his checkbook.

Much of what transpired in the five weeks of mostly concentrated work was far more difficult—from the beginning. For Allen, it was essential to have Peter sing with him, but as they were about to head to the city to record, Peter delayed leaving. Allen shouted at him, "Peter, Miles has come all the way from London!"

Once in Manhattan, they went to Capitol Records' mid-town studio, where they recorded two tracks, but Peter was now on amphetamine. His voice—this particular "leper's voice" of his, as Allen characterized it—made them unusable. And while they laid down some beautiful cuts at a second session only three days later, Allen Klein— who'd been brought in by John Lennon to solve Apple's financial problems—was shutting down all of Zapple, and firing many in the larger office. Now Miles had a hotel bill at the Chelsea, Allen a studio bill at Capitol, and, as Miles put it, "all the Beatles had disappeared."

So now, with Zapple zapped, where to record? Miles recalled that Frank Zappa (no connection with record label) had spoken highly of Apostolic Studios, with its 12-track Scully taperecorder and wide range of microphones. The latter enabled Miles, as he told me, to "get good EQ [Equalizer] on Allen's voice and make it deeper." Allen himself was intrigued that his already deep voice could be made "basso profundo." This technical capacity was aesthetically significant: the power behind "Nurse's Song" (from *Experience*), one of the very strongest cuts, depends in good part on Allen's voice registering its lowest range, enhanced, as the nurse looks upon the playing young with sickening regret for her own spent youth.

Apostolic's offerings also represented an opportunity for Miles to deal with another problem. Though Peter could sing not only uniquely but beautifully at times, his amphetamine voice tended to dominate. Miles tried, at first diplomatically, to avoid having Peter on any of the recordings, but found Allen saying: "No, no, it has to be Peter"; "Peter's great, the songs depend on him"; "He has to hit the high notes when I can't." So Miles thought to deal with Peter's over-presence in the mixing, even though his voice was so loud he "leached onto all the other tracks anyway—you'd never get rid of him completely." Allen didn't warm to that approach either, and as his English supervisor wisely recognized, it was Allen's record.

Yet Allen was open to all adjustments Miles made to his own contributions: this was very much a learning period for him. In those days I recall Allen's telling people on the phone, "Could you hold the receiver closer to your mouth?" and in later years, at conferences, instructing other speakers in a booming voice, "Put your mouth closer to the mic! Bring your mouth closer to the mic! Hold your mouth . . ." Such imperatives are ironic considering that one of Miles's first efforts with Allen, back in June 1969, was showing him how to use a microphone: "He was constantly going off mic."

But how would all this rehearsing and recording be financed, without Apple/ Zapple's support? Allen covered many expenses (musician's pay, Miles's work, studio time, etc.)—all told, $10,000. It was a great burden to him; he was forever juggling accounts in much smaller amounts, trying to create cash on hand. Further, he was aware of the costliness of Peter's role. Once all recording was done and the two poets had returned to the farm in July, I heard Peter's angry charge: Allen, he claimed, had told someone that Peter (in his vocal errancy) had cost him $2,000 in recording expenses. "Well, it's true," Allen calmly replied.

Fortunately, there proved to be a silver lining in the Allen Klein storm-cloud that marked the beginning of the whole recording effort. As dust settled, Miles's friends Ron Kass and Peter Asher took major executive positions at MGM. Sessions with Allen completed, Miles offered them a lease on the tape for $10,000, whereby they could produce the album. Allen retained copyright, and by late September his $10,000 was returned, as an advance on the record.

And so by the spring of 1970, Allen Ginsberg, who only a year or two before knew little more than a few rudiments of music, would have a full-scale LP album out on a major label. But as Allen finished recording, a new challenge would be ready for all of us. Putting in a whole water system for a small pre-electric rural community— installing hydraulic ram and reservoir, burying a couple hundred feet of water pipes four and a half feet deep—would extend through summer and into fall.

□ □ □

WHILE MOST OF the sessions were taking place, I remained on East Hill with Julius— and the occasional visitor. Days were clear and quiet. Birds twittered, the breeze blew, Bessie mooed. No one yelled.

The garden *was* proving more bountiful than ever, to my delight. Already we were eating lettuce, radishes, spinach, peas, and pulling scallions straight from the ground. Now that it was warm I pushed the flat oblong seeds from squash family plants into the black-and-blond manure-and-straw pile I was keeping behind the barn. If this were successful, and we could expand it, we'd have less need of machinery (Ed's old tractor wasn't expected to last another year).

I was pleased, so far, with results in every direction, and almost enchanted by newfound quiet and simplicity. Then came a surprise, in the form of Larry Verzano and friends.

Larry: close-cropped brown hair, my height, broad-shouldered, slender, with a thin musketeerish moustache. A picture of agility, a natural cat-like presence of mind and sexiness. He'd worked as cowboy in the Southwest, gigolo in Miami; he made leather goods, and sported a fine pair of leather pants, the only ones I ever saw him in.

We'd met back in March 1968—in the Puerto Vallarta jail, where we and a couple dozen other gringos were taken from nearby beaches, streets, and homes. When the first night's darkness overtook the courtyard where the males were kept (women were confined to the cops' office) a guard carrying a shotgun climbed a ladder to the roof and stayed there till daybreak, looking down at us. I resented this potentially violent measure almost more than being in jail. As if we'd try to escape!

So I thought. After that first night, there was no more rooftop guard—as if the *comandante* had read my thoughts. He seemed to have realized—or assumed—we wouldn't try anything.

So I thought. When the third morning broke we saw Larry on the other side of the great barred door, in the corridor between the jail street door and the cops' office, carrying large bowls of honey and strawberries which he shared with guards and girls alike. Suddenly the *comandante* appeared and shoved him through the gate into the courtyard, whence he was escorted by a guard into the dungeon. He'd escaped the night before by climbing over the roof; he'd visited friends in Vallarta, and now was returning with sumptuous food—instead of the usual breakfast cup of *chocolaté*—for those left behind. Guards who didn't recognize him thought he was a visitor bringing breakfast; those who did congratulated him, slapped him on the shoulders in brotherly fashion, shook his hand. The *comandante* had to save face and put him in solitary for twenty-four hours.

Now—one quiet afternoon, June 1969—I happened to be walking past the front of the house toward the garden when I suddenly beheld an apparition. There, in front of the hammock we'd strung between two maples, on his quiet cat feet, stood Larry, a grin forming beneath the length of his long thin moustache as he watched my astonishment grow. And grow: two strangers—his friends evidently—swung and lolled and played in the hammock's web.

He and his companions had come from Oneonta, where they'd seen jailmate Bernie Mayo. He introduced a short blue-eyed fellow with curly blond hair, and a large shapely brunette: Barry Goldsmith and Robin Billet. Though I had good quiet times with my chum over the few days of their visit—at the end of which Allen and Peter returned—I became more involved with the two strangers than with Larry.

Robin was a belly dancer, and soon performed for me, shimmying and shaking her bare midriff, waving her arms above her head in serpentine coil and uncoil. Barry played guitar and sang, writing songs on loose sheets of paper which would sometimes fly away, lost to the breeze. They all had the clap and complained of pain urinating. But they also said it increased sex drive. "Let's fuck," Barry urged more than once but I turned him down. Eventually I gave in with Robin and we had some good times together even though I used rubbers. (Buying them in Crain's Pharmacy from white-haired Mr. Crain—white-haired Mrs. Crain in their home just upstairs—I may have held my breath.)

Right before they left, Allen, on a break from weeks of recording and mixing, joined in with us immediately as Barry performed. He liked Barry's guitar and lyrics; the two of them talked at some length about music, and about Dylan, whose accomplishment Barry aspired to. And now that Allen was newly expert in this area of art, he offered his own critique. (This was typical of Allen—a few years later, after summer weeks helping carpenters build a small house on land he shared with Gary, he exclaimed to people he ran into back on St. Mark's, "I'm a carpenter!" and explained that carpentry could do a lot for life's basic problems.)

But now his critique focused not so much on the music but the method: during one of Barry's extended searches for music to one of his lyrics, Allen exclaimed, "*This* is why you're not like Dylan! You don't keep track of what you write down!" A sheepish Barry returned to a song he'd sung only minutes before, and performed it again.

Town and City

T HOUGH I DIDN'T play very well, I was accepted onto the Cherry Valley softball team, and wore a blue short-sleeved shirt with sponsor HERITAGE INN emblazoned on back. Among the best players were slugging centerfielder Reggie Brown; big smiling Ernie Whiteman at first base; captain Dick Russo, good-looking and quick at shortstop; and his huge younger brother Gary, a standout scholar athlete at Cherry Valley Central School, in left. All were friendly toward me—and, I hope, I toward them—and no one asked probing questions. That spring afternoon on the phone when Dick mistook my "harrowing" for "heroin" was the only time I knew when their world and ours seemed to collide.

For much of my youth, baseball had been at its center, and even though I wasn't now performing anywhere near the level I wanted, two events that summer seemed—for a moment—to captivate my teammates. With two out in the ninth and Cherry Valley leading St. Johnville 3–2, I made a good catch at the plate of a strong throw from Reggie in deep center, tagging the runner just in time as he bit the dust.

The other event had nothing to do with play on the field. One of our games coincided with a visit from a lady friend from Boston, Saralee Stafford. In those days Saralee was waitressing, waiting to get into business college, and taking a few psychedelics. But that was unrelated to the way she was received by my Heritage Inn comrades when she accompanied me to the playing field early one evening. Pretty blue-eyed Saralee, with straight black hair, dark freckled skin and a lovely shape, was so utterly sexy it would've shown through a space suit—or Ed's big parka. Yet here she was in our hinterland, in tight black vinyl and black cotton, "normal" wear at least for certain groups of young people in the urban northeast. Was our national anthem about to be played? The level of quiet descending on both sides of the field before I even began to introduce her to my all-American comrades in blue and white was reverential.

□ □ □

EXCEPT FOR SOFTBALL and trips to town, I remained on East Hill the livelong day and night in May and most of June, hands full with garden, animals, and all else that came with long-awaited warm weather. On Memorial Day, Cherry Valley's parade to the cemetery was led by the American Legion's color guard, with two Gold Star mothers, firemen, and Scout groups. A new Vietnam memorial, honoring Clarence Baldwin, Cherry Valley's first victim, and Franz Tines, her second, was unveiled by Brownie Scouts at the Cherry Valley Central School flag pole. The Legion commander spoke, and the Reverend Maxfield Delight, whose daughter Joy had written us of her husband's plans to desert the navy, gave the benediction. The school band played the "Star-Spangled Banner."

When Cherry Valley Central—neighbor Charlene Graham was a senior there— held its sixty-fifth graduation ceremonies three weeks later, I attended. From the rear of the auditorium I watched boys and girls in blue and gold proceed to the stage in step with the Processional, Mendelssohn's "War March of the Priest," followed by a salute to the flag. Before Benediction and Recessional, three dozen young people had received diplomas, and Charlene (recently crowned Queen of Cherry Valley's Fire Department) a leadership award as well.

When I'd gotten Charlene's invitation, I doubted I'd go. Shy as I was, fearful (ever since I was a five-year-old *Amerikajin* in Occupied Japan) of being stared at, how could I, even with long hair shortened and beard trimmed for softball, insert myself in the midst of such an assemblage? Didn't I think the less they saw of us the better? Or, could I—sometimes as scared of contact itself as of being stared at—rise to the occasion like some funny sort of goodwill ambassador from East Hill?

□ □ □

AT THE BEGINNING of June, I'd written my sister:

> . . . I may be away 2-3 weeks in July on possible film assignment in Persia—don't know yet till I have an interview. Ask Mom & Dad to forward birth certificate & passport. Don't know when I'll be able get to NC again.

Of course "film assignment" and "Persia" sound rather grandiose—and indeed they were.

A week or so before writing, I took a phone call from someone named Bob Morris. He sounded somewhere between Allen's and Peter's age, and we got to talking. He was an old friend of Peter's, he said, and he dealt in Persian rugs and curios. When I mentioned filmmaking, he said he was thinking of having someone go with him on his next trip to Persia (the name sometimes used, in those days, for Iran), to record his travels and business. Would I like to do so?

I said sure, if I could get away. I explained that I worked only in small format 8-millimeter silent film, but that it could be blown up to 16, with soundtrack added—as I'd done with my first film, "Georgia." We planned to meet in early summer, in Manhattan, and talk further.

I asked Allen about possibly being away two or more weeks, at a time when the heart of the water system construction might begin. He was agreeable: Peter and Julius would be here; Stephen Bornstein, now in Mexico, might be coming back.

Peter told me of his own visit to the region six years earlier. Teheran was interesting but desolate: it didn't sound like he wanted to go back. And he told me about Bob Morris—who in 1958 was a patient at the Columbia Presbyterian Psychiatric Institute (where Allen had once spent nine months). Peter had been working there as a nurse; that's how they met. So that was why Allen seemed to chuckle silently when he heard me say the name!

So should I try and do it? Would it be for real?

"I donno," Allen answered. "You may as well try, if you think you wanna. We'll be OK."

Misgivings aside, I was up for it. I'd need smallpox revaccination, which was easily enough done at Bassett Hospital. But hearing back from Winston-Salem, I found my passport had expired. Accordingly, I cut my hair even shorter, cut my beard altogether, and posed for my "official" picture, suntanned but stiff in coat and tie—somewhat like my student council days, I imagined, back in high school at the American School in Japan, when I received the Citizenship Award from Ambassador Reischauer.

Everything seemed in place, except for one fundamental item. I had two good 8-millimeter cameras, one given me by Jonas three years earlier: my first. It was a small but heavy Revere, easily hand-held. It would always be of use (and of great sentimental value), but technically it was limited compared to the Camex, with its high quality zoom lens, rewind, and other features. It was clear which one I'd need for my Persian "film assignment."

I'd taken the Camex for repair several months earlier—and still didn't have it back. In early April I'd written Karl Heitz, who replied it was "presently at the factory" (in France), where it had been inspected. They submitted a bill for $47.70 that included round-trip air-mail postage. I promptly sent a check—then nearly two months passed. "If you're gonna come in anyway for Bob Morris," Allen suggested, "maybe we could go up to Robert Frank's—I've been rehearsing there—and he could try placing a call to the factory. We could ask him."

I went in for a tight couple of days in the city. First, I saw Bob Morris—tall, pudgy, balding—on a hot afternoon. Talking and drinking sangria, I lay around with him and several other younger men in his air-conditioned apartment, the exotically carpeted floor piled with Afghan and Persian pillows. Sensually, it was a pleasure, but professionally disappointing. His travel plans might be pushed back to the fall; we'd talk again.

With Allen I went to Apostolic Studios: a few enclosed rooms, fluorescent-lit, with a control booth and the large Scully, with its many cables. The engineer was a pleasant tee-shirted head from Atlanta; Paul Berkowitz, a young fellow with glasses, was tape operator. We watched—Miles and Jon Sholle joined us—while Ed Sanders stood in the center of the floor at the suspended mic and sang his "Jimmy Joe, the Hippybilly Boy" in one take. He was a large man, phlegmatic to the core, and sailed right through the recording without a tic. His affect was essentially the same afterward, even as he received Allen's praise.

One or two other musicians appeared, and Michael Aldrich (whom Allen would credit in liner notes with "Joint Administration") walked in. Over the next several hours they rehearsed a few numbers, Allen going over and over a few sticking points. Eventually we headed back to Allen's for the night, where I sat next to Michael as he wrote in his diary—which he then showed to me. He ended his account of the rehearsal asking, "Is Allen a perfectionist?"—and answering, "You bet!"

Late the next morning, I was walking with Allen down St. Mark's Place, Allen with his colorful red-and-white Greek cloth shoulder bag ("I like them to be big enough for an LP," he once said); coming our direction was a shortish man a few years older than I, with dark curly hair, cleft chin, tee-shirted. He had a friendly, almost exuberant aura: he seemed vigorous, healthy.

Allen introduced Abbie Hoffman, we shook hands, and they talked briefly. "You're interested in ecology, aren't you?" Abbie asked Allen. Abbie would spend the last years of his life on the lam, working for conservation in the St. Lawrence River area, but back in mid-1969 Manhattan, ecology was still a relatively new concern, even for antiwar folk.

We had to get on. Allen was taking me up to Robert Frank's before it was too late in the day to reach the French factory. In the spacious hardwood-floored apartment Allen introduced me to a small, dour, darkish man with peering eyes beneath a large forehead. The rest of his face seemed to recede beneath those dark inquiring eyes.

Throughout our visit I was struck by Frank's evident glumness—he almost never smiled. It wasn't that he was unfriendly; in fact, he spoke in almost a confidential tone: Allen was indeed an old honored friend. But something made him mirthless, and I, in my twenty-four years of largely comfortable life, wondered why. Didn't he have much to be of cheer about? Hadn't life rewarded him with considerable recognition of his accomplishment? I assumed that such would automatically translate into happiness. I didn't know that Robert and wife were breaking up around that very time. But looking back, that "glumness," it would seem, was basic to his brilliance.

It was time to connect with Camex. Refusing to be paid for the expense, Robert placed the call, and began: "Allô, je voudrais le département de la réparation . . ." He spoke several minutes, pausing, listening, interjecting, then hung up and turned to us. "They say they only just now got it. I asked them to get on it right away and send it back, it's been paid for."

I didn't know if I'd ever see my Camex again, let alone get to Persia or other far fields. But I'd never forget the effort Robert Frank made to help someone he'd only just met.

Independence Day

A FTER WINDING UP at Apostolic and visiting Louis and Edith in Paterson, Allen returned to idyllic East Hill. How stresses of recording and hubbub of the city must've contrasted with the scene he found there! He noted in his journal:

a white hen pecks along
tree-shade's edges &
stands silent surveying
sunlit yellow grass

Coming with Allen and Peter (who seemed still on speed) was Michael Aldrich, stopping a few days on return to Buffalo. Now I got to talk with him at length as I hadn't in the city.

He spoke of an event that was already proving historical. Allen and some of the "Apostles" were enjoying a quiet dinner at an Italian restaurant on Christopher Street; suddenly shouting came from outside. They got up, looked out. Down the block was a small bar named Stonewall. In front of it two Puerto Rican queens, in full drag, were being roughed up by several policemen.

Allen said to his companions, "Well, we oughta go over there and protect those guys." Peter put his hand on Allen's shoulder: "Allen, if you do that, the headline in *The New York Times* will be, 'Ginsberg Involved in Riot.'" Instead, as Michael recalled, Allen went back the next few days, joining marches and protests.

On East Hill, Michael was troubled by a concern he brought with him; luckily, I was able to ease his fears that our farm was a "homosexual commune." His first visit just before Thanksgiving 1968 had been too brief—and was focused on carrying out an extensive interview with Allen. Mike wasn't judgmental on the subject, as his admiration for Allen would suggest, but like many straight men of the day he still wrestled with some of the homophobia instilled in him as a child. He seemed a bright, earnest intellectual with a mind determined to come to grips with all in its path. "Oh, don't worry," I reassured. "Not everybody here is gay."

The next day—the Fourth of July—a phone call informed Allen that Dr. Harry Hermon, who was growing marijuana for medical research, had been busted for it by Texas police.

That afternoon, Michael wandered down into the lower pasture. He came upon Allen, seated amidst high grass, scrub bush, wildflower. Michael called to him—a hearty "Hello!"—but Allen's response wasn't welcoming: it was, simply, "Writing."

That evening in the dining room Allen gave Michael and others the proof in his pudding: a poem on the occasion of the arrest of Dr. Hermon. Mike would publish "Independence Day" in his *Marijuana Review*, with a dedication "For Harry Hermon, M.D./from friend/in time of mental war & Distress":

> Orange hawkeye stronger than thought winking above a thousand thin
>   grassblades–
> Dr. Hermon busted in Texas for green weed garden-grown
> licensed Federal, Municipal-cop-prosecuted . . .
> Sweet chirrup from bush top to bush top, orange wing'd
> birds' scratch-beaked telegraphy signalled to and fro buttercup earlets–
>
> . . . .
>
> Independence Day! the Cow's deep moo's an Aum!

The hawkeye was one of several wildflowers brightening midsummer fields. Studying some of our musty books from antique stores, draining Ed's brain, and venturing forth to discover things for himself, Allen had begun identifying by name a fair portion of our local flora. The phrase "hawkeye stronger than thought," appearing thrice as it does in the poem, seemed important to him. When I asked about it, he said, "I don't know what that means."

Lennon

I N EARLY JUNE I'd written my sister:

John Lennon, M.B.E. and Yoko Ono in Montreal trying to get into US . . . to do Benefit for UNICEF in Mad Sq G. & to be w/ Allen when he records for Apple this week in NY. Klein, Lennon's lawyer, arranged deal w/ Senator Goodell to be allowed entry if Lennon would appear w/ Goodell on TV & renounce drugs. Lennon of course refused. So they are "lying in" Montreal hotel bed calling friends for help. A. has been talking w/ Sen. Kennedy's office & maybe they will help. Or possible injunction brought against Justice Dept by a Washington lawyer.

I was angered by the Nixon White House and Immigration Office persecution of Lennon-Ono based on their October 1968 arrest in London for a small amount of hash (planted by police, Lennon said). I was gratified by Lennon's standing his ground, refusing to violate his conscience. Yet neither Allen nor Ted Kennedy—who may also have tried to help—was able to get John and Yoko in this time; it would be nearly a year before they entered the U.S.

At their last Montreal bed-in for peace, with up to fifty others in their room—including Timothy Leary, Tommy Smothers, and Hare Krishnas—they recorded what quickly became an anthem for the antiwar movement, "Give Peace a Chance." John's powerful refrain clarified antiwar intentions for both movement and its opposition; its breakthrough urge was akin to Allen's end-of-war proclamation in his 1966 "Wichita Vortex Sutra." Its truthful simplicity and repetition and urgency—its purity!—contained a strength that would out-argue, out-maneuver any military-bureaucratic rationalization for the war.

Or so I thought.

Several of us, including Allen, heard it soon after its release, on a bright midsummer's noon in front of the house. Someone had brought our little transistor radio from kitchen to porch; it blared forth in all its tinny AM might the sometimes kitschy, sometimes memorable pop tunes of the day: the Archies' "Sugar Sugar," Credence Clearwater's "Bad Moon Rising," even Elvis's "Suspicious Minds." But from Lennon's abrupt "Two—one, two, three, four" at the outset, through the awkward authenticity of the choral voices to his exclaimed "Beautiful!" at the end, this was different. In the song's mid-section recitation of names, we thought we could make out ". . . Norman Mailer Allen Ginsberg Hare Krishna . . ." I remember Allen saying afterward, "Allen Ginsberg, hm, well," then turning to other things. I think he was pleased.

Petey 'n' Julie

ROSEBUD ONCE TOLD me that when Barbara was looking after Julius, the three of them living together in the city, Julie had a dollar-a-day allowance. Typically, Rose said, he'd approach her or Barbara first thing in the morning, in deep Long Island tones, "Uh, can I have my dollar?"—then spend the bulk of the day in a coffee shop, smoking and nursing coffee upon coffee.

So Julius, if he wanted something badly, could act on it; he could communicate. But with rare exceptions (as with the M.D.'s just after the car crash, and later phases when he talked my head off) he almost never volunteered conversation, nor carried it further when someone else began it.

Of course I (like Peter) often relied on his help with daily chores and other farm tasks. He wouldn't—or couldn't—milk Bessie and the goats; I'd usually have to ask for help with other things, tell him what to do—even matters of daily ritual: "Go water the chickens and ducks, Julie." He'd do it quietly, with, it seemed, the utmost stoicism. His preferred state seemed one of rest (and who can blame him?) or relaxation (walking around downstairs, cup of coffee or hot water in hand). Usually no one minded, except when he seemed to flaunt his preference in the face of requests for help—as when an exasperated Allen pushed him out the door in the fall.

He and I usually got along in our own way, but I could become frustrated. One warm morning back in June, with just the two of us at the farm, we'd completed chores and were letting animals out; we'd stake the goats up in the meadow above the front yard, beneath the woods. I was hauling them—Brahma and Shiva and Shiva's kid whom we'd kept, the billy "Junior," who was now starting to grow big and rambunctious. All were feeling their oats. Naturally: it was a bright day; golden light seeped down upon us through high hardwoods. All nature was alive; bees buzzed; mayflies made halos in the rising light. Buttercups bloomed; may apples raised green umbrella leaves over white flowers; maple and ash had turned living green.

But I was becoming exasperated, trying to deal with (and being outwitted by) this hoofèd trio. Brahma and Shiva rose up on their rear legs and butted horns in play, then turned and tugged away from me when I pulled on the chains we'd attached to their collars—and which I was trying to hook to the divots in the ground. Who could blame them? It was a golden morning in June for them, too. But if we let them wander, there'd go our growing garden.

Julius, meanwhile, was simply standing there, watching. Again I pulled, again I was tugged—now in one direction, now two. And then Junior broke loose. Julie simply stood there. Without a thought I found myself yelling, "Julius, if you don't help, I'm gonna slug you!" We got the goats in place.

Of course, Julius didn't have to be there with any of us; no one was "staking" him on East Hill. What else he might've done, where he might've gone, I'm not sure. He was thirty-seven years old, and options seemed: asylum or something like it; work (he hadn't seemed to want a job, though he'd once applied as soda jerk); or remaining in Peter and Allen's care. His deaf mother, already saddled with young twins Marie and Lafcadio, wouldn't—or couldn't—have him. A couple years back he'd run away from his two guardians. Now he did so from me.

I don't know that it was my goat-tying threat that did it; in fact, I don't recall which event preceded the other. I think Julie took action simply because he suddenly had the means to do so. Sometime around summer's start the insurance money from our Thanksgiving car crash came in. We each (except Allen) received a check of $400 for our minor injuries. "Four hundred dollars buys four acres of land," Allen told me encouragingly (and typically—rather than saying I should pay him back the portion of my medical bills that he'd covered). I think I simply held on to mine, spending as needed. I soon found out what Julius was doing with some of his money.

One afternoon I heard a vehicle roll down the drive. It was a taxi cab from Cooperstown, and the driver was just emerging from behind the wheel. Approaching me, he asked, "Mr. Orlovsky?"

And so Julius Orlovsky, residing in the center of New York State, paid a visit to mother and brother and sister in Northport, Long Island—all through a short phone call to the only taxi company in the area, and $400. Rather, $75—each way. I did learn that much the following evening when he returned. But nothing more. For over twenty-four hours I'd remained in a state of guilt-infused tension, at times nearing panic, not knowing his whereabouts—even though Allen, when I reached him on the phone, said not to worry: Julie had disappeared before.

□ □ □

ANY WHYS AND wherefores regarding Julius can't be considered without taking account of his relationship with Peter, a year and a half his junior: his guardian, his boss, his tormentor. At some point in the winter, once my hand was well enough,

I'd drawn a cartoon of a moment at the farm, focused on Allen, seated in the impossibly small chair at the impossibly small phone table. Around him in the kitchen, Lee Crabtree's in long overcoat; Malcolm quivers on the linoleum; Tiger cat defecates while eating; Peter massages a dog; Julie, coffee in one hand and belly pushing out from under tee-shirt, blows studious smoke rings. In calm understatement Allen says into the receiver, ". . . psychologically, it's a complicated situation. . . ."

Now, some six months later, Peter seemed in another tailspin. With perhaps six consecutive weeks of amphetamine already up his arm, there was, for all we could tell, more to shoot.

He stomped about and yelled at all of us—Allen, Julius, Stephen (just returned from Mexico), and myself, with Julie sometimes taking the worst of it. Stephen stood up and shouted at him one day, "You're a fascist!"; Peter simply returned, "I am not!" and stomped away. Stephen's younger brother Peter, joining us for a spell, told me he saw Peter kicking Godly. Once, when Stephen and I were working in the field with Peter, he hoisted an uprooted fence post, brandishing it like a lance, threatening to heave it straight at us.

As tensions rose, I told Allen that if Peter came at me physically, slighter of frame though I was, I'd fight, try to beat him up. "I'll help," Allen offered readily, good-naturedly.

Around the same time, we'd reminded Allen of Peter's thirty-sixth birthday, and bought Peter ice cream, cake, wine, and a new pair of blue jeans. He'd given the jeans to Julius; a few mornings later I heard him command in his gruff voice, hemming and humming and breathing loud: "Take off those blue jeans, Joolie, they're mine, and put on yer own ku-lothes!"

Solemnly, Julius did as his larger brother said. Silently he pulled the blue denim from each leg, then stepped into a pair of plaid Bermuda shorts I'd given him. On an earlier visit Huncke had left me a pair of black Italian pointed-toe shoes he no longer wanted; finding them just a little small, I'd given them to Julie. Now he slipped sockless feet inside them.

And so Peter Orlovsky, bearded, overalled and broganed, hair returning fullforce from self-scalping at Christmas, led his older brother Julius, tee-shirted, shorted, and fancy-toed, out of the house—under the golden sun, for work in the field, the livelong day.

Mrs. Bornstein and the
Secretary of the Treasury

W AS THAT, THEN, the idea of the farm? Peter on amphetamine ordering around Julius in catatonia? That—at least Peter's angry addiction—had been part of the city situation the farm was created to relieve! Dealing with Peter's problem—and with Allen's perceptions of Peter's problem—was endlessly difficult. But in spite of that, farm work did get done. Outside of the question of Julie's will, his work under the imperatives of his younger brother could sometimes be quite productive: fences were repaired, earth was turned, animals cared for. But there were Peter's senseless tasks, too—like moving rocks from one place to another for no apparent reason—and there was the yelling.

This whole can of worms—the interrelationship between Allen, Peter, and Julius—was more than I could manage. It was my lot, I felt, to tackle more concrete problems. Just as everyone returned from the city, I was making my own evaluation of the farm's effectiveness, from several angles, in my red-and-black notebook. Computing feed costs for milk animals over a five-week period, I arrived at a total of $12.60, as compared with $27.36 for store-bought milk.

Of course, this didn't include the occasional vet visit, hay from October till April, barn repairs, etc., nor matters of enormous expense, such as the water system, not to mention simply feeding a house full of people that approached two dozen in summer. Nonetheless I was pleasantly surprised at the result of my little survey, and I imagine it served as a kind of consolation.

As to guests swelling our household, this summer was light compared to the one before, dominated by Barbara's visitors. Allen's recording essentially took up June, and construction of a water system (along with his worries as to how he'd ever pay for it) swallowed the summer from mid-July. Even so, we were seldom long without guests. Stephen's sixteen-year-old brother Peter stayed a fortnight, his mother accompanying him at first—she wanted to be sure he wasn't being homosexually debauched, Stephen told me. He and Stephen shared our attic; their mother put herself up for several days at a motel in town, then went back to Brooklyn.

Mrs. Bornstein had reason to fear. Back when Stephen (now twenty-one) was sixteen, she'd discovered he had a relationship with Allen. Determined to protect her son, she telephoned the poet. "But Mr. Greenberg, Mr. Greenberg," Stephen could hear her voice, loud with anxiety, burst from the receiver in Allen's hand. "You're a known homosexual. How could you!"

Nevertheless, in the summer of 1969, she approached all of us on East Hill with genuine good cheer. (The nightly buffer of a room at the Tryon Inn with swimming pool and running water may've helped.) And though she was older than all of us (except Ed), red-headed Maly—now fifty-nine—was still attractive, and in her own way a classy dame. "A Jewish Marlene Dietrich," her sons characterized her.

She was an active presence. Though some of Peter's behavior terrified her, she invited him and Julius to swim at her pool, where at Peter's direction Julie executed huge, exuberant cannonballs, one after another, and splattered all the surrounding area. (It was a cool day and no one else, fortunately, was poolside. But from within the Inn, just behind a large plate glass window, the white-shirted manager stared at this performance, shaking his head at a grown man acting like that.)

Maly mixed nicely with two weekend guests, journalist Kennett Love and lady friend Melinda Reed, a gorgeous younger woman with dark hair. Kennett had been Allen's classmate at Columbia; he'd co-founded the War Tax Resistance, which Allen, Dr. Spock, Joan Baez, and Pete Seeger had joined. Because of Allen's refusal to support the war with his taxes, the IRS, claiming Allen owed $1,488.68 for 1968 plus $21.25 interest, could—and would—seize his personal bank account. On July 16 he wrote Treasury Secretary David Kennedy, explaining and proposing alternatives:

> . . . I am not able to pay this money into our Treasury to be expended in the continuing illegal and immoral effort to kill or subdue more Vietnamese people.
>
> I have retained attorneys with regard to your claim against me and am instructing them to present the appropriate documents and authorities to your office. . . .
>
> . . . I spent all of the modest amount of money I earned last year keeping alive and helping others maintain their lives. . . . I am physically, mentally and morally unable to earn moneys to pay for the Vietnam war. Basic, traditional ethics of my profession of poetry prohibit me from assigning money earned incidental to the publication of literary compositions pronouncing the inhumanity and ungodliness and un-American nature of this war toward funding the very same war.

> . . . .

I am willing to pay your tax assessment by donating what money I will have to any
tax exempt program acceptable to your department which will benefit money-poor
Americans or protect natural resources wasted as consequence of war-haste.

I humbly request an appointment to meet with you with my attorney to discuss
the policy decision which you must soon make as to how the numbers of persons
who feel as I do are going to be treated by your department. We plan to offer
reasonable alternative to paying taxes supporting the Vietnam War. I can't live in
peace with myself and pay taxes into a fund which goes directly into the Vietnam
War. This prospect has made me physically ill. If our tax system is so inequitable
it cannot find a reasonable alternative such as payment of these taxes into a fund
which is not used in this war then I am willing to go to jail.

Showing the letter to Kennett and Melinda, Allen discussed its contents while
Mrs. Bornstein sat and listened. His reddish seal at the bottom of the first page, as well
as at the end, caught Kennett's eye; he asked if it were from a ring.

"It's a Tibetan seal—lightning bolt," Allen explained. "Has a little magic in it!
Lightning bolt or dorje—vajra prick—lightning bolt prick . . . Tantra. Cross-sectioned."

"Cross-sectioned?" Kennett asked.

"Well, I think at the moment of coming," Allen chuckled. "Flaming come."

That evening at dinner, Maly Bornstein connected the tax resistance discussions
with a new bee in her bonnet: Allen's beard. I wound a reel of tape onto Allen's
Uher and pushed the buttons for "Record." Her fixation allowed him to discourse on
those strong personal symbols of resistance in the late 1960s—beards and long hair.
She began by asking what he'd do if told he wouldn't have to pay taxes provided he
shaved his beard: "I'd shave my beard immediately," he responds. While Stephen
retrieves Dylan's *Bringing It All Back Home*, with its back cover shot of clean-shaven
Allen in top hat, Allen reports his having been bearded on and off over the years: "I
resent . . . *having* to have a beard because people want it or expect it." As Mali continues to press him on his motives, he points out the difficulty of shaving on the farm:
"You have to boil hot water and all that." When she reflects, "Must be very itchy and
uncomfortable on a hot day," he offers his final word on beards: "We've had 'em for
a hundred thousand years!" Only in the late nineteenth and early twentieth centuries,
and earlier eras such as the Roman Empire, has short hair dominated. One's hair and
beard, Allen says, "enunciates the whole animal-mammal reality."

Buck Rogers by Kerosene Lamp

W HEN KENNETT LOVE and Melinda had approached the house on arrival, Peter Orlovsky came hurtling out the door, barely ten feet from them, and threw up violently on the grass. Allen, following behind, explained in welcome, "He's had a bad night off speed." Somehow, Peter had either run out of amphetamine, or surrendered it, and now faced the writhing pain and sickness of crashing.

Meantime contractor Ed Smith and crew had just completed their first excavation down in the meadow, and results were there for all to see: a large crater-like hole where we'd soon start building a cinder block house for our hydraulic ram. A deep trench connected well and ram house site. It looked almost lunar.

Had his concerns been limited to East Hill Farm, life for Allen might've been easier. But national and international situations had grown worse: in May, dozens of G.I.'s were killed and several hundred wounded at Hamburger Hill, near the Laotian border. That same month, under orders from Governor Ronald Reagan, California National Guard stopped the development of a community garden, "People's Park," in Berkeley. Alameda County sheriff's deputies, sent by Reagan, fired not only tear gas but bullets and buckshot, killing one bystander and blinding another who'd tried to stop the rock-throwing at deputies. In June, the Weathermen, a new radical breakaway group from SDS, issued its first manifesto on U.S. imperialism and racism—a challenging, inspiring, righteous, and confusing document. Eight months later, a Weatherman bomb would accidentally detonate in the West Village, killing two people.

In Biafra, 500,000 had died in fighting or its effects: I was shocked by the spread I saw in *Life* magazine. Stephen made an etching inspired by the classic photograph of a large-headed emaciated child. I asked Allen what we—he—could do about it. "Maybe remind me every day the next couple of days," he returned. Jejune as I was, I magic-markered the figure 500,000 onto my forehead, leaving it there two days.

Poor Allen! It was hardly as if he were unaware or ungrieving of world situations—not to mention his own burdens. A few days earlier he'd entered in his journal:

Every morning I wake early in uncomfortable mental excitement, and try to ignore the dread of revolution in my body & sleep.

The economics of the farm images recurrent money-bills confusion—no rest,
how to pay 30,000 dollars break my mind's back & sell my soul & poesy for this
active land? . . .

Not paid my taxes the government'll get my Bank Account & typewriter—S.D.S.
& P.L.P. want violent overthrow of the violent economic tyrants. . . .

Ultimately, I wake in morn afraid of violent dispersal of my possessions, music
books mss. and household—

Retreat from fighting the State for fear of being fought back by the state.

And so feel guilty dreaming of the Crazies & Motherfuckers who having no
possessions and no material attachments are not compromised in sentimental
friendship with the FBI, Local Police, Newspapers, TV Talk Show Hosts . . .

While Kennett and Melinda—and Maly Bornstein—were with us, the U.S. was
about to reach the moon. At Maly's motel room in the afternoon, a few of us saw
the spacecraft land; a few others went to Ed's. For first human steps on lunar surface
seven hours later, nearly all of us were at Ed's.

Sunday night, July 20, Allen, Kennett, Melinda, Mrs. Bornstein, her two sons,
and I hiked up the rain-wet foggy hill to Ed's. Together we'd watch this never-before
event, this higher-tech vindication of America's humiliation by Sputnik eleven years
earlier, this stuff of dreams and science fiction novels and flights of poetry—in our
good neighbor's little shack, near his barn of bearded goats, on his nine-inch black-
and-white golf cart battery-driven TV.

We struggled for space in the tight, goat-musty quarters, in between obelisks
of *National Geographic*, around the wood stove, next to a wall of Ball-jarred green
beans. As far as I could tell in the slight kerosene and television light, Maly Bornstein,
very much a lady, wore a profoundly stunned expression as she beheld such conditions. We were as crowded as the men in *Apollo 11*: only Peter (and maybe Julius)
stayed home, "Groaning & Cursing in bed, relieved of the lunatic burden at last," as
Allen wrote in his poem "In a Moonlit Hermit's Cabin."

The small image on the tiny screen was fuzzy; it was hard to see what was going
on. But a spaceship did seem to be at rest upon some sort of a rough grey-white surface, and some body in an immensely thick, head-to-toe suit did seem to step onto that
surface. (I would be aghast the next day upon learning that we'd left a flag and boots
there—a kind of littering, I thought.)

Another squall of rain beat down on Ed's tarpaper roof, then let up. Buzz Aldrin
and his men were where they were to be, lunar time, and we'd seen what we'd come

to see. We bid Ed adieu and left, passed beneath his barn of sleeping Nubians, and traipsed downhill through wet knee-high grass under a now man-touched moon. Maly would return to the Tryon Inn, with water to flow onto her hands at the touch of a spigot, a soft carpet to sink her toes in, an electric lamp to read by. The rest of us carried flashlights to attic and bedrooms in East Hill farmhouse.

□ □ □

LATE IN THE day of the moon landing, but before the moon walk that night, *The New York Times* telephoned. For a feature on celebrity reactions, they asked Allen for his.

"I'm busy," he answered, "trying to get running water in my house."

Later, when Eugene called, Allen waxed warm and friendly, remembering the radio drama they'd listened to in childhood: "Yeah, it's just like Buck Rogers!" His poem on the occasion gave a full range of his attitudes about landing and take-off, but his comment to *The Times* was pertinent.

Now that Smith had done initial excavation, we—Stephen, Julius, a recovering Peter, and I—began our part of the plan. First, we had to get down to the dirty work. In high rubber boots we descended a ladder into water and muck at the bottom of the well, eight feet below ground. Hauling down buckets, we laid a flooring of gravel and stone, into which Smith then lowered the three 500-pound ceramic pipes. From the base of that lowest porcelain pipe a galvanized steel one would feed down to the ram; from the far end of the ram, a black plastic pipe would reach all the way up to the reservoir (to be buried underground, beyond our house).

In the area excavated for the ram house—eight feet deep, a rectangle six feet by nine—we began the main work, directed by Smith and assistant John Jackson. With shovels and rakes we fine-tuned Smith's excavation; using a plumb line we flattened the earth before laying concrete flooring.

Outside the underground area were piles of cement mortar mix and troughs where we mixed it with water. We dipped buckets into the well for water, then using a hoe mixed it with the cement; then lowered bucket upon bucket of mix down into the house area for whoever, flooring finished, was laying the cinder block walls. We traded these jobs around; we worked hard—Julius included. In between each level of cinder block went a half-inch topping of cement, which fixed one block in place with one set above it.

For nearly two weeks, unless it rained, we carried out this rough work through-out the day, under midsummer sun. Stephen, whose badly chafed hands wouldn't heal for a month, wondered if he'd ever paint again. Allen came down occasionally, cheered us on, even lent a hand. There was as much camaraderie on this project as there ever was on East Hill Farm, yet it also bore the characteristic stamp of individuals involved.

For example, an exchange between Peter Bornstein and Julius when Peter was mixing cement, Julius bringing him water: Julie had just unloaded half a bucket into the trough, and Peter mixed it in with the cement. Julius stood by, watching as he did so, another half bucket of water in hand.

Peter, finding the mix just slightly on the dry side, told him, "Julie, I need some more water for the concrete." Speechlessly, Julius looked his way—then asked, "How much?"

"Just a drop," Peter answered casually.

Julius carefully set his bucket down, looked back at Peter, pulled off his work glove, placed his index finger on the surface of the water, and taking a step toward Peter's trough, delicately, with utterly straight face, flipped the single drop down into it.

Once the ram house was built, Smith—a big man with a big easy smile, reminding me of James Dickey—began filling in the upturned earth around it with his bulldozer. But as he did so, we suddenly heard a "Crack!" We looked down at one of the brand-new concrete walls and saw a single, thin fissure running much of its length. As our collective "Uh-Oh" hung above our heads like a cartoon bubble, we watched him put his dozer into neutral and turn to us. "Didn't you put any rebar in?" he called over his idling engine.

We didn't know what rebar (steel reinforcing rods) was. What now? Simply hope and pray the crack wouldn't worsen and all our work collapse before we figured something out?

"You can have someone go down in there and put in some supports," Smith said, relieving some of our anxiety. "It should hold a while till then."

He then returned to trench-making, connecting well and ram house with reservoir site above our house. Site excavated, Smith lowered a prefabricated reservoir into place, pushed back the earth around it. Then he dug another hole for a septic tank near the south side of our house.

All this spanned a couple of months. It was early fall by the time the whole system was working, with water bursting at the turn of a handle in kitchen and bathroom sinks, flushing in newly installed bathroom toilet. (Later, we'd even get tub and shower.) It was amazing to behold: we'd installed a device nearly two centuries old to bring ourselves running water the same season man set foot on moon.

The ram wasn't "efficient" in the strictest sense: it pumped back uphill a fraction of the gravity-fed water pouring downhill into it. But it worked. And its measured dum-dum-dum—you could hear it in the house at night—proved more reassuring than I can say as the temperature dropped well below zero in dark of winter. Allen seemed especially taken with it all, and whenever guests arrived, he'd bring them down to the ram house, show it off, explain every detail. He was curious about even seemingly mundane matters such as plumbing, charmed by how things worked. He thought of the ram as a perpetual motion machine, and was intrigued by what for a long time—long before East Hill Farm—had struck him as the essential problem of plumbing: how do you make that final connection, pipe to pipe?

It was typical of Allen to wonder about such things, which never occurred to me: to see charming problems and challenges. When we finished the ram house, Stephen used a piece of copper tubing to inscribe on a slab of cement:

1969 A.D.
BUILT BY: GORDON BALL,
STEPHEN + PETER BORNSTEIN,
ALLEN GINSBERG, JOHN
JACKSON, JULIUS + PETER
ORLOVSKY, ED SMITH

Nearby, he made a second inscription. Above the Sanskrit "Om" and the Hebrew tetragram of unpronounceable letters (YHVH) for God, he entered:

COMMITTEE ON POETRY
    1969 A.D.
HAWKEYE STRONGER THAN THOUGHT

Huncke Returns

D URING WATER SYSTEM work we learned Huncke would rejoin us. It had been some months since those winter and early spring imbroglios over his and Louie's needles and junk, and that was the last I'd seen of him. I liked Huncke, even though I now contemplated his return with mixed feelings, mixed recollections.

For all his conning and dependence upon others, he remained intellectually independent and would take issue with Allen (or anyone else) whenever he chose. I remember one time at the kitchen table when Allen was fretting aloud about Biafra's upheaval and starvation: Huncke, recipient of possibly more generosity from Allen, over a greater period of time, than anyone on the planet, asked, "What makes it fall to you to solve the big problems of the world? What's so special about you?"

Because of frequent scabs and scars on his skin from shooting up, Huncke always carried a tube of Neosporin with him, which he eagerly recommended to anyone complaining of a skin problem. He had a "yukky," occasionally superstitious fear of disease from any physical involvement aside from shooting up or sex. "You can get amoebic dysentery," he informed me gravely, "from too much detergent left on dishes."

My most recent recollection of Huncke was of an exchange I'd had with Bert Crain, our friendly druggist on Main Street. Seated on a stool at his shiny black counter, I was enjoying a vanilla ice cream soda when he suddenly asked, "Herbert Huncke is a drug addict, isn't he?"

I thought for a split second, and realized I trusted Crain. "Yes," I answered. "How'd you know?"

"Every time I see him get off the bus it looks like he doesn't know how he'll put his feet down."

□ □ □

WHEN WE PICKED him up at the Greyhound in front of Crain's, Stephen asked Huncke what he'd done the night before.

"I shot up six bags of junk," he replied flatly.

We all knew Huncke was coming down from his last high, entering a spell—perhaps a long and rough one—of the pain and sickness of withdrawal. "Don't worry 'bout a thing, Herbie!" Peter urged him at the dinner table, with a chuckle that seemed to hint at *schadenfreude*.

But Huncke remained somber. Over the next few days he seldom appeared except at mealtime—in his bathrobe—or to heat a can of soup. He complained about how sick he was; Stephen gave him a massage.

One day when I stopped by the vet's, Doc Schaer greeted me with, "I see Huncke's back in the club now." When I mentioned it to Peter, he warned me—calmly—to be careful about confiding information to people like that. "Sometimes it pays to be a paranoid schizophrenic in cases like this," he said.

At one point, in Huncke's presence, I got into a small argument with Stephen, who was proposing Huncke as a model of immorality.

"Well, most people are more moral than Huncke," Stephen said, and I took exception. I resented Stephen's put-down, and Huncke thanked me for defending him.

Though he didn't help with the ram work, we saw Huncke every day; he was always there in the house, usually centrally located, whenever we returned. Every now and then, I'd get in some chitchat. On occasion he'd mention someone or something from his past. Of Billie Holiday: "Oh, she was *so* generous—whenever you needed money, she'd always give you some." Once he confided to me a particular physical effect of his years behind bars: "I got hemorrhoids from all that time in prison."

"Say, what are they, exactly?" I returned. "I always thought they were like barnacles."

Huncke eyed me in disbelief. "They're swellings of the blood vessels around your asshole. You get them from constipation, or sitting or squatting a lot in cold places."

"Oh."

He eyed me again. "Barnacles!" he chuckled, hazel eyes twinkling, a slight shake of the head, seeing me for the hopeless thing I was. "Barnacles!"

More than myself, more than Stephen or Allen, the person giving him the most attention in his days on the mend was Peter Bornstein. Young, tall, and lanky, he was so scared of Peter Orlovsky he wouldn't go to the outhouse if he saw him near. But he'd join Huncke at dining room or kitchen table whenever he had the chance. Listening avidly, he heard his worldly elder tell of days long before as he coddled Malcolm while lounging in his bathrobe, or, as health returned, dressed mostly in black. Peter would stare at that large head, that fascinating and finely drawn face that could at times look twelve and at times a hundred years old.

Peter listened raptly as Huncke, whom Kerouac had acclaimed as storyteller, spun tales: of how, for instance, he bought his first heroin legally over the counter in a dry goods store in Minnesota. Asked about his days on Times Square in the 1940s, Huncke exclaimed, "I was *Mayor* of Times Square!" Now, his hazel eyes bright and electric, his rich voice traveled in time while down in the meadow young bodies worked barechested in water and mud, and in the room above Allen labored through piles of paper. Now, with a young initiate taking in his every syllable, Herbert Huncke was Lord of the Manor.

Pausing for Poetry

F ROM TIME TO time Allen and I would discuss poets and poetry. More often, I'd ask questions, then listen, and, if lucky, remember.

"What's Ed Dorn's poetry like?" I asked one morning as we sat alone in the dining room.

Allen left his seat a moment, returned with *Gunslinger* in hand, and read from the beginning of Book I. Certainly he admired its elegance, and as I heard the crafted syllables take shape from his mouth, I had some sense of that, too—but little else.

I met in Mesilla
The Cautious Gunslinger
of impeccable personal smoothness
and slender leather encased hands
folded casually
to make his knock.
He would show you his map.

There is your domain.
Is it the domicile it looks to be
or simply a retinal block
of seats in,
he will flip the phrase
the theater of impatience.

"Are you following?" Allen asked.

"Yes," I lied.

He continued.

During my final semester at Davidson College, spring 1966, James Dickey visited campus. Many of my peers saw him as an easy fellow to get along with: a good old boy, in contrast to (as they saw her) hoity-toity Carolyn Kizer, who'd come in the fall. At that time, he was winning considerable attention in the media, and seemed much more accepted as mainstream than Allen.

"What do you think of Dickey?" I asked Allen one afternoon, two or three years later, as we walked with Peter just below the edge of the woods above our house. "Do you like him?"

"No—a hunter," came Allen's direct response. He didn't mention Dickey's lopsidedly unfavorable review of *Howl* in *Babel to Byzantium*, which I learned of later. But he did tell me of Dickey's being so "neurotic" that he turned his back on him when they came abreast of each other at a party.

More significant was a recent encounter with another poet. Back in the winter of 1956–57, Allen had brought poet Louis Simpson a generous sampling of works by Kerouac, Snyder, Denise Levertov, Robert Creeley, and others. Simpson, with Donald Hall and Robert Pack, was then editing *New Poets of England and America*. When it first appeared, the volume contained not a single work by any of those in Allen's sampling. Over a decade later, Allen ran into Hall, in his cups at a cocktail party. Hall, eyes moistening, looked Allen in the eye and told him, "You were right."

On East Hill, we had a copy of the Fantasy LP of Allen reading *Howl* (the 1959 Chicago reading, unfortunately not included in his 1994 four-CD set *Holy Soul Jelly Roll*). Listening to it on our little yellow battery-driven stereo, I was greatly affected by its charging railroad-train declamatory power. And the short, very different "Footnote to Howl" was at least as strong as the poem's first three parts.

"Were you crying when you read 'Footnote?'" I asked.

"Yes," he answered, "that was recorded separately, in the Fantasy studio. I'd been drinking wine and I wept at the truth and untruth of it."

On another occasion Allen showed me how he was changing part of a line in "Footnote." "Holy the jazzbands marijuana hipsters peace & junk & drums!" became "Holy the jazzbands marijuana hipsters peace peyote pipes & drums!"

"Junk's burned down too many scenes," he explained.

He admired the precision in some of Wordsworth's nature imagery, as in a daisy's ". . . star-shaped shadow, thrown / On the smooth surface of this naked stone!" Among elder contemporaries, he mentioned Basil Bunting and Ezra Pound. He spoke of the Northumbrian's *Briggflats* and of a recent taxi ride in which they expressed their mutual admiration. Bunting informed him that he was writing an article on him: "'You use too many words,'" he complained. "But my excuse was, 'That's how I talk,'" Allen told me.

At his May 1968 Albany reading, Allen had identified Ezra Pound as one of his four major influences. His appreciation included a virtue less noticed and more refined, perhaps, than those often associated with Pound—his lyrical gift. Allen quoted:

The blossoms of the apricot
Blow from the east to the west
And I have tried to keep them from falling.

Such tenderness—pathos, even—seemed easily lost amidst the erudition, didacticism, and spleen of Ezra Pound.

□ □ □

ALLEN AND I spoke on several occasions about music and poetry. Joining me a moment as I listened to a Doors album one afternoon, he offered, "Musically, many black blues are richer, more sophisticated."

Bob Dylan's work was another matter.

Not since being jailed in Mexico in 1968 (where, like on East Hill, someone had a small battery-operated player) had I listened to a Dylan album as intensely as I did these days at the farm. Back in that small, enclosed flagstone courtyard in Puerto Vallarta, blue sky and the spire of Iglesia de Nuestra Virgen de Guadalupe looming above, I played *Another Side of Bob Dylan* again and again. I loved "To Ramona"; and as if hearing the words for the first time, I reflected on the ironic inversion of "My Back Pages"—just as I puzzled as to my own feelings, under such circumstances, about the last line of "Ballad in Plain D," where the singer asks imprisoned friends, "'Are birds free from the chains of the skyway?'"

Now on East Hill I listened to the same album over and over again, being especially taken by the rhythmic power of "Black Crow Blues." Allen, coming downstairs to listen too, told me of his first hearing Dylan, after his return from India in 1963: how he was moved to tears when Al Aronowitz (later he'd say Charles Plymell) played him "Masters of War" by a new kid on the block.

His love and respect for Dylan was profound, but it wasn't indiscriminate. For instance, he claimed, rightly or wrongly, that in "Mr. Tambourine Man," "Yes, to dance beneath the diamond sky with one hand waving free" is not good poetry because it's "imprecise": "What," he asked, "is 'diamond sky'"?

Allen's perspectives typically challenged or surprised me: I was young and still in thrall to romantic love and sex, taking whatever seemed a love song (or love's rejection) at face value. But of "It Ain't Me Babe" Allen proposed, "I think he's talking to America." As our American war in Vietnam continued to escalate, many of Dylan's admirers seemed to expect him to come forth in messianic song and statement and stop our war. Allen's larger sense of the possible audience for one of his strongest songs now seemed especially apt, for as well as lover, "It ain't me you're lookin' for, babe" could apply to his nation of fans.

□ □ □

OUR DISCUSSIONS OF poetry weren't one-way. When I was writing something myself, poetry or prose, Allen was always available to read, comment, help revise.

Around summer 1969 I began looking to my roots across the Pacific, starting in Occupied Japan, 1950: I was five, dirt roads lined our neighborhood on the city's edge, open sewers ran along some city streets, bombed-out buildings stood here and there. In those first days I played with neighborhood children: scissors-paper-stone, hide-and-seek, baseball with bamboo stick and cloth ball. By the time I left for good—en route to college in 1962—the "economic miracle" of Japan was manifest.

And I'd barely noted its rise.

Mine had essentially been an Ugly American environment within the foreign business community as I was soon separated from first playmates by schooling and language. By 1969—seven years after leaving for good—I longed to return, to a Japan I scarcely knew. This was simultaneous with possible plans for Persia, and an earnest sense of commitment to Allen and the farm itself!

In the city during Allen's recording sessions, I'd stopped at a Japanese travel bureau. There I—banker's son who'd several times crossed the great waters with his parents on elegant American President Lines ships—was stunned to learn that lowly freighter fare was $800. But a different way of "returning" was through poetry, which intersected with East Hill through the interest I shared with Allen in haiku.

In my room at night I began studying a Japanese language text, and at my little antique secretary, I practiced the simple calligraphy of the two syllabaries, *katakana* and *hiragana*. I also continued, as I'd done infrequently the last year, writing short poems, mostly haiku or haiku-like. I'd shown one to Allen:

In the meadow
Drifting angels shiver
Their wings rustling the wheat

Reading it at our dining room table, he'd said, "Don't write on something you haven't seen"—meaning, of course, angels. But I was trying to express (via personification) the look of the wind blowing across high grass down in the meadow. I may have explained as much—or, more likely, was too shy to. In any case, Peter, entering the room, also read the poem, and reacted as Allen had. This insistence on grounding the sensory data of poetry in what was apprehended directly by the poet was akin to Allen's attitude toward postcard writing: "Don't send a postcard of something you haven't seen," he once cautioned.

Though I was disheartened by this response (and felt Allen himself contradicted this precept), I eventually wrote more short poems, especially midsummer 1969:

The knob of the new door we put on our house
Was turned by hands young and aged.

While I was milking,
I looked at her eye.
It did not reflect me.

Even the garden fails to quiet my talkative friend.

A brisk wind—
Feathers part,
Exposing the hen's behind.

Late night:
My pen makes *kana*,
An owl hoots from the forest.

Flies are very busy,
They lead short lives.

On top of a doghouse
Against a sunset:
One large male muscovy duck,
Roosting.

Later in the summer I showed some to Allen—and he went to work. Two examples:

On a silent grassy field,
the sound of a single man,
Hoeing.

**On a silent grassy field,
the clink of one man,
Hoeing.**

With no embarrassment
The mallard chases his lady,
Wanting to fuck.

With no embarrassment
The mallard chases his lady,
Wanting to mount.

As can be seen, sometimes Allen's improvements (as with the specifity of "clink" in the first) worked; sometimes they didn't. I didn't go to him all the time—in fact I'm not sure I went again—but I felt Allen, one of the great teachers of his day, was always there.

Easy Rider, Union Grove, Woodstock

S UMMER 1969—A YEAR after Chicago—the cultural divide between young and old, war supporters and war resisters, continued its mighty growth. For the young, its most obvious sign remained long hair, a form of subcultural "speech."

The significance of this tag and the anger with which it was met—unbelievable today—was manifest in countless ways, some highlighted in a film released in July, Peter Fonda's *Easy Rider.* I saw it on a visit to the city; though I wasn't so keen about it as a film, I appreciated its portrayal of the persecution of long-haired youth, its intensifying tragic power at the end. Such renderings were severe but dramatically justified and true-to-life, I felt.

Standards did change, and in time long hair would no longer represent a challenge, but then it critiqued rock-ribbed 1950s-based assumptions about America, military aggression, and sexual essence. "Long hair doesn't mean anything any more," Jon Sholle would say to me in San Francisco, August 1971. But that was two summers later—and San Francisco.

In fact, an incident taking place within our hinterland nearly three years after the summer of 1969 suggests how slow or even nonexistent—outside coastal seedbeds of cultural evolution—such change could be. Early in the spring of 1972, after I'd left the farm and was living in Chapel Hill, North Carolina, Peter and Denise drove the 1955 Oldsmobile down to visit. The highlight of our time together was to be our attendance at the Union Grove Fiddlers' Convention, a time-honored annual event some hundred miles away.

Driving there late of a rain-filled evening, we were trying to find our way but twenty miles from festival grounds, when through our streaming rear window a whirling, intensely powerful blue light penetrated our private space. Within seconds Peter and I were ordered out of the old grey Olds, and our driver's licenses taken by one of two county sheriff's officers. The one confronting me wore a broad-brimmed rain hat and bright, rubbery yellow raincoat: he was, in every inch of hair and skin, save fingers, protected from the heavy drops—and from revealing any bit of identity. Standing a foot away, he brought an oversized flashlight six inches from my eyes as I stood facing him, rain running through my long hair, down my wet face. Auroras of light bleached into my retinas before my lids closed in the tiniest squint.

He stood scrutinizing me, glancing back once or twice at the laminated card in his hand; I could hear only the mighty thrum of his idling engine, the pouring rain— and the pounding of my heart. Then he looked me in my wet, nearly blinded eyes and exclaimed, "You're a sorry-lookin' son of a bitch, Gordon!" I kept mouth shut, body still.

Before both licenses were returned and we were allowed (without apology or explanation) to proceed, I turned to look for Peter, the man whom, in spite of all the turmoil and trouble we'd been through on East Hill, I thought of as a kind of Billy Budd. There he was, a few feet away, thick long hair that reached halfway down his back all wet, spreadeagled against the driver's side of our Olds as the well-protected officer patted him down and rain fell.

Next day at the festival I learned local police were stopping out-of-state cars purely for the sake of harassing young long-hairs on the way there, perhaps in hope of turning up drugs, but in any case without legal cause. I gave an impassioned statement about our experience for a video being made of the convention—but never learned if it was used.

That such gatherings should require little in the way of police beyond assistance and security was suggested by a festival of enormous proportions held in mid-August 1969: I mean, of course, Woodstock. Allen had been invited to share a poetry tent there with Ed Sanders, but said he had too much work to go. And he wondered, "How would we deal with all the traffic? Who's gonna drive? How'll we get there?" I think we all had at least a slight police paranoia too, particularly since it was only eighty miles from East Hill.

Over three days we heard from friends on their way to or from Woodstock. We listened to radio reports of the festival that mentioned overt drug use without evident ill effect. Reacting to one such report, Huncke wished out loud he'd gone. "You just wanna score drugs!" Stephen interjected. Huncke took offense. "No I don't, and even if I thought of it, I didn't say it!"

But our days were hardly spent at odds with each other. Instead we had our own quietly social weekend, with a few guests. Meryl Mason was an attractive, gener- ous young woman involved in pottery-making and other crafts. (She and I had been together for a spell my senior year at all-male Davidson College; she had an easy- going personality, and her straight long dark hair, blue chambray and denim posed a vivid alternative to the bouffant hair, pleated skirts, and make-up that predominated among young women in nearby Charlotte.) She was outgoing and vigorous—so much so that she'd shown me, one sunny afternoon, how to get a ride on a freight: rather than jumping toward it from a standing-still position, run alongside at its own pace, then jump up on. Exhilarated, we did it together.

Her two or three days at the farm as Woodstock was about to commence were just as much fun. A lot of fucking, walking up into the woods and beyond, doing chores and garden work together; she even helped down at the ram house. Panda Manda, the little tortoise shell I was so fond of, had just had kittens, who now scampered across the straw-strewn barn floor and out into the large scary world; Meryl was as enamored of them as any of us. Only a few weeks earlier, Bessie had given us a red-and-white girl all sleek with birth; now she was making her own way around on flexible legs. Meryl marveled at baby Jennifer and seemed to like all us two-legged animals, too: she found Peter, now nearly a month removed from amphetamine, "cool." "I really hated to leave the farm," she wrote, once back in Norfolk, Virginia.

Also joining us was Allen's friend Elsa Dorfman from Cambridge, Massachusetts. Affable, good-hearted Ellie brought her Nikon and took a number of photographs. She went on a long walk with Allen, pausing to shoot him along the way, seated among distant hills. She reported that he told her, "'Gary Snyder says the next political movement is gonna be around the environment.'"

So we passed a pleasant, quiet but sociable enough weekend at our East Hill redoubt. Allen was relieved, as he wrote a friend afterward, not to be on stage yet again, and he was gratified by 400,000 young people gathering together over several days: he connected it with the Indian Kumbh Mela in which he and Peter had participated seven years earlier: a festive, peaceable, spiritual gathering, once every twelve years, bringing together two million people for two months. Of course, he said, as if it were a matter of common sense, no violent problems arose.

It was four months before Altamont.

Candy, Zucchinis, and War

MUCH OF JULY had been wet: humidity hung in the air, then electric storms split the heavens. Farmers complained of the effects on haying, which was often rendered impossible, since three days straight were needed for drying in the field. But their field corn (for silage) was ten feet high, our half-acre garden plot grew fat with green, and rain had little effect on our water works construction—except to make it muddier. August too started wet, then dried.

Meantime the weathers of love—or friendship—continued with their own variability. In April Candy had written again from San Francisco: she loved me (in a presumably universal way), she had a new boy friend ("Richard makes the strongest, gentlest magic of anyone I've ever met") and she warned:

> Gordon—I sincerely hope you're keeping your head high & not laying around getting into homosexual trists. I hope you have a new chick who loves you.

In May she said she and Richard were among "a dozen people who . . . function on the astral & spiritual planes as well as just physical & intellectual." When the two of them came east this summer, could they visit?

Three months later—eight months after leaving—she was back on East Hill. Without Richard.

One sunny day I picked up Candy at the Cooperstown bus—where I'd last seen her—and we hugged and kissed. She was cheery, long auburn hair vibrant as ever, and still shapely—if a couple pounds heavier. At the farm, she seemed impressed by the garden as well as all our formidable activity. I was pleased for her to see burgeoning rows (amidst healthy families of weeds) of Blue Lake green beans, Annie Oakley okra, and various giant, superabundant zucchini, ever-present at our nightly table.

The Agricultural Extension Service, which I'd continued to bother regarding our application for a pond, had approved it; bulldozing had begun just fifty yards to the west of the ram house. Down in the meadow sat Ed Smith on his backhoe, rocking it lightly back and forth as its huge metal mouth bit more earth. Nearby Allen, Peter, and Julius stood watching.

Through rising stalks of goldenrod waving in a sudden breeze, Candy and I made our way down to the side of Smith's huge trench. As we neared the threesome watching the large man on his immense machine, Allen turned to greet her. "You're like a big ghost!" he exclaimed, hugging. Julius remained silent. Peter was closer to Smith, who shifted his backhoe into idle and seemed to be glancing our way and speaking—though we could hardly hear. Afterward Peter told me what he heard him say as the wind took Candy's long bright hair: "Look at that hair! I'd like to have her lay down and walk right over it!"

"I thought of Vietnam!" Peter told me.

We spent a good several days together; she was pleased to be back and I was pleased seeing her again. "Things look pretty busy here!" she exclaimed, seeming surprised. She filled me in on life in San Francisco, family she'd soon see in Somerville, New Jersey. She helped with chores.

One night in the kitchen just before her arrival, we'd considered giving away some of our excess vegetables down in the city. And even selling them: it could make the farm more self-sufficient. "There's a market for organic vegetables," I offered. I thought I saw a light—a mischievous one—come on in Allen's head. Laughing, he proposed, "We could go down to Victory Market, buy up all their vegetables, take 'em to the city, sell 'em as 'Fresh Organic Produce! Straight from the Country!'" He laughed and laughed, chugging away from deep inside his chest. Huncke—conman extraordinaire (to borrow Dylan's later phrase for Allen)—sat there in his bathrobe, nursing a bowl of Campbell's Chicken Noodle. He stared blankly at his mirthful host, his own mouth open not in laughter but puzzling disbelief. "What's so funny?" he asked, lower lip protruding. "I don't see why you think it's so funny." His voice sounded thin against the echo of our laughter.

A few days later Candy, Stephen, and Peter Bornstein and I filled the trunk of Stephen's used Volvo with some of the humongous zucchini of which we were so proud, and set off for Manhattan. Once under way, all seemed fine, except we couldn't turn off the heater, and it was end-of-August hot-and-humid. Would we arrive with a trunk full of baked zucchini? We worried—but didn't dare try to stop and look on the New York Thruway. We all were semi-naked, arms and legs out windows, long before the George Washington Bridge.

We dropped Candy off to see a friend; she and I would reconnect that night. Stephen, Peter, and I parked on 1st Avenue and went, giant zukes in arms, to Pete's Spice, our source for organic grains and other staples.

Our effort was met with, "Are you kidding? When they get so big, the seeds are all hard! It's like eatin' watermelon!" Our wouldn't-be-partner in business pointed to their produce, so meek and modest by comparison: "This is how zucchinis are supposed to look!"

At a nearby fruit-and-vegetable stand a middle-aged Italian, apron on his front, responded with "Are you crazy?" Asking to cut one open, he pointed to the large seeds. "Look—nobody wants to eat that!" He stared at us, dumbfounded.

Well, we thought, we'll give them away. Surely there are plenty of city people, deprived and undernourished, who, amazed by such an impressive sight, such a rare gift, would eagerly take advantage of it. We went a few blocks, stood in partial shade near a plane tree. Not one person walking by, hippie, straight, or bum, accepted a zucchini as we stood there, five or so pounds of huge thick oblong green in each hand, calling out, "Free zucchini! Get some great zucchini straight from the country! Organically grown! No charge!" We turned one way, we turned the other; still no takers. Had our city population become so alienated, so suspicious, that they distrusted the precious gift of food? Was *this* why the Diggers folded? Finally, a small man in open-neck short-sleeve white shirt, sweating like everyone else, stopped to repeat what we already knew but resisted: "You guys crazy or somethin'! You don't eat BIG zucchini! Only the small ones! These things," he squeezed one of our prime specimens, "are just too hard!" We three looked at each other a final time as he left: it never bothered us at the farm.

Night came—a welcome relief—and in the morning I had to leave for a Cherry Valley softball game on Long Island. We white boys from upstate were playing the all-white Vamps of the North Bellmore Fire Department—an annual event because our manager Sal Russo had lived here before moving his family to Cherry Valley.

It was a bright afternoon, the field was good (with dugouts, even), the game was close enough to be interesting, and I was shocked to the core. The racial epithets the young firemen used on each other when they took the field matched any I ever heard anywhere: "You goddamned nigger! . . . What are you, a kinkhead?! . . . You niggerlover! . . . You goddamned black asshole!" (I'd never heard anything like such oaths from my own teammates or anyone we played in the Cherry Valley area.) I have no idea what the score of the game was, not even who won. But forty-two years later I would remember the words, as I would those few from Ed Smith down in the meadow, as I remember our nation torn by violence, by the aggression we brought into the world.

□ □ □

A LITTLE TIME passed, and Allen received a response to his letter to Treasury Secretary Kennedy explaining that he was "physically, mentally and morally unable to earn moneys to pay for the Vietnam War." To several of us at the dining room table, he read the word from Washington out loud. Its heart seemed something along the lines of "Don't worry. Your tax money could be going to something else, something other than the war." Several of us laughed and laughed—perhaps till we cried. It was a rare moment, those days: laughter on account of our war. The inescapable horror of Vietnam depressed all of us profoundly.

During the month of August, Allen's journal graphed a range of his psychic anxieties, farm to war to marijuana arrests:

August 15

I wake mornings breathing shallow, birds warbling in foggy light, my mind racing with eyes open or eyes closed trying to return to unconsciousness to escape fear—of body pain, of fatigue, of horses eating fences rotting squash leaves lost in green weedstalks—weeds round my life—I talk about God and don't see Him— talk about love and fear Peter—my belly tense, mind racing to the revolutionary doom of planet—morning after morning nervous breakdown a cheerless self with my desk accumulating energetic papers, money worry above all, pestered by dollar needs first time in 42 years on planet money's gotten under my skin & into my consciousness like bedbugs that wouldn't let me sleep in the city.

August 22 6:30 am

Yellow light at fringe of sky, clear blue dawn-dome out the wooden window at cock crow. . . .

. . . This morning Madeline Sinclair's arrest [Magdalene, wife of writer-activist John] *. . . & her helpless phone-call to me & Ed Sanders rose in mind at dawn with bird chirps in ear & scattered paw-jousting of four farm dogs on cool August morn in wet grass—I got up to pee on the lawn . . . John got busted last year sentenced last weeks to 9-10 years screaming in Court for passing two joints of pleasure grass to a secret agent of the state.*

Black Panther Bobbie Seale accused of ritual murder by the F.B.I.—Dave Dellinger & Abbie Hoffman to be tried for protesting police state war in Chicago— and in England a scientist's declared we tipped the planet-balance of irrevocable pollution. These thoughts at rising, dread at being pushed out of the body-image with mass jail, Buchenwald re-cycled, storm troopers invading the countryside, carbon monoxide starvation riot popular death.

August 26

My belly too fat, O ugly potshaped abdomen of masturbation and no babies because of world over population sleeping late in bed insomniac after cock crow as the earth chills toward Autumn—

. . . .

Letters piled up to be answered; taxes refused unpaid, Bank account seized; possessions piling the walls, books, manuscripts, loves a burden waiting attention while the mind would be free to fly to Stars or travel to Persia.

I have America has too many possessions to sleep peacefully in the morning, doze late while the birds twitter in the fog.

Meanwhile, Otsego County lost its twentieth son in combat in Vietnam. John K. Winslow, of nearby Hartwick, Sergeant in the United States Marine Corps, was on his second tour of duty. Wounded in combat on his first, he'd received the Purple Heart, then after recovery signed up for a return tour. Due for discharge later the same month, he was killed by friendly fire.

Ed's Story: The Short of It

E D URICH: CRUSTY, friendly, musty, smelling of goats ("You wouldn't want to walk downwind of him," a friend from town once said). Living apart from everyone, decades, yet helpful and even sociable to a fault. We'd see him every day; so would the Grahams. Weekdays he'd stop down by their 635-acre farm for their mail, just like for ours. Usually he'd show up around noon, and they'd feed him lunch. Then he'd pull one of the kitchen chairs over near the door and sit, waiting until he could see the mailman stop at their box—and go out and get theirs for them. Often he'd head for the barn, and do little things to help out. But as the Grahams' youngest son Wayne would tell me, "He'd say he was helping out, but he wasn't really doing too much." He'd come down Sundays too—in the morning.

Weekdays in town—for a dollar an hour, never more—he looked after Oakwood, the imposing six-towered Campbell family home. He tended flower beds for several elderly Cherry Valley women, including Judy Cannon's ancient "Aunt Bun," who lived in the Samuel B. Morse house on Montgomery Street. (They—Ed called her "Bunny"—had a special communications system involving her turning lights on so he'd know she'd risen and was OK of a morning. But he usually checked on her anyway.)

He was ever our friend, introducing us to phenomena we'd never known. Once, early on, Stephen and I—city boys to the core—came running uphill to his place, a new "find" in hand: we'd discovered "scallions" growing in the onion row—and the old man straightened us out. It was Ed who first pointed out to me marsh gas (what some call "foxfire"), one evening in the lower meadow, where a pale grey-bluish mist hovered and rose, eerie and slow, above scrub vegetation. "Witches boiling sap," Ed said: fungus gives a glow to decaying wood.

I'm not sure we could've survived without his cheery practical wisdom (not to mention the basically good press he must've given us in town): from water system to garden to goats to weather ("Ya see, low-lying nimbostratus clouds mean persistent rain or snow") to winter clothing.

"This is an eccentric," he showed me once as we worked on the engine of his ancient tractor. It was a roundish off-center metal device, kind of elliptical—but essential to the whole operation. There was the crux of it, there was the metaphor:

what wasn't "centered" or of familiar appearance might be as crucial as anything that was. It applied to Ed; it applied to the rest of us.

But what made him live as he did? Why the extreme sociability coupled with the peculiar "antisocial tendencies"? His nearest neighbors his goats, his small shack on a hill with its dim cramped interior, mountains of *National Geographics*, shelves of canned green beans; smells of kerosene, wood smoke, and those magnificent Nubians; that tiny battery-run TV.

And his wearing three shirts, almost regardless of the time of year. Building his driveway early on by stopping off at the roadside shale deposit just below the Beautiful View, every day on his way home: "That's 365 buckets a year," he'd say. Odd driving habits, recommended to others: turning the steering wheel of his big blue '64 Oldsmobile Delta 88 in the direction he needed to go before starting the engine; turning the engine off and coasting the final five yards to save gas.

Whatever his peculiarities, he was colorful and thoughtful. "The Untied Snakes," he sometimes called our increasingly war-mongering nation. In his own right he was a prophet: the World Bank was on its way to controlling everything—they were "the biggest crooks, and the biggest controller of the world economy. They'll have their monkey wrench in the cog wheels," he assured us. The next world war, he always said, would come out of the Mid-East.

Still, the basic mystery remained. No one—town or elsewhere—seemed to know, really, what brought Ed to his solitude on East Hill—and into everyone's midst. "Some people thought I was a German spy," he told me of his first appearance.

I thought I'd never learn what had motivated him, until one afternoon he simply told Stephen and me outright. We were visiting up at his place, and I don't know what made him do it. The telling was matter-of-fact, unembellished.

As he neared middle age while working as an engineer for the phone company in Valhalla, New York, he had a nervous breakdown. One afternoon he was driving a company truck with his supervisor (and best friend) riding shotgun; they were following another company truck loaded with telephone poles. In one split second, a pole slipped loose and rammed through their windshield, straight into the head of his friend.

We never asked further about it, and he never brought it up. Maybe it explains, to some degree, why one person could so separate himself from humanity, yet so profoundly want to be part of it.

"Death on All Fronts"

D URING THE SUMMER Allen received a letter from Gary Snyder proposing it might be time to sit down in front of bulldozers ripping up the earth for the sake of reckless development; Gary pinpointed "simpleminded boosterism" as an obstacle to the recognition of ecological needs.

Around the same time, we received a document on oversized paper in elegant hand, bearing over four dozen signatures, including those of Gary, Keith Lampe, and *Whole Earth Catalog* founder and publisher Stewart Brand. The "Unanimous Declaration of Interdependence" begins:

> When in the course of evolution it becomes necessary for one species to denounce the notion of independence from all the rest, and to assume among the powers of the earth, the interdependent station to which the natural laws of the cosmos have placed them. . . .

And it asserts that

> . . . whenever any behavior by members of one species becomes destructive. . . it is the function of other members of that species to alter or abolish such behavior and to re-establish the theme of interdependence with all life. . . .

Among the ten "repeated injuries and usurpations" the Declaration attributes to "People" are that they have:

- refused to recognize that they are interacting with other species in an evolutionary process.

- fouled the waters that all life partakes of.

- transformed the face of the earth to enhance their notion of independence from it and in so doing have interrupted many natural processes that they are dependent upon.

- massacred and extincted fellow species for their feathers and furs, for their skins and tusks.

- [continued to proliferate] *in such an irresponsible manner as to threaten the survival of all species.*

- *warred upon one another which has brought great sorrow to themselves and vast destruction to the homes and the food supplies of many living things.*

Once early on, discussing individual, concrete applications of ecological concerns, Allen reported, "Peter and I say, 'Each telephone call burns a flower.'" Of course, Allen—who'd already written the poem "I Am a Victim of Telephone"—spent more time on the phone than anyone I ever knew, but it was typically spent (as his poem suggests) on behalf of others. Nevertheless, here lay the rub, of which Allen was very much aware: supporting ecology in principle was one thing; living one's life without violating ecological commitments was something else.

Allen's poem "Death on All Fronts" meets the problem of ecological ideals and ecological reality head-on. After the coming of warm weather some of our hens had begun looking a little scroungy. They stopped laying, started spending more time than usual dusting in the shallow depressions they made in the ground near the front of their house. Finally, we learned—Ed came onto the case—that they must have lice. They could be treated with arsenic spray, and so we sprayed: lice down, hens and eggs up.

Then early one morning entering the chicken house, Peter saw fifty rats run for cover: they'd been feeding around the trough on the floor where we gave the chickens "scratch feed" of corn and other grains. Down at the Agway we got some Warfarin, little yellowish pellets of poison in small brown cardboard boxes, and spread them about: apparently, chickens wouldn't be interested, but rats would be. And, said Ed, they'd end up dying of thirst.

Meanwhile, an old friend of Allen's who'd once worked as an exterminator returned to the U.S. from England. He didn't come up Cherry Valley way, but Allen went down to the city and visited William S. Burroughs at the Chelsea. One evening they dined at the Quixote Restaurant next to the hotel, then visited Huncke, who'd recently left the farm for a narrow little room with Louie in the Broadway Central. As Allen would often do over the years when visiting Burroughs, he returned with new phrases to quote. One was the subtitle of a poem he wrote a week later:

Death on All Fronts

"The Planet is Finished"

A new moon looks down on our sick sweet planet
Orion's chased the Immovable Bear halfway across the sky
from winter to winter. I wake, earlier in bed, fly corpses
cover gas lit sheets, my head aches, left temple
brain fibre throbbing for Death I Created on all Fronts.
Poisoned rats in the Chickenhouse and myriad lice
Sprayed with white arsenics filtering to the brook, City Cockroaches
stomped on Country kitchen floors. No babies for me.
Cut earth boys & girl hordes by half & breathe free
say Revolutionary expert Computers. . . .
I called in Exterminator Who soaked the Wall floor with
bed-bug death-oil: Who'll soak my brain with death-oil?
I wake before dawn, dreading my wooden possessions,
my gnostic books, my loud mouth, old loves silent, charms
turned to image money, my body sexless fat, Father dying,
Earth Cities poisoned at war, my art hopeless—
Mind fragmented—and still abstract—Pain in
left temple living death—

As Allen had been acutely aware for decades, there's no escaping death on our planet—and even seemingly benign attempts at promoting life and health can have their own deadly effects: the country's no refuge from the essential conditions of cities; our aspirations, East Hill and elsewhere, prove frail, vain, mortal.

I once marveled at some compost as I took it out to the pile: some richly colored, miraculous-looking iridescent fungus matter had spread across more familiar items overnight. "There's no stopping life on this planet," I exclaimed to myself.

What I still only dimly recognized—and was far from accepting—was that the same was true of death.

Sinclair's Gulag

S OMETIME IN THE early 1980s Allen told me of his attempt to discuss Reagan-era civil rights and censorship problems with a State Department man who simply didn't want to hear of it: "You should be concerned about the Soviets in Afghanistan!"

But for much of his life Allen *was* concerned about the malfeasances of Soviet and other authoritarian governments East and West. That's how he got kicked out of Cuba and Czechoslovakia in 1965! And in the late '60s, he told me of dissidents in the Soviet Union, specifying the situations of several recently arrested: poet Aleksandr Ginzburg, for example, had been jailed for giving his cafeteria card to a friend.

Though Vietnam was in some sense our own Holocaust, I don't propose there was an American equivalent of Stalin's extermination of 15 million. But as time passed I noticed on both sides of the Iron Curtain some correspondence of state methods in apprehending citizens who spoke against it. In the U.S., such arrests were facilitated by drug laws, especially those against marijuana.

John Sinclair was a young polymath in Detroit who in 1966 had published in pamphlet form Allen's "Prose Contribution to the Cuban Revolution." Since then he'd founded the White Panther Party to resist America's escalating war and racism, managed the rock 'n' roll group MC5, and written poetry, prose, and propaganda. His White Panthers ran anti-amphetamine and drug education programs as he spoke out for marijuana and psychedelics and for building a "Woodstock Nation."

He'd been busted before, but a 1966 arrest for possession—giving two joints to an undercover agent in his commune—resulted, three years later, in a nine-and-a-half to ten-year sentence. Early in the fall, he was being sent to a maximum security prison in northernmost Michigan, 500 miles from friends and family in the Detroit area. A petition urging his release began:

John Sinclair . . . has been sentenced to 10 years in prison for the "crime" of possessing two marijuana cigarettes. The only evidence . . . was manufactured by the Detroit Narcotics Bureau 3 months after Detective Lt. Warner Stringfellow had threatened to "get" John Sinclair. At no time was John Sinclair arrested with marijuana in his possession. . . .

He'd been refused bail on appeal. As he wrote Allen from his maximum security cell, ". . . the sales/dispensing charge was *thrown out* by trial judge on grounds of entrapment, then he kept the evidence illegally obtained and tried me for possessing it. . . ."

Allen's efforts to secure Sinclair's release were unremitting. He contributed $1,400 toward his defense; the second week of October he'd give several days of benefits in Detroit and Ann Arbor. But Sinclair's growing radicalization, unsurprising once his extraordinary punishment and confinement began, left Allen unnerved. Just before leaving, he'd written in his journal: "John Sinclair his letter says Guerilla Warfare supplant Love Fire, & here I gotta go get him out of jail? Jesus Jack!"

Sinclair's recent endorsement of violence against an armed and murderous state was hardly unique. A colleague wrote: "We carried signs and protested . . . and they beat us and jailed us." There was, after all, not "merely" the police debacle of Chicago 1968 and that city's deaf ear to permit applications in months preceding the convention; there was also People's Park in May 1969, where deputies acting ultimately under orders from Reagan (who said, "If it takes a bloodbath, let's get it over with. No more appeasement") killed one, wounded others. There was that first manifesto from the Weather Underground in June, calling for fighting the "pigs," strategizing world-wide revolution and the creation of "many Vietnams which will dismember and dispose of U.S. imperialism"; and there was, month after month—even though Nixon had called for "Vietnamization" and begun troop withdrawal—our continuing escalation of war. Before Americans wholly withdrew over five years later, Nixon had dropped more bombs than anyone in history: he outbombed LBJ; he outbombed Hitler.

Such matters had devastating effects, of course, upon all of us—not to mention those surrounded by armed guards and cold steel. And how "bad"—in the conventional, sanctioned consciousness of those days—was John Sinclair's "crime"? In 1968, in California alone, more than 50,000 people had been arrested for marijuana possession. Though in our era attitudes have remained less than enlightened toward this still-illegal substance (consider the vehement resistance of late great Tobacco Man Jesse Helms to even medical marijuana), our comparative tolerance might make some wonder how so many arrests, and such severe punishment as Sinclair's, could've taken place. For an eloquent indication of attitudes and assumptions making such things possible, look up "Marijuana" in the *New York Times Index* for 1969. You will be told to

See Drug Addiction.

Late Summer, Early Fall

D ENISE AND PENNY were up again for a while, and so we were two couples at the farm; Allen and Julius were the odd men out. Penny and I would see each other on and off; by early November Denise would move in for good. Both women had their gifts—Denise in music, Penny in art. We had a sewing machine which they used from time to time, and Penny was starting to teach herself to sight-read piano sheet music. "Gold diggers," Ed called them jovially, to their faces. I didn't quite see why. Allen enjoyed the sound of their giggles.

When these young women—Denise turned eighteen in the summer, Penny was a bit older—had first come in the spring they'd brought meat with them; Peter and I stir-fried it into our standard regimen of kasha, mushrooms, and vegetables. The last was a new item to Denise; over time, Peter showed both of them how to cook.

Denise's wasn't the classic female figure—large head, compact torso—but she was attractive in her own right. Thirty-three years later, a portly grey-haired Peter would exclaim, "She was so sexy!" as he recalled her in tight shorts in the garden, index finger to lips, looking his direction. Penny was prettier, in a "Sad-Eyed Lady of the Lowlands" sort of way. "You have the best ass on the farm," Huncke told me in late September as he was leaving for a spell. "I do?" I answered, then blushed at my vain misinterpretation as he burst into mock rage: "Oh, just listen to you! Get outta here!"

□ □ □

WHILE ALLEN WAS in the city, Cartwright returned with fellow junkie Dennis Lee. They were shooting heroin, developing big open sores on their arms. Not without some dread of public consequences, I drove them to Bassett Hospital, where they were treated with antibiotics. Later I heard from Patti Benson, who worked for Dr. Olson: "The doctors here know what caused those sores." Louie and Dennis left soon.

□ □ □

AFTER THE RECORDING sessions, with twenty-two of the forty-six *Songs of Innocence* and *Songs of Experience* on acetate, Allen wasn't working as intensively on Blake. But he did continue, refining further some pieces he'd already set to music, notating new ones. A late summer entry in my journal, written as my watch neared midnight, reads:

Organ playing beneath my bed—
No sleep for me tonight!

Yet I loved his renderings. I loved the sublime righteousness of Blake's second "Holy Thursday":

Is this a holy thing to see
In a rich and fruitful land,
Babes reduc'd to misery,
Fed with cold and usurous hand?

Is that trembling cry a song?
Can it be a song of joy?
And so many children poor?
It is a land of poverty!

Eventually, Allen would complete the music for all remaining "Songs." One for the future was "The Tyger": I heard him say several times he hadn't set it to music yet, "because that's the revolution."

He typically devoted a portion of each day to studying *The New York Times*, with an eye for New York City, domestic, and international news—and anything related to drugs. One Sunday near summer's end he'd seen Helen Vendler's review of his *Planet News*. He wrote in his journal:

A bring-down review in the Sunday Times Books—Planet News *denounced for being too planetary or too personally detailed by lady aesthetic reviewer. . . .*

"Gee that chick dragged me," he wrote Ferlinghetti. When I had a look later on, Vendler seemed unable to value Allen's juxtaposition of personal and "planetary," and so missed the distressing urgency of the political and ecological dimensions of his "news."

Vendler's critique appeared on the same page as Kenneth Rexroth's appreciation of Philip Whalen's *On Bear's Head*. A few weeks later he wrote Philip, whom he cherished as friend and poet, a lengthy letter rich in everyday details and preoccupations:

Leaves turning bloodshot gold, I just got up brewed coffee & read 3 pages Of Time
& the River *. . . cow mooing in the barn & goat complaining out barn window,
this being chilly week barndoors are closed first time for season—so Peter came
downstairs in red felt hat & overalls followed by Julius sleepy eyed & big-bellied in
middle of kitchen floor—now they're out milking & I came upstairs with coffecup
to clean out desk, go thru my giant grassy files to make a package for Leary's latest
lawyer's use . . . four peaceful days left, then I go out on reading tour . . . all week
raise money for John Sinclair . . . then go running round the country. This kind of
jumping around is schedul'd till next May on and off returning here for a month at
a time. By then I should have piled up enuf money to pay off all farm improvements
& not go anywhere anymore but Japan or India. Farm is such easy place to stay put
I might wind up buried here for years.*

. . . .

*Farm & quiet art (now having learned enuf music to notate & improvise with
chords) should be enough to occupy my declining years but the nagging horror
of planetary apocalypse billions of starving people murdering each other & the
electronic paranoia of continual revolutionary busts & Bullshit & police violence
intrudes on morning coffee and A.M. dreams, & keeps my stomach in a state of
turmoil & my head buzzing with unwritten letters to the Times. The only time I feel
really OK is if I write poesy about it or whatever rises deeper-thoughted, but I am
increasingly interrupted by phonecalls from the city full of conspiracy trial news or
other busts or squeaks & screams from garbage-drowning Manhattos—or endless
mailboxfulls of woe—*

□ □ □

GREGORY WAS BACK awhile, and he and I became what you'd really call friends,
going into town together, staying up talking.

> Hi-diddle-dee-dee,
> A beggar's life
> For me!
> A silk top hat
> And a silver cane . . .

I'd sing, at his inspiration, after *Pinnochio*, and he'd correct me as to whose sort of life it was: "A *Poet's*!" We were the Fox and the Cat.

Hoping to rejoin Belle permanently, he seemed to follow her around desperately. Shortly he left for Santa Fe, where she was resettling. His last night he and Allen hauled dirty laundry into the Cherry Valley laundromat, where (as they washed and dried and sorted) they read together the Platonist Thomas Taylor, who influenced Blake. After their return I stayed up all night in his attic lair talking with Gregory about his upcoming trip, excited for him—then drove him to Albany the next day.

Ten days later, he returned, in fringed buckskin jacket. He was picking up Indian lore, and told us how when they hunted buffalo they became buffalo. One afternoon, he in new fringe, I in overalls, brogans and straw hat, we posed side-by-side for a photo in front of the house. White hens scratched near our feet and a mostly obscured straw-hatted Julius stood behind us on the porch. "I look like a pumpkin!" Gregory complained, beholding the print.

□ □ □

MY FRIEND MERYL Mason, who'd been up Woodstock weekend, sent me a pair of fine, brand-new cowboy boots. But when I tried them on, they wouldn't fit. If only my foot were half a size smaller, I thought—and Julius came to mind.

"Julie," I asked, knocking on the pine-paneled door next to mine, gift in hand, "would you like a pair of nice cowboy boots?" Except for sneakers and the insulated Ball brand rubber boots for midwinter, did he have any footwear other than those fancy pointed-toes from Huncke? He tried on the shiny new boots; they fit; I felt good. "OK, Julie. Keep 'em—they're yours." I watched him put them on and saw him wear them a few times.

In those pre-running water days, we each had a large empty mason or mayonnaise jar in our room, so we didn't have to stumble downstairs and out the door to pee in the middle of the night. When I entered Julie's some days after being so pleased with my own generosity, I didn't notice either kind of jar. But there, set neatly side by side, toes to outer wall, were the new cowboy boots. Full of pee.

Inside the house when it rained, Julius would talk with Panda Manda (whom the girls called "Motorhead" because of her purr), telling her he'd be getting a job in an ice cream factory; Peter would play *The Velvet Underground & Nico* with the Warhol banana on the cover.

As autumn neared, our harvest continued bountiful, with many quart jars of green beans canned; now sober winter squash followed the prodigal zucchini. Some tomatoes ripened before frost; others we wrapped in newspaper or set on window sills, as before. Fall lettuce, as well as potatoes and onions, made it in time. A box of ladybugs I'd ordered in the spring had helped control aphids and other pests; we could carry in cabbage, broccoli, Brussels sprouts. We even passed around a few ears of our own sweet corn at dinner. I was delighted.

Godly and his lady friend Sadeyes had puppies; we kept one, calling her Radha, after one of Krishna's consorts. New ducklings graced the now well-protected chicken yard; hens seemed healthier thanks to dreadful arsenic. Junior, the growing "juvenile delinquent" male kid, was looming larger and larger, getting long, slithery red hard-ons, knocking his short but growing horns with Brahma and Shiva, butting at us when he felt like it, nibbling pines in front of the house and getting into the garden at every chance.

Some mornings Allen would spoon a soft-boiled egg from an egg cup (one of his particular delights) as he continued reading *Of Time and the River*. (He especially admired its great opening description of the train entering the station.) We just now had running water in the kitchen sink; before long there'd be a big deep utility sink and toilet in the bathroom. Soon the water was even hot, thanks to a "Jetglas Water Heater" from Suburban Propane. By late January, there'd be a tub; mid-February, a shower stall. And thanks to the Extension Service, there was now a pond down in the lower meadow, a couple hundred feet below the barn, nearly ready, all excavated and shaped, with an overflow spout. Next spring I'd stock it with blue gills and small-mouth bass.

□ □ □

WORK ON DILAPIDATED farm structures was ongoing. Before skilled carpenter Jim Bell joined us in November, Peter, with Julius's dutiful help, took on the task of putting up new sections of siding on the barn. Allen recorded one episode of their effort and its psychodynamics:

> *Last night at suppertime standing by the barn arguing with Peter—Julius up on aluminum ladder taking down the old boards so's they could insulate with tarpaper first before re-lining barn with fresh wood. Dark fallen, Peter yelling at Julius & climbing the ladder tearing down the boards. Inside the house the table set & Huncke & I angry that Peter wouldn't come and eat. Julius afraid to come in because of his fury, & Peter screaming at me in the dusk.*

Allen's perspective, on East Hill Farm and most other subjects, remained troubled. Consider a September journal entry:

A knot in my solar plexus yesterday all day, tremorous knot of anxiety that made me think of stomach cancer my karma—

Hardly a morning since I've been on the farm that I've woken to delight in dewey grass and birds' warble & ducklings' peeps.

Two days later he focused on the larger world of politics, including the recently announced U.S. anti-marijuana campaign (Operation Intercept) with Mexico, as well as domestic crises:

All out war on Grass plotted at the Border by wide-hipped prexy of Mexico & US, with chemical defoliants & gas dogs & sensors invented by NASA.

Black Panthers' offices in cities everywhere burned, white lawyers desks overloaded, barristers rushing by airplane every direction.

Costs 1500 for transcript of John Sinclair's trial, nobody got the money.

Dellinger Hoffman & Rubin & Hayden & Bobby Seale and not me not Ed Sanders on trial for Chicago Conspiracy, last year's political convention.

Directing Operation Intercept were deputy Attorney General Richard Kleindienst and assistant Secretary of the Treasury (and Allen's Columbia schoolmate) Gene Rossides. Rossides brought with him to the task his special assistant, G. Gordon Liddy.

The Last of Kerouac

B Y MID-SEPTEMBER ALLEN had finished a project that evolved from a Paterson visit in early July: studying a manuscript of Louis's poems, commenting, suggesting, editing, and offering help with publishing; then three weeks writing the introduction to Louie's second book, *Morning in Spring*. Boldly he addressed his elder's old-fashioned taste for rhyme, thereby coming to a kind of reconciliation: "Confrontation with Louis Ginsberg's Poems," he called it.

Soon a larger challenge arrived on his desk. In early October he told his diary of a relatively short piece of prose he'd just read. It was the last writing Jack Kerouac would publish before death:

> *Kerouac's essay in Capitol Newspaper Post, "After Me, the Deluge," flooded mind awakening—all day flotsam his imagery yesterday car riding to Albany—hate the revolutionaries & every pacifist Dellinger & hate the bureaucrats, like his father.*

Allen then left for Detroit, thinking of the words of an old friend seemingly imprisoned by his own ill-will, to try to rescue John Sinclair, a young man in maximum security turning angrier.

After nearly a week raising $4,500 on Sinclair's behalf, he flew to Buffalo, joining Ferlinghetti, who was reading there, and Robert Creeley, who taught there. Creeley then drove them to East Hill.

Over the course of the trip, they picked up a hitchhiking college couple, who sat with Allen in the back. True to form, Allen engaged the young man and woman in conversation, asking about their lives.

The guy quizzed back: "Who are you?"

Allen answered, "Who do you think I am?"

"Some kind of English professor."

"Well, then who do you think that guy is?" Allen asked, pointing to Lawrence in front.

"A businessman." Creeley, it seemed, was a forest ranger.

□ □ □

GREGORY CONTINUED IN residence; when the three travelers showed up, we all had dinner. Kerouac's "After Me" became a major topic of discussion: the *Post* wanted a response from Allen. Now, as Peter and I washed dishes, Allen asked everyone what he should do. Creeley later told me what I couldn't hear over our clatter of silver, plastic, and blessed running water:

> Allen felt it was a no win situation, that if he said anything in seeming attack on Jack's sense of the young, that would be a public attack on an old friend—and not to respond would seem equally no good . . . he'd be tacitly agreeing they should all be put in the army. I think it was then he also told of how Jack would call him up to advise him of the classic Great Jewish Conspiracy, and when Allen would answer he had heard nothing about it and he was after all a Jew, Jack would answer, you'd be the last to know, they wouldn't tell you, etc. In other words, Allen was emphasizing, as I recall, that Jack was very rightwing and pretty much otherwise out of it. So what to do?
>
> . . . Lawrence who was still hurting from the treatment he got in Big Sur just shrugged and said it was typical of Jack's disposition at that point. . . .
>
> Gregory—charmingly as ever—said something like, we've got to have both sides of the story, Jack's is one, etc. Anyhow we were all, I think, put off by Jack's adamant impatience with anything that confronted "law and order" in such manner as the young then did. . . . General consensus was that Jack had come a bleak long way from the person we'd all once known.

It was otherwise a good weekend visit, and the weather was moderate. We took a group photograph toward the side of the sloping front yard overlooking Ed's meadow. In back stands tee-shirted Julius, arms close to body as if noticing a slight chill. Ferlinghetti, beret capping head, looks straight into camera. I'm in bowl haircut; at my left, Allen in new blue denim jacket. He's elbow-to-elbow with Creeley next to him, being careful (maybe both are) not to impose any palsy-walsy arm-around-the-shoulder that might intrude on the other. Allen's alert, interested, dignified; Creeley has his own one-eyed dignity, dress shirt buttoned at top. Down in front, next to dogs Sadeyes and Radha, are Gregory and Peter. Corso, on tilting white lawn chair, huddles in buckskin jacket. Peter, in blanket-draped rocking chair from front porch, has turned his face from camera to dogs, as if to call or speak.

Within a day or so the pleasant gathering broke up. Ferlinghetti bussed to New York, and the morning of Tuesday, October 21, Creeley drove back to Buffalo.

Shortly after he left, Gregory and Peter and I were down in the kitchen with Allen, near the little round three-legged telephone table and big Kalamazoo. It was mid-morning. What happened next took just a few minutes, but has frozen in memory:

The phone rings.

Allen answers. He seems to be listening very closely and talks a little, intermittently. Solemnly, calmly, quietly. I don't know who's calling, though I'll learn it's Al Aronowitz. I hear Allen say "Stella." I know it has something to do with Kerouac.

After a short spell Allen rises from the little chair at the table, receiver next to phone.

Peter and Gregory and I remain standing on the kitchen linoleum, fixed, watching him.

He takes a couple of steps toward us, into the center of the kitchen. He says, "Jack Kerouac is dead. Earlier this morning. Internal bleeding." Then he returns to the phone. Solemn, calm, quiet.

Then Gregory gets on the line, and begins sobbing, sobbing, sobbing. He recalls his most affectionate moments with Jack: "Yes, I was Raphael, he was the saint."

The rest of us talk quietly a few more minutes. Then I notice as he walks toward the dining room table that Allen's eye is moist, there's a single tear on his cheek.

He continues speaking very quietly, and being silent too.

Later that afternoon Allen and Gregory went for a walk, and carved Jack's initials on a tree above the house, "in the name of American poetry," Gregory said. Allen spent much of the time on the phone; later Gregory came up to me: "Let's go down to the liquor store, Gordon, and get some good stuff. We're not gonna drink rotgut tonight; my friend has died!" We got into the Olds, left for town.

By six in the evening, we were back in the kitchen and Gregory was mixing martinis, handing them out grandly in cup and glass and mug. Even Julius took one. Gregory's mood had turned expansive. He slapped me on the back and said to Allen and Peter, "Oh, he's really one of the family, now, isn't he? This kid's one of us now!"

The next day I drove the three of them through the rain to the Albany airport, past Memory's Garden, a cemetery on the edge of Albany whose name Allen would adapt for the title of a poem written in the aftermath of death and funeral.

Allen had a scheduled reading at Yale that night; he and Peter and Gregory would go on to Lowell from New Haven. At the ticket counter, there was some confusion as Allen asked for the tickets—reserved just the day before—for his companions: Gregory in large hand-me-down overcoat, Peter long-haired and bearded in red felt hat, farm duds.

In those days you could make such late arrangements more easily, much less expensively than today. But now, at the counter, there seemed to be some of sort of problem, and Allen, in denim and corduroy, red-and-white Greek bag on shoulder, became flustered. Two middle-aged women stood immediately behind, staring at him and his pals.

The matter was put to rest within a couple of minutes, and so, tickets in hand, we turned to walk away. As we did, I heard one woman exclaim to the other: "You wouldn't think they could afford to fly!"

THREE

Life Goes On

Death's Aftermath

1:30 AM, OCT. 22, 1969, some fifteen hours after learning of Jack's death, Allen recorded:

> *Two watches ticking in the dark, fly buzz at the black window, telephone calls all day to Florida and Old Saybrook, Lucien, Creeley, Louis—"drinking heavily" and "your letter made him feel bad" said Stella—*
>
> *All last nite . . . in bed brooding re Kerouac's "After Me, the Deluge" at middle of morning watch I woke realizing he was right, that the meat suffering in the middle of existence was a sensitive pain greater than any political anger or hope, as I also lay in bed dying*
>
> *Walking with Gregory in bare treed October ash woods—winds blowing brown sere leafs at feet—talking of dead Jack—the sky an old familiar place with fragrant eyebrow clouds passing overhead in Fall Current. . . .*
>
> *At dusk I went out to the pasture & saw thru Kerouac's eyes the sun set on the first dusk after his death.*
>
> *Didn't live much longer than beloved Neal—another year & half—*
>
> *Gregory woke at midnite to cry—he didn't really want to go so soon—from the attick—*

Ten or so hours after Allen made that entry, I saw him and Peter and Gregory off at the Albany airport. Back on East Hill, I wrote a friend who once admired Kerouac, telling how I'd thought of him on October 21.

I soon discovered that my excitable pal was outraged. Shortly after sending him my letter, I received a single-spaced typed seventeen-inch-long sheet. He began by saying he'd started to write me, too, but soon launched into a condemnation of Allen, accusing him "and his whole entourage" of murder. It asked me to "kindly tell him" there's "one not-so-dumb kid out here" who sees the self-glorification Allen revels in publicly as he leaves his old friend behind—to die. "He [Kerouac] was weak, he was limited as an artist, he possessed a third-rate intellect and absolutely no discipline," my friend offered.

When Allen returned from funeral days in Lowell and a stop in New York, he told me that Kerouac, dead and embalmed, "looked like a doll" in his coffin. And I showed him my friend's letter. "He sounds like some of his critics," he observed as he came to his judgment of Kerouac.

Vietnam Again

O N THE TRIP to Lowell, Gregory had managed to score some Seconal. Before long he was in as bad shape as I'd seen him since the summer of 1968, stumbling up and down the stairs. He'd taken thirteen capsules at once, he claimed, and began hassling Peter and me. Clumsily. Droolingly.

Late one afternoon in the kitchen, Gregory in fringed buckskin started screaming at Peter. Peter took it awhile, then grabbed him by the back of his leather collar, hauled him out the door, and lobbed him onto the flagstones immediately in front of the house. I saw Gregory's head hit stone. He soon—amazingly—picked himself up, seemingly without serious injury, and quietly re-entered the house. He left within a couple days.

A week later—mid-November—a postcard addressed to "Gordon and Peter" arrived from New Mexico. Its brief message began without a greeting:

Thanks for my stay there—sorry if I came on sick but all is well now—We'll see you Xmass for sure—

Love,
Gregory

Of course, our interpersonal strife on East Hill wasn't even a pale shadow of the larger violence on planet Earth. As Gregory's enduring friend Allen had written earlier, after the night Peter yelled at both Allen and Julius, "If Peter & I can't get along, how can Jews & Arabs? How can any war end?"

Though many Americans appeared to support our war, resistance was intensifying. Nixon had been elected promising peace on a "secret plan"; so far, along with the start of Vietnamization, two troop withdrawals totaling 60,000 men were being carried out; later in the fall, his re-instatement of a draft lottery would take effect. But he'd also begun his secret, illegal "Operation Menu" bombing of Cambodia, which would unload twice the tonnage of bombs dropped on Japan in World War II. Reports surfaced of troop unrest, including racial antagonism, low morale, resistance to combat orders, "fragging" of officers, and use of quality drugs from the region. More Americans and Asians were being killed; South Vietnamese government and troops alike appeared increasingly less capable and respectable. Ho Chi Minh's death in early September left North Vietnam unfazed—as did Nixon's threats of even more severe aggression.

A new strategy was now manifest within the antiwar movement: involve all the people in expressing opposition. On October 15, a nationwide Moratorium had taken place: huge gatherings in cities; ringing of church bells; candlelight vigils; reading the names of Americans dead; chanting "Give Peace a Chance."

Asked in late September about the coming protest, Nixon had boasted, "Under no circumstances will I be affected whatever by it." Five days before the national observance, he'd declared, "I'm not going to be the first American president to lose a war." On Moratorium Day, peaceful demonstrators, including Coretta Scott King, appeared en masse before the White House.

A far smaller, far different demonstration had been held a week earlier in Chicago. The Weathermen, vowing to "bring the war home" with a "Second Battle of Chicago," carried out violent protests designed to fulfill the promise of Chicago 1968. Beginning on the second anniversary of Che Guevara's death, a few hundred young men and women trashed property in the exclusive Gold Coast area of the city. On East Hill we discussed the report of some of the helmeted young "Women's Militia" breaking into tears as they struggled with police. Allen exclaimed, "How tender!"

The huge demonstrations of October 15 had seemed to tell Nixon he couldn't ignore a strengthening antiwar movement's demand for a much quicker end to war. Then on November 3, claiming that complete withdrawal without time and deliberation would bring a "disaster of immense magnitude," Nixon made—according to polls taken afterward—a highly effective speech to the nation. He pleaded:

> To you, the great silent majority of my fellow Americans—I ask for your support. Let us be united for peace. Let us be united against defeat. Because let us understand: North Vietnam cannot defeat or humiliate the United States. Only Americans can do that.

I greatly resented this punch below the belt which further divided our nation as it dishonored millions of Americans who wanted the killing stopped now. But the move proved popular, and was only the beginning: the inaccuracy of the concept "silent majority" was soon followed by numerous other obscurantist phrases appealing to ignorance and ill-will, including the depiction of war protestors as "an effete corps of impudent snobs." Month after coming month, these epithets were mouthed by Vice President Spiro T. Agnew in his attacks on dissent and the nation's media.

△ Allen at the organ, August 1969. Right edge of frame, Peter's abdomen above shorts with dish towel tucked in.

△ Edge of front yard: Ed Urich (gesturing), Allen to the right. Dogs Radha (left) and her father, Godly. August 1970.

△ Farmhouse from front yard with flagstones, front porch (Peter's room is immediately to rear), Ed's clematis trellis rising from flower bed. Woodshed we built extends from right rear of Peter's room. Attic dormer window, above bed where Barbara (and later the Bremsers) slept, is open. Allen made altar at foot of bed after Barbara left. August 1970.

△ Herbert Huncke, Allen Ginsberg, New Year's, 1976, Allen's East 12th Street apartment.

◁ October 18 or 19, 1969. Front yard, facing up toward Ed Urich's. Rear, left to right: Julius Orlovsky, Lawrence Ferlinghetti, Gordon Ball, Allen Ginsberg, Robert Creeley. Front: dogs Sadeye and daughter Radha; Gregory Corso, Peter Orlovsky.

△ At Albert Hall, London, after press conference to announce the International Poetry Reading to be held there. Left to right: Allen Ginsberg, Barbara Rubin, Kate Heliczer (back to camera) Michael Horovitz, Simon Watson-Taylor, Lawrence Ferlinghetti. June 1965.

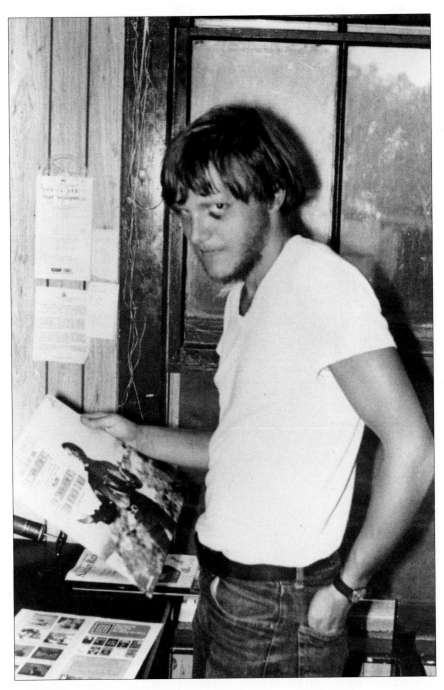

△ Gordon with black eye, July 1970.

△ Autumn 1969. Gregory in New Mexico buckskin; Gordon in brogans and overalls, in front of house on flagstones.

△ February 1971: Peter with Shiva and kid in living room; recording tapes, gerbil cage, KLH stereo on shelves.

◁ Candy and Gordon in backyard, summer 1968.

▽ Kitchen, August 1970. Julius stands at gas stove, perhaps boiling more hot water for drinking. To left, Kalamazoo wood and coal stove.

△ March 1973: Gordon Ball, Allen Ginsberg, East Hill front yard, two years after I left. Allen had recently slipped on ice on flagstones, broken leg.

△ Peter and Allen, March 1973.

△ My wife-to-be Kathleen, myself, Julius Orlovsky, upper front yard, November 1974.

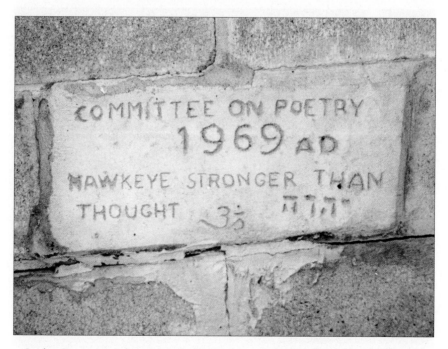

△ Stephen Bornstein's "plaque" inscribed in ram house wall at conclusion of our work, summer 1969.

△ My cartoon of a winter 1969 moment at the farm: Allen in Kalamazoo College sweatshirt on phone; Lee Crabtree in overcoat; Julius in tee-shirt blows smoke rings and drinks hot liquid; Malcolm cat totters; Tiger cat defecates while eating; Peter massages dog.

△ Allen and Gregory, summer 1970, front porch with Ed's clematis trellis.

△ Attic, facing south, c. 1973.

△ Allen at work at dining room table, daisy print tablecloth. On wall, poster of twelvefold cycle of interdependent co-origination; piano at rear, c. 1973.

△ Allen at the chopping block, kitchen table, liquid propane range to left. Summer 1970.

△ Peter Orlovsky at chicken house, July 1970; Allen behind him, leaning into doorway. "Ed's meadow" at left. In her earliest days Don't Bite Me the pig was kept in Peter and Denise's room in one of the two wooden cages.

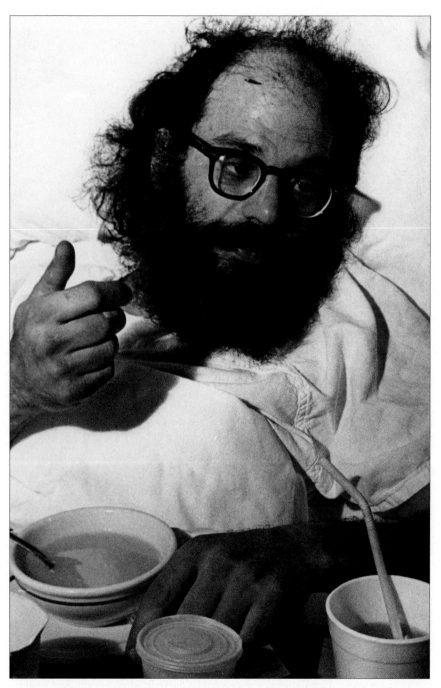

△ Allen in Albany Memorial Hospital bed after car crash, c. November 30, 1968.

△ Carl Solomon atop haystack, August 1970. 8-millimeter frame enlargement.

△ Assembling windcharger, June 1970. From top: Rosebud's friend Andy; Ray Bremser (shirtless). Extreme lower left of frame: Peter Orlovsky's hands, with electric cable and metal clamp. Lower center: Allen Ginsberg, with raised index finger; Rosebud; to right, Rose's father Juan Feliu. 8-millimeter frame enlargement.

△ Allen and his *New York Times*, "vegetarian" shoe with crepe sole, green rocker from front porch. Ed Urich in background under maple tree approaches from his meadow. Late August or early September 1970. 8-millimeter frame enlargement.

△ Ed's Billy, with five-foot-wide horns. 8-millimeter frame enlargement.

△ Stephen Bornstein and Bessie. Late summer 1968.

Such was the battle for America's heart. A second moratorium November 13–15 brought out even greater numbers of Americans in generally much worse weather. In Washington 40,000 marched silently from Arlington National Cemetery to the White House, each bearing a candle and a sign with the name of a slain American or a destroyed Vietnamese village. *Village Voice* writer Clarence Funnye described part of that evening:

> Hour after hour names were called out into the night, slicing through the cold rainy air across the helmets of marines guarding their President from his people, then bouncing with just a faint, faint echo off the wet, white walls of the White House.

That same day, the story of the massacre at My Lai twenty months earlier appeared at last in print.

□ □ □

IN TINY ECKER Hollow near Cobleskill, a mother received a letter from her son recently arrived in Vietnam, giving his address; the same day, a telegram announced his death. Clarence Baldwin, whose death was Cherry Valley's first, was awarded the Conspicuous Service Cross fifteen months later. His mother accepted the medal, which came with a ribbon and a certificate.

In the press, the moratoriums weren't playing well. There were ads for "Our President's Program for Vietnam," and in "Working for Peace?" Cobleskill's *Times Journal* editorialized:

> We weren't happy to read the Communistic propaganda passed out by students at the peace Moratorium. . . . We wonder if the students realized just what the words meant which they had signed their names to.
>
> Two [sic] quote a few sentences, "Imperialism is the system by which the American ruling class uses military and police force to insure economic and political control over the people of the world. . . . America's biggest mistake . . . black people are forced to fight a war that is not theirs; is the most barbarous fascist means to sow terror and carry out mass slaughter . . . a civil war between north and south but the U.S. is an aggressor with no cause.
>
> ". . . It is up to us to bring the government of the United States to its knees. . . . to support the stopping of the war in Viet Nam at all cost. . . ."

. . . We can't believe that the majority of our young people would fall for this Communistic propaganda. . . . We suggest that they remove themselves from our midst—we don't want them. Perhaps they would find a bigger welcome in Hanoi.

Weeks later, Second Lieutenant Terrance Graves, twenty-two, who grew up in Otsego County and played baseball for Cooperstown, was awarded the Medal of Honor posthumously, for saving Marine comrades under fire. He had a fiancée; he'd been head of the National Honor Society chapter and a star athlete in high school. His father, once an officer in the Navy, had been principal at Edmisten Central School, to which he'd returned a month earlier for the funeral of one of his former students, also killed in Vietnam.

Lieutenant Graves's medal was presented to his family, with his fiancée present, in Washington. The presentation was made by Vice President Spiro T. Agnew.

Bessie's Callers

F OR SEVERAL WEEKS we'd had a problem with Bessie: she'd stopped giving milk after her calf Jennifer was weaned. When Claude Graham explained that we had to get her pregnant for production to resume, we invited a local bull to visit.

Gingerly we ushered Bessie's hornèd hombre, her massive mate-to-be, down the aisle of the barn and into that last stall on the left. In its corner stood Bessie, watching in silence. We latched the railinged door. The space enclosed was small, but Bessie began walking away from her guest, sidestepping him. The bull, studious and determined, kept approaching her, trying to mount but slipping off, trying to mount but slipping off; every time she slithered out from under. He nearly broke the railing as his half-ton of muscle and water and blood and bone thundered and caromed against wood and earth. Reluctantly, we brought the visit to an end.

So what to do? We were stymied. Ed said it was time for an artificial inseminator. And so—the connection made by phone—Mr. Edward S. Egnaczyk drove up in his truck. He handed us a hardbound volume of pictures of numerous stud bulls, accompanied by identifications and descriptions.

Can you judge a bull by its looks? Predict its priapic performance? We looked over the weighty anthology, puzzling at page after page of mighty images: who would be best for our Bessie? (Did she, especially after her recent experience, even want anyone at this point?) And how could we tell? One bull looked as good as . . .

Peter solved the problem. He took the stud book over to Bessie. Raising it before her face, he told her to pick the one she liked best. "Come on, Bessie, give the one you like a nice little lick, just a little lick now, my girl, tell us, tell Petey with your great big wet red tongue, oh yass!" he urged. Bessie turned from eyeing the flies that flew away as her tail swiped them off her back, and did literally let those great huge eyeballs in all their liquid living shining darkness roll up toward what was being held inches above her broad wet nose. Keeping the book erect, Peter began turning pages, slowly, one at a time, giving her a good look at one before going on to the next. I have no idea what Mr. Egnaczyk, standing there silent in rain hat, rubber boots, and horn-rimmed glasses, thought. But we watched, amazed, as our Jersey Bessie did raise her head slightly, open her mouth, unroll her large bright tongue, and make contact with one glossy page bearing the image of one impressive fellow.

Inside of a week Mr. E. was back, insemination apparatus in hand; far better than his mighty predecessor, this modest fellow carried out his mission. I wrote him a check for $7; by late next summer Bessie had a newborn calf.

Late Autumn on East Hill

P ETER HAD LONG had a special relationship with Bessie. Often he'd nuzzle her, hand-feed her ears of corn, and kiss her, uttering lovey-doveys. And when Miles, done with post-production for Allen's album, was up briefly in the fall, he recorded a special in-house visit:

> Yesterday Bessie the cow came into the kitchen and had some cake, fed to her by ecstatic Peter who kissed her and slapped her all over. Even Julie smiled. Bessie ate some red apples before leaving. Her shy calf wouldn't come in but peered frightened round the open kitchen door with sad brown eyes, a little perpetual tear on her cheek, the sadness of cows.

While Peter cooed and cackled over his special guest, Allen kept exclaiming, "Take her out, take her out! She mustn't come in here! She'll come in again without being asked!"

Autumn 1969 on East Hill, with the exception of Kerouac's death and the interlude of difficulties with Gregory, was mostly quiet. Huncke had stayed two months, kicking, virtually without incident. He stole six of fifteen Darvons I'd been prescribed for a back injury; I shrugged it off, "That's Huncke."

□ □ □

TWICE, UNINVITED STRANGERS showed up. One unusually warm autumn night— late, about 11:00—several hippies pulled up in a car, asking to enter the house. We were still downstairs.

Allen didn't complain at the intrusion. He invited them to sit with us at the dining room table, under amber gaslight, then asked them—one or two women, one or two men—their purpose.

"We wanted to ask you for $1,000. We want to organize our lives, get a farm, settle down. That's how we'll use it."

I sat there listening, watching, struck by their audacity, wondering how Allen would respond. And wondering too if some less benign purpose could be afoot.

"I don't have $1,000," Allen told them. It was true, of course. After putting up the $10,000 to make the Blake record, he'd borrowed nearly $3,000 from Peter.

Thanks to Miles's arrangement, that $10,000 would be reimbursed—but it hadn't happened yet.

With strangers walking in with such a bold request so late at night, I would've expected some friction, but as Allen continued talking calmly with the uninviteds, I began to realize there'd be none. Eventually, they left.

Another evening we were surprised by a young man around twenty, slender in dark hair and glasses, accompanied by his mother, who introduced him as "brilliant." Apparently they simply wanted to connect with Allen and one or two other "heavies" (Marshall McLuhan in Toronto was the next intended victim), so the boy could be presented, demonstrate his brilliance, and thereby have a base for further communication, a leg up in the world. As with the hippie group, Allen remained calm, tolerant, and, if without enthusiasm, welcoming. I never heard of mother or son again.

Not that I sought to. I had, of course, my own preoccupations. I was now half-done editing my diaristic film on East Hill Farm. In silent regular 8-millimeter, I could edit on a single viewer with rewinds in my room: all was manual and mechanical, except the small bulb inside the viewer, which took batteries.

At the same time, I was continuing to try to get my Camex movie camera back from repair in France: despite Robert Frank's call in late June, it hadn't arrived. In mid-July, I'd written Saint-Lazare Réparations in Paris, and received an answer nearly two months later: on the Frank call their employee had misunderstood my name, confusing me with another client, but now I could rest assured that my camera would be sent in perfect working order, air mail, the end of July. Finally Allen's Miami lawyer friend Ricky Smith wrote, demanding repair of camera or return of payments I'd already made along with $400, the value of the camera. (Eventually—I don't know how many more months—I got my Camex back. Repaired.)

What did uninvited guests and my efforts to get my camera have in common? Allen's attitude: of tolerance toward strangers, even intrusive and foolish ones; of generosity toward friends, which doubtless played a role in how people who were originally his friends treated me. I don't think I was a generous person; nevertheless, through Allen's example, in ways direct and indirect, I began—slowly—to change.

□ □ □

JUST A LITTLE older than I, Jim Bell was a friend of Creeley's and had shown up on his recommendation. He was quite tall, all-American looking with short red curly hair and freckles, in good shape from years of carpentry and construction. Peter, who insisted on arm wrestling him, lost both match and rematch.

Pete and I were shocked when Jim said his pay would be $5.00 an hour (minimum wage was $1.30), but his work, which we assisted, was good. He stayed most of a month, helping with a range of projects including adding support to the ram house. He reinforced the barn by installing a turnbuckle, a large metal belt device depending on tightly screwed tension to keep hayloft walls from collapsing.

Personally, he was cheery and easy to get along with, and playful too. He'd tease Denise by making scary sounds of a vampire bat late at night. "Whomp whump whomp whump," he'd sound in the dark from one end of the house, just loud enough to be heard—and then hear the frightened eighteen-year-old's delighted titter. And he was good for community relations: he joined the Cherry Valley basketball team, scoring as much as seventy-four points in one game. And his team play brought an additional opportunity for Jim, a rare one for any resident of East Hill Farm: showers. Warm showers.

□ □ □

ONE DAY A letter arrived for Allen from Huncke, whom he was trying to help get into a methadone program. He began:

What can I say that will make any sense regarding Jack. Poor Jack—who should still be alive. Oh well—such is the way of this whole business—it never makes sense—I'm still around and Jack is gone.

I called the "Farm" recently and spoke with Gordon. I had nothing of any significance to speak of—just wanted to say hello.

Huncke asked Allen to "call tonight *whenever* you arrive home": "it doesn't make any difference about the hour." Closing, he urged, "Please call"; a postscript pleaded, "Call *without fail. Please.*"

□ □ □

MEANWHILE, WAR AND resistance to it persisted; the trial for the Chicago Eight had begun, with many lesser-known individuals also being jailed for their efforts to stop our country's aggression. On a related front, severe penalties for even the possession of marijuana were being enforced upon many thousands. I thought—assuming all of us on East Hill didn't get locked up!—I should prepare for the possibility of visiting friends in jail. How to ensure ease of access to lethally guarded cold steel fluorescent-lit interiors?

In underground press ads I'd noticed that a church—Universal Life, Inc., in Modesto, California—offered mail-order ordinations: you simply asked for the ordination certificate, filled in name and date, and returned it: you'd get back your ordination, signed by the Reverend Kirby J. Hensley, Doctor of Divinity. The Church explained itself:

> *The ULC has no doctrine itself. It only believes in that which is right. We believe that everyone has a right to his own conviction and a right to express it. We recognize everyone's belief.*

That, I thought, is for me. In a matter of weeks, I became a minister.

Not that I was then satisfied. Anxieties and yearnings showed in other directions, and I put pen to them, too—and even spoke of them to Allen. I was depressed, and didn't know what to do about it: what did he do under such circumstances?

"The first thing I do every morning when I get up," he answered, "is make my bed."

□ □ □

MY ANXIETY, HOWEVER, persisted. I woke one morning feeling bad about something I'd done in college. Running the student union film program (which, with such works as Jack Smith's *Flaming Creatures*, generated some controversy on that Presbyterian campus), I was in a sometimes unfriendly relationship with union staff. When they shipped a feature film back to its distributor before showdate, I angrily displayed a poster, explaining that we couldn't show Agnes Varda's *Cleo from 5 to 7* because of their "incredible incompetence." Now, realizing my harsh error, I wrote a letter of apology, and, forgiven, felt better.

But life for this needy Narcissus remained psychologically unsettled: there was my on-again off-again love life; there was the larger question of what I was doing in life itself. Should I make adapting to Peter Orlovsky my life's work? Though Peter already seemed better thanks to Denise, what if he should return to amphetamine mania? Though I loved Allen and for that matter greatly admired Peter in certain ways, I yearned for women; staying on the farm didn't offer the opportunity of meeting many. And wasn't I curious, at twenty-four, about seeing some of the rest of the world—if not getting to Persia, returning to Japan?

Back in the summer of 1967, at Shirley Clarke's rooftop party at the Chelsea, Candy and I had met an executive with Columbia Motion Pictures in Chicago. Hitching through the Midwest a couple months later en route to Mexico, we stayed with Jack Scanlon. Now, in the uncertainty of my future at the farm I wrote our well-placed friend, explaining I "wanna explore the planet before I'm old," but also asking if I might "work for Columbia in some capacity."

Meanwhile, I maintained or renewed contact with lady friends. Or made new ones: former Davidson art instructor Preston Faggart, now working in a Santa Claus photo studio for the Christmas season, left his bohemian apartment uptown for a short weekend, bringing with him his neighbor Ella Radocy. It proved good all around: when he left, Preston took one of little tortoise shell Panda Manda kitties with him, then wrote how he loved everyone there. Meantime pretty Ella—a student at CCNY, so pretty I kissed her at first sight, right in front of Crain's Pharmacy—and I made plans to meet again.

I kept in irregular touch with Saralee Stafford, the striking young woman who spun heads at our softball game in June. As I look now at her letters from summer and fall 1969—little stationery cards adorned with floral paisleys—it's hard to figure why I apparently didn't ask her back. Though there were gaps in her correspondence as well as mention of a roundtrip to California and an unspecified medical problem, there were also lines like, "Meanwhile write often—even though I don't I think about you often," and, "Whenever you want me to come back to visit with you & milk the goats—call or write & I'll be there."

Before Christmas, she was in Sausalito.

□ □ □

I'D KNOWN FOR a long time that a former girl friend, Anna Marie Felner, lived in Syracuse, where she'd moved from Charlotte, North Carolina, and our first meetings when I was at Davidson.

She'd gone to Syracuse University, then dropped out and worked for the large insurance company Mutual of New York. I'd spent much of summer 1966 with her, but when I left for New York in September, I thought our parting was for good—and soon I was taken up with Candy, psychedelics, Jonas Mekas, and much else.

Now, over three years later, nearly a year after Candy's departure, I thought of Anna Marie more frequently: her long blonde hair, green cat-like eyes, pale skin—the good times we'd had, notwithstanding the bad. She was straighter than I, not appreciative of drugs—except alcohol. But she was only eighty miles away: I didn't let differences stop me.

I wrote in early November, and heard back shortly: she was working in New York the rest of the month, and would then return to Syracuse, where she lived with her mother. Would I like to spend the first December weekend there?

Enter Bremser, Enter Snyder:
A Happy Thanksgiving

" **J** UST LOOK FOR a Bowery bum."

The second week of November, Allen was off again on fund-raising readings, and poet Ray Bremser was due on East Hill. Allen's goodhearted characterization—so I'd recognize Ray down at the bus—had come just before his departure.

A week earlier, Allen had received the following from Saint Lucy County Jail, Fort Pierce, Florida:

> Bonnie has left me & the State Department flew me to Miami—i'm destitute & in a bit of trouble—my Mother is dead. You are my only friend; so, forgive me for imposing again—i need some money to pay fines for drunk/disorderly & Breaking the Peace. $150 dollars would cover it, and the fare to New York—I'd never be able to get thru georgia & the Carolinas in my shape—had an accident in Guatemala, broken shoulder, 4 ribs, elbow, little finger & sprains:
>
> Please help me return to New York—i'll pay you back because i'm going to work when i'm back in the city. Necessary you send Money Orders, if possible!
>
> Let me know soon—sorry again, but desperate:
>
> > hope you are well,
> > i'm anxious to see & hear
> > you again,
> >
> > > Best love,
> > > Ray

Neither Allen nor I knew that Ray's mother Gertrude remained very much alive in New Jersey.

□ □ □

FROM AGE EIGHTEEN, Ray had spent some years in reformatory and prison on charges including armed robbery. In the fall of 1969 he'd returned to the U.S. from Guatemala, where he and wife Bonnie and daughter Georgia had gone months before, and was most recently in a Florida jail on a lesser count.

I was sitting on a black leather-topped stool visiting with friendly Bert Crain behind his soda fountain counter when the big, broad-windshielded Greyhound shuddered to a stop out front. Its accordion door whooshed open, and out stepped a tall, skinny, hatchet-faced man with dark curly hair and beard going grey, long limbs covered by a worn-looking overcoat. With him was Barbara, a somewhat pretty younger woman he introduced as "my nurse." From the first Bremser was friendly, outgoing, animated, jovial.

Back in 1967 I'd seen an ad for his second book, *Angel*, in *The Village Voice*. The "Angel" was Bonnie. Daughter of an undersecretary in the Department of Commerce, she was to eventually join us as she also made her way back from Guatemala with their two-year-old child.

There was much in the way of history I didn't know: at Bremser's Hoboken apartment Allen had listened to Ray Charles ("blues shout blind on the phonograph") shortly before writing the main part of *Kaddish*. Nor had I noted Dylan's nod to Ray in the "11 Outlined Epitaphs" jacket sleeve of his *The Times They Are A-Changin'*: ". . . love songs of Allen Ginsberg / an' jail songs of Ray Bremser / the narrow tunes of Modigliani. . . ."

In person, Ray was vivid and unforgettable, manifesting the features acclaimed in his poetry: "mouth-blow," Allen once characterized it; "powerful curious Hoboken language, crank-blat phrasing" that demonstrated his "spectacular oral gifts among contemporary poets." Soon, around our dining room table, outdoors, or in the car, our new resident could be found in typical high dithyrambic mode—whatever the subject at hand.

He was generous with his poems, and in coming months wrote a couple—one entitled "The Noble All" ("for Gordon Ball")—that he gave to me. And, as suggested in various references in his poetry, his mother occupied a special place in his heart. When Thanksgiving neared, Ray left to join her for the holiday.

Meanwhile Allen had most recently been back in the New York area, reading at Princeton, Great Neck, and St. Mark's Church before connecting with Gary Snyder. Sandwiched between Gotham Book Mart reception and party at computer genius David Padwa's, they read together at the 92nd Street Y. It was the first time Allen and Gary had seen each other since Snyder's return from his dozen years in Japan. Now Gary would join us for the holiday.

Also en route was Stephen Bornstein, who was continuing technical illustration work, and film editor friend Margaret Horwath. Lexicographer David Rattray joined the attic crew for a night or two. And Huncke, leaving his small narrow Broadway

Central room, was making a grand return with two middle-aged women, R'lene Dahlberg (who, divorced from novelist Edward Dahlberg, taught English at Peter Stuyvesant High) and art historian Ela Kokkinen. The three drove up in R'lene's white convertible, bringing a great big turkey with them.

It was always good seeing Huncke; in a sense, he never took his leave of you. Perhaps as much as any other character, he clung, not in his alleged parasitism, but his color: his rich, intimate midnight voice, his confidence, warmth; those hazel eyes meeting yours, his lore, his curiosity—his endless storytelling. He was a chameleon, infinitely adaptable, infinitely himself, from prison to penthouse to dive, from east Texas lowland farm with Burroughs in the '40s to the top of East Hill with the rest of us a generation later.

Peter (Denise returned home for the holiday) and I spent much of an evening preparing for guests, making beds with fresh sheets, cleaning the house. Such relatively personalized housekeeping was a rare event on East Hill, and it was still somewhat unusual for Peter and me to be working together. I asked Pete to do his special "hospital ties" on the sheets, and he asked for help in clearing space, rearranging furniture.

Once Huncke settled down on Jonas's old Danish modern sofa in the living room, he wanted to know what was new. I was as shy and brooding as ever, and could be hesitant with even the most general question put me directly—but not if it came from Huncke.

"Well, the best news I've got is Denise," I said, alluding to the difference she'd made with Peter. Huncke nodded in affirmation and we continued to chat, the circle expanding as R'lene and Ela joined us.

Only the next day did I learn that Huncke had brought Allen and Peter Thanksgiving gifts.

"Huncke gave me a bag of junk last night," Allen told me, grinning, "and so I took my annual shot of junk."

I was dumbfounded. All this time we'd been struggling to keep the house free of needle drugs—at Allen's insistence—and then he so casually accepted this from the arch-culprit to whom he'd read the riot act again and again? But I held my tongue.

Huncke was presumably relishing his moment of triumph, the brilliance of his buy-out, when Gary arrived. Stephen, who'd already talked with Gary before I met him, exclaimed to me, "He's so rational!" I remember Snyder saying, as we discussed the music of the day, "I don't see anything wrong with Janis Joplin killing herself to belt out a song, but the great black blues singers didn't have to do that."

Gary was shortish, wiry, small blue ring in left ear, knapsack over shoulder. He had slender, almost Asiatic eyes; his long light brown hair was pulled back. He gave an impression of great physical strength and psychic alertness—and of being at ease with everyone. We showed him around, and Allen took him on walks far and near, up to Ed's, down to the ram. He seemed impressed by the broad lay of the land around the house, the long lower meadow running down to the stream, and the green state forest ridge rising beyond. Rather than feeling cramped by our modest home, Gary—after more than a decade in Japan—appreciated the charm of its smallness, the intimate feeling it gave.

Indoors, he demonstrated the Padmasambhava bowing mantra. He began standing straight up, palms in *gassho* or *namaste* (prayer position) above his forehead. Chanting the mantra—"om ah hum vajra guru padma siddhi hum"—he then made a full prostration down onto our kitchen linoleum.

Near the end of the weekend, he and I and a couple of women who'd recently arrived joined Allen for a small orgy in Allen's room. Though Allen described it two months later in a letter to Whalen as a "big orgy organized by him [Gary]," I remember a small affair with Allen doing some directing: "Get that cigarette out of your mouth!" he exclaimed in the darkness, when one participant, struck by a moment's hesitation, seemed to use her Camel filter as defensive prop. (A year and a half later, when Allen and Gary and I found ourselves in a similar situation, Gary chuckled, "Whenever I'm with you, Allen, things always get sexy. I don't know why that is!")

I don't recall who cooked R'lene and Ela's huge turkey, but everyone at the table seemed in high spirits: Stephen was robust; his friend Margaret was having such a great time she later wrote a thank you note proclaiming it "the most wonderful Thanksgiving weekend I've ever had." R'lene was always smart, convivial; Huncke was Huncke, and Allen his usual calm and generous center. Jim Bell talked with Gary about Buddhism, likening the moment he drops the ball through the net to nirvana.

And it was Jim's birthday; we celebrated with a cake at meal's end. Everyone—Peter and maybe even Julius—was merry; it was worlds away from Thanksgiving 1968.

Anna Marie Again

S OON ALLEN WAS off once more—University of Massachusetts at Amherst, Bard College, and Princeton, where he rejoined Gary. The week following, he'd return to Chicago, testify at the Conspiracy trial.

And one weekend in early December I was heading eighty miles west on Route 20 for two days with Anna Marie. Our relationship from late my junior year of college through summer after graduation had been more rocky than tender. Now—essentially the first time we'd seen each other since—how would things fare? Had I reason to expect anything better? Was it wise even to contact her again?

What was the problem? Coupled with my own insufficiencies (sheltered childhood, selfishness, immaturity), she still suffered her father's desertion when she was a child, and had hoped to marry me, even by hook or crook. And I, still a virgin at twenty, not interested in marriage, but definitely interested in getting laid, had succeeded with her—and found that nice enough indeed. I tried to keep the relationship, after a fashion—if I could resist the marital pressure.

But the togetherness was scarcely real, and after I left for New York in the fall of 1966 and discovered all that was going on there, what little connection might've remained collapsed in great detail. Yet here I was, on a cold December twilight in 1969, knocking at the door of one of many identical two-bedroom apartments in middle-class Kensington Manor, in a Syracuse suburb.

"I always knew you'd come back," she said, taking me indoors. Same long blonde hair; same catlike eyes; same sense of welcome. We had a great weekend, her mother thoughtfully in the distant background. We spent a good part of our time together in bed.

"I could make love to you twenty-three hours a day," I told her at one point.

"And the other hour?"

"Eat," I said.

She'd been raised a Catholic and that had made for some unease with sex. But now she was relaxed and tender, and her blonde hair, green eyes, and pale skin excited me as ever.

Though she was still "straight" in some respects, we had things in common. She liked poetry; we recited some from my copy of Ray Bremser's *Poems of Madness*, particularly the "Blues for Bonnie," with its line "GOD GAVE ME TO BONNIE" about a woman neither of us had met. But her taste in verse was actually more sophisticated; I still have a card she sent six months later, in which she quotes a Creeley poem:

Love comes quietly,
finally, drops
about me, on me,
in the old ways.

What did I know
thinking myself
able to go
alone all the way.

Driving back that Sunday, I wondered what was in store. I still had some doubts about having renewed things, but we'd had such a good time they didn't seem to matter. And I'd invited her to visit me—soon. Yet how could life at East Hill Farm possibly please her? For Anna Marie, who'd seemed moralistic about most drugs, to be stuck (possibly snowbound!) for a weekend or more with people Allen once characterized as "archetypal dope fiends"! And no electricity!

Soon, it seemed, I'd find out.

It Only Grows Worse

WHEN THE FIRST Moratorium was observed in cities and towns across the nation in mid-October, even political prisoners participated—in a courtroom. The Chicago Eight (Seven, after Bobby Seale was bound, gagged, and tried separately) wore black arm bands and carried a large Viet Cong flag. Abbie Hoffman also carried a small American flag; David Dellinger attempted to read the names of Illinois victims of the war.

On this as many other occasions, the sympathies of seventy-four-year-old judge Julius Hoffman were clearly with the prosecution; he allowed nothing he perceived as anti-government in his courtroom. When Allen appeared, the marvel was as much in the behavior of Hoffman and Chief Prosecutor Thomas Foran, as it was in Allen's calm, generosity, and accuracy. At times Judge and Prosecutor seemed like giggling little boys; at others they were willfully, scoldingly uncomprehending of the witness's lucid remarks, recitations of verse from memory, demonstrations of "Om" and "Hare Krishna," and patient explanations. Allen's words, akin to Dylan's theme in "The Times They Are A-Changin'," went defiantly unheeded.

Following testimony, Allen returned to his fourth floor walk-up in New York, where he composed liner notes for Blake music fueled by Chicago Apocalypse 1968. He held to his vision of Blake's idealized, pacific Albion blooming into life, charged by poetry's power to free it from the crushing machinery of war and "mind-forged manacles." But by late 1969, things weren't going well for counter-culture or New Left: the wonder of Woodstock was accompanied by the locking away of John Sinclair for a decade, and the second of the two enormously successful Moratoriums took place as the FBI arrested four in their twenties and thirties for bombing eight city buildings. Hell's Angels guards murdered a man at the Rolling Stones' Altamont concert; Chicago police killed Black Panther Fred Hampton and others while they slept.

Then, one December evening on East Hill, Allen and I got into the old grey-and-white Olds and I drove him to the bus for the city and further readings. As we waited inside Crain's hospitable pharmacy, we gazed upon the magazine rack. The cover of the new *Life* magazine, a black-and-white close-up of the recently arrested Charles Manson, highlighted his eyes' eerie gleam. Its heading announced "The Love and Terror Cult" and listed its contents:

The man who was their leader
The charge of multiple murder
The dark edge of hippie life

"Shit!" Allen said. "Now Manson's blown the scene for everyone."

South at Christmas

A S 1969 NEARED its end, Allen and I—separately—headed for the Southland. In Miami to read with his father, he was cut short at a benefit for a local underground journalist convicted of obscenity when authorities, thinking they heard obscenity in Allen's poetry, pulled the plug. Allen sued the city, won, and gave a full reading a week later.

I headed home for Christmas with family in Winston-Salem, leaving Peter, Denise, Julius, Ray, and Barbara at the farm. If I'd had any hesitation about leaving, or being gone for more than a brief visit, it was surely erased by a letter from my sister Maylee a month earlier. "Dearest Gordon," she began:

> *How about coming for a week including Xmas? We'd all love it, especially Mother &*
> *Daddy—and I hope very much you can ... it is a happy time we'd like to share—also*
> *there are several people I think would enjoy meeting you & vice versa.*
>
> *... it would be very special if you can come—please do and I'll try to bring you*
> *up to date then.*

Her closing word was "Please."

When I answered yes, she wrote again: "The boys said Hallelujah when I told them."

□ □ □

"THE BOYS"—NEPHEWS Louis, fourteen, Paul, twelve, and Steve, five—did seem pleased to see me. When it was warm enough we shot baskets in front of the garage, even little Stevie taking a mighty turn with his enormous orange burden. I listened to music with Louis—early Beatles, Doors—in his room upstairs, where close to his stereo sat a locked glass box with a three-foot boa constrictor on a bed of pebbles. A volunteer at the nearby Nature Science Center, Louis was a budding herpetologist.

I didn't then know the problems created by the presence of his pet, but eventually learned from Maylee: she worried that a boa was in the same house as her infant daughter; furthermore, easygoing Louis sometimes forgot to not only lock but close its box. Even our elderly parents, when they visited, were enlisted in the hunt for the errant boa; once Louis, who bred white mice to feed his pet, allowed a pregnant female to escape; another time as he walked upstairs, white mouse in pocket, the mouse fell out and he unknowingly stepped on it, flattening it and leaving its carcass for Mom to discover.

We all took turns holding baby Missy, just over a year old and pushing about on her own. But what met the eye wasn't the whole story. At six months the little girl had begun experiencing up to 150 seizures a day, intermittently, for four months. After extensive in-hospital examinations, no explanations were offered, but the pediatric neurologist reported that the effect (retardation) of such seizures was typically severe.

Christmas Day itself was near mayhem: portable pachinko machine, radio, new basketball, candies, dozens of other gifts. Maylee, her husband Harold, and I exchanged presents. I gave them the Fantasy LP of *Howl*, with Allen's wonderful declamatory Chicago 1959 reading. I was surprised by much more: a Beatles coloring book, candy, a shirt, cigarettes, a kaleidoscope, and Kenneth Patchen's *Because It Is*.

I may not have been the only one surprised, however. I doubt my sister's conservative husband had much use for *Howl*, special as that recording was. But *Howl* did get a listen on Christmas Day. My brother Edgar and his wife Paula, visiting from Raleigh, came over. Edgar trekked up to my attic-like room and I lowered the black vinyl onto the turntable of the portable player. Edgar, serious, sober, professor of economics at the state university—horn-rims, tweed coat, striped tie—settled down on the nearby bed and listened. We heard the poem's three main parts, then I moved the needle to the "Footnote," which I found so moving. At the end, Edgar exclaimed, "Oh, he's an evangelist!"

My visits with my parents were sad—my father still uncommunicative, aloof; my mother still reserved, but open as a baby bird's mouth compared to my father. Little by little—it wasn't so bad yet—she continued to fail with what we'd be told was Alzheimer's Syndrome. Daisy Belle's grey hair was neatly composed in a bun from weekly trips to the beauty parlor, and she was as poised as ever. But occasionally she had trouble completing sentences or recalling a name, and might stammer as she tried. I sat there, on the comfortable, graceful couch of their new home, or in the hurly-burly of my sister's, not knowing what to do.

For Christmas I gave my mother and father the 1903 Sears Roebuck catalog, recently reissued as nostalgia novelty item. Through an artifact of the world around the time of their births, I hoped for a better connection with them in the present. I don't know that it worked.

At a physical with our family doctor, I mentioned a difficulty I'd had for some time: insomnia. He prescribed something I'd only recently heard of, from Gregory, who'd pronounced it part of his current pharmacopoeia: a tranquilizer called valium. In the course of checking me over Dr. Harris asked, "Do you smoke marijuana?"

"No," I lied.

"That's good, because if you do, you could get hooked."

□ □ □

THE HIGH POINT of my time away from East Hill was yet to come: Ria, a pretty brunette biology major at Wake Forest College. I'd met her when I was at Davidson and she an eager fourteen; we corresponded, but I held myself back. Now for both of us restraint flew out the window.

We had a mad Christmas night, the next day and the next night before I headed north. We were ecstatic, sex seemed as good as it could ever get, again and again, and we spoke of her coming up to East Hill in spring and summer.

While we were together I played a recent 45 rpm record, "*Je t'aime . . . moi non plus*" by Jane Birkin and Serge Gainsbourg (it had been written by Gainsbourg for Brigitte Bardot, with whom he'd first recorded it). Against a sort of French-night-club instrumental theme one hears a female and a male voice, close-up and intimate, beginning with the female:

"*Je t'aime! Je t'aime! O je t'aime!*"

"*Moi non plus!*"

"*O mon amour!*"

Along with the words comes a track of heavy breathing associated with two people fucking, as well as a melodic vocal, begun by Serge, repeated by Jane: "*Je vais et je viens / Entres tes reins. . . .*" It concludes with Jane's climax at the end, "*O! Mainenant! Bien!*" Silly and sleazy as it may now sound to a fading sexagenarian—not to mention many of today's readers—it was, 1969–1970, "our song."

But soon our romantic, erotic idyll came to an end. Ria, warm, generous, smart, and emotional, would write passionately the next couple of months, before time and distance cooled us both. But now it was a torrid goodbye at the Cherry Street station as the big machine puffed its airbrakes like some humongous cat ready to fight. Then, green duffel squeezed amidst other luggage below, I was aboard, waving goodbye, heading for New York twelve hours away—and the dawn bus to East Hill Farm.

A Surprise Awaits Me

WHILE I WAS gone, one of the worst snowstorms in many years blanketed Cherry Valley. Starting Christmas night, with fourteen inches already on the ground, twenty-eight more fell in a day and a half.

Returning December 30, I was shocked by what I could see through the mud- and snow-spattered Greyhound windshield as we crawled into town. All sidestreets were thick with white; Main Street itself was down to one lane, sandwiched between towering snowbanks, with just enough space shoveled out on one side for parking. Except directly in front of some stores, sidewalks hadn't been cleared. If you wanted to walk anywhere—*sans* snowshoes—one-lane Main Street was the royal road.

From Crain's I called East Hill; Peter said it was still uncleared all the way down to the mailbox. They were snowbound. Assuming I could get there, did they need anything? No, just get yourself back, if you can: they'd stocked up at Victory Market Christmas Day, and we had our own milk and a few eggs.

With Bert Crain's help, I located someone heading out Lancaster Street, which like Main was now single lane. "You can leave your bag here," Crain said, "and come back for it later. You'll have a lot of snow to make your way through." I thanked him and took my ride with good people whose names and faces I've long forgotten.

Getting off at the mailbox, I looked up Wilson Road, that first leg of my journey on foot. It was so deep in white there was no demarcation between roadside brush and the road itself. I set out, uphill, slogging each step through cold snow high as my waist. I was grateful for Crain's thoughtful generosity, and appreciated more than ever the value of snowshoes. Oh for a pair now!

I made it that four-tenths of a mile uphill to Schoolhouse Corners. The worst was over, I thought, because the rest would be more or less on a level or even slightly downhill. As I turned onto Kniskern Road, I thought I could make out, to one side, the dim shape of our big Olds, buried under frozen white.

Once I saw a break in woods lining Kniskern, I cut through for a direct route. I could see our tiny farm at a great white distance. It was cold, maybe just above zero. The sun shone distant from a blue sky, reflecting on the bright snow. I had to squint.

But unlike roads, meadows of course hadn't been cleared. As I started putting one foot down then another, through snow that was now even higher, I sank farther down with every step. I pressed on, but soon began running out of breath. My heart pounded in my ears. The house seemed no closer than on first sight. Lovely as the day was, the scene was desolate and still: no sign of "life" but sun and sky and dormant woody trees and majestic still evergreens and our distant little asbestos-shingled home. The pounding of my heart was relentless. I realized I could die under golden sun and blue sky.

I stopped, undid my parka hood, loosened its tie around my neck, and caught my breath. I waited, then started again—at a slower pace. Finally, fifty feet from the house, Godly came rushing toward me, lightly, over the snow. I made it.

It was my birthday: I was a very young twenty-five years old.

So Here I Am Again

IN SPITE OF the enormous storm all at the farm seemed OK: the barn had its mammal-and-straw-and-manure warmth; Bessie and the goats and Lash were OK; chickens and ducks were surviving in their petite bungalow annex. The ram still ran: I could hear that wonderful reassuring beat in the bathroom. Julius was solemn, no more than usual; Peter and Denise seemed basically jovial; Ray was still there with "nurse" Barbara. (The two couples seemed very separate—but that wasn't a problem, and days of tumultuous Corso appeared long past.) His Miami lawsuit in process, Allen had taken his parents to Haiti for a week—and was on to a couple more readings in the South before returning.

As far as I could tell, any real difficulty lay within me. Full of doubts as to my own situation and future, full of the impact of a week with my family (Ria the exceptionally bright light): my mother's slow decline, my father's remove, the vague sense of disapproval I got or imagined; my sister's middle-class home dominated by more children, one handicapped, than she could manage; dominated above all by her much older husband's laconic disposition. With no discussion of our war countenanced at all: it was the enormous historical fact of the day—as the Depression was in its time— yet deemed inappropriate to speak of. I was struck by my oldest nephew Louis's love of wildlife—compared to many other middle-class kids, he seemed beatific in that way. Yet I worried about the influence of his father's sometimes uncharitable outlook.

I wrote my sister a week later:

> . . . My thoughts are torn returning here mostly out of anguish for mother and father and . . . need to be near them as they live their last years. I don't want 25 years growing estrangement to continue & do want them to have my love & give them solace & more. I've considered moving there or nearby & a job (do you have ideas?) as my farm mood is ever vacillating. . . .

So I should be back on East Hill instead? I remained, it seemed, more out of love for Allen—for the simple joy of his company, for what I learned from him—than anything else (devotion to farm and garden and animals notwithstanding). Was I, with an A.B. in English and a highly refined, strangely aristocratic upbringing in an already largely vanished foreign world-within-a-world, much better prepared for the

American workaday realm than Julius? Workaday and war seemed socially, economically, and culturally enmeshed, aggression in Vietnam a sign of fundamental corruption at the core. Many Americans still, even after two Moratoriums and 36,000 of our own people sacrificed, seemed to ignore it, keep it beyond the realm of moral consideration, as if it would upset their daily 9-to-5, their car and interstate and gasoline happiness. Even my beloved Ria would soon use the phrase "government bloopers" regarding our war.

Of course, I failed to recognize my own self-indulgence, self-absorption. Inscribing my yearbook at the end of my freshman year, one of the few instructors I admired had cited the value of devotion to something greater than one's self. Now I had the benefit of Allen and much else—and I had as well my commitment to East Hill. Yet those college yearbook words must've felt uncomfortable.

So what did I do—socially—returning to the farm on the cusp of the New Year, doubtful and uncertain? Allen would be back, but not for ten days. Peter and Denise were now across the tiny hall from me, where Huncke and Louie once were—Peter's room downstairs was too cold in mid-winter. But I seldom talked personally (certainly not intimately) with Peter, and though communication was easier—more fun—with Denise, the fact remained that the two of them were alive in the world of love: young love, Peter's age notwithstanding. Daily, they were two kids in riotous tumbling play, one of them just happening to be twice as old as the other. After so much of what I'd seen at the farm, it was a wonder, a blessing to behold.

I could talk with Julius, but that was usually one-way; I could laugh with Ray. Barbara and I could talk, and did. And went to bed—but no good came of that.

Of course, Peter and I had work to do. A couple days after I returned, the snow plow pushed up from the paved road to the top of the hill at Schoolhouse Corners. Shovels on shoulders, snowshoes on feet, Pete and I made it out to where the Olds was parked, submerged under near-fathoms of snow, and began digging it out. Then we'd have to shovel out our yellow jeep truck with its small snow plow front, and try to get it going again.

And every day, shovel snow, shovel more snow from around the house, between house and chicken house and barn, get Julius's help. Then more snow fell . . . and I worried if the rest of the road could be cleared and Suburban Propane make it in before we ran out of gas.

Some days I went on walks with Godly. Or back into the barn, to Brahma and Shiva in their stalls, where I lay down on their thick straw, looking up or over at them a foot or two away, watching their jaws turn as they chewed cud, studying their visible breath flee their nostrils, studying my own, enjoying our mutual warm mammal-hood. Then I'd get back up, shovel manure (after boiling water to loosen it up from the freeze), start chores, or return to the house and plan next year's garden or write a letter, or get the Kalamazoo going again; or cuddle Panda Manda; or joke with Julius and Ray; or shovel snow, shovel snow, shovel snow.

Under a Cold Moon

I N ONE AREA of activity—planning our next garden—I became inspired. As I reviewed problems of seasons past and contemplated spring, summer, and fall of 1970, I began writing Dr. Norman J. Curtis, the regional agricultural expert, with questions. Almost every night, sometimes till past 11, I consulted and took notes from J. I. Rodale's encyclopedic *How to Grow Organic Fruits and Vegetables* and his *Organic Gardening* magazine. I started with early crops; moved to what was required around the pond; considered needs for an orchard, then mushrooms; and concluded with late crops and herbs. I diagrammed portions of the garden, with spaces between rows calibrated for specific plant needs and the width of a used rototiller we'd recently acquired. I ordered seeds early, pushing tiny peppers-to-be into little cardboard containers of vermiculite I set on windowsills; started watermelons and muskmelons and Danish Ballhead and All Seasons cabbage.

I spent many a night from December's end through May 10 in such research and preparation. But one night—Friday, January 9—definitely interrupted spring garden study. The extraordinary accumulation of snow that greeted my return had in no way diminished; cold temperatures and new snowfalls had seen it increase. (A state of emergency was declared for the area through January 6.) We'd dug out the Olds, but after new snowfalls the road crew had been unable to make it up to Schoolhouse Corners, six-tenths of a mile from our house. If we were to go anywhere, it had to be on foot a good ways through deep snow.

Around one in the afternoon, Peter and I were downstairs when we heard footsteps above. Ray and Barbara appeared in coats, scarves, and woolly hats: they were, in bums' fashion characteristic of us all, royally dressed.

And Ray was expansive, grinning in toothless joy. "We're goin' to brave the elements! Ya see, we thought it would be good for us to get out, and get some things for the house—some groceries, ya know. We'll even go to Cooperstown, so we can get more—"

"Well, I don't know, Ray," Peter began with a husky sigh as he and I exchanged looks. He was stacking dishes; I was laying a little more coal into the Kalamazoo. "We don't need that much—"

"Yeah, I'm not sure it's a good idea," I put in.

"But there may be another big storm comin' in a couple days, so it wouldn't hurt, right? An'—an'—I'll get a pint of wine for each of us! Maybe even one for Julie!" With a chuckle he eyed the silent man who stood smoking by the dining room window without response.

Peter and I acquiesced—after all, what could we do? Chain Ray down? Allowing time for likely delays and having to drive slowly under these conditions, I told myself they should be back by five.

The afternoon passed quietly, except that Peter and Denise, playing like the kids in love they were, banged into the front door and knocked out a panel of glass we had to replace with plastic. When 5:00 PM came and skies darkened, there was no sign of Ray or Barbara.

Then the phone rang.

It was Barbara, at a neighbor's several miles away. The links of one tire chain had broken, and when they stopped to look, the engine died and wouldn't start again. They'd already called Howie Fassett; he couldn't come immediately, but would when he could.

Hour after hour passed as sky cleared, moon rose, and temperature nudged zero. By 10:30, we'd already banked the Kalamazoo for the night when Barbara, small paper bag in crook of arm, pushed open the front door. Her face was flush with cold; from knees down, her coat and legs were caked in snow. She was exhausted.

Ray, she explained, was in the Olds back at Schoolhouse Corners, with several more bags of groceries. Fassett had charged the battery, but Ray was "totally smashed," couldn't move, and so was just sitting—or lying—there in the unheated Olds.

Peter and I had to act, quickly. If left there Ray could not only suffer frostbite, but, conceivably, die. While Peter went to the garage for our toboggan, I set out for Ed's, hoping he'd be awake: we needed his snowshoes to go with our pair. As I trudged uphill, the cold moon cast eerie blue light on Ed's white meadow.

Luckily, the hermit was up—kerosene lamp on—and when I explained my mission he seemed worried about Ray. I headed back with the snowshoes, and we strapped them on and started out, moving across the elevated white with ease.

At the Olds we hauled Ray out of the backseat. He seemed to be feeling utterly fine, but couldn't stand up. He tilted in all directions, collapsing this way and that, a six-foot-plus dangling man without a bone in his body. Dealing with him ordinarily would've been difficult, even for the two of us; with huge snowshoes on, it was more so.

Ray raised his arms to embrace Peter, exclaiming, "Oh Peter, I love you!" Peter cursed, "Goddamnit, Ray, stand up!" and Ray fell into my arms. I pushed and pulled him upright and tried to steady him against the car. Peter tried slapping him into sobriety, but it was no use. Ray continued carrying on, tilting this way and that, proclaiming his love for Peter, falling toward him again and again. Then suddenly I saw my companion's gloved hand coming in hard against Ray's chin. Down went Ray. I took his legs, Peter his arms, and we lifted him—already curled into a fetal position—over onto the toboggan. Then we reached in again for paper bags—they were full to bursting—and set them squarely beyond Ray's boots. And so we started hauling one embryonic man and several inanimate bags all the way back to our warm house, under a cold moon.

□ □ □

OF COURSE, RAY might've died had he stayed overnight in the Olds (which he seemed to have every intention of doing). As it was, he suffered frostbite on two fingers and his left wrist was sprained. When we pulled and pushed and lifted him inside the house, Ed was there: he'd come down to help.

Ray had gone to Cooperstown because in those days you could get terpin hydrate (cough syrup with codeine) over the counter. But you had to sign for it, and he was already at risk of burning down Crain's Pharmacy. In a few hours he'd consumed a whole bottle of terpin hydrate and all the wine. I never did learn if he'd gotten the wine for Julius.

For what was left of the night, I worried "only" about how much propane we had left. I hadn't been able to shovel down to the gas tank gauge, but I estimated it was only 30% full. Roman Killmeier, head of the road crew, had said they'd plow down our drive on Monday—now two and a half days away.

Sunday afternoon I dug and uncovered the gauge: 25%. I began to feel desperate: I'd heard again from Killmeier, who promised county bulldozer in morning and village snow plow at lunchtime—but that was if it didn't snow Sunday night. I estimated animal feed supply at one week's. If roads were cleared, would the Olds—given its recent failure—start again so we could get into town for more? Could Fassett fix our broken chains?

Anna Marie on East Hill

"SINCE YOU LEFT Sunday I've really missed you."

So wrote Anna Marie Felner from Syracuse back in December, the day after our first weekend together in three years. "Without you it was occasionally lonely, but with you for a short time, it was another sorrow."

I'm not sure how much I took those words to heart. In any case, I did indeed want to see her again—regardless of my relationship with Ria back in Winston-Salem. And so one mid-January weekend, just after Allen had returned, Anna Marie came to East Hill.

It wasn't easy, logistically. As usual winter took its toll, brought its own surprises. With light wet snow falling I waited long for her Saturday afternoon at Crain's, but eventually she made it: car trouble, and heavier snow in Syracuse. We got home OK, but entering our house I was on edge: how would Anna Marie fare in an environment so radically different from her usual middle-class milieu? I was sure she had some apprehensions, too. Back in the old days, I'd wondered and worried about Peter, who could seem so unaccepting of all of us. Now, though fond of him, I still felt some uneasiness, even with bizarre amphetamine days gone for the present. As it turned out, Peter, like everyone else except Julius in his solitude, was welcoming.

Upstairs, as Anna Marie and I, bag in hand, squeezed through the narrow door into my room, we tripped against each other; I dropped the bag, grabbed her by the waist and we stumbled onto the bed, laughing and tickling. Then lips touched lips and hands reached down and clothes came off.

"So this is your place," she said as we dressed before returning downstairs. Her eyes seemed to take in my small dark cherry wood secretary with its gardening books, *Cheiro's Book of Numbers*, Melville's *The Confidence Man*, and other works; its empty mayonnaise jar in the corner for peeing late at night (anachronistic now that we'd just gotten a toilet downstairs); the glossy poster of a blue Krishna blowing a flute.

Then followed an evening with Ray at the dining room table, as Peter and Denise went to their room; and a few late night minutes with Allen. (Recently on Ed's inspiration we'd hooked up a small black-and-white Sony TV to two car batteries, but tonight no one was watching it.)

I think Anna Marie was intrigued by Bremser, who was in a far better mode than the night of his toboggan ride. He was eminently sociable; he was Ray the charmer, Ray the performer. Except for her amused laughter my blonde green-eyed friend sat there quietly while the older, hirsute man of constant grin and seamless gab held forth.

"Now my mother, Gertrude, she used to work in a condom factory," he offered, eyeing both of us brightly, "Joisey" foghorn fairly booming through bearded lips. "So when I was a kid the house was filled with free samples, and we used condoms for everything. The milk bottle had a condom over the top! Everything that could be closed with a condom, she closed with a condom." And merrily he bragged, eyes a-twinkle, syllables spit forth from between toothless gums, "Ya know, the best blow jobs are done by people without no teeth!"

The evening went well, Ray getting up a number of times for more grass, beer, and even whisky. Perhaps from years with blacks in and out of confinement, perhaps from other circumstances, Ray seemed vaguely negroid, his vocal "crank-blat" jive gushing forth with all the intensity of a late night DJ. He once lived with the great jazz drummer Elvin Jones; and as he reported to Anna Marie on doing heroin with Ray Charles: "Damn! That blind man could shoot up faster than anyone I ever saw!"

Later in the night Anna Marie and I went back down for a snack. It was so cold we both were in sleeping gear, she in flannel P.J.'s. At the dining room table we found Allen, who invited us to join him. We soon got onto the subject of Vietnam; for Anna Marie's sake Allen gave some reasons why our war was wrong. In the midst of some back-and-forth she characterized herself as "arguing about Vietnam in my pajamas." I wasn't amused, for I was utterly sober on the subject of Vietnam, and felt she hardly acknowledged the horror of what we were up to there. It had turned into a most pleasant visit, except that as with every situation, the subject of the war—the intrusion of the war, the grotesqueness of our American war in Vietnam—was inescapable.

The next day after late afternoon chores I took Anna Marie in our jeep truck, snow plow on the bed because it had fallen loose from the front, back to her Chevy at Crain's. But it wouldn't start. Howie Fassett was open, but wasn't able to jump-start it; he towed it to his Mobil station and thawed its starter. It turned over. We kissed goodbye; "It was different than I expected," she said.

On the way back, about halfway up East Hill I suddenly heard an enormous "CLINK!" behind me, and discovered that the snow plow had slipped off the back of the jeep, and now lay in the middle of the road. It weighed several hundred pounds, but I managed to push and shove it onto the side of the road, then turned around and drove back into town, presenting myself once more at Fassett's. Howie followed me back up, lifted the plow with his motorized chain, then chained it onto the jeep's frame.

I'd scarcely gone another quarter of a mile when, passing Myron's, I saw him and Carl La Salle approaching the road, shovels on shoulders. In newly hardened snow at the sharp curve beyond the Beautiful View—high white banks each side of the bend—Carl's "cool" '57 Chevy Bel Air with no front bumper had collided (nobody was hurt) with the Grahams' big battleship '63 Oldsmobile Delta 88. I drove them to Carl's crumpled shiny hulk: engine pushed against fire wall, the Bel Air was totally wrecked. We chained it to the back of the jeep and I towed it to Myron's front yard. For once, I was able to help some of the good people around us.

"My Best Friend" & Others

N O SOONER WAS Anna Marie gone than other guests joined us. Adam Lawson, a learned ecologist from the Southwest, stayed several days, but was beset by flu the whole time. At first Allen (himself not well with Bell's Palsy and stomach complaints) seemed to be constantly running up to the attic to tend to his guest ("That's what I get for thinking to drain his brain!" Allen later exclaimed).

Then Peter assumed that role. Whenever he needed one thing or another, Lawson—dark haired, moustachioed, and awash with sneezes, coughs, and wheezes— would ring the little Yamabushi Zen sect bell on the attic altar. "You called, Adam?" I can still hear Pete yell from two floors below, the irony in his voice lost on none of us. Then he'd bound two flights up, after stopping in the kitchen to boil water for tea, find the medication of the hour, or toast some bread on the Kalamazoo or propane stove top. Even I went up once, and gave Adam the massage he requested.

Lawson improved a bit, just enough to join us downstairs for a meal or two, including a great dinner Peter made with corn and matzo balls and a soba, mushroom, and bean curd soup. But even on Adam's day of departure, misery seemed still his domain: he was so thick in the midst of it I thought we'd never get him out of the house in time for the bus. Just to make it to the car he'd have to tromp through deep snow; he stood on one foot and then the other to get out of his slippers and into the boots we offered. That done, a horrified look suddenly crossed his face as he shouted, "These boots are wet!" Bending down, he shook and tugged his feet free.

Fortunately, Peter intervened. Reaching down to the rejected boots, he picked up one and then the other, pushing his hand inside to the bottom, holding them up close to Lawson's face, rotating and tilting their tops for him to peer down inside.

"No, no, see? There's nothing wrong with these boots, Adam! They're good boots! A *little* moist, a *little* moist! But they'll do you fine!"

Actually, they were rather wet, from use the day before. But our stricken guest had little choice this his final hour in the Snow Belt before heading back to the warm, dry, and merciful Southwest. And so Dr. Adam Lawson stood there in front of the Kalamazoo, first on one foot then the other, his suffering body stuffed into long underwear, padded parka, sweaters and scarves, hands extended in mittens. He seemed not far from whimpering or all-out decomposing as Saint Peter bent to one knee and nudged one wool-covered foot and then the other into a rubber boot. An insulated rubber boot.

□ □ □

THE SAME WEEK, poet and graduate student Allen De Loach, on his way back to Buffalo from the city, stopped over to drop off Lucien Carr, the only person I ever heard Ginsberg refer to as "my best friend." Late in the day Peter and Allen drove into Cherry Valley to pick them up, Allen back in the open bed of the jeep in twenty-degree weather, so his guests could sit in the cab with Peter.

I devoted the first half of the next day—6:30 AM to 1:30 PM—to trying to get four vehicles going, including the ancient Ford County Squire station wagon we'd recently bought from Eugene, as well as De Loach's VW camper.

Lucien stayed a few days. He'd been built up so in my mind, from Allen's nuggets of recollections and one or two photographic images from Columbia, that I was initially disappointed. Jejune as I was, I'd expected someone resembling a Rimbaud-like visionary youth of extraordinary good looks—forgetting that such a creature had manifested out of Allen's dreams a quarter century earlier. Nor did I know Lucien had only recently quit alcohol—"lush," Allen called the affliction—after years of drinking.

I'd been taken aback by this middle-aged fellow with brown hair, a walrus-like moustache, and a seemingly practical disposition, but I soon came to appreciate Allen's "best friend." Lucien—who'd challenged young Allen that he didn't even know the masses he intended to save—was a down-to-earth, straight-shooting, good and generous man. As I drove him to the Cooperstown bus, I felt close enough to share with him my growing uncertainties over staying at the farm. I asked about working at United Press, where he was night bureau chief. "If you want to start the way I did," he answered immediately, referring to days as copy boy.

It was good having Lucien there, but I later wondered what it was like for Allen, having his oldest friend in his newest home. His journal entry on Lucien's last night graphs his musings:

> *A pipe full of hash at midnight lie down in attic "God is the Intersection point of all dimensions of being & non-being" . . . arrived as definition . . . then slept, headache & depression, first time bethought me after reading "Golden lads & girls all must as chimney sweepers come to dust" and "Brightness falls from the air/ Queens have*

died young and fair/Beauty is but a flower/which wrinkles will devour" Gordon in his bedroom of the old age of my desire, Lucien asleep in bed in my room quiet & I alone upstairs for the night.

Yevtushenko Writes

O NE AFTERNOON AS Ed unloaded mail onto the dining room table, a business envelope from Doubleday & Company floated out. It contained two letters, the first from an editor enclosing a poem by Yevgeny Yevtushenko with English translation. The editor asked Allen for his own translation, for a volume of Yevtushenko's poems.

The second was handwritten in Spanish, the one language its author and Allen had in common:

To Mr. Ginsberg

Querrido Bastard Allen!

Por fabor, no rompe mis cajones e busca un poco tiempo para andarme en question del libro "Las Mansanas Robadas." Tengo una poema con el titulo "Corrida," que es una poema muy Ginsbergiana e me parece para ti sera muy facil traducirlo realmente tu perderas solamente dos dias. Yo se que la vida es muy corta e dos dias libres tal vez hay que inventar. Inventa los, por fabor! Mandame por fabor tu ultimo libro e no olvida marcar algunos poemas para traducir los. Escribas me. . . .

Todos tu recuerdan aqui.

Eugenyo Evtushenko.

Here's my rough translation of Yevtushenko's Spanish, which is charming but not without a few problems which I've attempted to solve:

Dear Bastard Allen!

Please, don't break my balls and look for a little time to help me with a question for the book "Stolen Apples." I have a poem titled "Corrida," which is a very Ginsbergian poem and it seems to me for you will be very easy to translate it. Really, you will lose only two days. I know that life is very short and two free days perhaps have to be invented. Invent them, please! Send me please your last book and don't forget to mark some poems to be translated. Write me. . . .

All remember you here.

Allen seemed pleased to get it—not the work of it, certainly (the line-by-line translation was sixteen pages), but the collegial honor of it (including Yevgeny's offer to translate Allen). And of course it furthered their relationship, begun in Moscow 1965 encounters. He showed it to me; he showed it to Peter and Denise. When he asked for it back from Peter and Denise, they couldn't find it. Allen slapped his skull, groaned, and worried aloud; Peter and Denise tried to calm him, "We're still looking, we're still looking!"

Out the lovers' single window facing the front yard, small mountains of snow shimmered bright as golden light rushed through the pane. But no light had fallen upon the message from Moscow.

An antique bureau took up some of the space in their small room; then there was their low comfy, rumpled double bed, clothes and papers and *New York Times* and books here and there; the small sarod Peter had purchased on their recent New York trip; the right-handed banjo left-handed Peter had gotten from Sears Roebuck; and Denise's guitar: all amidst the whole ambience of their romp and play—she in tee-shirt and panties, he now a big gruff cigarette-smoking teddy bear in overalls, seeming without a care in the world. They laughed, they teased each other: I'd never seen Peter more relaxed, even as he'd scramble into action, with all the earnestness of a big bumbling cartoon character, to join the search.

For a long time, no one could find the letter, and if Allen ever did work on a translation, it didn't make it into the volume. A year later Yevtushenko wrote Allen again, pleading for his translation; a month later still, I spoke briefly with Yevtushenko when he was in Chapel Hill for a reading—though I didn't ask about letter or poem. But a lady friend who spent the evening with him reported no broken balls.

A Quick Night with Harry, Without John and Yoko

C OME FEBRUARY, ALLEN'S stomach trouble was diagnosed as hiatus hernia—easily treated with antacids—and he was making progress transcribing recent notebook poems before serious traveling in March. He seemed to enjoy being settled and working in a now peaceful, quiet old farmhouse surrounded by five feet of snow—so much so that he turned down an attractive invitation and offered it to me instead.

It was for the private opening of an exhibit at the Lee Nordness Gallery, of John Lennon's lithographs, *Bag One*, and Yoko's book, *Grapefruit*. The artists, the invitation reported, were expected to attend.

Since I'd be admitted with one guest, I called the best musician I knew. Would Jon Sholle like to take in this unusual opening?

But Jon wasn't keen on Lennon, so I asked Harry Smith. Gnomish, horn-rimmed, hunchbacked, wispy grey beard and hair, Smith was sought after in his small room at the Chelsea by a wide variety of folk—aspiring rock stars, record producers, friends, filmmakers, poets, young kids looking for an older man of cantankerous arcane wisdom. (And, by bill collectors: he lived in a state of indigence which would've been total were it not for the generosity of people like Jonas, Panna Grady, and Allen.)

This magician-filmmaker, artist, ethnomusicologist, and recorder-editor of the landmark *Anthology of American Folk Music*, which influenced many including Dylan, consumed very little food, outside of occasional egg and dairy diets. And vodka, marijuana, and pharmaceuticals supplied him by a psychiatrist friend who paid Harry to see him.

Comically cynical or morbid ("Home is where you hang yourself," he once said; "I'm not my sunny Hawaiian self," he told me on another occasion), he kept all of us—friends, supporters, startled strangers alike—on our toes with unpredictable comic insults. Miles was once on the elevator with Harry in the Chelsea when Jonas—who could sometimes seem aloof—stepped aboard. Greetings (at a minimum, on Jonas's part) and introductions were exchanged and then Harry offered, "He doesn't speak English. He's Lithuanian. He never learned."

On February 2, 1970, I sat with Harry in the backseat of a taxi hurtling up to East 75th. He was uncomprehending. "Why'd you ask me?" he wanted to know. "One genius deserves another," I answered, imagining John Lennon Meets Harry Smith.

At the small gallery, we had to take our shoes off to enter the exhibit area: its floor was covered (Yoko's idea) with what was then a new product, bubble wrap. Straight ahead we could see smartly dressed people moving gingerly about, peering into framed works of art, their stockinged feet going "Pop!" with every step. But we had one little problem. Harry, never particularly careful of his person, had worn no socks—and didn't want to go barefoot. Propping myself against the door frame, I reached down and pulled mine off, then squatted down and pulled them up and over his little feet. Then we happily entered the show, popping all the way.

We were all fairly elbow-to-elbow. We didn't know many of the others there, but that didn't matter—the champagne was abundant. Harry stood observing and drinking; I drank and shot, for I brought my movie camera with me. More guests poured through the small entrance, their stockinged feet shorn of shoes: Jonas with Bolex; Salvador Dali with moustache and cane. When it was announced that John and Yoko had been unable to leave London because she'd again miscarried, I fought and squeezed my way to John's agent to deliver a handwritten message from Allen, full of praise for their peacemaking art.

The lithographs, when not blocked by warm bodies, maintained their steady unflinching gaze back at us through unreflecting glass. The art was good (or good enough), minimalist, and funny: mainly fine-lined love scenes of John and Yoko, single or solo: a medium close-up of Yoko, her left hand between her legs; Yoko with legs spread, from pubic level; lovemaking with a third partner; John eating Yoko, who rests languidly on one arm; Yoko sucking John; the two of them clothed, sitting up, bedding-in for peace before an array of news photographers and journalists.

And I, the picture of sobriety most days on the farm, was becoming drunk—so much so that late in the evening, as the swelling crowd turned the room even warmer, I felt inspired and began unbuttoning my plaid long-sleeved farmboy shirt. I freed my arms from its sleeves, then started tugging my tee-shirt over my head.

Suddenly I heard Harry, in his most prim nasal voice, exclaim, "Now, Gordon, stop it! You're going too far! And you're drunk!" We left soon, in drunkenness, chaos, delight.

Our little evening had a tiny epilogue. No sooner was I back at the farm than I heard from Lynn Aycock, a friend from North Carolina newly arrived at the Chelsea. She'd just met, she said, this funny, cool little cat named Harry Smith.

"Do you know Gordon Ball?" she'd asked him.
"I'm standing here in his socks!"

Midwinter Medley: A Grab Bag

WINTER REMAINED INESCAPABLE. The Monday after the moonlight to-do with Ray, when I'd worried so about supplies holding out and gas coming in, I'd written in my diary:

> . . . *plows came w/ dozer. Dozer turned back 200' from house. . . . I ran to plow &*
> *caught up w/ it & they explained unable to go further—county said 200' private.*
> *Gas truck due but didn't show. Then Killmeier called—county in error—road is*
> *county; would plow all way Tues. a.m.*
>
> *Which they did, P & J & me got Jeep started & moved out but Ford would*
> *not start. County helped, pulled Ford out of way. Then chores & arrival of feed*
> *from Lipe's & P & me hit hay & J took last 2 of eleven 100-pound bags to barn on*
> *toboggan.*

A few nights later: "Worried bout pipes as it's coldest night yet, -11°, 40 mph winds, merciless."

□ □ □

HARVEY BROWN, OWNER of the small Frontier Press and admirer of Olson, Huncke, and others, gave Committee on Poetry, Inc., a large sum of money to be distributed ("as charity tax zap," Allen wrote Whalen) among various writers and musicians, including Don Cherry ($7,500), Ornette Coleman ($10,000), Herbert Huncke ($6,000), Ed Sanders ($5,000). Over the next few weeks Allen sent out a number of Committee on Poetry checks to grantees; on the windy morning when he and I left the house with the first batch, he dropped the envelopes opening the door to the jeep, and half a dozen checks totaling over $25,000 went skittering across the snow. We recaptured all of them.

□ □ □

LOUIE CARTWRIGHT HAD evidently written Allen that he wanted to return, for on February 10 Allen wrote:

Dear Louis—

Peter slightly ill . . . Ray Bremser requiring care, Gordon has hands full and is overloaded with cares—

I am clinging to desk working & have only 3 weeks to do what I can writing before long trip—

I know you need care, love, fidelity & friendship as much as I do or more and were I alone I guess I'd be more open—Meanwhile the work here is about as much as we can keep organized still—

Enclosed some money [$25] may help a little. I'll see you in time dont be mad at me—trying to keep things balanced

Love,
—Allen

□ □ □

JOINING US AROUND the second week of February was a quiet, tall, slender young man with glasses, long sandy brown hair, short beard. Gary Getz, who'd met Allen once before, came with his guitar from the Catholic Worker farm in Tivoly, New York, his last place of refuge. He jammed with Allen, helped him with his Blake, taught him more about music, suggested making a "mantric refrain" of the last lines of "Spring" and the "Nurse's Song" of *Innocence*. Those refrains became not only a staple of Allen's readings in later years, but a signature part of his presentation. Gary always seemed basically friendly, but he was so quiet—except for one night when drunk he poured out his feelings at the dining room table—that I hardly got to know him well. And then one day—after about a month—he was gone. He was fleeing the draft.

□ □ □

AT THE END of February, Brahma gave birth to three kids, but in the middle of an extremely cold night. One suffered frozen ears (which repaired) and frozen hoofs (one got better, the other turned into a shortened stub), and she grew up smaller than all the rest. Ed named her Cosset, for she always followed us around, full of good cheer. Because of her limping devotion to humans, we never had to stake her to keep her from the garden.

Valentines

I N LATE NIGHT loneliness, I sent out many valentines; Ray joked to Allen, "Gordon's sent 335 valentines & got none in return!" "You'll get 335 next year," Allen said, looking my way. In fact, Allen and I mailed one together to John and Yoko: he seemed to like the idea when I suggested it. As if worried the gallery message I took might not have made it their way, he wrote an enthusiastic note. And I got three valentines in return, including one from Anna Marie and one from Ed.

Down in Cherry Valley, the most beautiful girl—by far—was a young high school student, Joanna Fromm: breathtaking face and shapely figure, dark eyes and hair. I first noticed her back in the fall, and so did Gregory, who was first to accost her. As we drove slowly down Main Street one day he saw her on the sidewalk and shouted out the window in loud city voice, "YOU'RE BEAUTIFUL!" as we rolled by, her stunned eyes suddenly catching ours.

Come Valentine's Day, I was driving the yellow jeep truck through town; Denise (who knew how I prized Joanna's beauty, though I'd never approached her) was riding with me. It was a bright mild day; we saw Joanna, lovely as ever, seeming to pause in thought near the corner. As I made the turn Denise suddenly stuck her head out her open window, shouting exuberantly—I can still see the poor younger girl's shocked loveliness—"Happy Valentine's with love and kisses from Gordon!"

Denise was always keen on others developing relationships, and sometimes teased Julius about his having a girl friend (in Denise's fantasy) named Lulu Radonsky. Julius would sit there sternly, lips tight in speechlessness, not taking the bait. And I? I never did open my mouth and speak to the most beautiful girl in town. I saw her only once again, when I was driving one of the back roads that summer—suddenly there she was, sitting near a fellow on the front porch of what may have been her home. Their eyes met mine. It was a small shack of a house, as primitive as you would see in those parts, and I thought I better keep moving.

News from Chicago

T HE MAJOR NATIONAL event these winter weeks was the Chicago Seven trial. The word "conspiracy" had amused Allen, for etymologically it means "breathing together."

As soon as he sent the trial to jury, Judge Julius Hoffman made an unprecedented move: he sentenced two defendants to over two years apiece for contempt, two more to around a year. Next day he gave defense counsel Bill Kunstler four years, counsel Leonard Weinglass one, and issued contempt citations to the three other defendants. All told, defendants and two counsels were given over fifteen years for contempt. These actions were unprecedented and legally questionable: contempt citations must be given on the spot rather than at the end of a trial, and be issued in writing, with those cited having a chance to respond in writing, with the opportunity of trial by a different judge. And, as the Supreme Court had ruled in 1968, no one can be imprisoned more than six months without trial by jury.

Such stipulations evidently held no sway with Judge Hoffman, and the jury, after several days' deliberation without knowing of the Judge's actions, came to a compromise which cleared the Seven of conspiracy, but convicted five of trying to promote riot individually. Allen was of course upset by this debacle; hearing of the contempt citations gave him a sense of foreboding. I can still recall one of his rare moments of anger with his lawyer brother as they argued over Chicago on the phone.

After the jury's verdict, on the day of final sentencing, most of those found guilty responded with ringing statements, including Rennie Davis's threat, on getting out, to "move right next door to [chief prosecutor] Mr. Foran and . . . turn his kids into revolutionaries." Even Allen's father Louis, with whom he'd argue bitterly over Black Panthers, radicalism, and the Mid-East, was troubled. A journal entry by Allen after the five convicted defendants were given five years each (concurrent with contempt sentences) has the relatively conservative Louie calling the heavy sentence "outrageous . . . unconscionable, vindictive," and Judge Hoffmann provocative.

But many in America were otherwise persuaded. As Mr. Foran explained to the Boosters Club of a Roman Catholic high school shortly after final sentencing, "We've lost our kids to the freaking fag revolution . . ."

Julius in the Garden of Eden

I 'M NOT SURE of the time, exactly; it was still winter on East Hill, and Peter was around, Denise in Queens. I planned a visit to the city, a semi-final check-up, I hoped, with bone specialist Dr. Mayer. And, since I'd edited the first part of my 8-millimeter *Farm Diary*—an hour's film—I wanted Jonas to see it.

Julius heard me discuss my plans; later when the two of us were alone he said out of the blue, "I wanna go witchya." He'd made such a plea once before, and I brushed it off: taking Julie would change the whole character of the journey; I'd have to look after him constantly; I wouldn't feel I could circulate freely, and certainly couldn't visit lady friends.

On the other hand I wanted good things for Julius. Several months earlier I'd bought him a Frankie Lane album: in his infrequent periods of volubility and singing, Frankie Lane numbers—"Ghost Riders in the Sky," "Midnight Rambler"—were favorites. Within days, long days with a pleased Julius setting vinyl to turntable again and again, I heard Allen offer, "Say, Gordon, that Frankie Lane album was a stroke of genius."

Now I was about to answer Julie, reflexively, that it couldn't be done—no question. Then I stopped myself: why not? "OK," I suddenly heard myself say; I was sort of inspired by this novel idea. I knew his psychiatrist, Dr. Greenspan, would want to see him, and told him so. He agreed. We'd be traveling partners.

The date—only a few days away—was set, and Julius's behavior changed dramatically. He'd gone from extreme noncommunicativeness and even sullenness to almost prancing about the house, singing, asking questions, sharing his thoughts out loud whether anyone wanted to listen or not.

The morning of our departure I lowered a reel of tape onto the Uher. Though we'd just learned Peter was ill, and we'd have to delay leaving, Julius's spirits remained elevated, his eagerness to depart every bit as strong.

"The sun's comin' out again! The sun's comin' out again!" he cackled madly. "Toot toot tootsie goodbye / Toot toot tootsie don't cry," he sang, lifting up meowing Panda Manda. He asked Allen if he knew where the Garden of Eden was ("Why yes, right here!"). He started whistling "Blue Moon," burped, and continued. He asked Ed—he was going to ride into Cherry Valley with him—what he thought about the

Garden of Eden ("I don't think about it"), sang and whistled some more, and told Ed, "We'll go into town and see all the women, OK?"

He called for "ice cream and bananas. A lot of ice cream and bananas, whipped cream. And steam and everything" after Ed and Allen discussed food and drink for the afflicted Peter. He sang all the lines to "Blue Moon." ("Like a faded antique Italian opera singer," Allen commented; "Like the Mills Brothers," said Julius.) He shifted into falsetto and tremolo, he whistled with elegant fluted trills and variations; then, by the time the hot water kettle (for Peter's medicinal tea) began its ascending whistle, his unfettered voice trailed off as he started out the door.

□ □ □

AFTER THE GARDEN of Eden, New York would be anticlimactic. Well, almost.

Peter was decidedly better the next morning, so we were able to leave that afternoon. It was an unusual journey. Dr. Mayer told me my hand and wrist were doing well, given the injury. It took all of two minutes; Julie was still puffing on his ciggyboo when I returned to the waiting room.

Night found us in Jonas's room at the Chelsea as I screened that first reel of *Farm Diary*. There we all were in the early days: Myron plowing, Candy raising an earthworm from the freshly turned soil; Peter relaxing; Ed advising; Allen chanting; Julius sawing wood in slo mo; Enrique in the sunset; Huncke washing his face outdoors; Julius hauling water; Bessie arriving; Peter nuzzling Bessie; snow piling up. . . .

"I tink in time dis may develop a patina," Jonas said; "If not, you'll have to carry more vater."

The next morning we were due up at Dr. Greenspan's on Central Park. I woke, and Julius was gone. He returned close to noon. To one of the basic questions about Julius—did he recognize what he didn't verbally acknowledge?—this event (and others like it) gave clear answer.

We dropped by Robert Frank's spacious 86th Street home in the rather grand Arbuthnot. But Robert and sculptor wife Mary had broken up; only she was there. In the fall Mary had paid a weekend visit to the farm, riding up with Allen. She wasn't a fan of his Blake; she told me he'd sung all the way up, putting her to sleep "because it was so boring." But I loved his music—and liked her; she was interesting and attractive. She invited us into her kitchen and I sat down and began talking eagerly. Julius, settling himself into a chair, coffee in hand, remained silent. The subject turned to drugs, and Mary spoke as if she were a stranger to them—perhaps she worried for her children.

"Oh, I think they—marijuana, psychedelics—are as essential as sex," I offered.

Of course my words had an undertone that wasn't subtle. I was indeed hoping we could make it. As we continued talking and I began fantasizing how to realize my hopes while ensuring that Julie remained comfortably settled, I suddenly heard my companion: "I wanna go see my old man."

It turned out Oleg Orlovsky, long divorced from Kate, lived in a one-room apartment a few blocks away. I was exasperated, but didn't feel I could "let" Julius, who'd gotten lost a number of times (several months once) with Allen and Peter, go off by himself. In any case, I was responsible for him. Figuratively cursing under my breath, I wished Mary well and thanked her. Julie and I left.

Within minutes we were squeezing into a short narrow space at the end of which sat a smiling, white-haired man with a big nose. Behind a pair of glasses his eyes were a lively blue. He wore a white shirt and dark dress pants: like his apartment he seemed basically neat and clean, presentable. He had a small single bed and dresser and a few other appointments but that was it. Like Peter in his sociable moods, he liked to talk.

I sat; Julius, though there was space to sit, stood and—except for hellos—kept quiet. Oleg's talk centered on cavalry officer days. I mentioned my fall from Penny; he explained that the way to stop a runaway horse is to pull strong and quick on either side of the reins, back and forth. His own worst experience on horseback, he confided, was trying to ride on ice one wintry day in Smolensk: his horse couldn't keep his balance because of metal shoes, and Oleg fell, breaking his leg.

He told of being in the Crimea and fleeing the Red Army, making his eventual way toward the United States. The best cure for a cold, he offered, ". . . is cocaine. It cleans your nasal passages right out." Coming from the mouth of Oleg, with all his tradition and rank and experience, I reasoned, it must be true; at the very first sign of a cold, I'd have to be open-minded, give it a try.

Then, almost as abruptly as we'd arrived, we were leaving; Julius had decided the visit had gone on long enough. It afforded me very little insight into what the two men once had in the way of a relationship. All I could see was that Julius wanted to maintain it, even in the most elementary fashion. That Peter, some years later, could seem hugely depressed when Oleg told him, on the publication of his *Clean Asshole Poems and Smiling Vegetable Songs*, that he was "the world's biggest pornographer," suggested how sensitive the Orlovsky boys were to their father's opinions.

Before Julius and I were to rise at 5:00 AM to get to Port Authority in time for the 6:00 bus, one more social occasion awaited us. I hadn't seen my friends Diane and Bob Patterson since the end of March 1968, when Candy and I were there, and boyish

Bob, red-haired and freckled, had rushed in all a-glow with the news that Johnson wouldn't run again.

Now I called on them once more, and introduced Julius as we settled down, shoes off, in close quarters on the many pillows in their narrow, dark reddish-lit room, and began smoking some nice strong hash. Typically when Candy and I had visited in the past, we'd all end up making love.

Now, talk subsiding, the effects of the hash rising, I began making out with Diane, then fucking. In the darkness Bob watched—and, I assume, so did Julius, who, true to form, had remained silent after introductions. When I began easing away from Diane, she whispered, "Ask him."

Quietly I asked Julie, "Do you want to get laid, or would you like to smoke some more, or—?"

"I wanna get laid," he answered immediately.

And so I settled back upon a pillow against the wall and watched as Julius Orlovsky rose to his feet, shimmied out of his pants, leaving on tee-shirt and long-sleeved shirt, and took a couple of short steps in his stockinged-feet toward Diane. Then he was down in front of her and upon her and without foreplay starting, matter-of-factly, to pump.

My alarm the next morning was a few minutes late, but we made it to Port Authority just in time. Not long after the bus wheezed its way out of the city, dawn began to break.

Me & Peter

I WAS ALWAYS going back and forth in my mind about Julius's brother Peter. He was a wonder to be seen and heard; on amphetamine, a terror to be dreaded. And I was by nature hypersensitive to personal acceptance or rejection, and perhaps most of all that of mercurial, mighty Peter. I was given to feelings of insufficiency and guilt when it might've been useful to at least consider a statement Gregory once made, that Peter "doesn't like people." Shortly after this period I wrote:

> How many guitars or other instruments has Peter had & broken or lost or given back (?)—The guitar Dylan gave him—which he broke or gave away—the banjo he broke—& do you think he's got no musical brilliance?—It just comes shinin' thru!
>
> Recall the early Mar. '70 nite on amphetamine he played atop the snow-covered barn lean-to roof the Star Spangled Banner & improvised apostrophe to farm life, "The Asparagus."

Despite earlier assurance from Allen that Peter had accepted me "into the cosmic family"—and though Peter was now mostly off amphetamine—I still wondered, worried, if he cared for me—or anyone else.

My flailings at coming to an understanding of Peter also suggested how hard it can be to know someone. Decades later Peter shared with me a couple of things that were at odds with what Allen had told me of his earlier history. His 1953 statement to the officer who'd found him reading Erich Fromm hadn't been "An army is an army against love," but "An army at war is an army against love." But that wasn't all: the statement hadn't led to his discharge; instead, it was an incident which took place off-base. Enlisted man Orlovsky, drunk, was approached by an officer, who forced himself upon him. Peter reported the incident, and said he'd like to be discharged.

□ □ □

PETER HAD DREAMED a scheme of putting in a door at the rear of the cellar to facilitate bringing in vegetables for winter storage. I opposed this, for it would entail scooping out the four-feet-plus of earth that protected the cellar and made it viable for storage to begin with. But Peter saw it as a great improvement, allowing us to haul whole wheelbarrow loads of vegetables in at one time. I argued against it, but didn't persist. And so Don Winslow, mason, came up and did the work on the foundation, and the door was put in. The approach of winter would find us placing horse manure on top of tar paper around the outside of the house, to try to compensate for the expected lower temperatures in the now-exposed cellar, as well as help warm the house. We'd refill the area in front of the door with four and a half feet of earth, to be removed in spring.

In general, my inclination was low-tech: to move more toward raising crops without plowing, with composting. My behind-the-barn experiment—growing squash in the pile of manure and straw we tossed out from barn stalls—was encouraging. But Peter looked to get a tractor (and there were indeed times in which one in much better condition than Ed's was needed). Eventually, he'd get two.

Besides the Peter of bold plans, there was the Peter of laze and relaxation, who often manifested when he wasn't on speed. I remember Allen speaking to him as he lounged on his bedsheets, simply resting or reading *The New York Times*, about work that might be done that day.

"Allen!" he exclaimed, in mock urgency and earnestness, "Don't you realize today is one of the *holiest holidays*?! And you're talking about *work*? *Allen*! Hmpf! Hmpf! Golly tamale!"

Allen would be left standing in the door, a little sheepishly, "Well, I just thought . . ."

Whenever Peter returned to his amphetamine frenzy, Allen would grow as depressed as anyone. When Peter was off speed, Allen waxed more optimistic than anyone. To friends he'd write lines like "Peter off amphetamine a year now," when to us it would seem just a few months.

Perhaps for some readers there seems little doubt: Peter should be, as Barbara had vehemently proposed, dispatched to an institution. But for many of us, he remained a conundrum.

I loved Peter; I admired him; I also sometimes feared him, sometimes hated him. Often, I was on edge.

And things would grow worse.

Eclipse & Bomb

A S SPRING NEARED, Allen joined brother Eugene and his wife Connie and their children for a look at a solar blackout, billed as "the eclipse of the century," from one of the prime viewing areas in Tidewater Virginia—the football field at Old Dominion University. This full eclipse was indeed impressive, gratifying the many who turned out for it—"Sun's white diamond / ringed by black moon," Allen entered in his journal March 7.

Years later Connie gave the occasion added dimension:

I remember Allen alternately not wanting to be recognized, or not wanting to be made anything over, and seemingly a little annoyed, and obviously wanting to be recognized—standing up and striding around.

At one point Allen and my five children and I were walking down the street near the college, and a young person came up to him [as if to talk at length] *and Allen said, very annoyedly, "Can't you see I'm with my family?!" And I was wondering if the young person thought he had a wife and five children.*

While still at the field, Allen was interviewed by a local journalist—and persistently distracted by an intruder who challenged his view of our war in Vietnam. As Allen turned to go, according to Norfolk reporter Tim Morton, he took a farewell glimpse of the sun and offered, "'Beyond everybody's guff, here was something old and real. I felt like I was going to cry.'"

□ □ □

MEANWHILE, NORTH VIETNAMESE and rebellious Pathet Lao had recently retaken the Plain of Jars, and it was revealed that several hundred American lives had been lost in Laos the last six years—but Nixon explained that we had no ground combat troops there, and no plans for any.

Barry Miles, who'd produced Allen's Blake album, had returned to New York to work for *Crawdaddy* magazine. Just twenty-four hours before the eclipse, Miles was awakened by enormous explosions. One block away, on West 11th near 5th Avenue, a four-story townhouse was destroyed by these midday blasts. Miles assumed—and first news stories suggested—it was a gas leak.

A few days later a large store of dynamite and two bodies were found in the wreckage. One corpse was unidentified; the other was that of Theodore Gold, a leader of the spring 1968 student uprising at Columbia and, more recently, a Weatherman. Bomb-making had apparently been in process. A week later, en route to read in the Midwest, Allen had written a long poem, "Friday the Thirteenth." "Blasts rip Newspaper Gray Manahatta's mid day Air Spires," it begins, before asking in lament:

> What prayer restores freshness to eastern meadow, soil to cindered acres,
>   hemlock to rusty hillside,
> transparency to Passaic streambed, Blue whale multitudes to coral gulfs—
> What mantra bring back my mother from Madhouse, Private Brakefield from
>   Leavenworth, Neal from the Streets of Hades,
> Hampton, King, Gold, murdered suicided millions from the War-torn fields of
>   Sheol...
>
> ....
>
> What can Poetry do, how flowers survive, how man see right mind
>   multitude, hear his heart's music, feel cockjoys, taste
> ancient natural grain-bread and sweet vegetables, smell his own baby body's
>   tender neck skin
> when 60% State Money goes to heaven on gas clouds burning off War
>   Machine Smokestacks?
>
> When Violence floods the State from above....

During the same week, Henry A. Kissinger, President Nixon's premier advisor for foreign affairs, told a French interviewer he expected peace in Vietnam "in the first term of this administration."

In less than two months, Nixon would invade Cambodia.

Panda's Gone

MY TWO SHORT diary entries tell the tale of sudden death of Panda Manda, tortoise shell cat beloved by both silent Julius and me:

March 10 [Tuesday]:

She fought for her life as I went after her, she'd never resisted so strongly, but I got her into the burlap bag & Ray & I took Panda & the 2 other cats [for spaying] to the Vet's Monday. I said she'd never forgive me as we left her there, caged. Wed. Dr. Schaer phoned she died of heart failure, on the op. table, couldn't take the ether.

Was that cat a little weak and sensitive? The black and gold one?

No.

Well, she couldn't take the ether. She died of heart failure on the operating table.

March 14:

Today we put her to rest in our Milson cemetery under the apple boughs. Got body, wrapped in newspaper & inside a box, from vet's, & Peter & I dug thru snow & laid box down & re-covered & marked w/ furring lath. The sight of her body—I uncovered it before digging, & even had my camera in pocket to film—put me thru a change that probably means the end of tears that have flowed afternoon & evening since Wed. she died. As I would cry then I'd see her live, Panda-ing, licking herself, talking purring, moving sex, lovely, the most beautiful cat, unique, perched on the top window of the front door at night, orange nose against pane, yellow eyes & orange forehead streak, nite's blackness behind her; those images go racing thru my mind less now, for now I know a Panda that is dead, a still being, paws tightened under chin, I can't even say if her eyes were closed—but dead being—& after the initial gasp I gave seeing her thus knowledge entered of a new Panda, the only Panda now, a still one, boxed & covered w/ soil & snow under the apple boughs.

Guests in Early Spring

E ASTER SUNDAY WAS early that year: March 29. Come Good Friday, Ella Radocy was back for the extended weekend. Unfortunately, I had a bad cold, but Ella didn't seem to mind. We spent her whole visit, basically, in bed, "fucking madly," as I wrote in my diary, and even managed a hit of acid apiece. I was still so sick when time came for her to go I stayed in bed; Denise and Peter took her to the bus. After they returned, Denise reported, "Ella said you were the best fuck she ever had." Denise was a good friend and eager confidante, and such rare words cheered me despite my illness.

Soon it was the first of April, thirteen inches of snow were on the ground (more than in fifty years, Ed said), and two new people were with us on East Hill: Bonnie Bremser and daughter Georgia had arrived from Guatemala. (Nurse Barbara had left a few weeks earlier.) A letter had preceded them:

Dear Gordon Ball—

Ray tells me you just experienced a new arrival, a baby goat. I hope we won't be too much trouble for you, Georgia & me. I am looking forward to having lots of work to do cause I get very domineering otherwise. Georgia respects noone I'm sorry to say.

I want to bring a wonderful friend with me and want to know beforehand if it is allright with you. There is no problem of space if Ray doesn't mind her sleeping with us, we all sleep in the same room here which turns out better for the baby. Connie has some kind of authority over her, perhaps because she is the "madrina" godmother.

I hope that you will tell Ray to say yes to the lawyer who will certify my invitation to her, which is needed to get a visa for her.

As I am part of the family here I hope that she would be welcomed as my sister wherever I go. I hope also that this is not a problem for you and if it is that we can work it out.

Ray says there's a lot of love there, there is here too thanks to God.

Bonnie

When Bonnie and Georgia arrived, inexplicably no *madrina* was with them. In coming weeks and months I never found Bonnie domineering, but helpful, and by late April we'd be working together on a major project over several days. Down in the lower meadow beyond the barn was the new pond, completed just last fall. It was medium-sized, a quarter acre, and with surrounding banks rising several feet from the earth was like a thick-rimmed bowl. And those banks, which played a crucial supporting role, needed tilling, fertilizing, seeding. I'd collected soil samples and sent them to Dr. Curtis in Cobleskill for his analysis: the pond needed no lime, but two bags of urea, three each of organic phosphorous and magnesium. Then it had to be seeded with seven pounds of birdsfoot trefoil (after inoculating, with an ounce of sodium molybdate in water), fifteen pounds of red fescue, and a half-bushel of oats. The deep-rooted fescue was especially valuable to protect against erosion.

Working together under a warm sun, Bonnie and I tilled and seeded the whole area. Negotiating the roto-tiller at steep angles up and down the sides of the bank was difficult, but I persisted. And Bonnie worked right with me. That was fortunate, for hardly anyone else was then on East Hill: Allen was off reading, Peter and Denise in the city. Julius may've felt unsuited for the tiller; and Ray, though he'd help some in the garden, usually had to quit after a little because of bursitis.

Presumably Ray looked after Georgia while her mother and I worked. Georgia was a cute sprite-like two-year-old (soon to turn three) with golden brown ringlets; considering all the goings-on at the farm that summer, she managed (thanks essentially to Bonnie) to stay out of harm's way. But it couldn't have been much fun for her being the only child in a house full of needy grown-ups.

From her and Georgia's arrival till their departure with Ray in October, I never grew really close with Bonnie. Nonetheless we had a few good times together early on: a wild night of dancing in our underwear in the living room, little portable record player full blast. Another night she and I sat together on my bed talking; during a brief lull she leaned over and kissed my forehead. I didn't respond. It wasn't out of any feelings of loyalty to Ray; I simply didn't feel amorous.

I think our not coming closer had to do with mutual shyness, and the advent of warm weather. Though we sometimes shared outdoor work (as at the pond), we also went our separate ways; she often took over in the kitchen; and she had both Georgia and Ray to look after. She was tall and pretty; she was sensible, straightforward, educated, and resourceful. And I remember her fondly.

Enter the FBI

B Y MID-APRIL WINTER'S thaw, encouraged by recent rains, was upon us. The temperature reached a balmy forty-eight; islands of snow still covered some slices of land, puddles or streams claimed much of the rest. The road leading down toward our house was a wreck of brown ooze.

One afternoon I noticed a nondescript car paused up that road, about a hundred yards away. The driver got out, seemed to be looking around. Perhaps he was stymied by potholes and enormous puddles I'd barely negotiated in the jeep the day before. Did he need help? Was he trying to come see us? Better check.

"FBI," the man said, removing a small wallet from the breast pocket of his plaid sport coat, thrusting badge and identification inches from my chin. I glanced behind him into the front seat, where another man sat, silently. A third was in the back. Windows were down.

"They're with the Bureau of Criminal Investigation," offered the man in plaid, making a brief gesture to his car-bound colleagues. "Do you know an individual named Gary Getz?"

I didn't want to appear that I was hiding anything, and so decided to be conversational, without divulging anything they might not already know. I wanted them to think I was being as cooperative as I could, so as to have no basis for venturing closer to our home—or returning.

"Oh." I paused. Then, as if suddenly experiencing a return of memory, "Yes, I did meet him."

"And what's your name?"

"Gordon Ball."

"Was Mr. Getz ever here?" My questioner had taken out a small notepad and ball pen.

"Oh, yes, that's right—he was here on a very short visit, a while back."

Every now and then, I'd glance back to our house in the distance. I could see Ed and Peter standing in front of it, looking up our way. They seemed to be conferring. Then Peter began walking toward us.

Meanwhile my interlocutor wasn't done with me:

"Where did he go?"

"I don't know exactly. I'm not sure he mentioned. He came and went so quickly, you know." My eyes fell upon the agent's wrist, which bore a new-fangled sort of watch with several extra dials and an insert for month and day. Holding my gaze I asked, "Can you get your watch to tell you the day and the month?"

"Yes." He didn't appreciate my effort at distraction.

"Wow."

Meantime Peter was nearing us, worry on his face. Coming abreast of me, he tugged my upper arm and whispered huskily in my ear, "Ed says you've got a guilt complex! Don't talk with these guys!"

"What's your name?"

"Peter Orlovsky!"

"Do you know someone named Gary Getz?"

"Never heard of him!" My comrade was emphatic.

Our guest continued with me. "Have you received any correspondence from him since he left?

"No, not a word. I wondered where he was."

"Did you know he was running from the draft?"

"No! Really?"

"Would it help refresh your memory if we went down into the house?" he said, looking to our frail asbestos-sided structure down below.

"No," I answered immediately.

"Do you know anyone who'd know his whereabouts?"

"Golly, no—he's such a quiet fellow, you know, I didn't think of his having many friends."

I could see by now the exasperation—no, the resignation—written on my interviewer's face.

"If you ever," he offered, handing me a card, "hear of or from him, would you contact our Albany office immediately?"

"I'd be happy to."

Taking a long, slow and welcome extra breath, I helped them negotiate mud and potholes as, gingerly, they made their 180-degree turn. I was happy to.

The next day, I heard from Ed that the three gentlemen had returned to Cherry Valley, where they'd gone to the post office and tried to interview the two men behind the counter: did they remember handling any mail for one Gary Getz up our way, had they ever seen such a one in the post office or elsewhere around town? Call it small-town recalcitrance, call it loyalty to the kindly new neighbor in their midst, call it gratitude (rumor had it that before Allen, with his mountains of mail, came to town, the post office was going to be closed). They refused to be interviewed.

Anna Marie & Me: At Odds

T HROUGH MUCH OF 1970, things remained on-again, off-again with Anna Marie, the main problem from my perspective being our differences over Vietnam. After a mid-February visit I wrote with a strange admixture of righteous anger and affection:

I'm torn between happiness you give me & our gulf of understanding of genocide & destruction of all forms of life in Vietnam. "Can I see another's woe, / And not feel sorrow too?" Do you wish to be napalmed? Do you wish to see your loved ones die aflamed? If not then why wish it on others?

Otherwise I'm very happy being w/ you & hope you feel same—please return next weekend. I told you before I do not you alone love but grant me your sweet presence again & allow our differences to work out.

Love
Gordon

Evidently I communicated no further for a month, then received a big greeting card, the word "SEX" in huge raised green fuzzy capital letters filling its narrow vertical face. Inside, the printed message asked, "How's that for a St. Patrick's Day thought?" Beneath it Anna Marie had written simply, "Have you died recently?" and signed her initials.

Our correspondence picked up again.

But before long Ella Radocy was back for a visit, bringing that morning's *New York Times*, which told of the Beatles' break-up. The afternoon mail brought a short note: Had I been busy, Anna Marie asked. A month later, a decidedly cool message— Would I return her sweater, left a good three months ago?

It was signed in her full name: first, middle, last.

Cambodia, Campus, Catastrophe

"Don't worry about divisiveness. Having drawn the sword, don't take it out–stick it in hard . . . No defensiveness."

—PRESIDENT RICHARD M. NIXON

B Y SPRING 1970, colleges and universities had become centers of growing unrest. On April 30, only ten days after announcing further troop withdrawals and claiming, "We finally have in sight the just peace we are seeking," Richard Nixon announced that we'd invaded Cambodia—despite concerns among cabinet members and minimal consultation with others in Washington. On national TV he explained the invasion's purpose—to protect our troops and help end the war by attacking Vietnamese strongholds across the border. He commented:

My fellow Americans, we live in an age of anarchy, both abroad and at home. We see mindless attacks on all the great institutions which have been created by free civilizations in the last 500 years. Even here in the United States, great universities are being systematically destroyed.

. . . .

I would rather be a one-term president and do what I believe was right than to be a two-term president at the cost of seeing America become a second-rate power and to see this nation accept the first defeat in its proud 190-year history.

Simultaneously, henchman Spiro T. Agnew was pounding the bully pulpit, railing against negative "elitists." The invasion discovered no Vietnamese; soon, four aides to Henry Kissinger resigned, and 200 employees of the State Department signed a petition in opposition.

In New Haven, as Bobby Seale and eight other Black Panthers awaited trial on murder, kidnapping, and conspiracy in a courthouse two blocks from Yale, 4,000 Marines and 8,000 National Guard, as well as city and campus cops, were ready for a May Day devoted to supporting those on trial. (News of the Cambodia invasion the night before added urgency to the cause: 15,000 more protestors poured in.) Abbie

Hoffman, Jerry Rubin, and David Dellinger were featured speakers; also speaking, though known to only a handful of others ahead of time, was French novelist Jean Genet.

Allen was captivated by Genet's appearance and presentation, and would soon arrange for and introduce City Lights's publication of his text, calling for "delicacy of heart." Allen seemed amused—enchanted—as he beheld huge Panther Deputy Information Minister Elbert Howard, known as Big Man, reading the English translation for the "short, round headed, white skull'd, pink faced" Frenchman "with energetic cigar, drest in Amerindian style brown leather-thonged Jacket."

But that evening, as Allen sang "The Ecchoing Green" during his reading, tear gas was fired on the Green, forcing many to flee, including Cherry Valley native Beekman Cannon, then Master of Yale's Jonathan Edwards College. Allen remained long enough to calm much of the exiting crowd by chanting the Padmasambhava mantra.

□ □ □

IN THE FIRST days after Cambodia, there were strikes on one-third of America's campuses, as well as other expressions of outrage. The burning of the ROTC building at Kent State University resulted in Ohio Governor James Rhodes calling in the National Guard, vowing to "eradicate" the dissenters, who were, he claimed, "worse than the brown-shirts."

Then, on May 4, four students were killed and eleven wounded by the Guard at Kent State.

Nixon deplored the deaths, blaming the students: "This should remind us all once again that when dissent turns to violence it invites tragedy."

"Nixon acts as if the kids had it coming," the father of slain Jeffrey Glenn Miller would say. Sandra Lee Scheuer was killed while walking to class. Allison Krause was an honor student. Bill Schroeder, an ROTC scholar who wrote poetry, had attended the rally to see what it was like. Like many of his peers, he thought the Guard had no live ammunition.

Eleven months later, Allen and I visited Kent State for several days. While we were there one of our hosts informed us, "Most of the townspeople thought the students deserved it."

Miles Settles In

S UE: TALL, SLENDER, pretty; straight dirty blonde hair and blue eyes, with that sallow complexion the English sometimes favor. Friendly, talky. Not above anyone else: one of us. Miles: my height, slight of build, blond longish hair, serious horn-rims, friendly. Incisive. The weather warmer now, Peter and Denise moved back downstairs, behind the porch, beyond the pantry; Miles and Sue moved in right across from me.

We had our separate areas of work—once a very small electric system operating off a windcharger was set up, Miles would be in the living room where the numerous reel-to-reel tapes and recording machines were, and I'd be out of the house. But we'd often talk together, and Sue always helped in the garden. (A professional chef who'd run a London restaurant, she made a major kitchen contribution as well.) I so liked their accents I sometimes started speaking in my own version of one before stopping myself.

What Miles shared with me of his life at Indica Books and other sites in London was captivating—including gleanings from the ways of the Beatles: "Who writes it sings it," he informed me. Watching Allen set Blake to music reminded him of McCartney creating music for Lennon lyrics. John, he told me, was "crazy": "He had a 16-millimeter movie camera he painted all kinds of psychedelic patterns and colors." Once, Miles said, when Lennon was depressed, Derek Taylor, publicist at Apple, talked with him, told him he was worth something, raised his spirit so he could move out of despair.

Besides his own work in a variety of fields, Miles had recorded Olson and Bukowski and other poets, published Frank O'Hara and Diane Di Prima. "My role seems to be to help other people do their work," he said, handing me a copy he'd made of the soundtrack for one of my earliest films.

Before leaving England, he'd put his six companies into "voluntary liquidation." I think on East Hill he was relieved to be free of book shop and art gallery and the *International Times*, which he edited. Having hosted Allen in London 1965, having produced *Allen Ginsberg/William Blake: Songs of Innocence and Experience by William Blake, tuned by Allen Ginsberg*, he was looking forward to working with Allen a good half year.

He arrived on East Hill bearing seventeen years of Allen's tapes—to catalogue and edit all of Ginsberg's recorded poetry, so as to assemble a multi-album box set of the best versions of each poem. But there was one small problem: we had no electrical system on the farm—not until a young genius from Apostolic, Paul Berkowitz, came up in early June. We dug a long trench from our house to the ram house (batteries would be stored down there with the ram, way below frost line), and buried cable. Paul—slender, black hair, glasses—and Miles built a six-foot wooden stand, the base for the windcharger's metal tower; Paul then put together a converter and installed a diode to start the small windcharger.

But for the month or more until that came to pass, Barry Miles, of Apple Records, newspaper founder and gallery owner, publisher and recorder of poets, *copain* of one of the Beatles, had to make do with the electricity available from extremely heavy car batteries down in the bottom of the ram house: they had to be hauled back, twice a week, to Myron's for recharging. He did so with verve.

Planting Season, Again at Last! But . . .

"**B**LOSSOM BY BLOSSOM the spring begins," wrote Swinburne. And spring had come to East Hill once more. Dandelions yellowed the greening land; daffodils raised bright heads; pear trees and lilacs were soon to bloom, and before long we'd see pink and white apple blossoms.

And so, at last, I could apply all those book-and-paper labors of a winter's night, all those seed orders; I could transplant all those Fertl-Cubes, most of which had sprouted healthy green in windowsills. Would our garden be the best yet? I was determined.

I'd had every area of land to be cultivated tested. We'd opened up a second large field, a whole acre beyond the Milsons' cemetery. In the fall—on Dr. Curtis's recommendation—we'd sow a cover of timothy climax, birdsfoot trefoil, oats, and wheat, to be turned under in spring as green manure. It was mainly Peter's field, for he envisioned soybeans (as well as corn and tomatoes) on a large scale—even though I thought them not worth the trouble: unless parboiled first, the beans were so difficult to remove from the pod.

In between plowing and tilling we spread nutrients and lime. Field One, our traditional half-acre near the house, took sixteen bags of dolomite limestone; Field Two was neediest in potassium. In a quarter-acre area beyond the stone wall in the upper meadow above the house, we planned plum trees, peaches, apples, and pears, as well as seventy-five strawberry plants, dozens of asparagus, and raspberries and grapes. But could fruit trees withstand ferocious winters, tearing winds? This upper slope offered sunlight and good drainage—but also exposure to winds.

After tilling the half-acre near the house I prepared for each vegetable one-by-one. For peas we needed an additional 300 pounds apiece of greensand, bone meal, and granite dust. Following Rodale, I planted cabbage in the center of the garden where pumpkins and watermelons had been, to avoid being near cabbage family plants of 1969.

The past two years our carrots—more like orange toothpicks—had been a great disappointment; to my mind, it was caused by the relatively rocky, unrefined soil. Now, on my knees, hands sifting and pushing through it, I spent hours carefully clearing out rocks and breaking up clods that had escaped tilling. Surely I was the picture of a madman! But there was method in this microscopic madness, for now those swaths of earth were fine, flat, friable. I even got a rare compliment from Peter as he strode by one morning: "Looks like a table-top there, Gordon!"

As I looked back on garden and orchard and field, all seemed right with the world of East Hill—the world that wasn't Cambodia, Vietnam, Kent State. But there had been an inevitable consequence of several winter and early spring trips to the city that Peter and Denise had made for family, musical, and medical reasons: Peter had scored amphetamine, and was once more stomping about, shouting at this person and that: more frenzied, frenetic activity.

Joy Delight, the minister's daughter, was briefly back in town. Her Navy husband Dennis had gone AWOL, then turned himself in, and was serving time in the brig before being discharged. I'd liked her from the first; now she came up to East Hill one warm spring day. We walked into the upper meadow just below the woods, took off our clothes and started making love. But Peter was stomping around and yelling down below, and I couldn't go through with it.

Early in May I wrote in my diary, "I am so miserable! So sensitive to Peter's stubbornness, his loud-mouthedness, & so tired of feeling good/bad for his ill humor! I want to be happy again, once I was."

Family

W HILE I WAS involved with the vagaries of East Hill Farm, I also had my mind on family down South: my aging parents, mother ailing with still-undiagnosed (and largely unknown) Alzheimer's, my loving, expressive older sister, my quiet older brother. I wondered about my future, whether I could make a greater connection between my life and theirs.

My father (sixty-nine on March 6) and mother (sixty-four a week later) celebrated their birthdays early in the spring. I'd written my father happy birthday, sent him Snyder's "Four Changes" vision of a healthier planet. I telephoned him and my mother, as well. Within a week he answered:

Dear Gordon:—

It is nice to be remembered. We were glad to hear your voice and to know that you are well.

Re the essay birthday greeting, I would not agree that there are too many human beings. The trouble, I think, is distribution. New York City is crowded—your area of New York state is very sparsely settled.

Distribution of human beings, of capital goods is a field wide open for study, research and correction. Economists for many years have recommended such studies.

Florida was windy but sun was nice. Uncle Elwoods' Parkinson's disease is improving with L Dopo treatment.

All well here.
Love, Daddy Gordon

Then one warm golden morning around the time I was reacting to Peter in my diary, I wrote my sister. Chickens clucked out my window, gentle golden light beamed in, but I was deeply unhappy, thinking about home, parents, family—and myself. Maylee answered immediately:

Dearest Gordon,

I didn't get to see Allen G. [at Duke] because of the big snow and frigid weather. I had my bag packed and a reservation so it was a disappointment. I had a cake for him but it would not keep long enough to mail—a carrot & vegetable cake. Please give him my greetings.

Thanks for your remembrance of birthdays and anniversaries. Mother and Daddy are particularly appreciative, especially Mother. They are fine. Mother does well most of the time but forgets some. We see or talk to them everyday. You wrote after you were here Xmas that you were sort of torn leaving them and had thought of returning to this area and getting some kind of job so that you might share their remaining time and bring them your love & solace, and asked my opinion. . . . a difficult subject to write about and human experience in words on paper is imperfect. I think you could be a lot of comfort and your love would be appreciated if you were closer—but, and please don't misunderstand me, I wonder if you are willing to make the concessions all this would involve. Daddy can be argumentative and critical of everyone but especially is he over people whom he considers not to have a decent job or dress as he thinks they should. You know this about him as well as I. You would at least partially (as I've attempted to do) have to fit into their scheme of things or I believe they & you would be unhappy. All of this may work itself out in your life . . . and there may come a time when you want to do this—but I warn you as one who has been there—you love them and want to please them so you accompany them to church or the Twin City Club for lunch occasionally, and don't discuss ideas too different from theirs. They are products of their time just as we are of ours. You listen politely, cut your hair, wear a suit, give them affection and loyalty and then go your own way in some form of compromise. None of it, of course, ever approaches the ideal—which exists only in imagination, poetry, or memory. But it can be pretty damn fine even so.

. . . Mother gets awfully mixed up sometimes. It has nearly broken my heart. The condition of course is there all the time but sometimes the evidence of it seems to come and go. She was wondering if a certain lady had died and I had to remind her we had visited with that lady just the day before.

I love you,
Maylee

Two months after my mother's birthday, my father put her words on paper:

Dear Gordon:—

You were very sweet to remember me on "My Day." Your lovely card . . . arrived on Friday and the beautiful pin came on Saturday.

I had a very good day. Daddy and I went to church and then to Georgia Avenue [my sister's home] for dinner. Maylee and Harold had prepared a real repast. All are well.

We wish you could have seen the lovely dogwood and azalea while they were in blossom. Next year I will get Daddy to take some pictures.

Again my thanks and best wishes to you. Please write us.

Daddy joins in Best wishes,

Love,
Mother

In a small box in the lower left corner were a few cursive lines in my mother's hand:

Dictated to Daddy
My arthritis is acting
u up,

Love Love
Morther

Two Tense Encounters

B Y LATE MAY earth and fields were fat with green, and the air was warm; soon fireflies would grace our evenings. We advertised in the community weekly, *The Pennysaver*, to find homes for two of Brahma's growing kids. Allen, back in the saddle answering mail again, wrote fifty-three letters and thirty-two postcards in a single weekend. And Sally Grossman, wife of Dylan's manager Albert, wrote Allen, "Fish emulsion produces miracle growth"; I ordered a large bottle of Alaska Fish Fertilizer for $6.50, as well as boxes of ladybugs to eat up aphids. Strawberry plants were in the ground at the bottom of the orchard area, and baby fruit trees would be coming our way. Peter set all the asparagus beds—he was full of energy now—and most of us were miserable.

Things came to a head when I brought to the garden many of the burlap feed bags piling up in the barn. Using rocks to hold them down, I laid them out flat to control weeds between vegetable rows. Then one bright morning Sue Miles and I were working side-by-side, kneeling between rows, when overalled Peter strode by, manic on speed.

"Gordon!" he shouted in rant-like voice from twenty feet away, "I may need those burlap bags. You better put 'em back in the barn," and continued on, single-minded brogans clomping the live earth.

Fight him? Refuse? Sue looked at me sympathetically, shaking her head a little, smiling haplessly. I gathered up the bags.

But I could no longer stand Peter's browbeating. (Thinking now to leave before the end of the year, I'd mentioned as much to Allen.) And I wasn't alone. Denise, the person now closest of all to Peter Orlovsky, had reached the end of her rope.

Shortly after the burlap incident Denise and I went to Allen. As soon as I exclaimed, "I don't want to live this way anymore!" Denise followed with, "I don't want to either!"

In a matter of moments, Allen approached Peter under the midday sun. Peter was striding back to the far field, long arms and big hands swinging, solemn Julius in tow.

"Say, Peter," Allen tried, drawing near, "could we talk a few minutes? Now do you realize—" He wore his long-sleeved dark green work shirt and jeans and little grey "vegetarian" crepe-soled shoes.

Without pause Peter answered gruffly, "Sorry, Allen, I gotta plant beans!"

"Just for a minute, Peter—"

Orlovsky came to a halt. "Do you want me to stop and talk, or do you want me to plant beans?" he shouted back.

Both were squinting at each other, Allen through his horn-rims. Peter, not waiting for an answer, turned heel and was striding off again.

"Come on, Julie!" he called, and his older brother bent his serious head and followed him to the far field.

A Happy Family?

S TRANGE AS IT may seem, every now and then Peter on amphetamine could go through alternating phases of outright hostility and relative sociability (or at least reduced antagonism). Sometimes he'd be "offstage," working in the far field, which I took as his assertion of independence, that he could do something for himself (with regular help from Julius and Denise, and on occasion the rest of us). And there may have been spells in which he'd reduce speed intake or even crash a couple days before going back on.

He may have cooled it some after the bean-planting confrontation: at every sign of even the slightest respite, Allen characteristically seemed to take heart. Cheerily coming out to the main garden plot one morning as several of us pulled weeds and hoed, he exclaimed, "Serfs! Ha! Ha!" Back inside he wrote Whalen, "Farm all lush green, planting done now & I'm upstairs scribbling instead of pushing peas in mamma earth's labia." On May 30 he told Gary Snyder, "All well I'm absolutely happy."

Indeed, despite my earlier expressions of dread and misery, my own notes suggest some special moments:

Just had a nice make out w/ Allen, following very good one & long discussion of nite before. I love him very much.

The swim in the pond today was as beautiful as the grass Huncke brought up the other weekend—what a reason to stay!

I might've mentioned the small rivulets of cold every few feet—they came from springs emptying into the pond—a delightful sensation accompanying every swim. Soon we'd stock it with twenty-five large mouth bass and 250 blue gills I'd ordered from Brown's Trout Reserve, and could feel them nibble and brush against us.

Now several members of Denise's family—sister Rosebud, father Juan, Rose's four-year-old son Harley, and her boy friend Andy—came up. Rose brought with her her deaf Dalmatian, Mirabelle, who'd become a permanent resident.

Denise feared that her father, a retired longshoreman, would discover she and Peter were sleeping together. She was not just thoroughly prepared but eager to show and tell him that she was in the attic and Peter in the farthest part of the house, down in his room off porch and pantry.

I was there when they all arrived, and took in some of the conversation between Juan and his welcoming daughter.

As soon as they began walking down the drive toward the house, her father asked, "Where does everyone sleep?"

"That's Peter's room," Denise pointed out, nearing it, "and I sleep in the attic, and Allen—"

"Why," Juan interrupted, voice thick with concern, "don't you sleep together?"

□ □ □

MY CAMEX HAD at last been returned, repaired, and a number of the shots I took during the visit remain vivid to me today:

Rose and I play and laugh and hug. Bracelets on her wrist, cigarette in hand.

Julius sits indoors, rocking slowly in the green rocker. Blue chambray shirt, sleeves rolled up, near window, hands crossed together, just above his belly, somber.

Ray Bremser in white tee shirt, long arms, elbow on table eating soup, reading newspaper magazine, wiping mouth with napkin, black-and-white beard, talking, rough-skinned. Peter in silhouette on the phone, a kind of bobtail haircut. Characteristic large abrupt motions.

A long shot from the meadow above the house; superimpositions of trees, early morning light.

In the chicken yard, Peter throws a bucket of water at a fleeing Allen.

Sunset over the evergreen ridge of the state forest land.

Rose and Juan, she in panties, long-sleeve pink silky shirt.

Andy in close-up, long brown hair beyond shoulders, wet as if from swimming. He and Rose kiss and hug.

A close-up of Ray, looking like an old man, talking, gesturing.

White clouds; blue sky.

A crescent moon.

I assume Juan enjoyed his few days with us; I know one aspect of his stay impressed him enormously. Many years later Rose would tell me she'd heard her father exclaim as he looked out the attic window his first morning, "An entirely nude woman!" His eyes were cast upon Bonnie Bremser, walking naked to the pond for a swim.

He must've repeated it a hundred times over the years, Rose told me; he even returned to the image as he lay dying.

Farm, Town, City, Farm

B EFORE LONG HUNCKE was up again, briefly. I didn't get to see much of him; I'd been planning a trip of my own. Things on East Hill seemed OK: garden plants were outgrowing weeds; we'd found homes for all baby goats (except little Cosset, whom we'd keep); though there were still some dreadful moments, Peter was for the time being in some sort of "cruise" mode; Allen was home, making do; Miles and Sue were attentive. I'd take off for several days, first to Bearsville (near Woodstock), then the city and a final look from bone doctor Mayer.

Cheri and I had been writing each other, but not without difficulty. She was moving from one address to another; I misplaced her new one. Letters forwarded arrived late; one I misaddressed was returned. Now she was staying with her parents—and that made me hesitant. She arranged to move from them while I'd be in town, but more missed messages followed and I saw her not at all.

I had much to do. I'd stop overnight at the Bearsville home of Sally and Albert Grossman. She was still young and beautiful; he had long white hair and wore little glasses and was called "Grandma Benjamin Franklin" by Gregory. They had a skilled gardener; Allen seemed to like the idea of my seeing his handiwork for myself. Scheduling me a visit, he offered, "Maybe you can make it with her," as he went to phone Sally.

But when I got there just before dusk on an abnormally cool day, she was away. Nonetheless I got a good look at their garden, and was as impressed as I thought I'd be: it was smaller-scale than ours, but weedless, every inch carefully tended, a *House and Garden* showcase of raised rows. The quiet, the order of it!

In my room that I night I fleshed out my moments there:

All alone, a big room, me & the color TV, Mets ballgame on. Why, in all houses of the rich in which I've stayed, a certain paucity seems to accompany the grandeur decorum & quiet. One feels small, as if the house were the master of all w/in it. At Panna Grady's huge apt. I would walk to a Nedick's for a hamburger & a glass of water & wait for the next party for food. In X's the plumbing was broken, refrigerator sparse & an evening meal could be eaten out. Here I shared skinny lamb chop w/ Michi,

Japanese housekeeper, & salad & milk & 1 beer each, prepared by effervescent French maid Yvette & retired to bedroom chilled & no extra blanket in sight.

But the relief from the mania of the farm! & the tender neat garden of Miller fresh in evening mist. & now to sleep, to try a.m. aid 77 yr old taciturn Miller in gdn before leaving 11:15 for bus NY.

In the city Dr. Mayer seemed pleased with my wrist and sent me on my way. I saw Ella Radocy before she left for Europe, got in visits with R'lene Dahlberg and Lucien Carr and Alene Lee. Sophie Clark was healthy and glowing a year after her abortion. I was hoping for things to turn romantic, but she evidently wasn't. "I guess she doesn't find me attractive," I said, reporting our encounter to Allen after I was back. "You're as beautiful as she is!" he exclaimed.

I saw *The Strawberry Statement*, a big Hollywood film capitalizing on student unrest: sympathetic to the basic cause, but sappy. And, in a small room at NYU, *Peace Love 2 Hours: Taos 1970: The Communes*. A paean to living close to the earth, overall it reminded me of something I knew all too well: how hard it was for a group of people to make things work. The two young fellows who presented the film blamed others for problems. And those they blamed were seen on screen blaming others.

I got Allen's mail, voluminous as ever, from Stuyvesant Station on 14th near Avenue A. My last afternoon there, walking up 6th Avenue just below 8th Street, I came to a sidewalk table seeking support for political prisoners.

"Are you including people in jail on drug possession charges?" I asked, as I signed the petition.

"No," came the response.

Why this mental block? I wondered in silent exasperation. How long would it take for drugs to be recognized in their political context?

□ □ □

WHEN I RETURNED to East Hill, the big news was that Paul Berkowitz had been up, and we now had electricity: or, a moderate amount of it. I hoped it would be enough for Miles's work, for me to use my 8-millimeter movie projector.

There'd been good rains; all that was green was bursting big. White peonies were just starting to bloom on the front lawn; down in the meadow daisies and black-eyed Susans budded among the blossomed buttercups. Black Godly dog and his blue tick paramour Sadeyes ran up to greet me; I put my bag up and we went for a run. Then I went for hoe and shovel, headed to the garden.

There was other news. Huncke's visit had gone well; no scandalous blow-up as in days of yore. He'd gone on a long walk with Allen and others down to the beaver dam beyond the lower meadow and become distressed when his city clothes got spattered with mud and whatnot. One of his walking companions exclaimed, "You couldn't get a more incongruous person in the countryside!"

One news item was shocking: Sue Miles had left—for good. Her English friend Christie Johnson had visited; after being there a day or so she'd asked Sue, "Are you *mad*? What are you *doing* here?" That earnest query from an old friend made the difference. When Paul took the bus back to the city, Sue was at his side.

Relationships

THE BREAK-UP HAD been coming for some time. Before East Hill they'd both been having affairs; by the time they arrived things were near dead-end.

In the room across from mine, Miles and Sue were immediately next to Allen's. In the fullest sense: the heads of his bed and theirs abutted the same wall, in the middle of which was a door no longer in use: they were scarcely an inch apart. They could hear, they felt, virtually every movement in the other room. After they'd been with us a short while, Allen complained to Miles, "I can't hear you fucking!"

Astonished and outraged to begin with, and English on top of that, the two guests stuffed newspapers around the edges of the doorframe, but it was of course a futile effort, for they weren't fucking; they were breaking up.

□ □ □

OTHERS SOON JOINED us. Rick Fields, friend and high school trackmate with Barbara Rubin's brother, was a Harvard graduate who'd later distinguish himself with a number of books on Buddhism; Ann Buchanan was a friend of Allen's from San Francisco 1963, when she and poet Charles Plymell were close and Neal Cassady was around and they shared a house on Gough Street.

Rick and Ann had pulled up—slowly—one bright June day in her old grey milk truck. It looked decrepit; from the first Allen worried it would be abandoned here, his home turned into a gathering of vehicles squatting on cinder blocks. The truck was Ann and Rick's home: they'd been traveling around upstate New York, working on one or two other farms, often sleeping in the truck. The driver stood at the steering wheel, and there was a single "shotgun" seat for a passenger; in the small space behind the wheel, a mattress, a handmade bookcase with books, and shelving. Very slow-moving, it took nearly an hour to make the five miles to town.

Rick was dark-haired, hairy-chested, an inch or so shorter than I, calm, friendly. Ann was pretty with black hair, large dark eyes, a becoming neck. Her breasts were small but nicely shaped, and when she worked in the field her nipples often showed through her tee-shirt. She held herself erect, was quiet-voiced, deep-voiced, intent.

I don't at all mean Ann hadn't a sense of humor, but she was serious and direct about everything. At some point after San Francisco 1963, living in Guadalajara with

Rick, she wrote a long, absorbed letter to Maretta Greer, giving considerable attention to sex and meditation, exploring the spiritual dimensions of sexual intimacy.

In late June 1970 on East Hill, both Ann and Rick worked in daily earnest in
garden and field. I remember a morning replacing fence posts with Rick: taking a
break, we lay back on meadow grass under a pleasant blue sky, birds twittering from
overhanging maples. Simultaneously we happened to cast our eyes in the same direction, and there was Ann, bent over, hoeing vigorously in the garden. Rick looked at
me, eyes twinkling, and, using a term I scarcely knew at the time, offered, "Nice thing,
women's liberation!"

A week or so passed. Ann was spending more time—when she wasn't at work—
up in the hay loft of our barn. Rick and she seemed to be growing apart. One quiet
bright Sunday afternoon—everyone else was inside, as if enjoying a siesta—I went out
to the barn, up to the hay loft, and found her there. I sat down on the hay with her;
we began talking. After a few moments I was suddenly hearing, "I'd like to make love
with you." She did.

For a couple of weeks in early summer 1970 Ann and I were together, sleeping in
my room. But then she grew disaffected: "Our fucking's gotten too mechanical," she
complained. She moved across the hall, in with Miles.

Peter in Crisis

T HE BEANS AND burlap-bag encounters of late May proved only tiny engagements compared to the crisis to come. Sometimes during late winter months
we'd all watched that little black-and-white TV, but with warmer weather Peter had
moved it and its batteries from the living room into his downstairs room. And now
he'd just destroyed it by plunging our "harpoon" post hole digger through its screen—
I thought out of anger with himself for watching it; Miles thought out of paranoia that
it was watching him. In a few days he bought a replacement, only to destroy it as well.

Knowing he must have speed hidden someplace or some places (likely not his
room, because of Denise's watchful eye), Allen and I searched and searched. To our
surprise we came upon some underneath the eaves in the barn: high on the wall where
two beams met in Lash the old horse's stall, a clear plastic bag with familiar white
crystal-like powder. We returned to the house, Allen grimly holding the evidence.
Peter was in the kitchen. He and Allen went through the pantry and into his room.

Peter later burned the rest of the speed—we hoped—in the trash. Later still I
heard he'd devoted much of $10,000 from selling Allen's, Kerouac's, and Cassady's
letters, to amphetamine.

The last weekend in June, Louis and Edith were up. They both seemed well, Louis
at seventy-five, Edith at sixty-four. Louie, who'd seemed to stare to the point of self-
embarrassment at Candy's large breasts back in 1968, offered appreciative comments
about city mini-skirts in 1970.

It was a pleasant but short visit. One afternoon just after they left, Peter, perhaps
still crashing after speed, was getting drunk on wine. I don't recall our purpose, but
Allen and I were taking various measurements on the house, and Peter followed us
around, at a distance. We were calling out numbers to each other, inside to out, which
Peter repeated, parodying our calls. Then, as dusk came and supper time with it, Peter
utterly broke down in front of the house. Most of us were already at the table, but we
came out to see him lying in front of the porch, as if he were about to do push-ups,
only proceeding instead to bang and bump the side of his head against the flagstones.

This was not an event of an instant; it went on throughout our meal, and beyond,
as various of us got up from the table to try to calm Peter as he lay there alternately
muttering, moaning, banging his head, cursing himself for using speed.

"Everything belongs to you!" he shouted at Allen. "Everything belongs to you!" (Much later, Allen would tell me he bought Peter a plot of twenty acres because of this lament.)

When Allen returned to the table, he said to me, "Go get your camera and film Peter." Miles, seated kittycorner to me at the table, recorded the scene in his journal:

"No, I couldn't," said Gordon. "Peter's a friend."

"He'll thank you for it later, if he gets over it. And maybe it'll show someone else what speed'll do to you! You should film it. It's real. It's much more real than all those sunsets and trees you film . . ." Allen was quite insistent.

Gordon slowly shook his head and crouched low over the table, not looking up. Allen raised his voice, almost shouting, "That's what being a filmmaker is about. Showing things as they are. Well that's Peter out there groaning. That's how he is!"

Allen was suffering almost as much as Peter.

"Yeah. Go-wan. Why not?" demanded Denise. She had done everything possible.

I remained seated. At some point Allen, true to his aesthetic commitment to "reality," must have brought the portable Sony out near Peter. There's a recording of Peter, with occasional interjections from Allen, as he lies outside. His voice is not the truly gruff "leper's voice" he sometimes used, which sounded akin to the demon's in the 1974 film *The Exorcist*; rather, it's a more comic nasal one with grunts and groans, against the chirping of one or two birds. And it's a drunken one. Words—when he speaks words—are hard to distinguish, but we can hear him tell Allen, "Go on, beat it, will you now?! . . . I got nothing, I got nothing!"

And, hysterically, "It—it—it don't mean nothin'. I'd like to bash my skull!"

A little later when Allen asks soft and tender, "Why are you so unhappy?" Peter challenges, "What've I got to be happy about?"

"Your youth," Allen specifies. "You've got a girl friend, you've got all of nature, you got the whole earth to play with."

But Peter remains unassuaged; between hiccups he announces, "I think I'll kill myself."

Allen urges him not to.

"It don't matter," Peter insists.

"Yes it does!" Allen insists, "It matters to me . . . I'd cry!"

"Big deal!"

"Well, that's the biggest deal there is, when you get a broken heart."

Leary

IN FEBRUARY WE'D learned that Timothy Leary (who'd been arrested on drug charges at least fourteen times in five years) was convicted for possession of two joints which, Allen understood, were planted in the ashtray of his car by a California cop. Calling Leary "an insidious and detrimental influence on society," Judge Byron McMillan denied bail. Allen sat himself down at our little round telephone table and dictated a telegram to the judge:

> Pray release the pioneer psychologist Timothy Leary on normal bond till sentencing. He is considered by many good people to hold honorable if controversial opinions and it is not useful to deny bond and abruptly jail so famous a theorist for his unpopular views—such an imprisonment is proper neither to science nor to jurisprudence.

Leary remained jailed. At the same time, he was tried again for his original 1965 Laredo, Texas, arrest in which he'd claimed ownership of the half-ounce of marijuana found on his eighteen-year-old daughter. Judge Ben C. Connally gave him ten years for "smuggling" that tiny amount of pot into the U.S.; Judge McMillan then sentenced Leary to one to ten years for his California "offense." The sentences were set consecutively, meaning that Leary was liable to spend up to twenty years in jail for less than one ounce of grass. Both judges, according to Allen's later preface to Leary's *Jail Notes*, "agreed with government lawyers' boorish language that Dr. Leary was 'a menace to the community.'"

Allen continued to support Leary in various ways. In March, he sent a $500 check to his wife, Rosemary; in April, he "starred" in a San Francisco "freedom festival" and "Om Orgy" benefit, and with promoter Bill Graham planned a large benefit later. His journal pages contain numerous addresses for Leary, courts and judges, and a number of lawyers, as well as a list of rock bands (including Jefferson Airplane, Janis Joplin, Grateful Dead) for benefits.

At the Village Gate in May, Allen argued with Abbie Hoffman, who was on acid and denounced Ginsberg as a "CIA agent," claiming, "They'll never let Leary out; you're looking for a religious martyr but this is political revolution & he—a prisoner

of War, a political prisoner." Several days later, after Supreme Court Justice William
O. Douglas (Leary's "last recourse") denied bail, Allen sent Rosemary another $500.

Complaining that "Leary's bail denial [was] scarcely registered or recorded in
Press," Allen wrote his father:

> . . . the Supreme Court is not obeying Constitution which guarantees bail, especially
> on so petty offenses as 2 "roach" bust. . . .
>
> Leary is active Pacifist influence on Change. By this violent conspiracy or
> stupidity the govt. has now created a situation where there is no longer recourse
> to law. Also Abbey Hoffman's prophecy proved true last week. Given seriousness of
> repression on Leary—he's now a "Political Prisoner"—I see myself as less safe as well.
> . . . What has happened to Leary is happening to hundreds of thousands all over
> U.S.—250,000 pot busts a year you know—plus the rest of the slaughter & violence
> from above? There will be no way of preventing violent reaction to this violence of
> repression. . . .

In early July he typed a long letter to Leary at the California Men's Colony, San
Luis Obispo. Having read Leary's *Jail Notes* manuscript, Allen offered his imprisoned
colleague a primer on writing: cut "those judicious longwinded the's"; "'Of's are very
often useless legal echo style." It was a Poundian's directive to economy of language
and appreciation of vowels ("Lately I find attention to vowels, awareness of vowel-
density of talk flow is a good way to guide condensation. . . ."). Citing Kerouac's
"rhythmic-voweled ear," it corrected excerpts from Leary's own prose. I imagine it
was more than his correspondent sought to know.

At the heart of Allen's letter were legal concerns, based on his view that Leary
was caught in the jaws of a system not merely all-powerful but "violently corrupt,
and no recourse in sight." Allen told him of having discussed his "Socratic" situation
with former Attorney General Ramsey Clark, and alluded to Clark's confirmation of
what Lucien had told him two years earlier: that J. Edgar Hoover had recorded, and
made illicit use of, Martin Luther King's risqué activities at a hotel. Clark also supported Allen's

> . . . theory that most narcotics agents tend to push, which I had documented from
> NY Times last 4 years, he . . . said he'd indicted 32 out of 80 Federal agents ("all he
> had evidentiary proof against") for hankey pankey & that history of such corruption
> went back quarter century to his knowledge.

He praised Leary's apparent optimism and urged him, "Yes stay visit farm anytime that's what it's for." And updated him on East Hill, particularly on Peter (now, without speed, gaining weight) and himself:

Peter's in & out of focus depending on the week, right now fine & acre garden's acme summer green, new moon, misty day over tomato plants, he's sawing top off steel barrel to put fenceposts inside soak w/ creosote for cows who've been in garden dawn-raid, need barbwire, right now he's calling Julius help, birds chirping at suppertime//I have several months free here trying to detoxify my brain after months travelling & reading newspapers & social activity. . . .

Forty-one years later, looking over these draconian prosecutions and persecutions of an individual by a state sullied and ignorant at heart—it seems almost unbelievable. In a nation which can appear gifted with lack of historical knowledge (how many Americans connect the 1979 Iranian seizure of their embassy with the 1953 U.S.-aided overthrow of Mossadeq?) it seems pertinent to remember the circumstance of Timothy Leary, the man whom Allen would call "the archetypal man without a country."

Alcohol, Garden & Pond

AFTER LOUIS AND Edith had gone, Allen tenderly wrote his aging father, "You left your blue sweater & rubbers here—shall I send them to you? That's yr old familiar babyblue sweater."

More visitors arrived. Mary Beach and Claude Pelieu, Allen's French translators, escaped the inversions taking place in the city for a couple weeks translating *Planet News*. Mary was an American painter who'd lived decades in France, knew the language fluently, and was related to Sylvia Beach, first publisher of Joyce's *Ulysses*. Claude was a poet, painter, and collage artist. They'd often work outdoors with Allen, under high maples near the garden, which was now luxuriant, thanks to our hard work. As the scene appears in my movie footage, it seems idyllic: Allen in a fuzzy, puffy red hat, brim-backward; Claude bare-chested in striped bell bottoms, Mary in shirt and pants and onyx ring on index finger—all in glasses, chairs pulled close, laps of weighty papers.

Coming with the Pelieus were poet and printer Charles Plymell, Pamela Beach Plymell (Mary's daughter), and their baby, Elizabeth. Charles had known Allen since San Francisco 1963, and had ridden with him and Peter and Julius some of their way cross-country in the VW bus, winter 1966.

Still more guests showed up, including poet John Giorno, star of Warhol's six-hour *Sleep*, the creator of New York's "Dial-A-Poem." With him came filmmaker Wynn Chamberlain, whose *Brand X* feature, which Jonas called "the first entertainment film of the Woodstock Nation, or maybe the last entertainment film of the Nixon nation," had just opened in Manhattan at the Elgin.

But the grandest guest of all was Gregory, whom I picked up at the bus, Alexander Worth's *Russia at War* under his arm. He gave Allen Mario Puzo's *The Godfather*; reading it, Allen commented, "How awful the Italians are!" To which Gregory responded, "The Italians aren't the same in Italy. They don't come on macho. They're more elegant, more gentle."

But if anyone thought that once Gregory arrived our lives would be enriched with discussions of history and culture added to poetry, translation, and agronomy, they were mistaken. Certainly there were pleasant moments, and Gregory's company could sometimes be inspiring. "As long as I live, / Movie stars will die," I'd written in my diary soon after his return. (Gregory, who loved to quote himself, had no doubt quoted it again; and I admired the line.) Miles told me of one afternoon in the kitchen as Gregory (whom Claude called "Zucchini Face") cooked up an Italian storm, opera playing loud. The chef called to him, "Miles, you've been to Europe! You know what good food is! You know it has to be *al dente*!" He put down Peter, "this idiot Orlovsky who cooks the spaghetti until it's mush!"

Thanks in good part to Denise, Peter was more or less on the mend after his June breakdown—except that, with Ray, he was drinking heavily. Allen had announced that not just needle drugs but alcohol must be banned. (When Ray inadvertently sprayed everything close by snapping open a beer, Allen asked him to clean it up, reminding him, "There is, you know, a basic sort of rule, there's no alcohol in the house, sort of, you know that . . . no alcohol because people are in such terrible condition with alcohol here.")

Perhaps Corso's having just learned of this ban led him to hold forth—drunk and drooling—at dinner his first evening back: "I came to the farm to kill Allen."

"Eat your spaghetti," Allen shot back without even looking up. It was no great flap—but it was merely the beginning.

Early one quiet evening Miles headed down to the pond, thinking to sit by water's edge and enjoy a Camel. To his surprise, there on the surface of the pond—recently stocked with bass and blue gills—floated seven or eight beer cans.

Miles reported what he'd seen. Allen, very upset, assembled nearly everyone at the pond to behold the evidence and determine the cause. It seemed Ray and Gregory had walked to Cherry Valley. (Back roads and paths could shorten the distance, but still it was a few miles each way, and steep on the return.) They bought two or more six-packs, then walked back, tossing cans roadside as they finished them (thus furthering the reputation of Committee on Poetry, Inc., in the community). Gregory initially denied it, but once all was obvious, as Allen put it in his journal, "their smiling faces turned snarling & screaming at each other at dusk." Gregory shouted abuse at him and Ray broke down, cried, and promised never again. And Allen, Miles reported, "turned his big sad eyes" on Gregory.

Nostalgia and Acrimony:
An Interlude

S HORTLY AFTER THE floating beer cans, Allen taperecorded a scene in the dining room. Ostensibly a work session on "Wales Visitation" with poor Claude
and Mary, it became an exchange between Allen and Gregory. Though early on
Gregory asserted "Allen . . . I'm gettin' rid of all of you . . . in a matter of two weeks.
. . . you'll have peace here," he was soon drawing pictures for Georgia Bremser: a
Tyrannosaurus Rex, an ant, a pussy cat; Georgia herself. . . . Then a poets' dialogue
of sweet recollections (on Allen's part) became disputed recollections (on Gregory's),
with further threats from our guest.

Allen often responded to Gregory with humor, as in, "Thank God, I was so worried for a minute!" when Corso offered gratuitously, "I'll protect you from anything,
Al. Anybody fucks with you, Al, I'm on your side!"

But as typical with the mercurial Corso, he soon turned sour. Part of it may
have been misunderstanding: Allen recalled once screwing Gregory; Gregory insisted
Allen tried but couldn't, and so blew him instead. Allen took that as rejection: "You
wouldn't acknowledge our relationship! I mean, not only have you . . . cursed me all
these years, but you've refused to recognize what we had together!" Gregory challenged Allen's practice of taperecording, called him "motherfucker" and "asshole,"
and again said he'd kill him.

Gregory said he'd come to help Allen, and proposed he "get rid of" "the Bremsers,
the Orlovskys." (He—Gregory—would look after Julius.) He warned Allen to "watch
that motherfucker" Peter "with . . . his fat belly and ass sticking out." He told Allen to
head for the South Seas, rather than grow old with Ed the Hermit: "Hermit, shit! The
fucker's always out there feeling women's asses! All day! That hermit!"

Amidst such widespread human failure, what then was the way to be? That was
"the real goods," as manifested by Corso himself:

*The real goods is to be like a man like me who really doesn't know his next move,
but his next move is anywhere. But you don't have that choice, you don't have that
option.*

To which Allen returned wearily, "Right. You're tellin' me."

Why put up with such abuse? Others would've sent Gregory packing. It took the extraordinary affection and loyalty Allen felt for his friends, whose work he admired. It took his natural inclination to mythologize, romanticize—a faculty without which a poem like *Howl* might never have been written. It took his extraordinary—some would say foolish—love.

The tape also includes discussion of a recent incident when Corso shouted insults at Mary Beach: Ray Bremser, roused to chivalry, knocked the cigarette out of Gregory's mouth, and Gregory responded by slapping him. Gregory explained he was "only here for a week's happiness . . . I don't use fists."

But why, as Gregory himself asked, record such things? For literary history, for good or ill. When I consider excesses of Corso and a few others, yes, some Beats seem offensive boors: "mayhem and disaster" might be an only slightly hyperbolic characterization of their legacy. When I consider their best work—not to mention Allen's generosity and saintliness—I'm given inspiration and models to follow. Recordings, like mental imprints known as memory, can help bridge—or widen—the distance between real and ideal.

A Black Eye

I N THE AFTERMATH of these events with Gregory at center, Allen had written Ferlinghetti that there'd been "several wild screaming drunk explosions . . . we'll all kick his ass if he starts again."

More guests were coming. Cheri had been due the weekend of July 11, but missing that 6:00 AM bus, promised to make it the next Saturday. Paul Berkowitz, who with Miles had installed the windcharger, was returning. (The charger was producing less electricity than expected—we'd still have to climb the eight feet down to the bottom of the ram house, test battery levels, then sometimes haul the heavy batteries back up for charging at Myron's.) And Miles's friend from London, Steve Abrams, who in 1967 had taken a full page in the *London Times* (with signatures by the Beatles) to call for legal marijuana, would examine Allen's dope files.

Cheri did make it up, and we spent some special time together during the day. She now beheld the farm for the first time in all its green bounty. She was wholly a city girl (a Bronx one, to boot); as I gave her a tour, she mistook ducks for geese, and stepped on my prized carrots.

"Being in the barn with you or out in the garden is the first time I've experienced animals and growing vegetables so directly," she wrote the next week, adding, "It's the first time I've had the weather prophesized to me the way Ed did when he told us 'It's rain on the way this evening.'"

But the day wasn't a good one for Gregory—nor, because of him, for others. Early on he browbeat Bonnie. In the afternoon, he and some others went on a walk. It was hot and most of them were drinking. Gregory was taking in three or four times as much as anyone else, and he picked on Mary Beach, calling her a "cunt." (She was able to handle it, respond in kind.)

Dusk was falling when everyone returned. Gregory—as people sometimes do, realizing they alone are drunk—became resentful. Steve Abrams had to be back in New York in the morning, and I was set to drive him to the 8:56 bus. Gregory asked me to buy him a six-pack while I was in town.

I declined: "Gregory, I can't do that; Allen says you're not allowed to have any beer or alcohol."

"Fucking Ginzy doesn't rule my life!" he shouted.

I was heading through the kitchen; Gregory was on its edge, near the dining room. You're being ridiculous, Gregory, I thought. But I also thought it important not to verbalize that. I moved past him and headed toward the door. As I laid hand to handle I felt a great sudden pressure against my left eye: it was turning into liquid, and something weighty was clasping onto my back. Gregory had come after me, punching me from behind with his left fist in my left eye.

Miles and Rick pulled him off, threw him to the floor. Miles said Gregory had been "flailing like a madman" at my head and squealing. He swung at Miles, knocking his glasses across the room. Almost everyone suddenly assembled around the front door, spilling out onto the flagstones, urging that Gregory be put on the bus with Steve. But Allen was no keener on that than I imagine Steve was. He hesitated.

Meanwhile, Gregory denied having given me a black eye. "How," he asked, "could you give a guy a black eye from behind?" And there I was, with a swollen purplish-blue eye.

And there was time passing as a huddle of voices rose in gathering darkness—and fireflies began their modest silent show against the vulgar human hubbub. Cheri ran some cold water in a bowl, got a washcloth, and we went upstairs.

Through my window we—I with Cheri's cool wet cloth on my eye—could hear voices rise as we lay in bed. Gregory now shifted from denying he'd done it to claiming I'd come at him. I heard Allen exclaim, again and again, "But Gregory! To hit someone is unforgivable!" Cheri dipped the cloth in the cool water and wrung it, replaced it on my swollen flesh. Excited voices rang in the night: assertion, accusation, denial, fabrication.

Ann, true to form, calmly, firmly asserted herself, saying Gregory should go as soon as possible; Gregory returned, "How can you listen to her, Allen, that woman has slept with all these guys! She's a whore! A slut!" I couldn't believe how stupid he was making himself appear. He was insulting everyone; after Miles and Paul returned from taking Steve to the bus, he insulted Miles too.

Cheri lay there with me, reading, loving me, silent.

Later, the heated group dispersed; everyone more or less retired. Gregory went up to his room and Ray Bremser, drunk, climbed to his and Bonnie's bed in the attic. Then Ray began arguing with Bonnie, calling her a whore. Soon Gregory took a step out of his room—he was sharing Julius's, on the other side of the wall from mine—to the foot of the short ladder-like stairs leading to the attic. He shouted up, "Hey you fucking German, can you keep it down? Can you shut up, up there?" Ray and Bonnie were disturbing him; he was trying to sleep at last.

□ □ □

WE'D RESOLVED THAT if Gregory caused more trouble he should be asked to leave, but he wasn't. In the next day or two, I told Allen I was disappointed he hadn't kept that resolution, and he answered, "Well, I guess you should be disappointed." Only much later did the obvious occur to me: this was my karma, from not having defended Barbara two years earlier on the Fourth of July.

□ □ □

A LITTLE LATER, Allen and Gregory spoke about the matter, with Allen's recorder on. Corso offered that he "did not do it intentionally," for I "must have been facing him":

I never touch a man—only if they touch me . . . I feel for Gordon, I feel for Gordon, and I'm sorry the whole thing happened. I really am, I really am. I'm gettin' out tomorrow so I'm not gonna be a hangup here anymore.

But soon he was asking to come into Allen's room, then attacking him when turned down.

"No, I really want to go to work," Allen explained. "All you do in my room is abuse me." He accused Gregory of lying.

"This is the first time I ever struck a man, really," Gregory said, "and I'm happy that I gave him a black eye." He reminded Allen that he got the farm for poets. "I'm a poet," he said. "Where's his credentials?"

"He's a filmmaker," Allen answered. "But it's not a question of that . . . every time you've been here you've been a nuisance to everyone."

Corso explained that this was because "I'm very alive . . . everybody you got up here is Hare Krishna people, they're very dead."

It was, he allowed, "about time I gave the mark on somebody."

□ □ □

AFTER SEVERAL DAYS Gregory left for Buffalo, where Allen De Loach helped set him up in an apartment. Except briefly on one occasion, he didn't return to East Hill while I was there. But a month after the black eye, a handwritten letter arrived:

Dear Gordon—Such a goodness as you—a planter of life, a good man—forgive my sorrowful head—I have a deep respect for you, and it's a not-too-sad head as feels it. That was me that's awful to be, yet know there is also me what's poetry to be—And, of course, that you know of me, the best of me, and, of course, I am forgiven—Life

*was not good to me that day—I sorrow'd a lost love, a friend it was not my fortune
to farewell well.*

*Best stick to the muse and keep out of trouble—Who knows—I might be yet that
wise dream of me—a goodness for good friends, a life hard, yet your soil is soft and
food life grows there—*

Gregory kisses you,
a difficult friend,

Ye gods! and so simple too!

Many years later, not long before Gregory died, I asked him who his lost friend
was. He couldn't remember, and seemed shocked to learn he'd given me a black eye.

FOUR

Final Seasons

A Pig to the Rescue

O NE AFTERNOON PETER and Denise, accompanied by Miles, went searching for spare parts in a huge junk yard heaped with car corpses.

Nearby was a large red barn with countless chickens and pigs, pecking or rooting around metal skeletons. One cute little pale pink piglet—a "pure Yorkshire" Peter later wrote—captivated our searchers, and in minutes she was theirs. It would be Denise's birthday present: she was about to turn nineteen.

Giggling and cackling, they stuffed the pig into a bag and got into the car—then realized the larger problem looming. "Allen's gonna really freak out!" Denise said. And they immediately appreciated another difficulty—as Peter in his wonderful sweet poem, "Dont Bite Please" later wrote of his new passenger:

Squeek squalling & a squink winking
& pissing on our frunt seat surprised laps—

But Allen didn't freak out, and the little pig became one of the biggest stars at the farm. She didn't solve all Peter's problems, but she made an enormous difference in his life, becoming a focus of affection and nurturing for him and Denise—almost a child. The pig and hard work (often, overwork) became Peter's rehabilitation.

For a good while she stayed in their room with them, in one of those wooden cages for transporting chickens. In "Dont Bite Please" Peter tells it:

Feeding her 2 1/2 babey milk bottles &
put her in chicken-stick cage next to our bed
& for next 2 weeks early morning
we'd open top hatch & she would dart up 6 inches
all pure energy spring
right straight to tip of rubber nipple
& her mouth would clasp around it &
at count of 10 she would be franticalley looking
around for bottle no 2 & 3

But one day when Peter wanted to rub noses with "this little baby," the teething piglet bit him on his nose. She became known as "Don't Bite Please," or, as we often called her, "Don't Bite Me."

A pig, Peter tells us in his poem,

> . . . when happey or funney feeling will
> swing its self around off the ground
> 2 or 3 times & then dart a few feet
> & instantly freeze with spaced out eyes.

In my footage of the little low-slung porker's early days, she's as small as a baby puppy—the top of her head barely reaches the low point of Godly's torso. In the freshly mown front yard, Peter in red felt hat, brogans and overalls and big work-gloves reaching almost halfway up his forearm, dances a jig with the naked little pig. Quickly he moves around the front yard, she following, running back and forth, Peter stopping, pig running between his legs. He runs again, pig follows, catches up; Peter stops; Peter runs, stops, turns, runs, the pig turns, runs, follows, again and again.

In another scene a horseback rider in formal English riding hat and boots pays a visit. When he starts trotting away, Allen reaches down to the pig, lest she come near the horse. He picks her up in his arms, shoulders her like a baby.

By winter, when the pig weighed nearly as much as Denise, there were five members of the growing dog population (including Mirabelle the deaf Dalmatian) on East Hill. Peter's poem shows us of some of the basic relations between the two species:

> after filling the dog pan full,
> & out the hungrey blue dashes the pig
> with big split seconds gulping their food down.
> The dogs at first couldent believe their eyes
> at what was happening to their food
> because the pig was eating like 5 dogs rolled into one.
> The shepard bit off 2 inches of pigs curley tail
> to teach her the great all time lesson.
>> The deaf doumations nose
>> pointed right up to the pigs ass
>> & gobbled the shit up as it
>> came pipe streaming hot out
>> before it could fall into the snow.

The pig would raise her hind leg, Peter tells us, so he could scratch her, or "PLOP down so fast / letting me know it was scrach time." But eventually Peter would no longer be at the farm on a regular basis; something had to be done about all the animals. So Don't Bite Me had to be given away. And in the poem he bids her adieu:

Goodby my friendly babey,
You were lean & clean as a big pine neddle that
fell into my hands by surprise.

Bedroom Visits

O N THE FARM we had the entire seventy acres and woods and hills beyond to wander in: that was fortunate, for there wasn't much space in our house. Denise and Peter, with a room beyond the pantry, might have been best situated. Even so on occasion we'd hear—to our pleasure—their voices raised in song, Denise's guitar, and left-handed Peter's right-handed banjo.

Excepting the Bremsers in the attic, Miles and Ann may've had as little privacy as anyone. And as I recall one or two events, it appears both Allen and I were to blame.

I have in mind not only Allen's complaint, when Sue was still there, about not being able to hear as he wanted through the walls. A little later he came in one day while Miles was still in bed and thrust toward his face an after-death photo of Charles Olson (a friend of Miles's, as well as Allen's). "Ha! I bet that'll make you lose your hard-on!" Allen exclaimed.

For some months on and off I'd been concerned about a strange phenomenon: on ejaculation, blood would sometimes appear in my semen. It wasn't consistent, but it was frequent enough to make me concerned, especially one summer night when it seemed quite pronounced. Anna Marie—she and I had patched things up—was with me for the weekend and noted it and worried too.

I felt close to Miles; I took the liberty of going across the hall to his and Ann's room for . . . for—consultation? I'm of course embarrassed and ashamed now, but I think yes, I wanted a friend's opinion, and yes, I must've been to some extent showing off, like exhibiting a war wound. In any case, I did it, a concerned Anna Marie close behind: both of us naked, I knocked on the mostly closed door.

Miles called us in. They were under the sheets, he near the dim kerosene lamp near the door, Ann farther back in shadows near the wall. I entered, flashlight in one hand, cock in other. Whatever he must've felt, Miles managed at least to display concern as he brought his face close—without coming too, too close, proper Englishman that he was—and made an analysis.

Actually, he also seemed worried on my behalf. What followed was a discussion of the situation from several angles, including (of course) asking Anna Marie if she were having a period (she wasn't) and wondering if the penis had a bone. In a few days the problem would be solved, for at Bassett Hospital I'd be diagnosed with a treatable urinary tract infection.

But meanwhile, Allen, whom we could hear in his room padding about, shuffling papers, as he was wont to do, also appeared at Miles's door. He'd been getting some petitions together, and realizing that four people were right at hand, saw an opportunity.

Now he too entered the kerosene- and flashlight-illuminated darkness, papers in one hand, papers in the other. He handed out one petition against sonic booms over forests, another on saving whales; each of us took them and signed dutifully. He was pleased; he thanked us and we talked a bit; then he shuffled back to his own midnight chambers, getting them ready to mail.

There was just one discrepancy. On the petition against sonic booms, Allen had forged Julius's signature—as well as signing twice himself. Why? Because on the one for the whales, Allen had inscribed the first line, and Julius had followed. Julie did so with beautiful lettering, precisely on top of Allen's own signature, rendering both illegible.

The Farm at Midsummer

N ow wildflowers were out full force: orange day lilies lined the roadside; bedstraws made their fine white sprays; wild parsnip reached its full yellow height; Queen Anne's lace brightened every meadow. Elderberry bushes grew snowballs; purple clover darkened blue; black-eyed Susans and daisies bloomed for the long haul.

In the far field Peter's soybeans and corn and tomatoes grew big; our garden near the house was fat with food, and we had to work hard to keep back the weeds. Squash vines had started to run, and needed mulching. Cauliflower heads were growing, and their large inner leaves had to be pulled over them to protect from sunburn. Fences still needed work. There were successive plantings of short-term crops like radishes (a new China Rose variety, to withstand summer heat), midsummer plantings of fall crops turnips and kohlrabi. After end-of-June rains, the first half of July had been dry; luckily we'd moved a 250-gallon tub underneath a gutter spout, for hauling water from house to garden.

At the center of our plot, two seventy-five-foot rows of potatoes, Norland and Kennebec, were being ravaged by thousands of small orange bugs who chewed their leaves away. Squatting or on bended knees we'd slowly go after them, plant by plant, bug by bug, flicking them off into a bucket of kerosene. Three rows of peas neighboring the potatoes had produced their full; we hauled them up, used their nitrate-rich corpses for compost, and planted spinach for the fall and canning. We'd seeded more squash at the feet of corn for greater productivity, and both plants were doing well.

□ □ □

A month earlier several ducklings had hatched, but for some reason they all died; yet the mother continued sitting, weeks, under an old sled, eggs long gone.

□ □ □

Bessie was due to give birth the third week of August, and John Giorno, who seemed taken with the farm, would come back to witness the event. Our big swelling Jersey seemed to be doing fine, but not all was well in the animal kingdom. One bright day the body of Sadeyes, run over by the milk truck, was found on the road near the Grahams'. On hearing of it, Denise burst into tears. As we were burying the blue tick I stopped and took up my camera:

> A close-up frontal shot of dead Sadeyes, flies crawling over her tongue which hangs out one side of her closed mouth—you can see her front teeth. Her body's squeezed into a Kellogg's Corn Flakes carton, resting on a newspaper, left foot reaching up toward her face, maggots here and there. (Her body passed wind as we set her down.) The box lies next to her grave on top of a mound of piled dirt; as the camera cuts back we see Allen the grave digger, shovel in hand, more than knee-deep in burial hole.

□ □ □

ON JULY 22, we celebrated two birthdays with a cake: Denise's nineteenth, Bonnie's thirty-first. Though I admired both women, I remember thinking especially about the younger one on this occasion: how did Denise do it? The age difference between her and Peter was extraordinary; Denise still wasn't old enough to vote! And not only had she managed to put up with Peter's speed mania; because of her good influence he now seemed over his amphetamine problem. Even so, life with Peter could be minute-to-minute, and there was the constant care of his crazy brother—in a scene already rich with psychic complications and constantly colliding social dynamics. What character this young woman from Queens displayed on East Hill! What youthful vibrance! What resiliency! What love for Peter, and all living, growing things.

□ □ □

SOON MARETTA GREER called, asking Allen if she might return for a spell. Allen asked Peter, who stipulated, "As long as she works in the garden two hours every day." Soon Allen entered in his diary:

> Waking as every day for months in country, the heavy fear of police state continuous body depression at dawn—today Maretta Greer arriving by bus, kicked out of Pakistan—weeping on telephone—or Gregory in Buffalo solitary & drinking to angry tears—Sinclair in jail, revolutionary underground Press rolling out pretty-paged bad poetics—

□ □ □

GUESTS CONTINUED OUR way. One was Paris-born poet, translator, and anthropologist Nathaniel Tarn, a tall slender Englishman in his forties whom Miles knew from London. His first morning on East Hill he came bouncing downstairs, dressed head-to-toe in white sports clothes as if stopping at an English country house. Before sitting down to breakfast with others, he was suddenly stunned by what he saw out the window: there in the backyard was Peter, totally naked, spreading his legs, washing his ass.

□ □ □

LIKE EVERY SUMMER, we helped with haying down at Graham's. It was always fun: lots of itching and sweating and heavy lifting relieved by good camaraderie. Once in later years Wayne, the youngest Graham son, reminded me what haying with Peter on speed was like. After we loaded the wagon with twenty-five-pound bales and brought it beneath the upper-story hay mow (where it was 130 degrees), one man would place the bales one-by-one on a conveyor belt feeding up into the mow. The belt gripped the bales with metal teeth, each a yard apart. Typically the man in the mow would call "Three teeth" to the man below, referring to the interval between bales. That way the mow-man—who after laying hands on a bale had to turn and stack it five or six yards behind him—wouldn't work himself to death or die of heat exhaustion. Wayne—who was sixteen at the time—reported:

> When it was Peter's turn on the wagon, I'd call "Count three teeth." Peter would count three teeth, put a bale on; count two teeth, put a bale on; count one tooth, put a bale on—and then the bales would be tight one next to the other! You couldn't keep up with it in the mow, it'd kill you! . . . all you have time to do is grab the bale and give it a throw—no chance to place it. And you've got 100 bales up there, not stacked—you're jamming the whole works!

Having enough of conditions that could easily visit a heart attack upon a healthy man, Wayne would then trade places with Peter, whereupon he'd call down from the mow, "Bring 'em faster, bring 'em faster!"

□ □ □

ONE AFTERNOON SOMEONE (we often alternated) came back reporting that Ed had blabbed to the Grahams, "They all smoke marijuana up there." So much for our efforts at low-profile living and careful discretion!

□ □ □

ONE MORNING SEVERAL of us were gathered at Bert Crain's having ice cream sodas at the counter. Allen (who'd sometimes ask Crain to scoop him out a bag of cashews from their glass case, then stand there and consume the whole bag while talking with him) was with us, as was John Giorno, who was up for another pleasant visit. Crain's pretty, dark-haired daughter Nora, a young artist just graduated from the Rhode Island School of Design, came out and said hello. She told Giorno (who made sizable silk screens of his found poems) of her silkscreening, and Allen and I and Mr. Crain listened as the two artists talked of their work.

□ □ □

EARLIER IN JULY, Allen had entered in his journal:

> . . . Gordon up early emptying garbage, can hear cans rattle under bird chattery maple trees in white mist . . . my heart bare in left breast . . . body heavy in bed, sneeze, Burp into red brakie's kerchief, Kerouac dead . . . belly un-yoga'd a bit fat, Peter's bestial abdomenal bulge on porch last night, he yelled at Julius by the chickenhouse . . . my guilt I do no work on farm, Bonnie or Gordon emptying garbage feeding chickens 7 AM, they work for me, I capitalist provide the cash . . . not exactly lumpenproletariat as Cleaver defines the street Man of America . . . fat bellied groaning Om, no Revolutionary . . .

Outside & In

P OET ALLEN DE Loach: my height but bigger—chunky upper body, trim legs. Thick lips, soft Floridian accent. Black hair which he carefully combed, slicked back (comb in hip pocket, tight chinos). Trimmed moustache and broad goatee: a little Mephisthophelean.

He'd shot speed on the Lower East Side, and was now teaching while in graduate school at Buffalo, and editing the mimeographed avant-garde magazine *Intrepid*. He'd known Allen in the city and was one of his correspondents, often closing letters "Love & Doves."

On East Hill—a stopover between Buffalo and the city—he never stayed long. I always found him highly sociable, friendly; but not everyone was keen on him. Once when Allen and Miles rode with him to the city, he talked all the way (about how on speed he used to talk all the time); no one could get in a word. On another occasion Sue Miles once said, "He talks too much, isn't he a crushing bore?" and Allen answered, "Yes, but nobody's perfect."

Regardless of likeability, Allen De Loach did a very good thing at East Hill, and I am—many of us are—in his debt. With Nikon and tripod he set up photographs, at times with remote control (so he could be part of the picture); among them are some of the best visual images I've seen of the farm.

One, a widely grouped shot across the center of the front yard, depicts virtually everyone who was there—nineteen people—around noon on Thursday, July 30. A pressure cooker sits on the Coleman stove at right: we were canning outside, rather than make the small low-ceilinged kitchen even hotter. In the upper rear sits our tent, housing overflow guests.

De Loach and Corso were there only briefly, heading for Buffalo, taking Claude and Mary and the Plymells with them. Allen turned on the taperecorder as people began to assemble on the front lawn.

A Meher Baba photo with the legend "Don't worry, be happy," just arrived for Allen in the mail, is being passed around. As De Loach's group of subjects grows, he directs everyone to move back, calling Peter to join us. I film with my Camex. Bonnie worries her hands are too large. Allen had been anxious about Peter, and exclaims when he and Denise arrive, "There they are! They came!" Then he remembers, "Oh, the piggy!"—and Peter runs for her.

Then Allen remembers Julius: "Up in the manure pile," Denise answers. She calls to him. With much oinking the pig appears, and Bonnie exclaims, "The star!"

The shutter clicks.

Denise calls again, "Hey Julie, get outta the sun!"

□ □ □

DAYS WERE LONG and much was being done outside, but within the house there was no shortage of people, materiel, activity.

In the living room, Allen composed and arranged on the large A.B. Chase pedal organ as well as a smaller one; Jonas's old Danish Modern sofa, a paisley muslin spread thrown over it, remained accommodating. Bookshelves were graced with various volumes, including Gordon Wasson's recent *Soma*, on the fly agaric mushroom. And there were numerous tapes on which Miles was working. Nearby was his large Revox reel-to-reel taperecorder, Allen's Uher, a tape splicer, and two microphones. And there was the piano, recently moved from the dining room. All was overseen by a Tibetan thangka depicting the twelvefold cycle of interdependent co-origination, in a living room space anyone would consider small.

Taking up most of the dining room was the table where we'd squeeze up to twelve. A large map of Otsego County, a topographical one of the northeastern states, and a poster of astronomical constellations filled the walls. A sideboard was catch-all for condiments, newspapers, and mail of the moment, as well as home for a graceful, sturdy old dinner bell: sizable, handsome, bronze with wooden handle and a good strong high sound. A barometer—consulted frequently during winter—hung from the wall above.

New in the kitchen was a very large pickle crock, on top of which we'd recently relocated the cage where Joy, the lone gerbil, made her rattly rounds.

Miles and Ann had proposed that everyone pull their own weight in house and kitchen. We were hardly a commune, since Allen paid for everything, and though the garden was even better than last year, any dreams I had of making us self-supporting remained far-fetched. But in theory, at least, housework and cooking approached the communal.

Ray, as Miles has remembered, spent much of his time in the attic, generally coming down just to eat and then go back up, avoiding simple tasks he might've done like sweeping, cleaning, or helping in the kitchen. Miles and Ann brought this neg-ligence to Allen's attention, and Bonnie offered to do Ray's share. (In all likelihood, she already had.)

Miles, who'd never prepared entrée or side dish, had bought Julia Child's two-volume *Mastering the Art of French Cooking* in a used bookstore, and was cooking his way through all the vegetarian dishes. Thanks especially to Bonnie, we often had our own bread. And Bonnie borrowed an old churn—big, wooden, clumsy—and made butter.

There were tales of Peter—often vociferously vegetarian—going into Cherry Valley for meat, returning with chicken which he'd cook out of sight in the upper meadow on the little portable Coleman white gas stove. And poet Sidney Goldfarb, who stayed a week in late July, saw Peter walk into the kitchen one evening and slap a big steak into the frying pan, steam rising furiously. When expressions of concern arose (Allen: "But Peter, we're supposed to be vegetarian!") protein-hungry Peter, having worked mightily in the field all day, called back, "You don't know! You don't work all the time!"

But Peter's deviations from vegetarianism were seldom so public. On one occa-sion, Miles rode with him when, stores closed in Cherry Valley, he drove the forty miles to Oneonta for some chicken. "I didn't mind the lack of meat, but I would have enjoyed a bottle of wine with my meals," our adaptable English friend reported.

A Poet Visits, a Farmer Weeps

ANDY CLAUSEN WAS a young poet and working man, friend of Neal Cassady. He and his quiet pregnant wife Linda and small child were on their way back to California from Canada. Andy had some country music aspirations, and had written songs; after Cherry Valley they'd stop off in Nashville, maybe even look up Johnny Cash.

They drove down in an old green 1951 Chevy; though their stay was brief, Andy—husky and voluble, cowboy shirt and jeans, smoking White Owl cigars—was a vivid presence. Allen had read and liked his poetry; now young poet and elder host talked and argued, renewing disputes from several months earlier in correspondence. Andy was convinced that "a psychedelic-organic vision" was about to materialize, and encouraged Allen to try women again. He insisted, "The rednecks and the hippies are going to get together! . . . We gotta do a whole lot more fucking and making kids now!"

I shared some of Andy's elation that, as he put it, through psychedelics, "People with master's degrees and people from the street are in the same room talking about the same things." But Allen found him a bit naive, and shook his head: "You gotta watch it, you start soundin' a little fascist about dragging everyone into your hetero-sexual Eden."

It was good-spirited give-and-take, and that mood dominated Andy's stopover, even as he ate gefilte fish for the first time (and vomited); even as lexicographer David Rattray, also visiting, told him, "I like the way you use words—you use them just so slightly wrong!" (He took it in.) And even as he tried to figure out how to deal with Junior, our growing young male goat who butted everything in sight. (Hand him a leaf.)

When time came to leave the next evening, Allen and Peter, in their underpants, stood in the drive and pointed out constellations in the sky before walking Andy and family to their green automobile. Hand at the door handle, Clausen mentioned that in Nashville they'd try to visit Cash; Allen offered that he'd met him once. Peter disappeared for a minute and returned, bearing a giant zucchini. "Give this to Johnny Cash for us," he said.

Andy wondered what to do with this oversized green burden suddenly weighing down both hands. Then it occurred to him that perhaps it was his ticket of admission: "Johnny Cash, Allen Ginsberg and Peter Orlovsky want you to have this zucchini." A few nights later, he was standing at the front door of his mansion, waiting for it to open, huge squash in hand. It opened, but Cash wasn't there.

□ □ □

JUST BEFORE THE Clausen visit, I was involved in a new project. Early in the summer our old rototiller would simply not work, and couldn't be repaired; I took to using an ancient, manual, two-handled single-blade cultivator (the kind, in larger version, you see a mule pulling).

Then one day Ed proposed, "Ya know, that rototiller is dead. Louie Wickwire has a nifty little new one on sale down at Agway. It oughta do good."

Further garden space at the far edge of the main field could be used next spring; it could be turned now and seeded with a cover crop. We followed Ed's recommendation to get the bright red shiny machine. I was heartened; now I'd be able to turn that strip of soil, and not have to bother Myron, or even Claude Graham, with their big tractors (We'd long given up on Ed's ancient contraption.)

Full of confidence, eager with anticipation, I pulled the ignition string, set the heavy little glossy gizmo into forward gear, and negotiated its way up to the plot-to-be. The earth there had never—or not for a decade anyway—been turned, and its layer of more or less matted timothy was at first hard to get through. Then, try as I might, I discovered that I couldn't get the tiller to penetrate the earth itself—not sufficiently for really turning it. I tried; I tried. But the solid surface of the earth would scarcely break beneath the tiller's tines. Again and again, my fine new machine did little more than skate along the surface, making wrinkles and impressions.

And so finally I turned around this bright, noisy red wonder into which I'd put so much hope, and began guiding it back to the garage. I was so disheartened that one tear and then another came down my cheek, and by the time I returned to the house I was crying in earnest.

I'd been so preoccupied with my failed task I hadn't noticed that a new vehicle had pulled in up above where I was working: it was the '51 Chevy. When I entered the house there was Julius, simply standing in the center of the kitchen: nothing unusual about that. But I was surprised to see a young couple sitting with Allen at the dining room table. And there was Maretta, too, cigarette in hand, cup of tea in front of her. Everyone saw me. I turned my face away and headed upstairs immediately.

Moments after I came into my room Allen entered, putting his arms around me from behind, hugging me as he exclaimed, "Oh the weeping farmer! Oh the weeping farmer!"

The next day I tried something else; after all, I had nothing to lose. And succeeded. Against all odds, I managed to get Ed's ancient red tractor running for what was surely its final time; I plowed that strip, then brought that nifty little new machine back out to till. It did fine.

Solomon on the Haystack,
My Sister in the City

A FTER MY BURLAP bag encounter with Peter in the spring, I'd ordered bales of hay and straw from farmer Harold Hayes to use as mulch and compost. He delivered them to a spot on the far edge of our main plot, where they made a many-leveled pyramid, a ziggurat reaching over a dozen feet in the air; they were ideal for climbing, fun, and play—and for just sitting. Rick Fields meditated on them, Mirabelle seated behind him; Godly and Radha played, running up and down them; Allen observed, wrote, and read upon them; garter snakes burrowed a home in one end; and guests, including Carl Solomon, liked to climb them: I have a shot of tee-shirted, horn-rimmed, urban Solomon peering into the camera from atop a bale, happy on the hay.

Carl was large and tall, had a big head, and tended to hunch over. He was slender but potbellied, with a deep intellectual voice. This was his second visit; he'd come the summer before when I was with Candy in the city. Now, just after arriving on the morning bus, he telephoned his mother back in the Bronx, from Crain's. Allen, who was there to meet him, came on the line to again reassure his mom (he'd done so at length before Carl could leave) about her son's visit. That Ann Solomon wielded an awful power over Carl's life is shown in an anecdote told me decades later by John Tytell: when Solomon once fled Pilgrim State Hospital and made his way safely through the city back to his mother, she reported him to the police, and he was returned to Pilgrim State.

These days he was working in the Port Authority Bus Station bookstore. During his short stay at the farm, he and Allen seemed to get in some good talks; and Allen (who once complained that I didn't sneeze correctly) gave his friend instruction in personal hygiene, including toothbrushing and noseblowing.

Ever the literary man, Carl had looked at James Fenimore Cooper manuscripts in the Museum in Cooperstown on his first visit. Now, besides conversations and walks, he enjoyed not only our haystack but our pond; he'd return in the future, and fish there. Allen would name it Solomon Pond.

□ □ □

Around the end of the first week of August my sister Maylee wrote that she and Harold would soon be in New York. Older than I by ten years, Maylee was born in Shanghai, and had married at nineteen (Harold was then thirty-four). She'd left college after her freshman year for marriage and family, staying in Winston-Salem from 1954. (A friend of mine, looking at their wedding pictures, beholding childlike, dewy Maylee seated next to Harold, exclaimed, "What!? He's an old crow! How could your family let this happen?")

After meeting her in Winston the summer before her senior year at a New England prep school, Harold had romanced her from 800 miles south with letters, poems he admired, phone calls to her dorm, and multiple bouquets of a dozen roses. But after sixteen years as wife and mother of children she loved, she'd found life increasingly mundane and sedate, conversations even shorter, and adventure—intellectual and otherwise—nearly nil.

Now Harold was fifty. He was starting to think of retirement, and with four children, the youngest handicapped, was picking up a sideline: selling South American semi-precious stones. In New York he'd start the process by purchasing the stones, then carrying them home on Trailways.

I'd last seen my sister in the city three years earlier when in the flowering Summer of Love she visited Candy and me, telling Harold, "There is social history being made": she was making the trip with or without his approval. She was seldom so assertive.

I was eager to see Maylee (and wondered how my intelligent but decidedly rural and sometimes narrow brother-in-law would take to the city). She, I know, was looking forward to it, not just for our seeing each other but for the opportunity to take in museums and do some library research. (A course at a time while raising kids, she'd completed her B.A. and was now at work on a master's in history.)

Maylee's letter gave me two regrets. A small one was that she wouldn't have time to come to Cherry Valley: they'd have only three days. The other was immense, for Maylee reported that neurological tests recently given our mother suggested what was then called Alzheimer's Syndrome:

Mother . . . has a progressive brain degeneration for which nothing can be done. The Dr. could give no schedule as to how fast or slow this would progress.

She'd been willing to be examined for a brain tumor. Only Dr. Toole hadn't, Maylee reported, told my mother she had an organic brain destroyer. Informed merely that she had no brain cancer, Daisy Belle exclaimed, "I'm so relieved not to have a tumor!"

□ □ □

I CHECKED WITH Allen, said goodbye to everyone, and hurried in on the Greyhound. We had some good time together, including dinner in Chinatown with Jon Sholle and John Giorno. "We liked the young men at dinner last night," my brother-in-law surprised me with the next day, offering his hometown approval. I was staying at John's big loft at 222 Bowery, where he had large silk screens of some of his found poetry on the walls, such as this from the classifieds in underground papers, in large block stenciled lettering:

HUSBAND
SUCKS
AND TAKES IT
UP THE ASS.
WIFE
LOVES COUPLES
WITH BIG COCKS
AND HAIRY PUSSYS.
WILL SUCK
THEM DRY.

I took Maylee by 408 East 10th—I wanted her to see the neighborhood slum conditions and basic asceticism in which Allen chose to live. There was something righteous and didactic in me; given what I saw as her settled or complacent middle-class existence year after year I wanted her to know firsthand other standards—and to be exposed to Allen's values. I was being a bit of a zealot, especially considering that whatever lay in her heart there was little she could do about her circumstance—but I always felt there was more there, waiting to blossom: sometimes it seemed so. "Anyway, here's where the greatest poet in the world lives," I said as we entered the narrow foyer of his fourth-floor walk-up. Maylee noted the mattresses on the floor. I'd taken an acid trip the night before in which I'd relived my birth experience, and told her of it.

She and Harold and I went that evening to Wynn Chamberlain's *Brand X*. Taylor Mead was funny as always; Abbie Hoffman played a cop (who spoke happily into the camera while busy on the toilet); and there was a fucking scene at a Southern mansion with a big black guy and a fair flower of white maidenhood. I didn't wholly share the enthusiasm of Jonas's earlier blurb, however, for much of it seemed stereotyped.

I wondered how my family from the provinces, especially my brother-in-law, would take to the Southern depiction. But Harold offered not a word afterward.

I'd met him and Maylee at their 8:00 AM bus at Port Authority, and soon was seeing them off there late one afternoon. I now had a night left before returning to the farm, and took in a sexy farce by Lennox Raphael, whose *CHÉ* had been closed down for nudity on stage. His new work starred a young woman named Sandeville Hall (Sandy for short). She was very pretty; I went up to her afterward and we spoke; she was light-skinned and it was only then I discovered she was black. We had a good time talking and spent the night together.

Years later I learned of what happened my sister's last day in town, before we went to the bus station. She and Harold spent a couple of hours or more at the Metropolitan Museum of Art, in the Ancient China and Chinese Paintings collections; they beheld Egyptian Anubis, Greek Pan; they wandered among brilliant friezes, stone sarcophagi.

At the end of such age-old splendor, they traversed the length of the long large cafeteria for a late lunch. Once they were seated with their trays of meats and vegetables and rolls and salads, glasses of water and cups of coffee, once they'd gotten their napkins and apportioned their tableware, my sister lowered her face and wept.

Giorno and His Hongos

A LLEN AND I continued to hear from John Giorno, who'd return the day Bessie's calf was due. He sent a flyer on his "Bread Strike":

Stop eating bread until they end the Asian War, free Bobby Seale, Tim Leary, John Sinclair and all political prisoners, and repeal the laws against marijuana.

. . . watch the warehouses fill up with poisonous white bread and the bakeries cut production and the surplus of flour builds in the Mid-West and the farmers freak out and the flour mill and farm machinery stocks with lower earnings plunge on Wall Street. Bread is law and order. Stop consuming plastic white bread . . .

If they don't stop the war, free all political prisoners and the 300,000 kids in jail across the country on drug charges, extend the strike to all flour products. Give the wheat surplus to the hungry people in the third world.

I appreciated his idea and his use of the term "Asian War," though I wasn't keen on watching "farmers freak out." I looked forward to his return, and when he came we went on a long walk together, snagging apples off wild distant trees. With our basil, oregano, garlic, and tomatoes, he and Bonnie made a big batch of tomato sauce, canning a lot of it.

John loved the farm. For him it was a refuge from New York and all its entanglements, a special community of poets removed. His appreciation of each person there was strong: of hard-working Peter he noted, "One didn't talk to him so much." He was "in his own mode":

He came in late for dinner, he just worked. . . . We talked a little bit, but it was more like just being together. I mean that was the way the farm worked for me. Relaxing in the moment of being with everyone . . . rather than any direct interpersonal communication. . . .

And of course it wasn't just poets and friends. John thought it remarkable to

. . . have a farm and all those animals . . . to have a horse for no good reason, an old dead horse . . . and then the pig, you know, all of these things which were like

great little deities that had no function—they weren't being raised for meat or to
kill them, they were just like people.

Nor was he admiring from afar. His everyday chore was milking the goats; he'd
get up every morning at six or seven, he reminded me later with a sigh, "and milk
those stinky goats."

When he came in August John brought with him several psilocybin mushrooms
(*hongos*) from Mexico which he'd been given in New York. Allen and Maretta took
some, and went on a long walk. Allen summarized his situation in a journal poem:
"not got hi 1967–1970 till a mushroom / button yesterday divided the jewel ferns."
In a letter to Gary he expanded on this mushroom with a "silk-smooth purplish cap":

> . . . *absolutely easy, natural, not a trip i.e. no departure from any normal custom,*
> *you just eat some food, soma-esque food, but basically just regular body food that*
> *tastes like ordinary Jap dried mushroom if you soak it halfway & chew it—found*
> *myriad tiny fish making ripples in the green backwater behind the beaver dam,*
> *frog sitting haunch in mud, head stuck out looking around the woods where we*
> *passed—walked 6 hours all over neighbor's hills & found old woods familiar &*
> *neighbor lake set in valley below reminiscent of Tolkein landscape.*

I took mine, and stayed home, in the garden and down in the cellar. John's psilocybin mushrooms were, for me, subhallucinogenic and almost totally pleasant. But
not without some disorientation. At one point in the afternoon Miles was making suggestions about shelves I'd build to store the growing multitude of canned vegetables
and root crops over the winter. He didn't know I'd taken one or more of the *hongos.*
He was in the kitchen at the top of the cellar stairs; I'd gone down below, near the foot
of the stairs, where I'd build the shelves. We were calling back and forth with ideas
and demonstrations, when Georgia wandered down the steps toward me. Suddenly
I noticed that Miles was motioning in my direction with his curled index finger and
calling gently, in slightly raised voice, "Come up!"

I put my foot on the first step and heard him say, "No, I meant Georgia." At last
I understood. I reached for the little curly-haired three-year-old's hand, brought her
upstairs, concluded our discussion, and went about other tasks, with good energy,
sharp focus, and no further confusion.

My Girl, Allen's Nephew

A LAN EUGENE BROOKS, now fourteen, was named after his uncle (with different spelling) and father. He'd been to the farm in 1968 when his family picked Allen up for their trip to Mexico. Any the raccoon (long since disappeared) had just made himself part of our family, and Alan found East Hill intriguing. He wanted to return.

He was miserable, certainly, on Long Island. Early in the summer of 1970 he'd written his uncle that school is ". . . a big piece of shit. They want all the kids to be exactly the same . . ." During the whole academic year

> . . . there wasn't any antiwar demonstrating . . . but many kids had contests to see who could wear the most colorful peace-button and then after school they'd smash each other up. . . .

Now, a new school year nearing, Alan decided to return for several days. I was asked to go in and meet him in the city, bring him back on the bus.

Since I had a day there (the evening bus arrived around 2:00 AM), I got together with Sandy. The next morning we went up to West 147th Street, Harlem, and visited her mother in her small, neat, enclosed apartment at the front of a building, just below sidewalk level. "There are some undesirables" who try to move into their neighborhood, Sandy's mother told me. She was sedate, hair starting to grey. "But we manage to keep them out."

Evening found the two of us with Alan Brooks—slender, horned rims, long brown hair that often seemed to cover his eyes—in the company of John Giorno at his loft. My young charge and I would get a good night's sleep, rise at 5:00, and be at Port Authority before 6:00.

So I thought. Sandy was on speed. Long after lights were out, she kept walking around, singing songs, exclaiming, laughing. The loft was spacious and beds far apart, but it was easily loud enough to disturb others—I was especially worried about John. I tried and tried to quiet Sandy, and finally became so furious I did something I'd never done to anyone: circling both hands around her neck, I began to squeeze as I whispered loud, inches from her face, "WILL YOU SHUT UP?!" Eventually—but only eventually—she did.

In the meantime, young Alan was eager to take advantage of his moments in the big city. In the darkness, before I could see what he was doing, he made it out the door and down the stairs to the street. When I managed to catch up with him on the dismal midnight Bowery, I learned he'd just handed someone $15 for pills. I looked at them under a street lamp, and thought I could see "Bayer" inscribed. When I pressed him for details, it seemed he hadn't even asked what they were till after paying. The "dealer" had then exclaimed, "They're mescaline—a downer," and as he turned away, added, "Since you're so paranoid!"

"Mescaline's not a downer!" I shouted at Alan, seizing the pills, crushing them underfoot. I led him back into the loft—quietly.

Never was I as happy to rise at five as I was several hours later for the six o'clock bus.

Oh No! Oh No!

C AROLYN KARCHER: FRIEND since we were in grade school together, 1952, at the American School in Japan. Very bright and animated, she was virtually my soulmate during high school years. Valedictorian, she'd gone to Stanford, married her French tutor there, and moved to Washington, D.C., where he worked for the World Bank.

When they'd seen me at their wedding in 1965—long-haired, on the bum from Harvard summer school—she thought me a "lost soul," she confided later. But the next several years of cultural upheaval and escalating war had complicated that view. By the time I stopped in on my last trip South, Christmas 1969, we found much more in common, and I left them with a toke of hash to try. I was given, in those days, to making encouraging offerings of sacramental substances to straighter friends.

Now they were coming up Labor Day weekend. I'd shown them a few rolls of my *Farm Diary*, and of course had spoken with them about East Hill. Nonetheless I discovered later that they expected a commune with free sex, especially homosexuality. With many couple friends of theirs experimenting with "open" relationships, they were wondering about doing the same.

But (as was typically the case) what transpired during their stay differed from expectations. It was a quiet weekend; Miles, Ann, and the Bremsers were gone. We three went on a long walk on surrounding hills; we even made it down to the stream and beaver dam at the base of the state forest ridge, a relatively distant spot I seldom reached. After five years of marriage my two friends seemed still very much in love: they were physically affectionate, with much tenderness and occasional sweet whispers back and forth. At the same time, they were immensely curious about all they saw and heard.

In those days depictions of Allen in the media (not to mention among academics, when they deigned to recognize him) could be so bizarre people had little idea of the "real" individual. Not surprisingly, Carolyn and Martin seemed impressed by his culture and learning. At Stanford, Carolyn had specialized in Herman Melville, working with scholar H. Bruce Franklin, and was now writing a book on the nineteenth-century novelist. She and Allen had much to talk about, given Melville's importance to the poet early on; Allen could share his knowledge of Thomas Taylor and his influence on both William Blake and the American author.

Allen spoke of his current investigation of CIA involvement in opium traffic in Southeast Asia, then began asking Martin pointed, well-informed questions about the World Bank: Who were its shareholders? What governments were involved, and how? Denise cooked a great soybean casserole for dinner, and the visit seemed to be going fine—until early Sunday afternoon. It was then that Martin, an expert rider, saddled up old Lash, who almost never got any riderly attention. They'd just come out of the barn, and were at the edge of Ed's meadow, near an old wooden fence separating our land from his, and were about to cross the lawn and trot up the drive.

Most of the household happened to be out on the lawn at the time, but no one saw that Don't Bite Me—now a little piglet no more—was happily rooting in the earth near the base of the fence, inches from Lash's iron-shoed hooves. Lash also didn't see.

The next instant, as Peter recorded in "Dont Bite Please," "all 10 farm ears . . . heard the pig / . . . crying in english OH NO!" as iron came crushing down on bone. The pig screamed repeatedly: the sound of utter terror and utter pain, "Oh No!" over and over again. Blood flowed from her jaw. She stood frozen a moment, then ran; eventually she settled down, and we—in almost as much fright as she, with poor Martin looking mortified as he dismounted and led Lash back to the barn—helped her nestle on her side in some straw near the front of the house.

Peter, in overalled grimness, stood gazing down on his now silent charge, shaking his head; Denise, nearby, was pale. "It's dying!" he exclaimed in gruff unquestioning worry. "It's gonna die." But Doc Schaer arrived, pronounced it a broken jaw, treated her, and said she'd be all right in two weeks. "Leave her alone," he counseled, "just keep her as stationary as possible."

He was right. Carolyn and Martin were far more apologetic than needed—it wasn't their fault—and we got in some good time together before they had to leave. After returning to Washington Carolyn wrote:

> . . . the city was a real shock to us after getting back. My desk at the Library [of Congress] seemed incredibly unreal—insane—the first morning: couldn't believe I had committed myself to a pile of musty books, a neon light, & no windows all these years. Sick. Martin said he was overwhelmed with a similar feeling at the sight of the Bank as he rode up on his bike.

Meantime we were nursing Don't Bite Me for a fortnight: we fed her liquid corn meal, even beet juice; Julius took the sickle to some grass "for pigs barn breakfast." And Peter wrote in "Dont Bite Please":

Out the back barn door
a top 5 foot high manure pile ferment cooking
the pig streached laying in the fall
wisely getting sun warmth on her top side &
her other side from the manure
wile Denise put the pocket radio dialed
to Madem Butterfly & rock & roll
near the pure yorkshires ear
& we thought we saw a big wide smile
as if she was lissoning very intently
to all the sounds. . . .

Canada Calls

A LLEN HAD INVITED me on a short trip to McMaster University in Hamilton, Ontario, forty miles across the border from Niagara Falls, where he'd speak at a drug conference. Of course symposium discussion included the problem of police, but theory and talk were at least matched by our experience with law enforcement on the way to and from.

Heading west, we were stopped at a New York state highway patrol roadblock; I was asked for license and registration, which said our '55 Olds was owned by Committee on Poetry, Inc. "What kinda Committee is this?" the officer asked. "A foundation on the arts," I replied. After telling me to step on brakes, click turn signals, and press horn, the trooper queried, "Where you goin'?" Luckily, Allen answered "Buffalo": mention of crossing the border could invite further questions.

We were, of course, careful not to carry drugs when traveling. While certain aspects of the stop seemed routine, not everyone who came to the roadblock was being detained. We wondered afterward if we were stopped because of beards, long hair. In any case, Allen reflected, "Sure doesn't help to have all these kids yelling 'Pig!'"

As we drove through Niagara Falls, the town seemed dominated by a smell of sulfur. "Honeymooners come here for this rank smell?" Allen asked. "One look down the main street," he said, and "you can see it's owned by the Mafia." But I'd never seen the falls, and Allen made sure we went for a good long look on the way back. They were mightily impressive.

At the conference, in a large gymnasium one-third filled, Allen, in dark work shirt, flower print tie and jeans, spoke on psychedelics, police, and opiates—and chanted. While many seemed open to his arguments, there was some belittling by Marxists. Rising to his feet, one tall skinny fellow with glasses seized on the "silliness of Mr. Ginsberg," asserting the need to recognize "the real problems that most of the people in the world face":

> *All over the world people are struggling against exploitation, and they can't live by making speaking tours. . . . I think we should reject this kind of circus performance.*

Allen sought to clarify: the speaker's concern was that drugs weakened political effectiveness? If so, the recent Black Panther convention (the "Revolutionary People's Constitutional Convention") in Philadelphia, "in line with the gay liberation and women's liberation," had formally declared drug use "a definite part of the armamentarium of revolutionary liberation." He elaborated:

> *You can argue this point, but the stereotype that drugs lead to passivity is not an acceptable stereotype. . . . Remember, the confrontation in Chicago in '68 . . . was led and organized to a great extent by drug-oriented, psychedelically-inspired hippies. I don't actually so much approve of their specific tactics, but I would point that out. . . .*

Returning to the U.S. three mornings later, we were given a courteous exit by Canadian customs officers. Then, as we encountered the American, Allen kept his Sony on "Record" while we submitted to far more detailed interrogation (where we'd been, what we'd been doing, etc.) and inspection (of car trunk, personal belongings). It went through a couple of phases and lasted at least several minutes. I managed to keep my cool, while Allen remained cooperative, calm, and even somewhat cheery, humming softly to himself some of the time. "This happens a lot. Almost anybody with a beard, now," he confided to me just before his harmonium case was opened, contents examined. What seemed like it might be a crisis came when the officer saw the taperecorder, asked Allen to identify it, and wanted to know, "What're you doing now?"

Allen simply answered "Taperecording," and, reading the officer's mind, showed him how to shut it off. On finally driving away I exclaimed, "I had an urge to kill!" Allen allowed that such things happened "every time" with him; he'd even been made to strip sometimes.

We stopped in Buffalo and visited briefly with Allen De Loach and Gregory, walking around an old area of Main Street together, among huge ancient warehouses and dilapidated frame houses. Then, on the road again, I saw a state police light in my rear view mirror. Wondering once more why I was being stopped, I pulled off the road. Allen started the Sony. Huge trucks roared by.

Again I was asked for registration, and what Committee on Poetry, Inc., was, as well as where we "boys" were going. And to show that my signals worked. But the major question, coming when the trooper had gone to the front to check signals, was not at all standard. It was, "How'd you get your plate so banged up?" I didn't know what he was talking about, and had to get out and look. At the front of the car

I kneeled down to the license, saw one or two bends and a few dents (but numbering and lettering were entirely legible). As I raised back up I tried to satisfy his curiosity: "Driving country roads?"

But that was rejected. "Been pushin' a lot of other people?" the officer asked. I said I didn't know the cause; I'd never noticed it before. "Maybe stones from dirt roads?" I tried, being more explicit; that too was turned down. I gestured outward with raised open hands, puzzled. Finally, after several more exchanges, he let me go.

When I got back in Allen seemed amused—and moved, he said—by the earnestness of my response.

But even with police hassles on the road, there was much that was positive about our trip: we stayed in Toronto, visited a young people's club, got in a trip to woods and a waterfall. And I met a pretty woman, Wendy Rogosin, with whom I spent a night or two at her little home on Paradise Road. Throughout it all Allen maintained his usual good humor and generosity; as we neared East Hill he offered, "Thanks for the honeymoon!"

But the most positive moment of our whole journey had come without Allen's saying a word. One afternoon we were on our way up a flight of stairs at McMaster University when Allen noted a bit of graffiti on the yellow wall:

Power comes from the barrel of a gun

—Mao

Pausing, he removed a pen from his breast pocket and wrote beneath it:

Power comes from the imagination

—A. Ginsberg

East Hill Society

S OCIALLY SPEAKING, OUR "farm for used poets" continued to be a hodgepodge. But without a central threat or menace like Gregory, without Peter-on-speed, things were relatively benign. Rick Fields—who'd leave soon—and I did a couple of stints applepicking at nearby Sharon Orchards. It was odd and interesting work, climbing a long ladder into huge trees, large basket strapped onto chest, straining to grasp as many round red fruits as you could before having to climb back down, empty your full basket into a bin, then climb back up again, and again.

When scholar Ann Charters came to East Hill for two days, her impression was positive. Everyone seemed "very kind and hospitable," she later recalled; we had "heterogeneous agendas" but things seemed to be working out. Here was a place where Allen could keep Peter away from the city, as well as being spiritually healthy for Allen: he didn't have to be a public entity.

Ann took a number of photographs; Allen played her some Blake (in a few years she and husband Sam would produce his *First Blues* album, recorded by Harry Smith). Allen asked Ann about harmony and the work of an expert, Walter Piston. She talked with Bonnie about her writing, with Denise and Peter about music.

Of course, there was no way she could see each individual up close; as I recall people and events after the sad heart of August died, we continued very much at evens and odds—but we did continue.

In terms of fulfilling Peter's stipulation that she work if she returned, Maretta had indeed proved helpful in certain ways. She seemed more mature, perhaps, than when we'd last seen her—at her worst—a year and a half earlier. She taught Allen variations on some mantras, including Raghupati Raghav Rajaram (Ghandi's hymn on his March to the Sea) and the Prajna Paramita Sutra. Miles recorded them (Maretta solo, with her high, clear crisp voice; and with Allen, with his deep rich one). Allen was obviously pleased; in late August he'd written mutual friend Gary Snyder:

> *Maretta Greer here, back from street sadhu begging saddhana year in Rawalpendi*
> *... Very good shape, meditates & does mantra quietly all day like the Sakyapa old*
> *man did, she also reads extensively now, got herself together quite neat, everyone*

remarks on her beauty & quiet demeanor, & she helps out here & there with
gardening or canning or curry cooking—we take long silent walks in woods.

I saw her ascetic venturing to and studies in remote places, like some contemporary Isabelle Eberhardt, as praiseworthy, but not everyone was as keen on her as good old optimistic, generous (and forgiving!) Allen. For some it wasn't just her exoticism—perhaps it was her aristocratic bearing and relative restraint with common tasks others easily undertook. For Denise, with her working class background, she was an anathema; for Miles she was not only "phony" but "a complete sponge," "obviously a disturbed person": "She was so holy," he told me, "but I thought it was a complete pose." Sometimes he'd wait for days for enough stored energy for a few hours of editing Allen's tapes, only for Maretta to "blow it all by thoughtlessly playing Dylan records."

But for Bonnie Bremser she was worthy of admiration. To shy Bonnie, then doing hatha yoga some early mornings on the living room carpet without anybody knowing, Maretta was someone to look up to, admire. And, of course she never told her; the two women hardly spoke.

Unfortunately, I did a very bad thing one morning. Entering the house after chores, I poured the cow milk through a filter into glass half-gallon bottles in the kitchen sink—as usual. Then, carrying the large, just-emptied stainless steel milk pail, I entered the bathroom—as usual. There I saw Maretta—and she me—at the opposite end of the small room, on the toilet. The deep laundry tub sink (kitchen sink too shallow for what I'd do) was near me, to my left against the wall. I thought to myself, Well, work takes precedence. Eyes averted from Maretta, I proceeded to the sink, scrubbed the pail, and left.

Maretta suddenly appeared moments later in the kitchen. In her high-pitched voice she announced, loud and clear:

This is not aimed at anyone in particular, but I want everyone to know that when
I'm in the bathroom I need privacy and must not be disturbed!

Of course I was embarrassed; ashamed, even, though I didn't want to admit it at the time. She was in the right.

□ □ □

MEANWHILE, THE BREMSERS seemed to spend a good bit of time by themselves; Bonnie looked after Georgia, and a new young couple in Cherry Valley, Ross and Julie

Fullam, with a child Georgia's age, made for good social contact for mother and child. And Bonnie worked. But Ray continued to be, at times, a loud drunken nuisance. Miles wrote a portrayal of Ray and his relationship with Bonnie:

> *He sits all day in the attic, rolling up his Bugler tobacco, surrounded by dust and dead flies that it would not occur to him to clean up. He orders Bonnie around in a way that most women would find intolerable, particularly in these days of women's liberation. His refusal to do his share of the cooking is irksome and Bonnie saying that she will do it for him doesn't help. They seem to be from a different era, the embodiment of fifties male chauvinism, something in a time warp, and they keep themselves to themselves.*

Peter, Allen wrote Gary, was "strong & marvellously straight compared to last year." But beneath strength lay a problem: as Allen had written earlier in his diary, "Pete been ill, says work himself to sickness so he won't think of Speed." Peter would conceive of and take on huge projects, some of which (with Julius's help) he'd complete: fencing-in the far field. Some he wouldn't: building a separate house for the pig. Even a matter as comparatively small as the pickle crock tells a story: we'd acquired that enormous stone jar, and at Peter's instigation spent $100 on pickle-making ingredients, then made a near-lifetime supply of pickles—which barely took up a small slice of the bottom of the gigantic crock.

And even as Allen De Loach had taken that end-of-July group photo with pressure cooker on Coleman stove, a larger, twenty-one-quart pressure cooker was ordered from Montgomery Ward for $32. But such were human excesses, which Allen generally seemed able to absorb—if not always happily. On its most basic level—as refuge from the city for Peter—East Hill Farm was now working, with thanks, in good measure, to Denise. And Don't Bite Me.

Come late September, we were gifted with pleasant dry warm weather before sudden cold at month's end. The pig's jaw had repaired; she continued to grow and grow, rooting and snorting happily hither and thither. Images in my *Farm Diary* include a little vignette near the laundry line full of white sheets and colored towels. Allen's in the green red-tipped rocker, *The Times* on his lap, work shirt unbuttoned over tee-shirt. Peter's on the ground next to him, in pony tail, overalls, long white shirt sleeves rolled up, brogans. At arm's length he playfully offers a white hen a piece of bread. The whole scene's then disrupted by Don't Bite Me, now nearly enormous, with brown stains on her rear.

Later Allen pleasantly reads *The Times* in the same rocker, now moved to just in front of the house. Leisurely he turns the pages, frowning a bit as he settles into a particular article, rubbing lips and beard. Ed, in cap and windbreaker, canvas laundry bag in each hand, appears in the background, about to cross from his meadow onto our lawn, Godly and daughter Radha prancing at his heels, tails wagging, red tongues happily dangling.

Equilibrium, it seems, had been reached at East Hill Farm.

"Ecologue": The State of the Farm

I N THAT LETTER to Gary depicting a rehabilitated Maretta, Allen wrote in typical candor about his life and worries, in typical generosity about the farm's productivity:

> I wake every morning totally depressed, 4 or 5 am, Leary & Sinclair in jail in my mind, the weight of sustaining the farm heavy in light of apparent continuing disintegration of social order. Vast garden crops coming in, & we'll have canned 100 cases of vegetables . . . enough, really, for winter survival, I'm amazed to see—by the end of harvest. Great organic garden this year, 3rd year of Gordon Ball's experience & study—also planted orchard of fruit trees & permanent strawberry & asparagus beds on hill above house.

But as is often the case, things were more complicated than they seemed. Two pieces of Allen's writing, one a mid-August journal entry, the other a major poem written in September, highlight many of the practical difficulties at hand. Today, looking at some of both, I feel guilt, agreement, embarrassment, consternation:

> I wanna get rid of cows horse pig goat & simplify farm so's there's less work right now hydraulic ram needs daily adjustment dry august water level so low the ram drains the ceramic ground well-shaft of its minutely gallon & half flow, & stops. . . .
>
> Barn needs roof-slats tacked, tin to stop rain from wetting winter hay store, pig lady needs concrete floored pole sided pen, meadow needs barbed wire fencing, basement needs earth built up outside foundation wall to protect from winter wind the new built door & wall made of cinderblock we put in . . . If we don't get that wall heaped with earth or insulation as good as 4 feet below frost line, all the vegetables we're canning'll freeze crack & spoil & the dry punkins & zucchini'll crystallize in October to rot and a rabbit hutch need be built. Porch needs fixing. . . .
>
> Prune the useful apple trees, & fence the new planted orchard & strawberry & asparagus patch. Get a tractor to plow up some open fields before they get too filled with willow bushes & chokecherry so we can plant timothy & clover & hay for the milk bearing beasts. . . . Build a few hermits' huts here & there in woods or meadows by trees—

Of course, we accomplished only a fraction of such projects. Allen was facing his own anxiety and depression, as recorded repeatedly in journal entries (". . . remote & cowardly away from city I rot tied to my own karmic feebleness, caretaking Julius half resentfully, loving no one . . ."). But starting just before the Don't Bite Me disaster and continuing over three weeks, Allen wrote a long poem on the farm itself. He'd just been inspired by the "relax'd style" of Philip Whalen's new *Severance Pay*, and he and I had been reading some Virgil and Hesiod in those little compact hardcover Everyman editions. But given its juxtaposition of conditions on East Hill with those of nation and world, the relationship of his long "Ecologue" to classical models was sometimes direct, sometimes ironic.

I always admired its opening, its millennial reshaping of current history, its return of nature and tribe to life's core:

In a thousand years, if there's History
America'll be remembered as a nasty little Country
full of Pricks, thorny hothouse rose
Cultivated by the Yellow Gardeners.
"Chairman Mao" for all his politics, head of a Billion
                folk, important old & huge
        Nixon a dude, specialized on his industrial
                        Island, a clean paranoiac Mechanic—
Earth rolling round, epics on archaic tongues
                        fishermen telling island tales—
all autos rusted away,
                        trees everywhere.

A shift to East Hill: wind shapes maples, Bessie's in the corn. "Ecologue" (spelling unorthodox, to emphasize ecology) is suffused with lyrical renderings of bucolic life and matters of fact:

Horse by barbed wire licking salt,
                lifts his long head & neighs
        as I go down by willow thicket
                to find the 3-day-old heifer.
At bed in long grass, wet brown fur—
her mother stands, nose covered with a hundred flies.

Long-awaited rain has filled the well; the ram will work once more, "& water flow in kitchen sink tap." Georgia Bremser, reports the poet who sleeps some nights under the stars, is now outweighed by Don't Bite Me. And the pig herself is shoulder-to-shoulder with major figures and events in the human realm:

> Scratch her . . . under hind leg,
>> she flops over on her side sweetly grunting,
>> nosing in grass tuft roots, soft belly warm.

> Eldridge Cleaver exiled w/ bodyguards in Algiers
> Leary sleeping in an iron cell,
>> John Sinclair a year jailed in Marquette
> Each day's paper more violent—

Local as well as larger concerns are interrupted from time to time by brief hymns to classical models as only Allen can sing them:

> Bucolics & Eclogues!
>> Hesiod the beginning of the World,
>>> Virgil the end of his World—
> & Catullus sucked cock in the country
>> far from the Emperor's police.

"Hail to the Gods, who are given Consciousness. / Hail to Men Conscious of the Gods!" he hymns near poem's end. And there are little Williamsesque snapshots of everyday details:

> Fine rain-slant showering the gray porch
>> Returnable Ginger Ale Bottles
>>> on the wood rail, white paint flaked
>>>> off into orange flowered
>>>> blossoms

But time passes; it isn't simply sacred, cyclical: events take place, things change unpredictably. Don't Bite Me's jaw is broken; a pet rabbit escapes confinement and is killed by our dogs; the poet hears the Bremsers at odds just above him:

Man and wife, they weep in the attic
      after bitter voices,
            low voices threatening.

On farm and off, he sees "Millions of bodies in pain!" That phrase will recur as refrain in his great lament a year later, "September on Jessore Road."

And the farm itself? He now defines it, publicly, as never before:

The Farm's a lie!
      Madmen growing giant organic zucchini
           mulching asparagus, boiling tomatoes for Winter,
                drying beans, pickling cucumbers
                sweet & garlicked, salting cabbage for sauerkraut,
                canning fresh corn & tossing Bessie husks—

Bessie, broken through barbed wire again, batters sunflower stalks; and Timothy Leary, confined to prison in San Luis Obispo, California, bursts free, in high drama and complication:

. . . climbed the chainlink fence & two strands of
            barbedwire too
      This weekend, "Armed & Dangerous,"
          Signed with Weathermen!
          Has Revolution begun? World War III?

The question's rhetorical, but the singer won't leave his song without a diatribe on farm conditions:

Get rid of that old tractor or fix it!
          Cardboard boxes rotten in garageside rain!
Old broken City desks under the appletree! Cleanum
             up for firewood!
Where can we keep all summer's bottles?
          Gas pumps, broken mandolins, old tires—
            Ugly backyard—Shelf the garage!

Yet East Hill Farm works: fruits of its labor bless the dinner table, the ram pumps again, Ginsberg's at the organ, a lover's in his house. But as maple leaves turn and fall, the voice of doom returns: "Civilization's breaking down!" Fridge freezer's warm, toilet leaks; windcharger has no power. "Ecologue" concludes in anything but an idyllic or pastoral temper, quoting one of Kerouac's great haiku:

"Useless! useless! the heavy rain driving into the sea!"
Kerouac, Cassady, Olson ash & earth, Leary the Irish
                    coach on the lam,
Black Magicians screaming in anger Newark to Algiers,
How many bottles & cans piled up in our garbage pail?

Footnote to Leary

B Y MID-SEPTEMBER, TWO documents circulated in the underground press. One was from the Weathermen; the other, Timothy Leary. In "Communique # 4 From The Weatherman Underground," Bernardine Dohrn claimed for her group the "honor and pleasure" of helping "political prisoner" Leary escape from "the POW camp." And the former Harvard psychologist reported:

> The following statement was written in the POW camp and carried over the wall (in full sight of two gun trucks). I offer loving gratitude to my Sisters and Brothers in the Weatherman Underground who designed and executed my liberation. Rosemary and I are now with the Underground and we'll continue to stay high and wage the revolutionary war.
>
> There is the time for peace and the time for war.
>> There is the day of laughing Krishna and the day of Grim Shiva.
>> Brothers and Sisters, at this time let us have no more talk of peace.
>> The conflict which we have sought to avoid is upon us. A world-wide ecological religious warfare. Life vs. death.
>
> . . . .
>
> I declare that World War III is now being waged by shorthaired robots whose deliberate aim is to destroy the complex web of free wild life by imposition of mechanical order.
>
> . . . .
>
> You are part of the death apparatus or you belong to the network of free life.
>
> . . . .
>
> In this life struggle we use the ancient holy strategies of organic life: [Nine are listed; the ninth appears immediately below:]
>> Resist physically, robot agents who threaten life must be disarmed, disabled, disconnected by force . . . Arm yourself and shoot to live . . . Life is never violent. To shoot a genocidal robot policeman in the defense of life is a sacred act.

Listen Nixon. We were never that naive. We knew that flowers in your gun-barrels were risky. We too remember Munich and Auschwitz all too well as we chanted love and raised our Woodstock fingers in the gentle sign of peace.

. . . .

For the last seven months, I, a free, wild man, have been locked in POW camps. No living creature can survive in a cage. In my flight to freedom I leave behind a million brothers and sisters in the POW prisons of Quentin, Soledad, Con Thien . . .

. . . .

Listen, the hour is late. Total war is upon us. Fight to live or you'll die. Freedom is life. Freedom will live.

(signed) Timothy Leary

WARNING: I am armed and should be considered dangerous to anyone who threatens my life or my freedom.

And where was Leary now? Might he be on his way to East Hill? There was apparently a chance. If so, Allen told me, we had a code name for him: "Mr. Cow."

In earlier days Charles Olson had told Leary, "When the police come for you, you'll be welcome in my house." Now Olson was dead, and Leary might come our way. So there was an underground network—shaped by Weathermen? Where would we put him—up in the back room at Ed's? (That would make for quite a couple.) Would Mrs. Cow accompany him? I never knew how likely his arrival might be, only that it was a possibility. "If Leary does come," Allen warned me, "don't talk with him about acid; it'll be a busman's holiday."

Naturally, some of us were concerned about Leary's endorsement of violence following his dramatic Erroll Flynn–like escape. Of course, it was in self-defense; and of course, it was after spending most of the year incarcerated; and of course, it was after five years of persecution, fourteen arrests.

Allen, Miles, and I sat at the dining room table talking it over one evening. Even though I was nearing the end of my pacifist rope I wasn't sure what to make of Leary's position; Miles was in favor of it (of Leary's fighting back—not in random acts of violence); Allen had always been somewhat wary of his friend even as he supported him. ("Precisely what do you mean by drop out . . . for the millionth time?" he'd challenged over three years earlier.) Now he wanted to continue to help even as he was worried by talk of violence.

Soon we learned that Leary and Rosemary had just surfaced in Algiers, where they were joining Eldridge and Kathleen Cleaver. We were all relieved not to be seeing him on East Hill. But he stayed in our minds, especially in Allen's, both out of concern for his well-being, and for what he represented. In a sense, Leary's was everyone's problem in late 1970 America, given escalating violence at the top: how, by non-violent means, do you turn a warmongering giant peaceable? To the extent that we foregrounded aggression and pushed inquisitiveness to the rear, even off our stage, the case of Timothy Leary, I felt, was American Karma.

At Home in Autumn:
Politics, a Sylvan Scene & Guests

A ROUND THE TIME of "Ecologue" I was helping Allen organize some of his files. For many years, through knowing junkies like Huncke, reading such works as Alfred Lindesmith's *The Addict and the Law*, studying news reports in detail (saved in folder upon folder of "faded yellow press clippings"), and talking with numerous others from street and law enforcement alike, he'd become convinced that the criminal status of heroin addicts in America was a shell game supporting crime in the streets, often involving collusion of Mafia and police. Junkies were denied constitutional and medical rights to see doctors for their illness (addiction), a violation going back to Treasury Department interpretation of the 1914 Harrison Act, which was intended merely to register the flow of narcotics.

So in Allen's view, for politicians of 1970 who called so strenuously for more law 'n' order to combat rising crime-in-the streets, the first thing to do was to address the problem of illegalized citizens having to steal to treat a sickness, thereby accounting for half of street crime.

Abroad, Ginsberg found that our traditional support of often corrupt anti-communist leaders had resulted in a most peculiar circumstance in the Golden Triangle, where Thailand, Laos, and Burma meet. There the CIA was facilitating traffic in the cash crop, opium. And the great majority—83%—of opium and heroin entering the U.S. came from the Golden Triangle, not Turkey, as per standard government line: our involvement in Southeast Asia was contributing to our number one domestic problem. Restore medical rights of junkies and recognize the corruption in our Asian War, Allen would say, and we'll have peace in the streets, and peace in Southeast Asia. I was inspired by Allen's thought, insight, and labor, and wanted to do all I could to help set the record straight.

□ □ □

IN MY DIARY I wrote, mid-September:

Today Pete was mad, yelling at Denise
to scram, I know not why;

Removing tv batteries violently from his room—
Then appeared later in mine asking for another swig of wine, pleasantly, as he took
I patted his back, asked if he was alright, said yes, that he needed a new TV set.
Another one! (3!)

Perhaps this brief entry is given a bit of depth in my movie footage: a close-up of a cartoon Denise has drawn in chalk on a small blackboard, entitled "Peter getting inspired by *cartoons*." We see him in profile, pony tail, looking at a small TV atop their dresser, hand to mouth as if sucking thumb or finger.

□ □ □

IN LATE SEPTEMBER—a spell of warm weather had come—I shot an extended seven-minute sequence of Allen, nude, in the woods above our house. What exactly I had in mind, I don't know; looking at it today I'm stunned by his patience and generosity: it must've easily taken an hour, if not more. I believe I thought to present him as some sort of atavistic spirit of the woods—though I never asked him to take his glasses off. Nonetheless some shots are oddly interesting, and there are even moments of humor.

Right from the start, Don't Bite Me has joined us. Allen calls to her, clapping hands, bending over to pet. The pig, in utter concentration on her business at hand, makes her singleminded way through fallen leaves and upright ferns. I see that she does have, as Allen once wrote, "Satanic" ears: their winged shape resembles classic western depictions of the Devil's. Her face is totally smudged, and much of her body is too: she's been rooting with great devotion to the task. At various points Allen, who remains standing, assumes certain postures (even a modified yoga asana), gives a range of mudras, and holds on to a staff I'd given him. I shoot the pig through the "A" frame made by Allen's legs. The sun breaks through from above; Allen smiles, jerks his thumb back to the pig chewing busily away behind him. Mirabelle the deaf Dalmatian joins the scene; she takes a bite out of the pig, the pig goes after her. Don't Bite Me gets at Mirabelle's left ear, and pushes her: there's a lot of back and forth, round and round.

This extended sylvan sequence with naked Allen, naked pig, and naked dog cavorting on a bed of green ferns and orange fallen leaves is followed by a close-up of nature in another guise: amidst the lush greenery of our garden, a black garter snake with white stripe running along its mouth and down its sides arches its neck and consumes from the rear a plump and utterly helpless spotted frog. The frog's expression as he faces the camera, eyeballs bulging, pale flesh of lower jaw vibrating, is that of one prolonged big gulp. His little forearms dangle frozen while his body recedes from us, into the mouth of the snake.

□ □ □

WENDY ROGOSIN DROVE down from Toronto, and we seemed to spend a fair amount of time in bed, or so the filmic record suggests. Amidst the tongue-in-groove walls of my room we see her smoking; I'm evidently holding my Camex above us as she lies in my crotch, head just beneath my soft cock. Moments later I'm clothed, sitting in a chair in front of my door, grimly holding a sign bearing date and situation: SEPTEMBER 27, WENDY'S GONE.

Today, this melodrama baffles me; I don't remember caring *that* much for her. In any case, such self-absorption was soon interrupted, fortunately, by the lively appearance of R'lene Dahlberg and Huncke, who came up for a night or two while Allen was off reading downstate. Julius, Peter, Denise, Ray, Bonnie, Georgia, and I were there.

They arrived bearing two quart bottles of Meyers Rum. "Tonight after dinner," R'lene announced, "I'll make everyone hot toddies. All we need is this dark rum, boiling water, and of course you always have brown sugar, right?" Merrily she put the rum away with her things upstairs.

Early in the evening, Bonnie started dinner, complaining about having to shuck all the corn she was going to boil. R'lene—ever a glad and helpful presence—proposed, "You could just stick them in the oven, in their sheaths, and bake them." Bonnie did so.

But moments later Bonnie was vexed again as R'lene and Huncke—more or less a "number" now—walked out the door: she was taking him to dinner in Cooperstown, a nice place by the lake. Bonnie would miss her.

On return a few hours later, they were greeted at the door by Peter. "I've been a bad boy," he told R'lene with a hangdog face—but there was a trace of twinkle in those bleary blue eyes. It wasn't necessary to say he'd gone upstairs and laid hands on one of the two bottles—and made good use of it.

Smashed, he was funny. He proceeded to pick up odds and ends from the dining room table, humming, bouncing, and wobbling just a little. He brought out what remained of the bottle, which he and his two guests—who were upset at first but soon pacified—finished. Everyone slept well.

The Bremsers Set Forth

W HEN BONNIE HAD arrived with Georgia at the end of March, Allen told her the three of them were welcome six months. (For Ray, arriving earlier on East Hill, that would mean nearly a year.) By September's end half a year had elapsed, and soon they'd move into the Cherry Valley home of Ross and Julia Fullam.

Everyone had liked little Georgia; Gregory drew for her; Allen even, as an Ann Charters photograph shows, swang her, bare feet dangling, in the swing we hung from one of the maples on the front lawn. And Bonnie was generally accepted as the hardworking and intelligent person she was. But Ray was a different story.

He could certainly be amiable, but often difficult. In March I wrote in my diary, "Bremser drunk feverish & moaning upstairs while I sit abed contemplating my own mad loneliness." And in April—just five days after arrival of wife and child, I reported:

> Just took Ray's pills from him, he scored in C'town today visit Hospital w/ Ed Bonnie
> Georgia Denise, I feel like a creep. 1st time I betrayed him, of course that's his plea,
> it hits me, but I had to do it . . .

On a mild summer night I heard Ray shouting in the attic, "Bonnie you smell like a French whore!" Ray and a Cherry Valley friend with a car "burned down" all the drug stores in a thirty-mile radius for terpin hydrate. Andy Clausen (who became a friend and admirer of Bremser) later told me that during his visit he was told Ray had been temporarily banned from the farm for bad behavior. In any case, every six weeks or so, Ray took the bus to New York and/or Jersey City (where his mother lived) for a few days. Once, staying at Allen's apartment, he got so drunk he shat on the floor.

Of course, it was quiet, dependable Bonnie who had (or chose) to deal with such things more than anyone else. And what she later told me of her life at the farm was worse than I'd imagined. She'd been struck by the comparative austerity there—the emphasis on vegetarianism and (though far from realized) self-sufficiency—yet she saw that some had ways around official conditions, or seemingly better conditions to begin with. "Actually," she said, "I was a little jealous of everybody."

For one thing, she and Georgia and a frequently drunk Ray had their space in the attic, where other guests often camped out; I had my own room, Peter and Denise their hideaway off pantry and porch. Ray had his walks on the back roads to town, chugging forbidden beer as he carried it home. And Denise and Peter could hop in the car and go off and eat as they pleased.

And Bonnie herself? Thirty-three years later Bonnie (now Brenda Frazer) told me:

I wasn't happy. I sort of lost myself in the kitchen there. I wasn't really relating to anybody. I was just taking care of Georgia and cooking. For a while, it was really great. And then after a while I guess I started stepping on people's toes. Peter and Denise were like a little territorial—maybe I wasn't doin' things right or something. And Ray was always pushing me on to greater heights of cooking, "Do this tonight"—make some real elaborate thing.

There was a scene one night. I was making fried fish, and it was a hot day. And I didn't do a very good job of organizing the dinner, and Peter came in and started yelling at me that the kitchen was a mess and that I just basically couldn't do anything right. Everybody was there, everybody was waiting for dinner to come. And I was trying my best.

Of course I had this attitude that I was makin' a big sacrifice by doin' all this work, you know. And so it just floored me, and I didn't respond any way, I was not able to yell back or defend myself at all, I just sort of absorbed it, and it made me sick.

She wasn't even sure if she finished cooking the meal. In any case, neither Bonnie—preparing dinner for ten with a too-small kitchen table as well as stove—nor anyone else responded directly to Peter. "Allen came up to me afterward," she recalled, "and said, 'You took that very well'":

And I thought that was a kind of a compliment so that maybe I had done the right thing in just saying nothing. But I can't imagine that it was, because I was just defenseless, that was all. I wasn't articulate enough face-to-face or especially with a group of people there to tell him off.

Other problems threatened this economist's daughter. With considerable time spent in the kitchen, she was developing an eating disorder: "Sometimes I'd go down in the middle of the night, and I was just lovin' the whole wheat bread and all of the stuff I was cooking; just gobbling it up."

Perhaps worst of all, she thought she was pregnant; then, that she'd miscarried. In early August she spent two days in Bassett Hospital—and learned it was a false pregnancy.

Not having miscarried was a relief, but knowing she wasn't pregnant was a disappointment: "I had gotten my expectations up," she said, "that this baby was going to be a new start for Ray and me that would solidify the relationship."

It was good talking with Bonnie after a distance of decades. (We'd seen each other only once since the farm.) Perhaps—we had a long, long talk—we were making up for all that time on East Hill in which we two shy people seldom spoke at length. And, obtuse as I am, I found myself startled by something she told me. It made me wonder how little any of us in that small asbestos-shingled house might've understood each other.

At one point I asked Bonnie about one of my lady friends who'd visited that summer. "A girl friend?" she answered. "Well, if I knew about that, I was probably jealous, Gordon."

"Why?" I asked.

"Well you know I had a terrible crush on you then."

Works and Days in the Country, Violence in the City

R ECENTLY ANNA MARIE had sent a vacation card depicting Williamsburg's "Historic Berkeley Plantation," its face a placidly grazing handful of sheep on a well-groomed lawn afront a trim redbrick home. Her message was simply, "Perhaps in our old age we could settle somewhere here." Now, the first weekend in October, she was on East Hill. I'd recently given her a nice blouse, and she was sweetly making curtains for my room as if to encourage me to stay near. Then while out driving we learned of Janis Joplin's death by overdose. "Cheap thrills!" she exclaimed, to my consternation.

□ □ □

FROM THE TIME of Bremsers' departure we were blessed with warm dry weather and could continue harvesting with ease. We gathered many of the apples from ancient wild trees, taking them down to the Grahams who, great neighbors that they were, let us use their press. A large, gangly old wooden contraption, it had a big wooden central stick that when turned rotated a gear that brought about the squashing of the fruit—demanding work, but freshly pressed cider, one of the great joys of the earth, made it worth it. Peter became so involved in the process he'd stay and stay at the Grahams', into dusk, into night, until finally Denise would shout, "Peter! You're a cider nut! C'mon!"

I've a movie shot of Maretta in the garden near a wooden crate with some handsome carrots inside, and a little vignette shows several farm folk shucking corn: around a large pyramid-like pile of yellow-green ears, Julius sits upright on a chair borrowed from the dining room; little Georgia, atop the pile in white-collared grey dress, does her best to pitch in; Denise and overalled Peter remain on the ground; and the pig (in large rope harness now) roots happily, consuming many a tossed husk. Peter starts then stops sticking an ear into the pig's rear, just beneath her curled tail.

□ □ □

ALREADY ALLEN HAD been gone most of a week in Dallas, sitting meditation sixteen hours a day in his room at the Hilton, pronouncing silently "Guru Om" under the guidance of Ram Dass friend Swami Muktananda Paramahansa. The rest of the fall and through the winter, he'd continue sitting an hour a day. Leary's Weatherman letter, he'd explain, brought him to it.

Miles and Ann were moving to Allen's East 10th Street apartment, where Miles could more easily continue tape editing and cataloguing, without fear of electric loss and many other disruptions on East Hill. They'd contributed to its work, but I don't know how much of a sentimental attachment Miles or Ann might've developed to the farm. I do know, though, that Miles had been struck from the beginning by the difference between Cherry Valley and all he'd seen of America on previous visits. Arriving for a short stay back in 1969, he came from the city with Allen on the morning bus; I was there with the Olds to meet them. Allen insisted on showing him smalltown America: we entered Crain's Pharmacy, sat at the counter beneath the coffered ceiling, enjoyed sodas served up by amiable Mr. Crain. Then we walked and drove around our quiet, peaceable town before heading up East Hill.

Now, moving back to the city between Avenues C and D, Miles was entering a center of dramatically rising crime, much of it attributable to the need of New York's 100,000 junkies for $80 or $100 a day to support their habit. Why the dramatic rise? In the winter of 1971 *The Times* would report:

Many new young addicts say they began using heroin during the recent Federal crackdown on marijuana, which has made marijuana scarce while hard drugs remain plentiful.

. . . .

Doctors in widely separated cities report that they began to notice a sharp rise in youngsters seeking withdrawal treatment from heroin in the weeks following last fall's Operation Intercept to cut off the marijuana flow from Mexico.

At first, everything seemed to go well at 408 East 10th; Miles was now in touch with a whole electronics infrastructure that for months had been many miles away. And there was privacy.

Then one mild afternoon Miles and Ann returned from the supermarket. Like virtually all others in the heavily Puerto Rican neighborhood, Allen's building had no lock on the front door: anyone could enter; anyone could follow a resident in. Laden with provisions, Miles and Ann trudged up four flights. Just as he stuck his key in the lock of apartment 4-C, someone tapped him on the shoulder. Turning around, he found himself face-to-face with a fellow pointing a flat, short-barreled handgun at his head. A companion had Ann up against the wall with a knife.

No words were exchanged. The man with the gun quietly removed Miles's watch and wallet. But the two didn't stop there: they ordered him to let them inside. The one with the knife cut the phone, using its cord to tie up their victims. Miles and Ann sat on the bed, hands knotted behind them, while their guests ransacked Allen's humble flat.

They took taperecorders, a non-working TV, and a portable radio, which they stacked next to the door. Miles kept nervously chattering away; they kept asking, "Where's the money?" Miles answered, "If I had any money, do you think I'd be living here? If we had any money, we'd be in a hotel! I'm visiting from England and this is a friend's apartment—I don't have any money and there isn't any money here—"

Both men—they were black—were nervous, jerky. The one with the gun kept rubbing it against his thigh, the other lit a cigarette. Miles, who hadn't smoked for months, asked, "Can I have one?" The fellow reached over, stuck it between his teeth. Miles sensed they weren't going to kill or rape: they were junkies, looking for money.

Now and then his benefactor removed the cigarette from his mouth so he could exhale. Meanwhile Ann, who knew there'd been many rapes in the neighborhood, was keeping absolutely still, melting into the bookcase behind her.

Then they were made to stand up, and pushed into the small bathroom. "Don't come out," the guys warned, "'cause we're comin' back for a second load." They staggered out of the apartment with what they could carry, including Allen's Uher.

Miles and Ann wriggled free, sensing that their threat to return was only that. Miles slammed the door shut. And then, being English, he proposed calling the police.

"Don't bother—you know, it's pointless!" responded Ann, immediately.

But Miles was insistent: how, for example, would anyone know the crime rate's as high as it is? He knocked on the door of the old Puerto Rican lady next door, asking if he could phone police.

"Oh, I've been robbed seventeen times!" she exclaimed. "And they probably only live around the corner!"

So Miles didn't call. But he could no longer stay on 408 East 10th; he was, as he told me, "absolutely scared shitless." Before dusk fell, he and Ann were safe in the Chelsea, at a monthly rate.

□ □ □

BACK IN 1968, Allen had told me of how he was once coming up the stairs with a bag of groceries when someone approached with a knife. "'Oh, come on!'" Allen exclaimed, tugging suddenly at his bag, whereupon glass bottles of Coke popped out, crashing onto the step between them. The fellow turned and ran, in fright.

Once too some "friends" decided the Tibetan thangkas and artifacts he'd brought back from India were signs of being middle class, and so took it upon themselves to relieve him of that stigma.

Otherwise, he'd encountered no crime at 408 East 10th, and seemed unworried—for himself—by basic conditions. But I—like anyone—could see that the whole neighborhood was turning more violent, with abandoned buildings, burnt-out cars. ("The whole time we were there it was obvious we were going to get robbed," said Miles.) But when I used Miles and Ann's experience to suggest he look for another place, Allen was resistant: "What will they steal," he asked, "the teapot?"

He remained there, as it happened, another four years, until one twilight out on East 10th he was knocked down and robbed. Then, but only then, did Allen decide to move.

More Orlovskys

L ATE ONE OCTOBER weekend—Allen was in New Orleans, reading at Tulane— Peter and Denise drove to Long Island to bring Peter's family to East Hill.

Peter had long worried for them—on his first trip to Europe with Allen in 1957, he woke one morning troubled by Julius's continued stay in asylum; eventually, after confinement over a dozen years at Central Islip, his older brother was released into his and Allen's care. But there was still his mother, deaf four decades from a surgeon's drunken error—as Peter once put it, "She couldn't look people in the eye, she had to look 'em in the lips." Kate the cleaning woman moved her essentially fatherless five children from pitiful dwelling to pitiful dwelling, the family so impoverished they'd scavenge throwaways from vegetable carts.

She'd been born Katherine Schwartzen in Yonkers. Her father was a mechanic; her mother died early on. He then married a woman she couldn't stand, who brought her eleven step-brothers and step-sisters. At seventeen she ran away to the Village, carrying her typewriter: she would be a writer. She was very pretty, Peter told me.

In New York she first dated lawyers; then at the Wonderbread factory in Long Island City, she met a Russian ten or eleven years her senior: foreman Oleg Orlovsky. Soon they married; initially she continued writing, but things were turning out badly, and she wanted to write only of the good things in life. She lost her hearing; Oleg's new silk-screening business wasn't bringing the income they needed; the family grew. Her face remained partially paralyzed from the surgical debacle; she couldn't smile on the sagging side; she looked, she thought, like a witch. Oleg began having affairs, eating at restaurants, not bringing money home. Nights, they argued, throwing pots and pans. They began separate lives. . . .

And there were the children, Nicholas the eldest, living in upper Manhattan, where he delivered papers. Julius would turn thirty-nine in December; Peter was now thirty-seven; and there were the twenty-nine-year-old twins, Lafcadio and Marie. Lafcadio hadn't finished high school; Marie had tried nursing long ago. She and Laf had been home with mom nearly a dozen years now.

"What's Marie like?" I asked Peter before he and Denise left. "Well, she's shy, and I guess she's kinda pretty." He paused. "Maybe you and she'll like each other," he offered.

When we met, I could see a resemblance to Peter, but she wasn't pretty, and was more than shy—standoffish, as if permanently frightened, scarcely "socialized." Speaking to her I had the feeling I'd startled her; her responses could be loud, abrupt. Lafcadio was quiet, with pretty blue eyes; slender with flabby, flaccid skin. He didn't take care of himself, and in speech—I couldn't say "conversation"—he'd repeat what you just said (which, given his lack of personal hygiene, was often an order). You'd hear back, "Brush my teeth? Brush my teeth?" He'd look at you earnestly, pleading.

Even with her inability to hear I found Kate expressive, friendly. But to the righteous displeasure of Peter (ever the reformed sinner), she smoked cigarettes. At sixty-one she was a bit heavyset, brown-haired with some grey; one side of her face sagged from that long-ago injury. I liked her.

We took them to Cooperstown one afternoon, brought them by Myron's. We stopped at the Beautiful View, took in its panoramic vista. Back at the farm, Ed came down for a visit. Peter spent a lot of time making sure his family understood the lay of our land, physically and psychically, as if determined to assume the role Oleg abandoned long ago. I remember being upstairs in my room at night, hearing Peter shout (presumably for his mother's benefit), "I am a man! I am a man!" Likewise, I heard him repeat in a loud voice to Lafcadio, "Farming is the planting, cultivating, harvesting, and preserving of vegetables! Farming is the planting, cultivating . . . !"

When Peter and Denise left to return them to Northport, Lafcadio stayed. Peter, who sometimes imagined having a child with Denise to help with farm work (though she wanted none of that), at last had his young agricultural worker: or so it seemed. Would Laf be Louie to Peter's Huncke? How would he and Julius relate? Could East Hill be his salvation, like it was (given the givens) for one of his brothers? We'd see . . .

Another New Farmhand

MEANTIME ALLEN'S FOURTEEN-YEAR-OLD nephew Alan Brooks, having returned to Plainview, Long Island, from his late August visit, was miserable. He wrote me soon after going home. He had one close friend whom he loved, with whom he played guitar; otherwise, he reported, "I always feel useless in the shitty suburbs & I dont think this year is going to be different."

His father told me he continued unhappy at school, where he was being scape-goated, and had run away to the railway station: police brought him back. And Alan himself later told me, "School was filled with 'greasers,' leather-jacket-clad sharkies. Plus I was a dud at sports." It seemed something had to be done: why not return to Cherry Valley? But rather than Allen's multifarious scene, why not a stable family one? Asking around, Ed found a family—the Claggarts—with a large dairy farm in need of a hand. In return for labor, Alan would get room and board, go to school.

First he spent a weekend with us—just Julius, Peter, Lafcadio, Denise, and me; then we took him to Claggart's. Of course he was already an old hand in our company, having been through that disquieting night with Sandy and me, and having already seen the strangest things vis-à-vis Peter. Once, in 1967, Alan said, Peter had visited the Brookses' suburban home, fed his dog off his own plate, and then eaten the leftovers. He spent a few hours polishing curtain rods, and told everyone in the neighborhood he was married to his dog.

But Peter Orlovsky in the fall of 1970 was squarely on his feet. Once Alan joined us temporarily, Orlovsky saw to it that his latest charge—slight, slender, glasses, long hair in eyes—did this and did that, all the while calling him by two names: "Brooks!" and (as if Alan were Allen's son) "Junior!" But a few days with a more or less amiable Peter would surely be different from life on a "real" farm: I wondered how he'd fare.

It proved hard work indeed, as it would've for anyone—on top of going to school. His day began by seven every morning, milking cows, then working till seven at night after coming home. The first day, he was wakened at five to shovel silage. His muscles ached—but they developed.

The Cherry Valley school was much friendlier than his Long Island junior high, and (perhaps because many kids had farm commitments) no sports were required. The Claggarts were a pleasant family; he was a right-wing farmer in his early thirties; she was quite attractive. They had two children, one a daughter about Alan's age. They were barely making monthly payments on the farm, so Alan didn't get paid, but he did get $2 for lunch at school—which he spent on candy bars.

It was, Alan remembered decades later, "the only time in my life I've ever worked really hard." Who Alan's uncle was seemed of no concern to his hosts, but a couple of other items became sticking points. One was his long hair; Claggart was always on him to get it cut: anyone without a crewcut was a Communist.

The other point was, of course, our war. Alan told me that whenever Claggart's relatives visited, ". . . the first thing they'd ask us was 'What do you think about Vietnam?' and I'd say I was against it."

His opinion may have been the reason why Claggart's uncle, who drove the school bus, slammed the door in his face one morning, and wouldn't let him board. Or might it have been Alan's undressing his hosts' daughter one Sunday while her parents were at church?

Such events, as well as Alan's constant hunger, contributed to his departure. By Christmas fourteen-year-old Alan Eugene Brooks found himself boarding the bus for New York, "covered," as he told me, "with muscles, smelling like a barn, relieved to be free."

He'd left Long Island despising sports; the next semester, Alan Brooks ran track for Plainview Junior High.

Films, Music, Relationships

A NUTSHELL OF my work in film, until this time: when I invited Jonas to campus my last semester at Davidson College 1966, he brought with him that small regular 8-millimeter camera with which I made my first films. The nudity and sexuality in "Prunes," shown at heavily Presbyterian Davidson, upset many and got me fired (though at year's end) as head of the student union film program. "Georgia," shot impromptu and edited in-camera that summer, won Jonas's enthusiastic endorsement after I went to him in New York that fall, asking for work.

In New York 1966–67 I shot much other footage. Once Candy and I planned to leave for Mexico I made day-by-day takes, camera on tripod, out the window of Filmmakers' Cooperative where I worked, even as the young filmmaker replacing me, Ernie Gehr, was already coming in. And I completed a short silent lovemaking scene of Candy and another woman, "Revelation." When I ran into film critic P. Adams Sitney at a performance of a Richard Foreman play in Saratoga Springs, New York, summer 1970, he volunteered having seen "Revelation" and liking it.

Nonetheless I had an inferiority complex in general and specifically about my films. After all, there was Jonas's ambiguous remark on farm footage I'd shown him; there was Allen's criticism during Peter's headbanging; and later, after Jonas arranged for me to show my first year's farm footage at the Jewish Museum (taking the place of the Cinematheque), Allen would tell me that he'd heard the showing wasn't so good. It was seven years before I released a film again, and it took a dozen years to deal with what I'd shot in jail, Mexico 1968. Nearly a whole decade passed before Allen, Robert Frank, Jonas, and others offered extremely generous comments on my later work.

Meantime I did have this show, thanks to Jonas; and I was gratified: I wanted my films to be seen. I made up a flyers list of nearly fifty people, including family, Lucien, Carolyn Karcher, R'lene and Huncke; even Don Wilen, the Brooklyn accountant with whom Allen and I were now working because of IRS scrutiny of Committee on Poetry accounts.

Before the showing I heard from several from far away, including Gregory. On October 20, on a notecard whose color face depicted a nineteenth dynasty image from the Egyptian *Book of the Dead*, he wrote from Buffalo:

Dear Gordon—I would love to be in the city to see your films—maybe I can make it—gave reading here—I was really liked and it sort of encourages me to go on doing same—I've no agent like Al so it hard to git such gigs—but enough to know I have 'em rolling the aisles—like poesy readings can be real drag—stuffy over-bearing, serious—me I give 'em something to laugh about . . . with the serious—just like I am—funny, & serious—

. . . .

how's farm, and the gang? Pig big? I've ceased cursing mine fellow human lot— for the time being anyway—I just yell at Al because it be hard to worship an old buddy—like I'm ground roots and Christ he knows it—Tell Al that since I've no agent he could help by recommending me to where he reads. . . .

Love, Gregory

Pleased to hear from Gregory and everyone else, I wondered who, if anyone, from the city would make it all the way uptown to 95th for the show, on a holiday (Veterans' Day). Meantime, I asked Giorno about staying there. "Last time was really a drag with Sandy," John told me, and I knew he was right. Miles and Ann were at the Chelsea; I'd go back to Allen's, 408 East 10th.

It had been a while since I was in the city, and the last time (connecting with Alan Brooks) was essentially on farm business. Now I planned to spend two or three days besides the one of the showing.

I filled every minute. I saw Bunuel's *Tristana* at the 8th Street Playhouse; I saw Warhol's *Trash*, with Joe Dallesandro an impotent junkie, Holly Woodlawn his transvestite roommate. I loved the lowlife charm of it, with Holly's closing line after all plans and scams have failed, "Joe, let me suck your cock." At the 92nd Street YM-YWHA I took in a reading by John Ashbery, Kenneth Koch, Joseph Ceravolo, and others; I liked Ceravolo best for the intriguing flatness of one poem. I took Sandy to a matinee of the "Father of Bluegrass" Bill Monroe and his Bluegrass Boys at the McBurney YMCA on 23rd Street. (In those days bluegrass was far less recognized nationally than today, but I knew of Monroe through Jon Sholle.) There was a small, specialized audience of maybe fifty people on metal folding chairs, very "YMCA-ish." Sandy was the only black person there, and she won the door prize.

Frank Zappa and the Mothers of Invention were performing at the Fillmore East, and on Miles's recommendation I took that in rather than what I'd wanted to see,

Linda Ronstadt's concert at the Academy of Music. The Fillmore was packed, and Zappa responded to the many shouted-out titles of favorites with a dutiful, "We'll do our best to honor all requests." But I didn't appreciate (and never have) that whole Suzie Creamcheese social criticism put-down of young girls. Zappa and his music were clever and critical; I found myself yearning for the strong beauty of Ronstadt's voice.

And as to my own presentation: only a very small audience—ten or twelve?— were at the Jewish Museum. Sandy was one. Playwright Richard Foreman entered, carrying something of some weight in one hand. I went over to welcome him, thank him for coming; he explained, "I'm just returning this projector." Nevertheless, there were others, and they stayed through the whole silent showing of nearly an hour; afterward, a nice gathering at R'lene's, with Huncke, Sandy, a few friends of R'lene, and much merrymaking. I saw Sandy into a cab—we'd spend other nights together.

Then I rejoined R'lene on the sofa. We sat close, talked quietly, earnestly, intimately, into early hours, even though she had school to get up for: she always made me welcome. I told her I still didn't know if I ought to stay on East Hill; she told me the farm would always be Peter's. I wasn't concerned that the farm "belonged" to one person or another, but simply with the general direction of things. I was frustrated by some of Peter's projects: there was the new cellar door, exposing underground storage space to cold, and our having to refill that area with earth for winter. And Peter's intention to get a tractor in the near future, mine to move in the opposite direction, relying more on growing plants by composting. And, I now felt, I wasn't especially needed—Peter was determinedly on his feet, and he and Denise a happy couple. And I wanted and needed to do some things on my own—see more of the world, maybe enter graduate school (if I could get in, given my poor undergraduate academic record). I hadn't figured it out, but the basic thrust was there. Given her background and commitment to teaching, R'lene was of course sympathetic to further education. Her words didn't crystallize my thoughts overnight, but they may well have set their direction.

From this account of several days in New York, all seems relatively nice and neat: my showing, other films, girl friend, concerts. But as I visit my memory of forty-one years ago, I wonder: where was Cheri? Cheri who'd nursed me through my black eye, who was so smart, so sexy, and who seemed to always want to get together. Evidently Sandy was replacing her. But I thought I was fairly serious about Cheri, who certainly had her enchantments—what happened? I'm baffled.

Holding in hand surviving bits of correspondence—one a narrow piece of lined paper, typewritten; some handwritten in pencil or pen; various kinds of cutouts, sometimes with messages added on the reverse—I've tried to reconstruct. Soon after her return from the black eye weekend, she wrote:

dear gorden

enjoyed myself up there.

> *learnt that I feel a great tenderness towards you that makes me afraid to say anything to you at times; I get so afraid. when gregory hit you felt that I should have offered some words of comfort none came. setting by you and reading was the best I could do at the time. I'd like to build so words can come.*

. . . .

> *I found myself thinking about you a great deal. (what you'd want to eat, what we could do together . . . Incidently I found out I enjoy riding in a car with you when you drive (a mild but happy discovery as this turns to be a mild somehow love letter.)*

> *Bought a book today that shows some knitting stiches. want to make some scarves, mittens hats and vests. Pick a color write me what you want and I'll make you something if you like*

love Cheri

I'm sure I was moved by much of it—but was I scared by the domesticity of her knitting something for me?

In any case, in what may have been the last time I saw her in the city—and the last time I saw her at all—I recall a moment of conversation. She wasn't entirely sure about going on to law school; she liked working with kids, and might become a teacher. But as she imagined herself at work in the legal world, thinking up this crime and that punishment, she came out with something along the lines of, "And I think punishment for possession of acid should be limited to two years."

Though (true to form) I didn't respond, I was so offended at her endorsing the very idea of a penalty for possessing LSD that I may have let it cool our relationship—rather than simply discussing the matter with her. I was good at making moralistic judgments about people in those days. Even those I really felt for, fell for.

Two Thanksgivings

1

A COUPLE WEEKS before Thanksgiving, R'lene and Huncke had telephoned: they'd like to bring a big turkey up for the holiday. But Peter and Denise said no turkey—we were vegetarian now. Huncke and R'lene didn't come.

And Thanksgiving 1970, unlike both times before, was a quiet affair. I missed the hubbub and uproar, even with a fair number of guests: Eugene and Connie and their five kids joined us, Alan coming over from Claggart's. We had a good spread ready for them, but no meat. Lafcadio, seeing a plate full of dressing but no bird, asked over and over, "Stuffing? Where's the turkey?" He asked thirty times or more.

The next day Connie woke up first, saw no milk in the fridge, and—respecting Allen's request that kids be quiet in the morning—took her brood and Lafcadio into town, returning with store-bought milk just when we late-rising farmers were preparing to milk.

Allen then led Eugene and Connie into Peter and Denise's room, as if they were lying in state, as if they were John and Yoko. "It seemed important to Allen for us to see they were lovers," Connie said. Outside, Peter urged her to lean down and smell Don't Bite Me because she was "so clean." For a split second, Connie brought herself near. "We think of pigs as being very dirty but actually by nature they're very clean," Peter said. Connie found Peter correct, but Don't Bite Me had grown so big she was no longer a pig: she was now a hog.

2

As I SAW in the *Daily News* down at Crain's, Nixon had his own Thanksgiving, with turkey and much else. He and Pat and Tricia, as well as Mimi Eisenhower, hosted 106 "wounded servicemen and nurses," "some in wheelchairs." Some, I learned later from NBC correspondent Ford Rowan, were blind.

Nixon told his guests, "The White House belongs to all Americans, particularly those who have served with such distinction." He added, ". . . all Americans really can say this, in a sense, this is their home . . .We want you to feel its warmth and all its friendliness." One photograph featured Tricia near center foreground seated before a fruit cup topped with an erect strawberry, longish blonde hair neatly in place, as she gestured with both hands raised, broad grin across her face. The Army sergeant next to her, in class A blouse, bent his head toward her in total attention. The U.S. Marine Band, the article informed us, "played light musical airs."

□ □ □

THE OUTRAGE I felt at learning of such an event was mitigated some by an article in the *Times* a week later. Nixon was awarding four Young American Medals for bravery or public service. Acclaiming the honorees "fine young Americans who represent the very best in American youth," he added:

> We hear too much these days about the very small minority of young Americans who have lost faith in their country.
>
> We hear too little about the great majority of young Americans, young Americans who can display courage in their daily lives, who are willing to sacrifice and save the lives of others and young Americans who are motivated by idealism.

One recipient was nineteen-year-old Debra Jean Sweet, "a church worker from Madison" who'd organized a thirty-mile march by 3,000 Wisconsin high school students to feed poor children. She was being recognized for that, and "for her work in race relations."

When Nixon handed her her medal, she said, in a voice scarcely heard by journalists standing near, "'I find it hard to believe in your sincerity in giving the awards until you get us out of Vietnam.'"

Mr. Nixon, reported *The Times*, "seemed a bit taken aback."

This Thanksgiving season I gave thanks for nineteen-year-old Ms. Sweet.

Vermont and Back

I N 1967 RAY Mungo and friend Marshall Bloom had founded the Liberation News Service, which quickly became the center for news dissemination within the burgeoning underground press.

But before long LNS broke into factionalism, and Ray left to start a farm with friends and co-workers. Now located in Packer Corners, Vermont, it housed a goodly number of people and was supported mainly by his book contracts.

Of his LNS days he'd recently published *Famous Long Ago*; soon he'd bring out *Total Loss Farm* to keep his current project afloat. He was both a good writer and good talker, transporting me to a 1967 Bratislava conference where he and a few other American antiwar activists smoked grass with Viet Cong.

On a visit to East Hill Mungo had invited me their way, and when Allen was to read at Goddard College in Plainfield, he suggested, "Why not come with me, and you can go on to Mungo's from there?"

The last day in November a student picked us up for the reading that night. Once we were in the Green Mountain State, I remember riding along a two-lane road next to a stream, brown mountains of late autumn on both sides. And I remember being shameless: when Allen talked with our driver about his time at sea, I made a point of bringing up sex. It was partly because I'd been reading Irving Rosenthal's *Sheeper* with its criticism of Melville's lack of inevitable (as Rosenthal saw it) sex among men at sea. But it was largely to show I had a sexual bond with Allen—who, fortunately, wouldn't take my bait: "No, just being on the sea—the sea itself is so majestic."

At the reading I met a psychology major who was working in a day care center with emotionally disturbed children. Elise Greene was dark-haired and pretty and the next day I bid Allen adieu as he headed south to Scarsdale and several readings around New York with Louis.

I spent a day and a night with Elise in St. Johnsbury (where she had a small apartment) and we went to the one movie theater in town, where I saw a Barbra Streisand film for the first time; neither of us could believe the horrible voice and personality of the Streisand character and the general dumbness of the movie. We returned to Elise's place with better things to do. And promising to meet again (which we did, over half a year and 3,000 miles away).

At Total Loss Farm the next afternoon I was struck by its difference from East Hill—instead of a centering main house backed by a barn, with garage and chicken house nearby, old maples and low stone walls making graceful borders, it was more sprawling, with various buildings in various states of repair or construction or completion. The main house was a dark wooden two-story frame with a recently built single-story plastic-windowed extension. A barn and other buildings and a number of vehicles sat here and there in a pretty hillside wooded lot.

Everyone was welcoming, full of good cheer. As with many such situations, living there seemed focused on the physicality of the environment—the cold, the need for daylight, food, warmth. Ray—small, black hair, glasses—seemed to care about each of the people around him; and thanks to him as well as the general good faith and spirit of everyone else, Total Loss Farm was hardly living up to its name.

Ray had returned from Brattleboro with Kerouac's *Scripture of the Golden Eternity*, enthusing over it for anyone who'd listen. I spent the night downstairs on the couch, and though it wasn't far from their efficient Ashley stove, I woke up cold in the dark. Then I felt something land softly over me—it was a blanket, laid gently by Ray.

The next day John Wilton, an Australian from a group in Montague, Massachusetts (he worked for Boston's underground *Avatar*), drove me to the bus. Like most young people living communally, he had essentially no money. "Could you buy me a hamboogie?" he asked as we slid into a booth at a diner near the station. Unlike many others, I had a few dollars—thanks to Allen.

Because of the schedule, I had to overnight in Albany for the morning bus that took us to Crain's a little after eleven. I found a sort of "quality bum's hotel"—well, it was a small room with single bed, clean and quiet—near the station. Late that afternoon and well into the evening I sat up on the bed reading Gogol's *Dead Souls*, which has remained my favorite novel.

Likely I'd started it at the suggestion of Allen, who repeated Dostoyevsky's exclamation, "We all came out of Gogol's *Overcoat*!" The bed was narrow, the street outside was quiet, and I was there with Chichikov in mid-nineteenth-century Russia. Yet I was also on that narrow bed in that small quiet room, and I realized I loved being alone, I realized I was happy.

East Hill as Winter Nears

LOOKING AT MOVING images of the farm as real winter approached, I see that

Papa Duck stands amidst the snow on one leg, beautiful and impressive against a background of white. More snow descends, Papa just stoically holds it in. His ladies nearby squat and waddle on two.

Julius, barehanded in plaid shirt, tails out, saws wood in the snow—more's coming down—it's fairly thick on the trees now, building up on ground.

Here comes Ed in yellow waterproof parka, there goes Godly in the other direction behind him. Ed wears clip-on shades over his glasses, baseball hat brim bears a crust of white.

We'd built cribs around the outside base of the house, filling them with horseshit to add to the general warmth within. When true winter was here and it was hard getting out, we washed laundry in that deep sink in the bathroom. Really dirty clothes would be brought to a boil on the Kalamazoo.

Meanwhile, Peter and Lafcadio were often at odds as the anxious older brother tried to compel the extremely passive younger one into a regimen of action. Otherwise we mostly got along, the shared duties of extreme cold reducing differences. Except for the antipathy toward Maretta. When she was about to leave for a spell in the city, Peter unleashed an attack, shouting that instead of becoming a nurse like her mother, she was living off the starving.

"She's not a nurse!" Maretta yelled back. "You are hallucinating!"

Peter had been depressed by a letter from his own mother that day, but the feelings he seemed to share with Denise toward Maretta might well have come out anyway. On another occasion I overheard an exchange—I don't remember what precipitated it—between the two women along these lines:

D: No one here likes you!
M: Yes, Gordon does! He's nice to me—
D: Yes, he's nice to you, but he doesn't like you at all!

I didn't volunteer any clarification.

□ □ □

RETURNING TO THE farm, Allen noted in his journal that as he did his daily meditation he found his "mind moving over impossibly multitudinous mass of letters on my
desk unanswered, proofs, mss. to correct." He'd lost five years of poetry manuscripts
on a plane in the Caribbean in October—he'd have to cobble all of that back together.
And there was much else, including writing requests from *The New York Times*,
underground press books to read, poetry readings and classes to prepare, his tax
struggle with the IRS. . . .

I was helping him with his documentary history of junk illegalization and its
consequences; by Christmas, there'd be 325 mimeographed copies of an eighteen-
page, single-spaced annotated bibliography, "Compiled," as the cover read, "by Allen
Ginsberg/Scribe." Its title alone was twenty-five words long:

> *Documents on Police Bureaucracy's Conspiracy Against Human Rights of Opiate*
> *Addicts & Constitutional Rights of Medical Profession Causing Mass Breakdown of*
> *Urban Law & Order*

Chapters ranged from "Addiction Politics, 1922–1970" through the contempo-
raneous "CIA Involvement with Opium Traffic at Source."

□ □ □

AROUND THIS TIME Allen wrote Leary in Algiers that the "odd effect" of his
Weatherman "freedom manifesto" was Allen's now daily hour-long meditation practice. He recommended it for "Revolutionaries, counterrevolutionaries, & anybody
interested in my opinions." It was "no use," he said, "unless I'm doing it myself which
I am."

This original and strikingly apt response rhymes with his remark ("If the revolution's not spiritual, it's not worth it") I heard back in Albany 1968. The same basic
perspective held throughout his life: 1981's "Why I Meditate," a poem listing reasons
for the practice, concludes, "I sit for Jean-Arthur Rimbaud's Christmas on Earth / I
sit for world revolution."

As I continued assisting with "Documents on Police Bureaucracy's Conspiracy,"
I became more excited by this sort of journalistic information-gathering. And Allen
had recently bought me my own Sony cassette taperecorder which I'd use for further
ventures. Yet as I told my diary, I remained vexed:

I really shouldn't be here—want a social life, a place where I can . . . peacefully pursue projects. It's not Peter's fault he yells at Lafcadio—what an oppressive burden L is for P! But Peter's not going to put up w/ him forever. But still there's a certain "climate" which his psyche produces . . . —we've each our own directions, I'm a fool for not pursuing mine. Explore, discover, get to know as many phenomena available in this human world—there will always be the heaviness of Peter's psyche, w/ its assemblages of do's & don'ts prescribed for himself & others—he wants his own life & I want mine—tho I love him & respect him, & Denise, dearly.

I must do something else! Yet w/ Allen here I am involved in information exchange, there's a happy companionship of our 2 souls I feel, but there's always P's planet spinning in orbit near & parallel, & I think we should all have more room in the solar system.

▢ ▢ ▢

AT THE SAME time, I kept my relationships with both Sandy and Anna Marie. With Sandy it was passionate and tortured; with Anna Marie I felt an enormous gap in terms of our values regarding the rest of the world: it was as if she wanted only our relationship, apart from all else; as good as she was being to me, it worried me, angered me, scared me.

Sandy wrote a rhapsody beginning, "I too am a sensualist!" It (like some other letters) was full of sexual details, as were, I imagine, some of mine. And everyday life specifics: she'd gotten a new place to live, a tiny room on 71st Street; she'd have a small role in the next Warhol film; she was getting a new job as go-go dancer: "This time I'm wearing an auburn wig. It looks cute. Maybe I won't be so arrogant as a brunette & get fired so fast." She'd star in a new play by Wayne County (later Jayne County).

She was up: *After-Dark* gave her a whole page; she'd been down, worried with no period (it came late) I'd made her pregnant. And she was, at one point, furious at me for something I'd evidently said on my November visit:

I put you on a grand pedestal like a SEMI-GOD then when I thought enough time had passed I let you penetrate me so that I might belong to you. But, no! You didn't like my pink velvet pants or my blonde hair. . . .

"Why don't you dye your hair dark and be black like you are?" was the most preposterous unintelligent thing you said. . . . You even put me down for talking only of myself to my public. . . . Being a narcissist is wonderful despite the loneliness.

I'd asked for another picture of her; she closed by inserting a swatch of pubic hair with a note, "The pubic hairs are BLACK, anyway, 'like I really am?'" Yet she wanted to see me, and we'd get together again shortly.

Meantime, my feelings toward Anna Marie were almost as contradictory as Sandy's toward me. When she'd visited earlier in the fall, there was a huge strike at Syracuse's General Electric plant. At the dining room table she and Allen and I discussed the worsening situation. "Yeah," she offered, "some say the President will have to resolve it." Allen, evidently uncomprehending, asked "Of GE?" Of course Anna Marie answered "Nixon"—she was the only person I knew to refer to him by title.

And now here she was, making those curtains for my room, and for Christmas searching in New York for a pair of slippers like Peter's fur-lined moccasins. She'd also made a sweater for the baby recently born to Cooperstown friends Patti and Paul Benson. This persistent domesticity made me uncomfortable, at the least; I felt enclosed. I might not have minded if we had meaningful discussions of the issues of the day (or, to use a current expression, of "the elephant in the room"—our war): but she simply couldn't or wouldn't examine the conflict or question authority. She loved me, that was clear. She was much better as friend and lover than in earlier times, perhaps in part because we weren't seeing each other daily. But now I wasn't sure if I wanted that love, and all I took it to mean. I sought to break free, and wasn't sure how. . . .

Doctors, Patients, Brothers

B ASSETT HOSPITAL: WE'D been there often, I for injured wrist, Allen for flu; at one point when many of us seemed sick and he feared hepatitis, we all lined up for hemoglobin shots. I'd gone with Allen when Dr. Harvey Gurian, head of psychiatry, had invited him to speak to colleagues on the historical problem of Treasury Department intrusion in doctor-patient relationship and its relation to present-day crime in the streets. Bonnie had gone suspecting miscarriage; Louie Cartwright and friend had shown up with incriminating wounds up and down their arms. . . .

And when Peter had been in one of his late phases of amphetamine mania, we'd managed to talk him into going because of his right arm, where he usually shot up: much of it was dotted and striped with red infection. And he complained of weakness, of not feeling well. It was entirely unspoken, but I think many of us hoped for a diagnosis so dire he'd stay off speed forever.

On that occasion, I remained on East Hill. When the old Ford station wagon pulled back down the drive, the report was that Peter, introduced to the physician, announced, "I'm not feeling very strong these days," as he took his hand and nearly crunched it to pieces. Yes, the exam revealed, he had an infection, treatable with antibiotics. He was otherwise in good health.

Now it was Lafcadio's turn. Before East Hill, he'd spent years indoors, barely moving from one room to another; he hadn't brushed his teeth for ages, and it was about that long since seeing a doctor for any reason, let alone for a physical. We scheduled an appointment; I drove him over. Before the doctor entered, a nurse checked blood pressure, took temperature. Next was a blood sample.

Laf saw the needle. "Noo, noo," he muttered. He drew back. We tugged his plaid sleeve halfway up his pale slender arm. His eyes were a blue ghost's. He backed away and pushed at us, "Noo, noo." I held to him, but as the nurse advanced he resisted so much he lost his footing and fell hard to the floor. I hauled him up. Apparently the fall did the trick, convinced him this medical terror was inescapable. I felt horrible—but held him still by both arms. And the nurse got her bright red sample of Lafcadio's essence.

It must've been the same Russian constitution of his brother: no unexpected problems were discovered in the course of check-up and blood analysis. But back on East Hill, the psychic diagnosis wasn't positive. Peter ordered and ordered him around; Laf frequently stood there, repeating orders, questioning. Driven to the limits of frustration and anger, Peter eventually hauled off and hit him, blackening his eye.

Back when Peter was fourteen, Julius was the bodybuilding master, and could squat 360 pounds. He encouraged Peter to lift weights—it would clear up his asthma, he said—and he was right. Now Peter made Laf lift one-handed barbells, sometimes outdoors in late autumn snow. From a little distance I shot Laf lifting:

It's snowing. He wears a red hooded jacket-sweatshirt, zipped up (though not all the way tight to neck), there's frost on his beard. The laces at the top of his rubber boots are untied. He struggles to lift a barbell in his left hand, elbow crooking into his side, body bending backward awkwardly from his waist. Freeing his left, he reaches down with his right for another barbell. He looks miserable. He squints into the camera, bowl-cut hair almost in his eyes. He's a study in grim despair, lost, detached from what's going on; it's as if his body doesn't fit together, its parts not connected, mind separate from body. Intent on her own business, Don't Bite Me, her face a study in smudge and frosty white, pushes through the snow in front of him.

In a later shot, he seems the frozen sentry, outside the house near the window, beyond the little pine tree—both it and Lafcadio are accumulating snow. He's hunched over as whiteness descends, woolen cap on head, heavier coat this time but again not tightly closed at neck, right hand resting on a shovel, frost growing on beard and coat.

How could I tolerate such things? I may have felt that if I tried talking with Peter, little good would come—or I may have been chicken. In any case, once Allen returned to the farm—he'd been away awhile—he decided enough was enough. He took Peter and Lafcadio to Dr. Gurian for an evaluation of their relationship, then told me of Gurian's conclusion: "'It's obviously a sado-masochistic relationship!'" The two should be separated. And so it was determined that Peter's younger brother would have to leave East Hill Farm. Still more time would pass, but eventually, Lafcadio Orlovsky, farmhand for a season, would be returned to his mother.

South at Christmas Again

F OR THE HOLIDAYS Peter and Denise left for Queens and Long Island; I headed for Carolina. I went first, joining Allen in the city a night or two. (Allen would return to the farm before the others left; he, Maretta, and Julius would hold the fort.)

Allen and I went to a benefit showing of films (for Jonas's Cinematheque) by John and Yoko at the Elgin. The work I liked best was one by John, "Apotheosis," in which a camera was evidently placed in a balloon and slowly rose above a township—so, over a number of minutes, the gradual, graceful movement was from the midst of human affairs into cloud and mist and atmosphere and blue and silver upper atmosphere, the cosmic realm: at least that's how I remember it, its charm.

There were other films, including the main attraction of the night, "Up Your Legs Forever," an assemblage of 365 pairs of legs (each subject standing, unclothed, shot from beneath genitals to feet). "We asked everybody," Yoko told the *Village Voice*, "to donate their legs for peace."

Leaving the theater, Allen and I ran into someone Candy and I had known in 1967. It was Alan ("A.J.") Weberman, who was giving a weekly Dylanology course at the Alternate University, and had formed a "Dylan Liberation Front." Recently he'd written me on a typewriter:

> *Uhave t understand that Ive been nice (petting) Dylan for years, lovingly trying to cox him out of his shell but now man I am going to fight him for I see that I cannot do shit, man, as far as getting Dylan's head back together. He just invest a quarter of a million dollars in an office building in times squate—he's taking the $$$ from the hip community and giving it back to the establishment. He's a stoned PIG and I hate him for this along with many other things. Looking forward to seeing you tho, call 477-6243—you can crash here if you like.*

Now he began insisting, in words that seemed especially directed at Allen, that Dylan was a junky. Didn't the lyrics in "Country Pie" affirm that: "Saddle me up my big white goose / Tie me on 'er and turn her loose." But an upset Allen was just as insistent from his end: "Dylan is not a junky! Dylan is not a junky!"

□ □ □

I TOOK IN Sandy's play; watching her was delightful, but we were fighting; escaping the warm approaches of the director, I went to the cast party—a large affair—alone. I was talking with one of the actors when Holly Woodlawn came up and asked him, "Who the hell is this, he's so fabulous!" She and I danced a little, kissed a little; she mouthed, "Oh, you're beautiful!" at me, while the Rolling Stones played loud on the Victrola.

□ □ □

IN D.C. I stayed overnight with Carolyn and Martin Karcher, then joined two people for lunch the next day before going on to Winston-Salem. Bob Spearman and his family, who'd been active in the civil rights movement in Chapel Hill, had been friends ever since I came to the States for college. Now Bob was assistant to Justice Hugo Black at the Supreme Court. But the impetus for getting together at this time was my desire to connect with his roommate, NBC White House correspondent Ford Rowan, whom I admired for his tough questioning of Nixon at press conferences.

I brought a copy of Allen's "Documents on Police Bureaucracy's Conspiracy"; they seemed open to its basic thrust, and Ford asked that I send him one. He pronounced Vice President Ky's past involvement in opium smuggling, reported within Scribe Ginsberg's pages, as "very interesting." Leary's case came under discussion, but at my "Now that he's gone I guess Sinclair's the number one example of artistic or political censorship in the country," they asked, "Who's that?" I filled them in briefly. It still seemed that, in spite of the efforts of Allen and others, few outside the counterculture knew of Sinclair.

Ford spoke of recent Washington events. The U.S. had raided a prisoner-of-war camp in the North; no one—Vietnamese or American—was found. Nixon, awarding medals to some of the raiders, said there'd been a 50% chance of their death. That made you wonder, Ford said, what chance the prisoners—many of them likely infirm—would've had. Though Nixon's bombings had probably exceeded our total from previous wars combined (large areas of the North resembled the moon, reported *The Times*'s Harrison Salisbury), and further bombing "wasn't going to be very effective," it was all Nixon would feel there was to do.

□ □ □

MY SISTER MET me at the old downtown bus station on Cherry Street. Loving mother of four, she also lived as much as she could in a realm of recollection and books. In her blue Chevelle, the passenger side of the front seat was so piled with reading matter and kids' stuff I had to sit in the back. But we talked with each other just fine.

Christmas Day my mother and father joined us, and my brother and his wife came by with their daughter. I took out my Sony recorder. Edgar and Paula mentioned having played their LP of the Beatles' *Abbey Road* when our parents recently visited them in Raleigh; Paula exclaimed how my mother had liked Ringo's "Octopus's Garden." For Christmas they'd given my parents a tape of the album.

I asked my mother, "Tell us about 'Octopus's Garden.'"

But she was confused: "What?"

"Tell us about 'Octopus's Garden,' Mother," I asked again.

"I—I don't know anything about that," she worried.

"Oh, you don't know that song?" I tried.

"No, no."

Later, everyone else gone, a guest from Thailand—a young intern at Bowman Gray School of Medicine, where Maylee's husband sometimes gave a course—arrived for dinner. She seemed surprised when I asked about specific places such as Chieng Mai, but provided helpful information and wanted to know the basis for my familiarity.

"I've been studying CIA involvement in opium traffic in the Golden Triangle," I explained. All was quiet at the table; the instant that had just transpired was an historical first. At last! I'd brought up Vietnam, our malfeasance in Southeast Asia. I at age twenty-five had felt so inferior, almost criminal, in holding the views and convictions I did; at last I'd seen a green light to speak my mind a moment.

□ □ □

STAYING AT MY sister's, I palled around with my nephews and played with little Missy, now two. I hung out with my oldest nephew Louis, fifteen. My brother seemed now to oppose the war, and we talked about it, for the first time as one, with Louis. The three of us went by the Nature Science Museum, where Louis volunteered, projecting films, giving public presentations on dinosaurs and reptiles, feeding and caring for animals, cleaning up. I admired him.

My visit wasn't without a few light moments. At my parents' the next day, my father noted the headband (after Joe Dallesandro's in *Trash*) I now wore some of the time. He asked, "Why do you wear that, Gordon?"

"Keep hair out of my eyes."

"May I say something? I cut my hair."

Gordon Senior was chuckling. I don't know that I made as much of an effort at bridging the gap between us as he, but sometimes his efforts seemed pitiable. Asking if I'd been in the "beautiful" new Winston-Salem Convention Center, he told me, "They have so many shows there that would be of interest to you. Say, the gun show. And of interest to me is a good-sized coin show I took the boys to . . . I guess I wanted to stay longer than anyone else."

I was using my Sony as much as I could. I interviewed my sister about early family history, our father's father and mother and their growing family on the banks of the Ohio at century's turn; China when Maylee lived there; our father's preference to return abroad even after his POW experience; my sister's recent trip to Parkersburg, West Virginia, where we'd lived five years before joining our father in Tokyo.

Such moments were precious, but the dominant feeling of the trip was one of disjunction, sadness. My parents hadn't known I was coming—at least not when—until suddenly my sister brought me from the bus: my mother, seeing me through the door, burst into tears. But being paranoid, I worried that she wept because of how I looked, my long hair and beard the sign of an unacceptable station in life.

Much more affecting was her growing struggle to speak a complete sentence. Sometimes she could do so; sometimes it was a few deliberate or halting phrases, which she might repeat; other times, nice sociable "Um-hum"s.

One of our last days together was my birthday. We all laughed about mutual confusion of dates and ages. Then my father informed me, "You're twenty-six. Well, that's fine. Very good. You've had twenty-six very good years and no real serious accidents or illnesses, have there been?"

"No."

"What is your objective in life?"

"Find my objective."

He turned sympathetic, telling me he'd thought he'd be a teacher, then changed to business his sophomore year in college. "And after getting started in business I wondered whether I had done the right thing or not."

The kind of profession wasn't as important as "choosing one and making a good honest living. That's the important thing. And another important thing would be possibly the rearing of a family."

Whereupon Daisy Belle offered innocently in my direction, "You have a very nice family, don't you think?"

In characteristically stiff language he predicted his son would come to choose a profession and "will be at work and making a living and will be at the point where he'll need help in continuing, so he can take unto himself a wife."

I attempted to relieve tensions and take better advantage of our time together. "Well, tell me," I asked, "how it was when you and Mother first met. Actually, I don't even know how you met."

Daisy Belle was pleased; she began slowly with a "Well—" and a chuckle; my father promised "Well, I'll tell you a little of that."

"You came into the—" Daisy Belle paused for words as she looked at Gordon Senior, "my father's—" She paused again.

I helped: "Studio." Then my father took over—he wanted her father to photograph Gordon's senior class at Ravenswood High School, thirty miles from Parkersburg.

The doorbell rang; my father was gone a couple of minutes, long enough for Daisy Belle to say, "And I—he couldn't—I couldn't make him go away, you know?"

After his return my father grew resistant. Perhaps it was the long-term effect of two years of house arrest and concentration camp near Shanghai, which my sister said seemed to make him ever-cautious, given to hoarding food and supplies. Perhaps recording put him off—though I didn't sense that. In any case, soon he announced, "I'm not prepared to talk very much about our personal life, Edgar, uh Gordon."

Still, I tried: "This is for the family, this is not for the public."

But I got back, "Well, never mind, I don't want to go into that."

I used another tack: "I bet you've got lots of interesting things to tell me, Daddy."

"No, I haven't made up my mind yet whether I want to talk about a lot of interesting things or not . . ."

I turned again to my mother, who supplied a couple of details: "Well, when I saw him, I grabbed him." ("She shook hands with me," Gordon corrected.)

But soon he reaffirmed: "This question of how much of my many experiences I will speak of, or how much of them I will write of, that's a big question. I haven't made up my mind yet . . ."

□ □ □

I RETURNED TO my sister's, where Louis gave a reading of "Casey at the Bat" and his brother Paul played "Perpetual Mason" on the cello he'd been studying two years. Then before heading north I rode with my brother and wife and daughter for a short visit at their home in Raleigh. Edgar helped solve a problem with my Sony and gave me an earphone for it; Paula played the piano; and we all had fun with my seven-year-old niece. But at the Raleigh station I checked my big green duffel bag and stepped up into the warming Trailways bus not knowing where the greater pathos lay: in my mother's inability to speak, or my father's refusal.

A Visit with Barbara

O VER TWO YEARS had passed since Barbara Rubin left East Hill Farm; over two and a half since she'd brought us all there. I'd heard very little of her, especially following Candy's visit in Sharon Springs the month after her departure. Given the basic cataclysm of summer 1970 I'm not sure how much I even thought about her anymore. But my journal entries include a couple of dreams of Barbara—one way or another, she lingered in the psyche:

Back in the spring, in the midst of a "big sexy affair" I was having with Goldie Hawn, I learned that Barbara was the protagonist of a Jean Genet novel. In the fall, I was seated at a bar with a friend from college, when Barbara, hair curled up high, walked in "aggressively" and came over and kissed me, open-mouthed.

Well. The strange stuff of dreams! Stranger yet is that of everyday life. At some point early in winter Barbara called the farm. Peter answered, but—still stung, no doubt, from having learned through Allen that she'd have him in asylum—he immediately said, "Here's Denise."

Denise came on, then I. The news was big: Barbara Rubin—who'd once sought to wed Allen, Dylan, and the Beatles—was getting married, and we were all invited to the celebration in early February.

As it happened, I was soon able to see Barbara face-to-face. Taking a couple of days in New York on return from Carolina, I joined her—she was back around the city nowadays—for lunch at Ratner's on 2nd Avenue. Her head was scarved but her face had its old glow; I was happy for her. She was worlds away from the grim ghost who'd departed East Hill in September 1968.

At some point she'd also left the Satmar Hasidic group in Sharon Springs, later becoming involved with a Yeshiva in Far Rockaway centered around a Rabbi Shlomo Freifeld. It specialized in gathering together *Ba'alei t'shuva* (Jews who wanted to resume religious orthodoxy). Rabbi Freifeld's group included many a young person from the counterculture, especially those inclined to music.

At Far Rockaway she met Mordecai Levy, "a young rabbinical student," who I later learned was also a trumpet player. I heard only later, as well, that at a mere twenty-one he was four years younger than Barbara. But she seemed fundamentally happy. And though she'd committed herself to a community radically different from

East Hill's as well as the rest of contemporary society, she seemed essentially the same Barbara.

She also spoke of "Bobby," never pronouncing his famous last name. She'd been seeing him some, she began as blintzes and a bagel arrived.

"Oh, really?"

"Yes, going to his place on McDougal." (Dylan had moved back to the Village just over a year earlier.)

"We talk about Judaism. I've been trying to get him back into his roots. But also," she continued, "about him and his work and, uh, you know, what he thinks about things today."

"Oh?" I asked. What came next seemed an ironic reversal of her argument with Allen over Peter.

"I wonder about him. You see, I ask, 'Bobby, what about your fans? Didn't *they* make you what you are?' I tell him, 'Don't you owe them something, all those millions of people who buy your records?' He should give his money away.

"And I tell him, 'All that brilliance of *Blonde on Blonde* wasn't you, it was the amphetamine! Admit it!'"

In Barbara's eyes, he was now walled up in his home, remote from others. "He's down on everyone. We talk about politics and he says, 'Jerry Rubin is a punk! You don't expect me to care about people like him and Abbie Hoffman!'"

I sat there listening, taking it in. Though she appeared happy, I wondered what to make of it all, of the divide between East Hill and Far Rockaway, between pipe dreams of marriage and a real—and most traditional—wedding soon to come. Can her highly specialized chosen scene contain her? Can any? I sat there wondering in Ratner's, beholding Barbara Rubin talk excitedly once again.

Farmer Ginsberg

W HILE AWAY OVER the holidays, I twice called Allen at the farm. With three of us gone much of the time, was he really all right, like he'd said he'd be? Were farm hands Julius and Maretta and Lafcadio standing him in good stead?

Both times, he was positive. He seemed especially pleased to report, "Maretta lost the broom and I found it." It seemed a testament to his belief that everyone could work together, that mutual support was key to human relationship. (I didn't know it at the time, but the day after Christmas he wrote Gary Snyder, "Maretta getting more helpful round house after Peter started screaming at her she wasn't a saint she was lazy.")

A week later he graphed farm work and circumstance:

Woke peed downstairs shook down coalstove and added shovels of noisy coal to the red ember bed wondering interlocking dream life's meanings. . . . Repeated demands for money from Harry, Gregory as last nite by phone. . . . mid-morning darkness—have to get up in an hour and feed fitten' ration to cows, water them and goats and dogs and chickens and pig and horse, give animal hay and feed cats arguing with the pig and cleaning dung from stalls with Julius and Maretta.

A few hours later he resumed:

Woke went downstairs, Mirabelle black-and-white spotted Dalmatian with puppies in box under elevated wooden bed in Peter's room had shat all over rug—I'd fed her extra last nite—lost my head later and rubbed nose face and whole body in her dogshit, then regretted it, having to get on hands and knees, scrub carpet with soap and chlorox and bathe Mirabelle in bathtub after she's abandoned all rational hope and curled up alone in the hay, nose buried in brown stained short fur, trembling.

Every day's chores—feed fitten' ration to goats, cows, horse and pig, bucket of water for each, large and small leafs of hay-bale for each except pig who steals loose hay from goats—help Julius, clean cowflop and horse turds from stalls and pile it in wooden cribs around the house, wheelbarrowing hay-dung thru the snow from barn floor to house-side. Then empty water buckets, feed dogs mixing coffee-cans full of store-food with hot water brought from house, clean out chicken coop water trough and fill that with fresh water, give chickens and ducks (who among all 30 lay only one egg a day now dark wintering in coop) scratchfeed mostly corn, and laying mash. . . . Call horse back from snowy pasture and cajole him back to stall, bar it with lumber-plank since he's kicked out the stall door-hinge. Play with grunting pig who butts my knee with his nose and runs squealing after I kick him in the act of stealing goat hay—he fights with the dogs over their food, they snap and bark and drive him back inside . . . from their hay-strewn lean-to.

. . . .

Cow moos softly undertone waiting her feed bucket while horse paws and knocks his wooden door, pig squeals and grunts and noses into water buckets upsetting them, horned Nubian Junior goat snuffles and snorts and waves his brass-tipped horns—two lady goats pregnant, no milking to do, one brown stray dog pregnant by Godly the black father, one stumpy legged runt girl goat the sweetest nature in the barn, ears frostbit at birth and hoofs half clubbed, last winter's deathly freeze as she was born, Peter and Gordon Ball saved her and gave her five sisters and brothers away.

Pete's Mom & Pete & Me

I ADMIRED KATE Orlovsky. After visiting she sent me a small gift and thank you note; mentioning the Cooperstown trip, she hoped "to spend a whole day sometime in the future poking around there."

I never saw her again, but for a short while we remained in touch; she was ever the mother, ever appreciative of her son Peter. After she left she also wrote Allen (who'd missed their visit), reporting, worrying, and proposing:

Hello Allen,

Here's the extra pillows mentioned in note left under the old lumpy pillow. . . .

We enjoyed the farm visit tho brief & could not cover everything. For the working members it's a hard, rugged life. Fine if one has the youth & strength for it. We returned home feeling like a pair of rejuvenated people. (Pete threw much of my cigarettes away & was probably the better for that too.)

The kerosene lamps in your house upstairs worry me. In case one goes over accidentally, & a conflagration starts, do you have at least one (preferably 2) metal window ladders. These hook over the sill & one can climb right down thru the window to the ground. These would be comparatively in-expensive as the price goes by length. Of course, a longer length would be needed for one from the attic. Pete & Denise could go out the door from their diggings—but of course Pete would run up thru the whole house & burn his beard off. (I know him)—This calamity could be prevented by your having a loud gong upstairs. 2 gongs means "FIRE" & a single gong later means the last one has gone down. There ought to be a preparatory fire drill.

Well, I hope all goes well & you folks have a good winter. . . . my thoughts are up with you all very often.

Kate

At Christmas I sent her and Marie chocolates, then received a letter of some length, thanking me for "the most luxurious box of candy to come our way in a number of years." I'd hurt my back again shortly before their visit, and she remembered:

she was sending for a pamphlet on back ailments. Asking me to come see them, she reported on recent guests:

> *We had a Surprise visit from Denise & Peter during the Holidays & they both sure are full of health & get up & go. About the first thing Pete did was go right to where I had my last 2 good pkges of Camels, fish them out & rip them up. He always did have the knack of digging out anything & how he came by this, I'll never know.*

Back with Allen on the Farm

O NE NIGHT ON return I sat up late with Allen on his bed. Reading from texts, he talked about Pound, the effect of usury on art ("With usura the line grows thick," complains Canto XLV). A result, for example, was barocco; an analogy today would be pre-fab, cookie-cutting design, diminution of fine woodwork, all for the sake of quick profit: "Each house rhymes up and down the street, the same, like in Levittown," Allen said.

He linked that with a poem ("14," beginning "The groves are down/cut down") in the first section of Snyder's *Myths and Texts*, its felling of trees for Jevoah, the smoke from sawmill burners his incense. That is, Allen explained, Jevoah being "authoritarian, monopolistic, monolithic":

> When they got rid of polytheism and nature worship and substituted authoritarian Jehovah, they also began abstracting everything, including monoliths and treating the woods as so many feet of board lumber, rather than living trees to be carved with care, you know, and selected with care.

I filled him in on some of my holiday doings, including running into musician Bobby Neuwirth, Dylan pal and former road manager, late one night at Max's. (We'd known each other through Barbara, back at the Cinematheque in 1967.) He'd recently been in Nashville, where everyone liked him, he reported, because rednecks now think of long-hairs as superstars. He'd be performing at the Gaslight soon; he wanted me to tell Barbara to "please invite" him to her wedding—to sing.

Paul Morrisey was at Max's the same time; I didn't like him—thought him a snob—though I admired *Trash*, which was his fine work. But my mentioning him brought a query from Allen: "You don't have a 16-millimeter camera, do you?" When I said no, he wondered, "Should you?" He asked about cost, musing, "We shoulda gotten Gregory's . . ." He was still considering things for the farm on my behalf; I still hadn't determined my plans.

When he asked if I had, I specified only how "I got a boost playing journalist," talking with people, recording Ford Rowan and others. Allen exclaimed that that sort of first-hand journalistic investigation was "how I get involved"; he planned some more in March when he had a week's chair at the Institute for Policy Studies and several readings in the Washington area. He'd be talking to newsmen and people in the field, on drug law policy and practice, on CIA opium traffic connections.

Nut that I was, I reported, I spent some bus travel time not only listening (via earphone) to my recorded conversation with Rowan, but recording myself reading out loud some of "Documents on Police Bureaucracy's Conspiracy." I was so engrossed in it, I told Allen, that the bus had an accident without my even noticing: suddenly the driver was handing me a piece of paper, asking for testimony.

"It was really a gas playing journalist," I said.

"You know what's even a gassier gas ultimately?" Allen returned. "Occupying yourself" with yoga, meditation. Poetry was another avenue; film yet another: "In other words there's all these lines of communication possible."

The next day dawned bright and chill. By evening Allen would be in the air once more, bound for Detroit, again to put shoulder to wheel for John Sinclair. His mood was partly optimistic; New York state district attorneys had recently discussed the possibility of reducing the maximum sentence for possession of up to a quarter ounce of pot from a year to fifteen days, and reclassifying it from misdemeanor to violation: were that to ever happen, it would no longer be a criminal matter.

Meanwhile in Michigan, John Sinclair remained in prison, serving his nine and one half to ten years.

Sinclair and Other Matters

A FEW DAYS LATER—Saturday, January 16—Anna Marie was with me for the weekend. We were basically getting along, except for the awful chasm of our differences on the war. She wasn't a zealous supporter; she simply seemed not to grasp its horror. She appeared content with our being together, though I shuddered every time I thought her ultimate intention, as in early days, might be to marry me. She remained as physically attractive as ever, and was caring and sweet.

That evening we drove to Albany and picked up Allen; he was, as always, news and energy. He'd performed benefit readings for Sinclair and given pre-trial testimony in court. Sinclair, already serving the longest sentence for marijuana possession in the history of Michigan, was now to be tried for conspiracy in a 1968 bombing of a secret CIA office in Ann Arbor. (He eventually was cleared of the charge, the penalties for which were decidedly lower than those for marijuana possession.)

The evidence against him in this highly politicized case, Allen felt, was not legitimate; it all came from a young "crazy" who was trying to get out from under his own seven- to ten-year sentence for marijuana possession. Allen had much to report on this, the antiwar movement, and other topics. We had a whole hour and a half to talk—even sing—our way home.

Together at Western Michigan University in Kalamazoo, indefatigable poet (averaging four hours of sleep a night) and indefatigable lawyer William Kunstler raised $2,700; then by himself Allen raised another thousand with a four-hour reading in an Ann Arbor coffee shop. But Sinclair needed $40,000. Jane Fonda was raising funds, others were helping; Phil Ochs would give a benefit. It was at last becoming a national matter; *The Times* had a young reporter there.

In court, he was to testify on behalf of a motion that the young were inadequately represented on voter registration lists used in jury selection; that those older than forty, who make up most juries, could not judge fairly. To be a witness expert on youth culture, he had to demonstrate his qualifications by such things as "counting the number of readings I'd given and where, and how much I'd mixed with the students, and King of May in Czechoslovakia and involvement in the Be-Ins, and acquaintance with Dylan and the Beatles and Jagger . . ."

But the United States attorney challenged that; he asked Allen

. . . how many Boy Scout troops I had read to, how many Sunday schools I had read at, saying that I didn't represent anything like the majority of the youth culture . . . or couldn't speak for any of that, or didn't understand any of that, and God help the nation if I were the person that could be qualified as an expert on youth culture for American youth!

Ironically, that night before he was about to read, Allen said, "a beautiful young kid" came up to him and gave him his official Boy Scout knife.

Admitted as an expert, Allen testified the next day that it would be fairer for Sinclair to be judged by peers: the word "revolution" had many differing senses among the young, as opposed to the single meaning it might hold for an older person. "The common idea of the death of the planet by the end of the century" was "firmly implanted in minds of younger people," "motivating their thoughts and their ideas about character, sexual revolution, dress, behavior, and politics": it was a notion not affecting those "not likely necessarily to live out the end of the century anyway." Soon, however, the prosecution interrupted: "These are fantasies of an aging man who doesn't want to admit that he's lost his youth."

Press conference followed testimony; then, Allen said, he kissed Kunstler, getting "a big wild grin, and that came out all over the papers there." I asked Allen what kind of mood Kunstler—who'd led the Chicago defense—was in now. "Very tired," he answered: "He's defending everybody. The Berrigans, the Panthers here and there, involved with Angela Davis, he's helping out on John Sinclair. . . ."

Defense Attorney Leonard Weinglass got Allen past the guards for a few minutes with Sinclair. He'd been in solitary two or three weeks, but "looked good, strong. Very sensitive . . . a little nervous." Allen handed him a copy of "Documents on Police Bureaucracy's Conspiracy."

Allen connected with David Dellinger and antiwar colleagues. In light of Weatherman bulletins and other provocations, he told us, the feeling now among antiwar folk was away from violence, toward disciplined nonviolence, "giant peaceful demonstrations," civil disobedience: possibly a "sit-in around the White House with people refusing to leave until the war was over. . . ." Our talk shifted to music: guitar (which Anna Marie knew) and harmonium chords; harmony. Allen reported, "There's a really beautiful song by George Harrison" that had just come out. Anna Marie and I had already heard "My Sweet Lord."

They were playing it to death in Syracuse, she said, much as she liked it. "It's a great adaptation of 'Hare Krishna'" as chorus, Allen said. Before long he broke into singing "My Sweet Lord," mixing "Hare Krishna" with "Halleluja" as Harrison did. Anna Marie and I joined in, all of us joyous.

Nearing Cherry Valley, we ran into fog, but it merely slowed us a bit. Soon we were approaching the Beautiful View, wind starting to blow. We spoke of the relation of singer to lord in this hymn that was so "full of *bhakti*" (devotion), of the Hindu need to personalize *bhagavan* ("the ultimate nature of things") as opposed to the Buddhist void. Krishna worshippers were like Christians—like St. Francis—Allen said, worshipping their lord in all things; even like the Jews in their ritualization of each action, "so that everything is a sacred observance."

It was late by the time we crunched our way down the hard-packed drive, bag and harmonium in hand. No one was up in the house, all five dogs remained sound asleep, presumably, in barn and lean-to. I checked the Kalamazoo, banked it some, and we went upstairs for needed rest.

Anna Marie had not only driven the eighty miles from Syracuse earlier in the day, but a good part of the Albany roundtrip late at night. I was grateful for that and for the return leg of our drive with "My Sweet Lord." Possibly Allen's discussion of Sinclair and the movement had some effect, too—I wondered.

I felt so good about things that the next day I tried to bridge the gap with Anna Marie. Naively I brought up several specific issues—was one My Lai? Another simply the staggering number of human beings killed, the tonnage of our bombs dropped thus far? Nixon's egotism and *hubris*? The corruption of the regimes we supported?

But she and I couldn't, it seemed, have an effective discussion. Neither of us became heated; she simply didn't want to talk about such matters in any meaningful way. It made me sad: someone so kind to me, so tender especially recently, wouldn't recognize something so devastating. And it frustrated and even angered me, though I held my anger back: I simply didn't know what to do. I sat across from her on the bed as the sun illuminated the deep snow outside, and looked into her green eyes one last time. Then I gave up.

Brahma's Babies

NOT LONG AFTER Allen's return from Detroit, Brahma, our brown Swiss, gave birth. Some of us had come into the barn in the middle of an unusually cold day and discovered her tending three little kids on their bed of bright straw. "Baaa," she looked up at us as if pleading. "Mmmmm," one of the black-and-brown babes bleated. Ed's old Billy remained as active as ever!

But there was a problem. The ears of the babies, born wet, were frozen: evidently they'd entered this world a couple hours before we came in. Allen and Peter and I gathered close, debating what to do. Allen, who seemed particularly distressed, suggested getting warm water for them. I checked on the weakest one, who was lying down, made sure it was breathing, and proposed taking him inside, nursing him there. Godly began prancing about; Don't Bite Me (now well over a hundred pounds) showed up and began rooting. The tape I made intermixes the ring of Brahma's bell, pig grunts, baby baahs, Brahma's comforting closed-mouth Ummmms, and anxious human voices.

Allen repeated his concern over frozen ears, cold barn. Peter exclaimed, "What's wrong with short ears, then—that's all! What's wrong with short ears? What're you gonna do?" Allen went for warm water.

The doorway to the lean-to had been left open, letting in cold air. (We sometimes opened it for light amidst winter darkness, and sometimes the pig pushed it open.) There were cracks in a window not far from Brahma's stall, which was the outermost, at the very end of the barn.

Peter and I stapled plastic over the cracked window, then while I stayed with the goats, he nailed the lean-to door shut. Allen returned with warm water and towels for kids; I got drinking water for mother. Allen said, "Well, you know what the trouble is? We didn't get out here early enough to wipe off their ears. That's all our fault, then. In a way. What can we do about the ear thing?"

"It's not a complete necessity," Peter rejoined. "They don't really need their ears that much, do they?"

Allen remained deeply affected by what he saw. Listening to his voice, it's as if he's about to weep: "They're born wet . . . that's why the ears freeze. . . . They're frozen babies."

I told him Peter said he wiped the kids. Allen returned, "Well, he didn't. I mean he wiped them a little. . . . So they're not dry . . . it's incredible! It's too cruel. . . ." He and I wiped them with the warm water, then dried them with towels as best we could.

He asked if we had any form of heater; I was taken aback: "Heater? I wouldn't trust any kind of heater with all this hay." Then we hit upon an idea: Junior had the stall next to the two mother goats, with a full wall between them—it was warmer there. We'd relocate Brahma and her kids.

Now the weak one rose to its feet, crying. I brought her mouth to one of Brahma's teats; she started sucking. Allen watched, but worried again when he saw blood on its black fur: "What's the blood from?" But I reassured him—it was Brahma's.

Peter had Julius get a bale of hay for Brahma in her new stall. By now it was a couple hours till chore time. We went into the house, covered a portion of the living room floor with plastic and straw, brought Brahma and the kids in for the next two hours. All the kids suckled, all were warm and dry when we brought them and their mother back into the barn, into a warmer stall. We put up a barrier to keep the pig out, and checked on them later at night. In the morning, tails wagged, ears flapped, and the three kids did their best to nudge each other away from Brahma's two teats.

We were pleased; we poured hot water into Brahma's frozen pail, gave her more hay, extra fittin' ration. Then we took care of the other goats, the pig, Lash the old horse, Bessie the cow, calves Jennifer and Little Bess, the five dogs, and several cats. Then we went to the chicken house to tend to ducks and chickens.

Barbara's Wedding Celebration

B ARELY TWO WEEKS before the celebration, two invitations arrived from "Bracha & Mordecai Levy."

You are cordially invited

To	Shevah	Bracha's
	wedding	Celebration
Date	Feb. 2, 1971	
	[8th of Sh'vat, 5731]	
Time	Tuesday—8:00 p.m.	

Directions and a personal note, signed "Bracha" in Hebrew letters, were enclosed. The one to the five of us ("Peter, Julius, Denise, Gorden, and Ed") contained a brief but warm message; Allen's, an odd detail: "Bracha & Mordecai Levy please ask you to come to one wedding celebration for our friends. (Due to parental problems the wedding ceremony is being held privately). . . ."

I learned only many years later that the "parental problems" alluded to Mordecai's youthfulness and the fact that his parents (under his influence) had recently converted back to Orthodox Judaism, whereas Barbara's weren't religious.

As dusk fell Tuesday, February 2, 1971, several of us gathered at Allen's East 10th Street apartment: Maretta, Penny Rand, Allen, poet Simon Vinkenoog from Holland, and myself. Shortly Al Aronowitz was due to stop by in his station wagon, to give us a ride to the Far Rockaway synagogue. Simon was telling us about Holland's ways of dealing with heroin addiction when the phone rang and Penny answered. "Just a minute," she said, handing the receiver to Allen. Then she told me quietly, "It's Bob Dylan."

Allen and Dylan hadn't seen each other for a few years, though they'd spoken once or twice on the phone. Now the younger poet was telling his elder he'd be coming with Al.

Because there'd be no room in the station wagon—Dylan and Sara, all the Aronowitzes, plus Allen—Allen asked the rest of us to go in a taxi. We left, disappointed.

The cold winter's night ride seemed endless, through great stretches of land, down to a nethermost point of Long Island. But at Beth Midrash Sh'or Yoshuv, which consisted of a few spacious but low-ceilinged rooms prefaced by a foyer, all was warm. In that entrance area many milled about, lots of them middle-aged or older women. (I'd soon discover the sexes would be separated.) Hums of excited conversation played about; from a large inner room where men gathered one could hear music as well. Anticipation filled the air; the celebration would start soon.

Admiring as I was of his work, I was of course excited by the possibility of meeting Dylan. But the image I'd formed of him differed from reality. For me Dylan was some mad genius kid—relatively short, I imagined, with the intensity I saw in one of several Daniel Kramer photographs on the back cover of *Bringing It All Back Home*. There (above a short-haired Barbara massaging his head and Allen in top hat and tie) was a wide-framed shot with several people, including two security cops. Edge of frame, foreground, brows knit in a wholly different concentration from the others, a smallish figure with wild hair stares toward the camera. That was the look, those the dimensions in my mind.

Still in the foyer, I turned to see Stephen Bornstein, ebullient as ever, for the first time since skinnydipping in the pond last summer. We embraced and set to bringing each other up to date, though it was hard to hear for the din. Then Al Aronowitz, whom I hadn't seen for two years, came in from the street. We started catching up, and I strained as I had with Stephen over the hubbub. Just after Al went on into the room where men were gathering I noticed a young Jewish kid, about my height, approach from my right. He wore little granny glasses and a Russian cloth and fur hat with the ear flaps tied up, and had blue eyes. From those granny glasses I got the impression that he was trying to look a little hip, but maybe wasn't—yet yearned to be.

Just as he came abreast of Stephen and me and stuck out his hand, exuberantly, to Stephen, I realized who he was. They talked, recalling the Bay Area 1965, when Stephen was with Allen and Peter, and Dylan was performing. Now even more people milled around in this small vestibule, including at least several Jewish mothers beaming in admiration—I heard several bursts of "Look, Bobby's here!"

Then Stephen turned and introduced the two of us, but it continued to be hard to hear. We shook hands, exchanged greetings. I was struck by his blue eyes, not at all the "mad" ones I'd expected, and his "regular" build and size—his frame larger than mine, bigger bone structure, long fingers. We couldn't really hear each other—I couldn't hear him—but he smiled so easily, as on the *Nashville Skyline* cover, only much more fully, openly. He and Stephen resumed conversation a moment, then we all turned to go into the main room—only we men, of course.

Three white linen-covered tables were lined up together, one—the head—against a wall; the other two fed from it at either end along parallel walls. The women were confined to a room opposite the head table; throughout the evening various women, young and old, white turbaned Barbara and dark-haired Sara and many others, would frame the double-doorway, peering out at the goings-on and eminent guests in the large room. Standing on tiptoe on chairs, little orthodox girls managed to peer over the broad wooden barrier separating the two spaces, behold the extraordinary gathering.

Later I learned that within their own private space—there were a number of round tables—the women talked, ate, kissed, and hugged. It was all very happy. They cheered and honored Barbara: they danced with her, danced in front of her; it was her day of days, she was Queen.

In our larger space, it was like a "church basement" situation with metal folding chairs on a linoleum floor. At the center of the head table sat Rabbi Shlomo Freifeld, a large, broad fellow with huge beard, dark brown hair, black old-fashioned glasses. On his left, Allen; on his right, Dylan. Near them was Mordecai, Barbara's young and intense bearded groom, as well as Lester and Moishe, fathers of the newlyweds. There were fifty or sixty men in our room, all looking quite orthodox, in contrast to Simon and me, and even Stephen. All wore headpieces of some sort, whether small yarmulkes or broad black hats.

I sat next to Simon at one of the tables adjoining the head; Stephen was nearby, as was filmmaker friend Jerry Jofen, son of a distinguished rabbi (for which Jerry seemed to be accorded considerable deference). There were several scriptural readings, prayers and calls and responses; much of the evening was sparked by the wonderful leading sound of a cantor's plaintive melody, enriched by many voices and guitar, fiddle, accordion. The songs were of the earth, there was wailing, there was rising, there was soaring, there was falling. Ancient hopes for goodness and community and blessing came together this cold night far from Manhattan's material moil; wild whoops of joy rang out with loud fast clapping; there was foot stomping and shouted chants; there were slow, almost dirge-like pieces celebrating the sad dignity of a people's heart and history.

As I studied Freifeld, he seemed warm, vibrant, sweet, humble. And Allen looked as if he were responding to every aspect of word and music. But one of the world's greatest singer-musicians sat nearby, showing only the slightest response to the music: every so often his capped head moved a fraction of an inch, to one side or the other. Scarcely an expression crossed his face. I don't know what he was feeling, but it was as if he were extremely shy or ill at ease. (After all, he was next to the Rabbi, and all eyes from the facing room seemed aimed in his and Allen's direction.) I know what

I came to feel, as the music rose and fell in ageless sad tones, as a millennial people's efforts to know their God were renewed among this huddled hundred surrounded by cinder block walls: I began to weep just a little, and turned to Simon: "This is far out."

"The Jews have always been far out," he answered, his own eyes wet.

At the cry of "Chalah! Chalah!" ("The Bride! The Bride!") Barbara (Bracha), in shiny white Satmar turban and gown made by her husband's mother, was presented with Mordecai to Freifeld for his blessing. Freifeld intoned the Sheva Brachot (the Seven Blessings, for a wedding) with its "Soon, O Lord our God, may there be heard in the cities of Judah and in the streets of Jerusalem, a sound of gladness, a sound of joy, a sound of the bridegroom and sound of the bride, the sound of rejoicing . . ."

A cantor with guitar led a beautiful, haunting, and even mournful (in its reverence) "L'Cha Dodi," the ecstatic hymn to the bride, in Barbara's honor:

Come in peace, divinely crowned,
With joy and rejoicing
Amongst the faithful, loved by God,
Come in, Bride, come in, Bride.

Then many of the men (mostly from the head table, including Allen and Mordecai) moved to the center of the floor and began to dance, holding hands, in two or three circles, as music swirled about them. Allen danced with the others, their "beards pointing," as he later said; Dylan remained at the table, still undemonstrative except for the slightest movements of his head; still seemingly nervous, tentative. Finally Allen came back to the table and brought him onto the floor and they all danced hand-in-hand in a large ring with Rabbi Freifeld.

In the foyer at the end of the evening, Mordecai and I had a deep, silent extended exchange looking into each other's eyes. Then I ran into Al Aronowitz again. "Gordon, do you want to come back with us?" he asked.

"No," I answered, unprepared for a moment's decision I've regretted ever since. "I'll go back with Allen." Only later did I consider that Allen may have given up his seat, suggesting that Al ask me instead.

In any case, Barbara Rubin, friend to and influence on some of the great visionary artists of the day; Barbara Rubin, runaway teenager from Queens; Barbara Rubin, *Christmas on Earth* filmmaker, dreamer of her own Rimbaudian visions, was now married to young Mordecai Levy, their union sanctified and celebrated by one of the most traditional of the earth's religious movements. I was deeply moved.

In the City with Allen

S EVERAL OTHER OCCASIONS during this time I stayed on East 10th, late in the Cherry Valley era of my life, remain dear or amusing. Some involve Allen, for I felt particularly close with him then.

The day before Barbara's wedding reception Allen met with accountant Don Wilen to review Committee on Poetry farm books; I went with him to Wilen's Broadway office, checks in hand. That evening he brought me to the upper Park Avenue home of Morty and Lita Hornick, where we were among a handful of other dinner guests. Their apartment took up the whole floor of their building: Morty was in the high end of the drapery business, Lita a well-known literary and arts patron painted by Warhol. Everyone seemed very upper crust; it was quite pleasant, if a little stiff at times. Near the end, as if playing Allen's monkey, I demonstrated for our hosts some of the many daily pushups I was doing, inspired by Black Panther George Jackson. (In prison, he was performing hundreds a day.)

"Gordon, it's time to go," Allen said quietly.

□ □ □

ALLEN AND I went to a midnight showing at the Elgin of Alexandro Jodorowsky's *El Topo*, a surrealistic, violent morality play. At one point, as a man without arms bearing on his shoulders a man without legs appeared on screen, Allen whispered, "That's poetic—the armless man supported on the shoulders of the legless one."

On the way out, we ran into several people Allen knew: David Padwa, computer genius; *Realist* editor Paul Krassner; and Abbie Hoffman.

Padwa had first met Allen through Carl Solomon over two decades earlier. In 1960 he'd begun developing computer systems, then sold them to Xerox in 1966. Now we all went uptown to his home on 77th between Madison and Park: a townhouse of several stories connected by a beautiful winding staircase. He'd recently moved in after a year in India with Baba Ram Dass, and was a welcoming host.

Padwa and Krassner had once been briefly at odds, when a *Realist* cover some years earlier, parodying *Vogue* magazine, portrayed a fashion model (who happened to resemble Padwa's wife, model Danielle) as a transvestite. But that point of difference had vanished long ago with Krassner's apology.

Now there were weightier matters to discuss, as we sat late in the library, lights turned low. It must've been 2:30 AM when we arrived, and we were up much of the night. I remained quiet, listening.

We all worried about Nixon's repression of dissent and its likely escalation in the near future. Sinclair remained in prison; the Berrigans had just been arrested; resources for resistance were being spread thin with increasing court cases; preventive detention (holding suspects without bail) was being discussed as a possible strategy by Attorney General John Mitchell; the cry for "law 'n' order" was turning shrill.

All of us fantasized possible concentration camps for dissidents; only Padwa thought it would never be realized. He felt Allen was over the top on this, that it may've been after-effects of his experience as witness in the Chicago Seven trial; and, he felt, a lot of people had displaced paranoia from authorities cracking down on drug use. In any case, before dawn's first light we broke up, nothing resolved; David gave Allen and me a comfortable guest room upstairs. Only time would tell how Richard M. Nixon would respond to those challenging his conduct of the war.

□ □ □

SOME OF THE time I was out on my own; the night after Barbara's wedding reception I was seeing a pretty woman I'd just met who was active in women's liberation. We walked through West Village streets together, it was again a mild night, much energy in the air, the "sluff of boot-soles" on the pavement. And I remained so taken with what I'd seen and heard the night before at Far Rockaway I played some of my tape on my Sony as we walked; I wanted all Manhattan to hear such sounds from a special realm, like a latter-day kid with a ghetto blaster boom box, crazy fool that I was.

□ □ □

AT SOME POINT I went to a reading—by myself or with Allen, I don't remember—at the Poetry Project at St. Mark's Church, presided over by Anne Waldman in a long red Chinese dress. Shortly afterward I wrote in my diary:

> Anne Waldman,
> I don't know you,
> But I love you—
> I want to breathe on your cheek.
> I want to steal your poetry!

Julius Redux

WHEN HINDU PRIEST Saligram Sukla had visited East Hill in the fall of 1969 he performed a Shivite purification ceremony in our living room with fire, hashish, and chanting. Afterward, as Allen filled him on our scene, he explained, chuckling, "See, the reason that this place exists, probably," is Julius: "It was all built around him, really. He's the secret guru here!"

Allen had started his Uher, so we know Sukla's reply:

I'm so impressed by him! . . . I don't know why. I think I can just sit and look at him for days without getting bored. Like this morning I took some wine, gave it to him, just like those sadhus . . . he will drink, you know. He just took it and drank and gave it to me . . . so beautiful!

"Secret guru" or not, for many who came to the farm, Julius was an extraordinary center of interest. Now, as I neared my own exit from East Hill, I found myself given to further reflections, reports, and observations having to do with good ole Julie Woolie, mystifying Julius, inimitable Julius, exasperating Julius.

As Allen spoke with Sukla, his guest told him of a certain holy man at the Nepal ashram of his father, who held that "everything is illusion."

"That's exactly Julius's philosophy," Allen answered. "Peter and I haven't gone to India because we don't know what to do with Julius. Maybe we should bring Julius . . . to this ashram. . . . I think we would go to India if we could figure what—see, we can't leave Julius alone."

". . . I think he would be perfectly able to be settled there."

"Yeah but," Allen countered, "who tells people to do things? Like here we tell Julius to wash his face, or empty a pail, or make his bed, or get up."

But there was no problem, as Saligram saw it: ". . . when the time comes they react. Like early in the morning no one has to tell Julius to get up, go to the bathroom, do something . . ."

Of course the observations of an overnight visitor weren't wholly accurate. As one friend and neighbor remarked, "Julius wouldn't move unless you pushed him." Poet and former football player Sidney Goldfarb was once assigned by Peter to saw wood with Julius, using the long two-man saw. Goldfarb, a man of considerable patience as well as strength, pushed the saw through the surface of the log, all the way to Julius's side, where it remained in place for quite a bit of time as his partner contemplated the situation. Then Julie began to move the saw back toward Sidney, a tooth at a time. And so it went——the morning's work a half-inch dent in the wood.

Julius's appetite for cigarettes, food, and liquid of any variety was legend. Miles, who gave him smokes lest he sneak into his room for them, remembered how he had to be called in from the hot, sunny field if Peter forgot him; how some mornings he'd be told by several people to have breakfast, and so was "getting fatter and fatter!" Lucien watched him eat coffee grounds—and, once, jars of tainted green beans: he talked non-stop for hours, wiping out two decades of catatonic silence.

He seemed always to bear an institutional legacy of drinking anything he could. When there was no coffee, he could drink so much water it sloshed in his belly; Patti Benson remembers hearing it when he walked. Wayne Graham watched Julie drinking from the hot water kettle. Wayne said he'd known Julie for a year before ever hearing him say anything; it was "Got a cigarette?"

The second part of my *Farm Diary* records a June 1970 swim in the pond by several of us, preceded of course by stripping off our clothes: slowly and deliberately Julius unbuckles his jeans, slips out from boxer shorts, serious but seemingly pleased to be in the sun without having to work.

He had his own way of thumbing his nose when called to labor or follow conventional expectations. He was, at certain moments, entirely his own man, and the supreme individual among us, even as he did as he was told: he was the cut-up man of East Hill. Once Peter handed him a full bowl of dog food and told him to go outside and whistle. Julius left the kitchen, stood on the porch, bowl in hand, whistling a phrase from Beethoven's Fifth.

Another time, deliberately within Allen's eyesight, he blew his nose on the dish-cloth hanging next to the kitchen counter. It brought on a heated, earnest explanation by Allen of distinctions: hand towel, dish towel, handkerchief. On occasion, Allen could make a wonderful straight man, and Julius was one of the few who could lead him into it.

Ray told me that Julius went through a spell of answering the phone and not saying anything, just holding it and listening. It took his mother four or five hours to reach her son one night.

And Judy Cannon, from Glensfoot, the exquisite old family estate and dairy farm on the edge of town, remembered the first mention of him. Before committing to East

Hill, Allen called at Glensfoot: coming in the kitchen door one afternoon, he asked whether he'd be welcome in Cherry Valley if he moved there. He seemed to be looking for "a safe place to have a home for Julius."

Once settled on the farm, we'd sometimes stop by Glensfoot. And things would sometimes turn rocky: they could be, as Judy told me, "fairly scary in terms of my mother and Julius."

One event wasn't so. Julius locked himself in the downstairs bathroom; Allen went and stood outside the door, talking to him through it for an hour before he came back out. Allen explained to Judy and her mother, "We don't have any plumbing and Julius hasn't seen any for a long time."

But another evening Judy's fifty-seven-year-old mom said goodnight to family and East Hill guests alike, and went upstairs for bed. Entering her wholly darkened chamber, she suddenly sensed that in the middle of it, just a few feet away, stood another being. It was Julius. Just standing there.

Suddenly everyone downstairs heard "an incredible scream." Allen leapt up the stairs and brought Julius down. Allen seemed, Judy told me,

> . . . to be the person who mainly did things about Julius, and who appeared to have a real affection for him—although he might say "Come on, damnit!" he did it with a sense of not just "Here's a helpless person," but of "This is somebody you need to treat well and have an affection for." We all had a real liking for Allen in terms of his relationship with Julius.

A rare glimpse of Julius was provided one mid-February day when Denise and Peter had gone into Cherry Valley to stock up on provisions. Julie took advantage of his freedom, and I took out my taperecorder. At the dining room table, hesitating Hamlet-like before peanut butter, bread, tea, and a cake, sat Lafcadio. His left eye was black; he was pitiful.

For half an hour, Julius, in his low, gruff New York tones, performed the role of some interrogating officer or psychiatrist, perhaps repeating what had been once (or often) said to Julius himself. He strutted about the table, back and forth into the kitchen for more liquid. Only occasionally would there be the slightest murmur from Lafcadio, responding to some point of monologue. "Are you gonna be quiet, huh? Is that what it is?" Julie asked in frustration with his silent subject. At times he waxed almost surrealistic—"Would you like white snow or shovels or broomsticks or what?" Generally he seemed caught in his own circles of principled abstraction:

. . . you can't live forever. You have to settle down, relax a bit. You can't expect everybody to help you for nothing—don't you realize that? Or do you expect to get something for nothing—is that what it is? . . . Huh? . . .

Lafcadio? Don't you like your tea? Or you just want to throw it away, or what? . . . Hah? Why are you so silent? Do you think silence is going to help you? . . . You're living on your own, you've got yourself in support, where else do you think that you live? Do you think that you own the kitchen, or what? Upstairs, bedroom, attic? The Ginsberg residence? Or the Ball residence, or what? Or Denise's residence, or Peter's residence? Can't you make your mind up?

Lafcadio? . . . do you want to be investigated, or what? Or do you want to live in an asylum, for nothing? Is that it? You have to make your mind up. Nobody can help you. . . . There are all kinds of people around here absolutely doing things for nothing. You think that's good enjoyment? . . . Like bisecting peanut butter and bread and jelly and things like that?

. . . .

I can't suggest anything more helpful. . . . You can't expect me to digest everything. I'm so full myself. . . . I'm not doing you any harm any more than you're doing me harm. I like to live by myself sometimes too—when I have nothing to really live by. What do you think, huh? Or do you just want to live for nothing? For free, is that it? Do you wanna smoke a cigarette for free, you think? Very easy. Maybe you can find a hobby or card trick, or anything. I don't know what is really better. You have to tell me. . . .

. . . .

I can't graduate from nothing or to something for free. I have to pay for everything I do, don't you know that? Huh? I have to absolutely pay for everything I do. I'm not saying that I do very much. If you want to live for no help or hope, I can't think of anything any better than that because I think time is limited. You can have free gifts, you can have anything. You can have wrist watch, cup, peanut butter and bread and butter, tea, anything. But when you graduate then, you'll just have to graduate. Or else you'll just have to remain inborn. . . .

Or would you like to live some other place? . . . I can't think of anything better than that. As of now, anyway. Especially when time's limited, right? You like to live quiet, or what? . . . Do you think silencing things is helpful, or adjusting or

*getting out of things? . . . You'll have to suit yourself, because—heh, heh—in the final
analysis, two plus two do not help too much. If you know what I mean. Huh! I can't
suggest anything better. After all, even catatonics grow paranoid in your old age.
According to firsthand suggestion.*

Then Allen came downstairs, quickly taking things in—possibly he'd heard a
little of the monologue from his room. He asked Julius, "You getting any interest?"

"A little bit."

"What's he said?"

"Uh, he's got something wrong with his eye, I think."

"Yeah, he's got a black eye," said Allen, pointing out the obvious.

Allen returned upstairs, but soon was back to use the phone. As he did so, the
interrogation seemed to ebb—as if something of greater interest had captivated the
Inquisitor. When Allen hung up, Julius resumed with Lafcadio. Then suddenly we
heard Godly barking outside. Allen, looking out the front door and up the drive,
turned to Julie and announced, "The monsters are comin'!"

"Huh?" responded a dumbfounded Julius, wholly involved in his own
speechmaking.

"Monster Orlovsky!" Allen then pronounced. He intoned, "Hm! Vajra Guru
Padme Siddhi Hm," went back to the little telephone table, and began another long
distance call.

"Julie, open the door!" Denise called from just outside moments later. "Help
Peter—go get the stuff. Help Peter," she said, entering. Then Peter pushed in, shouting
his own commands, returning the Inquisitor to his accustomed role.

A Midwinter Miscellany

N THE LARGER world, we learned shortly before Barbara's wedding celebration that things had soured for Leary in Algiers: Eldridge Cleaver and Black Panther party members there had "busted" him and Rosemary at their home, putting them under "Panther protection." Condemning the "whole silly psychedelic movement which we've supported in the past," Cleaver pronounced psychedelics "harmful to our cause and counter-revolutionary." In a journal poem the second week of February Allen asked, "And what reply to Leary and Cleaver arguing in Alger, / Contending twixt armed Revolution and Mystic Mind Change . . . ?"

Back on East Hill, Godly had knocked up the Grahams' Queenie, an old Collie with burrs in her fur. ("Godly's gotta be curbed," Allen said. "Could we give him a vasectomy or something?") And Shiva gave birth to two robust kids on one of the mildest nights of the winter.

In the house we stayed warm and basically clean; after doing laundry in bathroom utility sink or boiling it on Kalamazoo, we'd fill a line strung cattycorner from the middle of one bathroom wall to another with towels, shirts, jeans, long underwear. We had plenty to eat; I took a photograph of Julius, in green work shirt, solemn and intent at his gruel—brown rice, cabbage, canned beets. In the corner behind him, next to and higher than the adjoining sideboard, rise stacked boxes of wide-mouth mason jars, each of them filled with our vegetables.

But in the face of such plenty, Allen worried: he was considering closing the place down for winter next year. He didn't want to, but he was concerned about his ability to continue going out raising money for it on the scale he had been. Moreover, every public breath he took, so to speak, in politically, paranoiacally charged conditions, could contribute to the misperception that he was a rabid revolutionary. Greater scrutiny beyond the present IRS attention could easily come from a government determined to crack down on dissent: not only did he feel guilty that others were going to jail for resisting the war; he could be next. "The whole political situation," he reminded us in February 1971, "is getting worse."

And, farm maintenance had continued expensive. Though (outside of cellar and foundation work) we no longer had major construction projects like the water system of 1969, we'd broken all records for guests last summer. Avoiding meat, however, was helping, as was our garden, with all our canning and storing. Yet we'd added animals, and more goats had just been born. We'd just had Bessie's older calf Jennifer inseminated, and now little stump-legged Cosset was pregnant! In any case, winter, with all its stress and bother and added expense, was an easy season to consider cutting back. Allen even contemplated dissolving Committee on Poetry. Though "I built it as craftily as possible w/ lawyers & accountants," he wrote Whalen, "Nixon's tax examiners already are costing me $3000 in lawyer's fees . . ."

Back in the summer Denise and Peter would sing and play in their room set off from the rest of the house, and unless one came close, they might not be heard. But now in winter they regrouped in the living room-dining room where it was warmer and where piano, organ, and (as long as Allen was there) harmonium were within reach. I liked hearing them, and recorded a dozen numbers. Even when not in his "leper's voice," some people didn't like Peter's singing: "Like some drunk pulled in off the street," a friend characterized it, "cracked and raucous." But I loved its robust quivery crustiness, stirring in its authenticity. When I introduced him at the start of a reading with Allen and Burroughs at Chapel Hill six years later, I called him "the most glorious rooster that ever crowed."

I was most inspired by Peter's "Wabash Cannonball," with Denise on piano and organ, and recorded several versions. They sang much else, including Allen's adaptations of the "Nurse's Song" of *Experience* and "The Lamb." Then Denise tuned her guitar to a drone and they did a couple of rags; for "Raghupati Raghav Rajaram" Denise was at the organ, Allen on finger cymbals.

□ □ □

WHEN EDWARD IGNACZYK of the American Breeder Service had come to inseminate Jennifer, he mentioned having a headache. After the insemination he said it came from getting hit by shrapnel during the Korean War: he lay on the ground four days before waking in an army field hospital.

Because of his injury, he was "nearly blind" with 20/300 vision in one eye, and thought one piece of shrapnel remained in his skull. I asked him what that war was all about.

"It wasn't worth a single life. The country wasn't worth it, the people didn't give a damn. It's the same as Vietnam, the people don't care."

"But," I countered, "it seems in Vietnam the people do care and they're entitled to live their own lives and they've had a thousand years of foreigners trying to tell them how, and furthermore, I wouldn't like foreign troops in my country burning villages."

"Yes," he agreed. Then he added, "The only way to deal with 'em is to kill 'em all, there're so many of 'em."

□ □ □

WHEN SHE'D WRITTEN me most recently, Kate Orlovsky reported "a good deal of apprehension & loneliness" regarding her youngest son, who'd spent so much of his life at home with her. A month or so later she—rather, Marie, since Kate was unable to hear—called the farm. I brought my Sony near the phone as Lafcadio stood in the kitchen, next to the Kalamazoo, a good fifteen minutes, basically answering questions. His end of the conversation included gists like:

Huh?

Yeah.

Uh.

Yeah, OK?

How is Mama?

Huh?

Mama?

Oh yeah, how am I?

Yeah, oh right.

The what?

Oh Gordon?

Do what, Medicaid? [enter Gordon]

G: Yes, you got Medicaid.

L: Oh, Medicaid.

Ask him if I got Medicaid.

G: Yes.

L: Yeah. What is that, Medicaid? Oh, Medicaid?

G: It'll pay for your hospital bills. It'll pay for your hospital bills.

L: What is that?

G: It pays for your hospital bills.

L: Oh, yeah . . . Medicaid. I didn't see any Medicaid bills, Medicaid papers. Yeah. Medicaid? Yeah . . . called up? Yeah. Medicaid.

If I get Medicaid.
Go to bed early?
Medicaid.
Uh.
. . . stay here then?
What are you doing at home now? Are you resting?
Yeah. OK.
Gordon's here.

While Laf was at the phone, I had things to do, upstairs and down. As I went my way, I could still hear, even if barely, his occasional brief comments and repetitions. Then, no longer even a syllable. After some minutes of silence, I returned to the kitchen to shut off the Sony.

To my surprise, there was Lafcadio, standing as before, receiver to ear. "Still on the phone?" I asked. "Yeah."

Acting on intuition, I gently took the receiver from his hand: a dial tone!

Saying Goodbye to Anna Marie

A MAZINGLY, I HADN'T wholly made up my mind about leaving East Hill even as late as the end of January. A diary entry records some of my ambivalence:

I gotta get away. I love Peter, think of him as friend—but there's too much irregularity here, too many interwoven levels of love joy hate frustration between him & Allen for me to see myself in any clear definite secure way towards them. Maybe go away a yr., let em see what they want to do—so much heavy intensity on Peter's shldrs—I think I can do nothing bout it—cept be available to help him when I'm here & when he wants it, & rest of time stay out of his way. He has been kind & strong to me.

What the entry doesn't specify is how the continuing relationship between Peter and Lafcadio must've bothered me. Certainly having a second extremely difficult brother on his hands was a severe burden for Peter, but his boot camp way of dealing with it was troubling.

Soon after Barbara's wedding celebration, I made up my mind finally: I'd leave East Hill Farm. Perhaps it was the celebration and its sense of other worlds being available, but I'm not sure any one last event triggered it—it merely seemed inevitable, based on my needs and the experiences of many months preceding.

I walked into his room and told Allen; he returned, "Would you like to come with me on my spring reading tour?" We'd go from several days at Kent State in early April through the Midwest and California, reach San Francisco by the month's end. "You can be my bodyguard," he joked.

What I'd do after that I wasn't sure; as a practicality I continued to have graduate school in the back of my mind. But I was excited by the immediate prospect, and pleased to return to San Francisco—America's most beautiful city—which I knew from short stopovers crossing America and the Pacific as a child.

During last days in New York in early February I saw Miles, Ann, Giorno, and other friends, said my goodbyes. Telling John I was leaving East Hill, I started to explain, "'Cause really the farm's for—" But he interrupted, eyes squinting with laughter as he finished my sentence: "—the Orlovsky boys!"

My relationship with Sandy had dissolved, as it evidently had with Cheri; I was keeping a friendship with Nora Crain, pharmacist Bert's daughter, who was now in

Boston; I was writing Elise Greene, whom I'd met at Goddard College. But Anna Marie was coming again for a weekend, and I had to tell her. I knew she'd be unhappy; was there some way of doing it less hurtfully than others? Thinking on it, I awaited her arrival.

Soon after she came, we headed to Paul and Patti Benson's in Cooperstown. He was a school teacher; she worked at Bassett Hospital. They'd been to the farm a few times, and were among our warm-shower hosts in early days. It was their baby for whom Anna Marie knitted a sweater.

On the way, I was still mulling things over: I should start by saying, "You know, Anna Marie, I've been thinking about doing something else . . ." Or, "I've got to tell you something you may not like." Or . . .

Instead, I found myself leaning against the counter of a comfortable kitchen, all of us having tea or coffee. And saying casually, "In a month or so I'm going to be leaving the farm and going with Allen on his reading tour to California."

I don't know that I faced Anna Marie directly as I said it. But she took it, as I remember, without outward sign of distress, and it became, for a brief time, a matter of appropriate social response with our hosts: what will you do there, where will you stay, who'll look after the farm, etc. Then, finishing our tea and coffee, we went on to other things.

□ □ □

OF COURSE, MY method of breaking the news was about the worst possible. The rest of the day and evening neither Anna Marie nor I spoke of it, but it hung there in both our minds.

We went down to Oneonta for the night. Bernie Mayo, my friend from jail in Mexico, had invited us to use his house while they were away. After a nice modest dinner at a restaurant, we went to the picture show, which was *Joe*: a middle-aged, middle-class father, distressed at his daughter's hippie life, ends up killing her. I thought it (like *Easy Rider*) revealed a truth about cultural bigotry in America, and wondered what Anna Marie thought—but chose not to ask.

Instead, we went quietly back to Bernie's, where we went quietly to bed. Anna Marie got into a pretty light green teddy, we lay down, turned off the lights. But I was frozen, immobile: if we made love, wouldn't it increase longing and disappointment? But she reached for me, brought me over, and we loved.

□ □ □

THE NEXT DAY, we were back on East Hill. Soon Anna Marie was gathering things together, ready to go. I walked with her a final time up the drive. We embraced, kissed, and embraced again. Then I moved back against a snowbank as she pulled out. And I saw tears streaming, just pouring down her face. Stricken, I made the beginning of a gesture as if to say, "Please don't cry," but she was gone.

I returned to the house, told Allen of it. He exclaimed, "Oh, she really loved you!"

Of course I was a heel—a heel's heel—for the way I did it. And Allen's response— moving in its direct sympathy and empathy—only added to my consideration of the error of my ways. Only much later did it occur to me that how I told Anna Marie goodbye was even more insensitive than how Candy had let her decision to leave travel the grapevine.

But soon the midwinter sun would begin to set, and Anna Marie would likely be halfway home. It was time to head for the barn, start on chores.

Snowmobiles

T HE PREVIOUS WINTER Allen recorded in his journal what he witnessed elsewhere in the area: "the gasoline/racket of snowmobiles chopping up the/black-
hilled fields." Come summer, there were snow mobile drag races at fairgrounds; come
winter, United States Snowmobile Association races.

Even tiny South Valley had formed a snowmobile club, the Piston Poppers. The
Times-Journal of Cobleskill headlined "World's Champs Booked for Races"; ads for
machines celebrated "292 ccs to a growling 3 cylinder 440" or claimed "This is the
Family Machine."

Of course, snowmobiles could be crucial in reaching families stranded after heavy
snows, and in other emergencies. But amidst all the shouting and bravura, the insult
and injury they caused were seldom mentioned. What might've seemed most obvious
(and, thereby, dissuading) were direct effects on humans: back injuries from bump-
ing along the ground; sprains, broken bones, lacerations from running into snow-
hidden obstructions such as rocks, stumps, fence posts, barbed wire. News articles
dutifully reporting snowmobile-related injuries, sometimes severe, even fatal, were
commonplace.

Then there was the aesthetic damage, as Allen noted, in sight and sound. And the
ecological: what was the cost in the well-being and peace of mind of deer and hosts
of other animals living in what had been the sanctuary of quiet white woods? And a
worse situation arose when individuals combined their *afición* for snowmobiling with
that for hunting. For some time in the winter of 1970–71 we'd noticed what we hadn't
heard at all our first winter: the *RRRRR*s of the machines bleating away hither and
yon, but usually in the distance, always out of sight. That, of course, was disturbing
enough for those accustomed to winter's blanketing quiet, beauty, and privacy.

One day a couple of snowmobilers pulled down our drive, nearly all the way to
our front door. I don't remember what for; most likely, to ask directions. But I remember some of the exchange.

Shocked, we'd gone out to see what was up. Once their immediate concern was
taken care of, we talked a minute. Rifles were attached to their machines; we inquired
about their hunting. They really loved it; one of them said that with their snowmobiles
"it was great sport": they could quickly penetrate a remote area where deer would

come. Then they'd just have to turn off their machines and sit quietly, and after a while the deer would likely appear. One of their machines was specially fitted to pull a small cart, evidently for carcasses.

I could feel Denise, nineteen-year-old vegetarian, lover of animals, simmering as she listened. But by a certain point she was no longer simmering; she was simply exclaiming, loud and firm, "*Some sport!*" and turning heel across our hard-packed walk, into the sanctuary of our house.

Last Footage

WHEN DENISE AND Peter were in town while Julius was delivering his mono-logue to Laf, the phone rang; Peter wanted to know if we needed anything else. Yes, I said: please get a roll of regular 8-millimeter silent color movie film at Crain's. It was widely available in those days.

That was the roll on which I shot most of my last moving images of the farm, after having assembled and edited the final part of *Farm Diary*. It includes a close-up, in front of the house, of Don't Bite Me and a little brown puppy nuzzling and nudging each other in the snow under bright sun. Denise in dark jersey and bright vest and Peter in tee-shirt and overalls appear in porch sunlight, happy.

Then we see the pig root in the snow, perhaps eating some food she'd been tossed, a dark brown woolen jacket draped over her back as she continues her all-consuming task.

Laf stands nearby in green work shirt and rubber boots, ankles pressed together. He wears only a tee-shirt under his work shirt, one sleeve unbuttoned. He removes the jacket from the pig, carefully brushes off some snow, and puts it on. Both his eyes are dark-ringed.

Snow tears furiously around the chicken house and its huge drifts and banks, piles up in front of our house as high as the porch roof gutters, scurries brilliant red at sunset over frozen pond and surrounding meadow.

Final shots on a second roll, likely of a later storm, show black windcharger and green ram house turning white; thick flakes fall leisurely upon bare branches, Ed's meadow, and the woods above. . . . Snow falling still, Peter's outdoors in blue overalls and bright burgundy shirt, sleeves rolled up to elbows. High in the air he tosses the puppy, catching him again and again. His beard's full, long hair in pony tail; his whole mood is hearty.

□ □ □

MEANTIME—EARLY MARCH now—Allen was in Washington for that fortnight of readings and meetings with journalists; in several days I'd be joining him. Later in the month I'd make a Carolina trip, then reconnect with him to head for Kent State.

He called East Hill the day after reading with his father at the Corcoran Gallery. "Guess who I had dinner with last night!" He could hardly contain himself.

I puzzled. "I don't know—who?"

"Richard Helms."

"Richard Helms, the—"

"Yes, head of CIA. I talked with him about my research and made a bet with him. If I was right and it's proven the CIA has supported opium traffic, he'll have to meditate an hour a day the rest of his life. I'll give him my dorje if I'm wrong."

"What did he say about your idea?"

"He said he didn't know anything about it, and that 'If my son thought I was involved in opium traffic he'd shoot me.'"

The Corcoran's Amy Huntington Block, who'd invited him to read and was his dinner party hostess, had greeted him with, "Our friends the Richard Helmses will be coming tonight." Not only were they at dinner; they came to the Corcoran, where Allen read "Pentagon Exorcism" and many a related poem, chanted Tibetan mantras, and displayed his dorje.

□ □ □

AND THEN CAME my day to leave. The day before I'd said farewell to friends in town, including Howie Fassett at the Mobil station and Bert Crain, and stopped at Myron Wiles's on the way back home. Now I went up to Ed's, stuck my head in his goat barn, saluted elegant-horned Billy and his two dams. In the hermit's small musty cabin, everything seemed as usual: stove and firewood, chair, magazines, rocker, TV. "I sure hope everything stays copasetic with you," he said, using one of his favorite words. "Don't forget me—send a postcard now and then, Pogo." I didn't forget. And I dedicated *Allen Verbatim* to him.

□ □ □

I WENT ON a last walk in the snow with Godly, then squeezed my priapic friend good-bye. I knew I might never see him again. I patted Radha and Mirabelle, threw some barks back at the puppies.

In the house I hugged Denise, hugged Peter. "Will you come back?" he asked. "I don't know." I put my arm around Julie-Woolie, brought him close. (Laf had recently been taken back to Northport.)

I'd crammed three years of extra clothing, papers, books, films, tapes into two footlockers which I'd return for later. Now with Peter's help I carried my full duffel bag and a suitcase up to the Olds, and laid them on the two 100-pound bags of feed we kept for traction in its spacious trunk. He'd take me to the afternoon bus in Cooperstown.

Then we came back down the drive, he to talk with Denise. I went into the barn. Just after entering I noted once more how all but the upper couple of inches of the San Francisco *Oracle* "Changes" cover (with images of Allen, Gary, Alan Watts, and Leary) that I'd tacked to the wall in our first months was now gone, into the mouths of goats. I went to the rear and sat down on the straw with Shiva and Brahma and their kids, their breaths fine bright steam hanging in air. I hugged little stump-legged Cosset, cheerful as ever in pregnancy, knuckled Junior several times on the forehead between his horns, and we both went "Baaah." I pulled off one glove to wipe my eyes. I patted Bessie and her young and old heifers, and Lash the horse, still on her ancient feet. Then I went to the chickens pecking happily at fittin' ration in the snow, and Papa Duck and his gals.

I returned to the house a final time, admired the grand Kalamazoo. And did I wave goodbye to Joy the Gerbil, still solitary in her treadmilled cage now on the shelf between the KLH record player and a carton of EverReady batteries, beneath many a boxed tape of declaimed poesy?

I went out onto the porch, set foot on the crunchy walk one more time, turned and glanced at the backyard and the old green garage where I once saw Barbara in pink nightgown weep. I started up toward Peter, who was already at the Olds, now thrumming in sturdy majesty. As I came abreast of the main plot of garden, it was still covered in white.

Epilogue

IN THOSE FIRST years East Hill had been, as Allen worried, a "giant White Elephant Poesy Household Farm." But not long after I left Peter and Denise began thinning things out; never again was it as full-scale as in its early seasons, with many animals, many guests. In July of 1971—I was in San Francisco, living at the Swiss-American across Broadway from City Lights Bookstore—I received a card from East Hill. Denise thanked me for two blues books I'd sent, reported the farm was quiet and that Godly, who'd been setting forth and impregnating all female dogs in the area, had been neutered. She'd turn twenty soon, and would celebrate with apple cider. And Peter added:

All is well—Garden growing—we gave Bettsy away to Tree Frog commune in Vermont so she is in good hands. Have a lot of garlic planted & gathering green mint for drying in winter tea Time. Take Care Love Peter

The goats and Jennifer had already gone; even old Lash, even Don't Bite Me would make their exits. As for the humans, Lafcadio stayed in Northport, but Julius remained with Peter and Denise for the time being. Denise's growing commitment to music required more time in the city as she eventually formed her own band, the Stimulators. Yet East Hill Farm remained a source of special, profound feeling for her. In late May 1971, before parting with Bessie and Jennifer, she'd written Allen, rhapsodizing on the beauty and uniqueness of the place: frogs were singing from the pond, there was lightning and thunder, cows ran back to the barn, mooing as their bells jangled. The farm was the best place to live on the East Coast; Denise for once felt at home. Confining city apartments make people crazy; here you can have sex outdoors wherever you like, beneath the sky, on the grass; you can work naked in the garden. She was saddened that few others were so fortunate.

Before the end of 1971 the farm was closed till spring—Peter and Denise chose to winter in the city, and Julius was relocated at the large public hospital in Binghamton. For several seasons Peter and Denise would raise magnificent crops (and Peter get his desired tractors). But as early as mid-June 1972 Peter himself was at the farm only intermittently: he wrote me he was there for "4 days of all garden seed planting, weelbarrowing Ed's great goat compost pile." East Hill was starting to become less of a year-round home; Allen, Peter, and Denise spent much of summer 1974 in the Sierras, building a small house on land shared with Gary Snyder.

Eventually—around the end of the 1970s—Peter and Denise split up. Meanwhile, various people became East Hill caretakers from time to time. Wayne Graham, who was there some of 1974 and 1975, also stayed from summer 1976 through summer 1978. Andy Clausen and his family moved in for a year in 1980. But otherwise the farm was becoming, increasingly, a warm-weather-only place. Bob Rosenthal, Allen's secretary from 1977, and co-executor of the Ginsberg Trust after Allen's death, worked mightily, with extremely limited funds, to keep it alive at all—mainly for summer weekend or week-long retreats. The pipes wore out, as Ed Smith had predicted, after twenty years; the water system failed and was not restored.

So East Hill Farm has served, in a highly marginal fashion, as refuge from the urban press of life, even unto today. Admittedly there were individuals—Gregory comes to mind—for whom it didn't "work": as Allen once said to Creeley, "They brought their problems with them." Though overall the farm met with only mixed results in providing refuge from urban entanglements, it did help (as did Denise) move Peter Orlovsky away from the crush of speed. The move didn't prove permanent—but Peter's reinvolvement with needle drugs came not on East Hill but after re-immersion in city life. And that (coupled with excessive drinking) proved his curse: in Jonas Mekas's video, *Scenes from Allen's Last 3 Days on Earth as a Spirit*, Peter—forty feet from Allen's corpse—tells Jonas

> . . . these last nine years I've been shooting coke and drinking vodka. I haven't been writing anything, I've been making a nuisance of myself. I've been clean for the last two and a half years. Not a drop of drinkin', and not a drop of druggin', and it's gonna be that till I die. And I plan to do a lot of writing, yes. Poetry, songs.

There were other good effects of this small community on a hill. For Bonnie Bremser, it encouraged her toward what became a career in soil science, and was the start of her involvement with Buddhism. She'd first noticed a difference in Allen after India and Japan 1963; at the farm she got to observe him up close. After she and Ray left, he continued to loan her Buddhist readings, including *The Life of Milarepa*.

Though he was visitor rather than long-term resident, the effect on John Giorno was similar in part to that on Bonnie—by a much different route. During a summer 1970 visit, John, as he'd done previously for years, asked Allen extensively about Buddhism and the nature of Mind.

In the kitchen one morning, having just come down from LSD the day before, John asked Allen one more question about the mind. Allen, standing only a foot and a half away, screamed at him: "Aaaagh! Stop asking me all these questions! Why don't you go to India and find out for yourself?" John felt slapped in the face; he saw stars. Angry at first, he then thought, "What a great idea! That's what I should do!"

It triggered his first trip to the East some months later, which in turn led to a lifelong commitment to Tibetan Buddhism.

On East Hill, Miles made his first recording of Louis Ginsberg recalling early Newark days, and so began his biography of Allen before he'd conceived of it. Many of us—myself, certainly—made lifelong friends there. I shot extensive movie footage, gathered impressions, stories, and artifacts, and began a life's work inspired by Allen.

To some degree, the farm during the summer of 1970 showed that intellectuals, poets, and "heads" (many were all three) could collaborate effectively in a cooperative agronomic effort. Of course (notions of self-sufficiency notwithstanding) it was never conceived of as a Brook Farm: there was Allen, providing economic support.

Allen—and Committee on Poetry, Inc.—survived the Nixon administration IRS scrutiny, and watched Spiro T. Agnew resign in 1973 under suspicion of bribery, then plead no contest to cheating on income tax. Nearly a year later, Richard M. Nixon quit in the disgrace of Watergate. America's war in Vietnam did come to an end; I hadn't believed it ever would.

Three days after a late 1971 benefit concert that featured John Lennon, Allen, and Ed Sanders, the Supreme Court of Michigan ordered John Sinclair released from prison: he'd served over twenty-eight months for giving two joints to an undercover agent. The Court agreed with Sinclair's argument that Michigan's pot laws were unconstitutional, and three months later his conviction was reversed. Though drug war mania remains active in the U.S. today as opiate illegalization and consequent black market profiteering continue, some of our policies on addiction seem almost enlightened—when compared with circumstances Allen and others brought to light over four decades ago. And though Richard Helms never got back to Allen about their bet, public exposure of the CIA-Golden Triangle connection by Allen, scholars Alfred W. McCoy, Peter Dale Scott, and others, may have helped end the war. In 1978 Charles Sulzberger, publisher of *The New York Times*, wrote Allen:

> *I fear I owe you an apology. I have been reading a succession of pieces about CIA involvement in the dope trade in South East Asia and I remember when you first*

*suggested I look into this I thought you were full of beans. Indeed you were right
and I acknowledge the fact plus sending my best personal wishes.*

In Cherry Valley, no one saw people from East Hill Farm more frequently than pharmacist Bert Crain, behind the counter at his drug store as the mighty Greyhound dropped off and picked up: Bremser in worn overcoat, Huncke looking where to put his feet down, Rachel Fleischman in disarray. . . . Allen bought the farm, Crain's daughter Nora later reported her father saying, "to get the two brothers out of the city." It had worked; the pharmacist had seen a change in Julius.

Except for his service in World War II, Bert had seldom been away from upstate New York. He had no comprehension of vegetarianism, Nora said. As strange as some of us must have seemed, he told her, "Those people never gave me any trouble." In fact, according to Nora, the effect of his almost daily contact was "enlightening."

Though their sense, accurate or inaccurate, of what was going on up on East Hill doubtless worried or exasperated some Cherry Valley residents, Allen's presence and contribution to the community seem to have been perceived as quite positive. Down at Glensfoot Farm Judy Cannon (who told me Allen's arrival had put to rest worries that the post office might close) said that his having moved there was "wonderful":

*There's a whole new population . . . who have all kinds of awareness and concern
for society and for the community and for each other. And everybody really liked
Allen: when he was first moving here he would go onto the main street and talk
to people. He made himself very accessible, and he talked about anything that
anybody asked him. People just absolutely closed ranks not to tell any outsiders
where he lived or even admit that he lived here—I mean the protection, the
unspoken protection—"Don't know anything about Allen Ginsberg" kind of attitude
that tourists or sightseers got if they tried to find out where he lived. Nobody would
tell 'em.*

Judy's politically conservative housekeeper happily played Allen's Blake music at their piano as the poet sang. Her usually "stuffy" mother invited him to dinner immediately upon meeting him; only their ancient Aunt Bun initially disapproved of the newcomer from the city, branding him a "social climber."

Charles and Pamela Plymell settled in town in 1970 and have remained active in the community ever since, with Cherry Valley Editions and much else. Anne Waldman's brother Carl and his wife Molly, after a stint caretaking the farm in 1972, bought their own place in the area. Since Allen's death a number of Cherry Valley arts festivals, organized by Breath Hand and others, have honored his memory.

And up on East Hill, Wayne Graham recalled never having questioned our war or other issues, until hearing Allen:

> *I used to call Allen "Farmer Allen." When I met him there was just my family and the farm, and not much else going on—that was the whole of my world. Once Allen was here I started to get ideas about everything else, and start actually questioning the rest of the world.*
>
> *The whole Buddhist thing—I remember his explaining that circle in the poster that hung on the wall* [the Tibetan "Time Wheel Mandala" of the "twelvefold chain of interdependent co-origination"] *explaining the different realms . . . the dorje. All that was enlightening for me, and just about as foreign as you could possibly get for a farm boy from upstate New York. But I was very glad I had the opportunity to experience that; it was a great awakening.*
>
> *Up until then you took the spin doctors' word for what they were sellin', and suddenly Allen came up with alternative ideas that made perfect sense. I had no doubt he was right about all this.*

□ □ □

LESS THAN A year after I left, one life reached its end. At the start of 1972 came a card from Allen, reporting:

> *Myron Wiles perished heart attack on front porch snowy midnite after his car got stuck at Beautiful View returning from Xmas party at the Grahams. . . .*

I heard later he was found frozen, door key in hand. Ed moved into his house the next summer, using just three rooms. I visited in 1974, and presented Ed—soon to turn seventy—with a copy of *Allen Verbatim*. He was well then, but in later years declined. He died of a heart attack early in 1985, "waiting," as Wayne told me, "for spring to come." He left his place to Wayne, and $250,000 in ATT stocks to the children of an Indiana cousin.

After Peter and Denise and I went to the Fiddler's Convention at Union Grove, North Carolina, in 1972, we stopped in at my sister's in Winston-Salem. Five years later Allen and Peter and I visited Maylee again. We brought my father over from the rest home a few blocks away; it was a month before he'd die. Allen gave him his finger cymbals and held his hand as together they sang Allen's Blake.

I continued to come to the city, staying at 408 East 10th and then (after Allen was mugged, and moved) at 437 East 12th. He and I hung out or worked on further projects, and until they broke up I always enjoyed time with Peter and Denise.

□ □ □

AND SO I did return to East Hill, as visitor, both early and late. In the last week of October 1972, I came with Allen; we were to go over the work I'd done on *Allen Verbatim*. Only two others were present, arriving separately: Japanese poet and mountain-climber Nanao Sakaki, and filmmaker and farm founder Barbara Rubin.

These were mild bright autumn days, and hearty Nanao, long-haired, bearded, wiry, wearing only shorts with a shirt, cheerily raked golden maple leaves. With equal gladness he meditated daily; I joined him once at afternoon's end; we sat silent an hour facing the setting sun over pond and state forest evergreen ridge. "I love meditation!" he exclaimed, exuberant, when it was over.

With Allen we went to look at the Milson tombstones next to lilac and apple. As we stood before them, Nanao turned to Allen: "And where is yours?"

Nanao had a beautiful voice and one night, standing in the middle of the small kitchen, he sang one after another traditional Japanese songs.

Meantime Barbara—as we called her again now that her marriage to Mordecai had broken up—was shooting a movie of Allen with her 16-millimeter Bolex. She kept requiring Allen's attention so she could shoot him doing this and doing that, until finally I spoke with Allen and he told her, "Gordon's getting anxious about the work we gotta do, and rightly so," and Barbara held off, amiably.

She was still vibrant, like the Barbara of yore. Yet a prediction Jonas had made on learning of her wedding twenty months earlier—"It vill last six months"—hadn't been terribly far off. She found Nanao attractive, but couldn't pronounce his given name. "Nanaa," she tried again and again, giggling. They became close.

That was the last time I saw her. A little over eight years later, I was married, and Kathleen and I were expecting a child in two months. I'd just completed all graduate work, was an instructor for several courses at Chapel Hill, and was on the market for a permanent teaching position. We received a card from R'lene Dahlberg, at whose Majorca home we'd honeymooned:

Many thanks for the pictures. I may look rotten, but the old Mobylette looks great. . . .

Huncke asked me to relay the information that Barbara Rubin is dead. She
apparently died recently. I didn't know her except by hearsay—for her involvement
with the farm. Huncke also sends his best wishes for you & Kathy.

□ □ □

IN CARL CARMER'S 1936 appreciation of upstate New York, *Listen for a Lonesome*
Drum: A York State Chronicle, we find the following observation of the region that
includes Cherry Valley:

> *Returned to it after many years I can understand more clearly than ever why this*
> *stretch of wrinkled land has held . . . more of men's mystic and psychic receptivity,*
> *perhaps I should say creative imaginings, than any other region in America.*

In her insistence, then, that East Hill Farm was "a *mystical* place," Barbara
would not, perhaps, have been speaking in isolation. Yet there was, of course, the
whole broad region—presumably most any site, on this basis, might be considered
"mystical."

In any case, looking back, Barbara in her mid-twenties was gifted with more
imaginative energy than she could begin to control. But she was groundless; she was
looking for that ground. She did well in a flurry of activity—much of which she generated. But the flurries were sometimes loopy; the mundane, the everyday more trying.
Yet that's only partly true, for there she was looking after Julius many months on her
own. As Jonas once said, she was the one person he knew who'd take in a bum from
the street. She found a place for herself, not in her marriage with Mordecai, but a little
later, through remarriage and an orthodox community in France. There she gave birth
to five children, dying after the birth of the fifth from an infection.

□ □ □

AS FOR THE bearers of the news of Barbara's death, my friends R'lene and Huncke:
When I was leaving the farm back in March 1971, Huncke, after months of waiting,
had received an even more generous grant from Harvey Brown: $9,000. R'lene invited
me to join them in the city for dinner at an excellent intimate restaurant, The Derby,
near her 3rd Avenue apartment. There we fantasized expansively about our travels.
Huncke was going around the world; he wanted especially to go to that consumer's
paradise, Hong Kong. He was concerned as to how he'd break it to Louie that he'd be
going alone. We spoke of meeting in Tangier, in London, or at R'lene's in Majorca.

Several months later I was with Allen in San Francisco. A telegram arrived for him from Louie Cartwright in Nepal: Louie was out of money, needing to get home. Huncke, too, had already run broke, and, I learned later, was saved by R'lene, who came to Nepal and took him back with her to Spain.

Huncke and I never did meet abroad. But in late March he wrote on a postcard depicting the Taj Mahal:

Greetings chum—

I have never in my life experienced anything quite like this trip. It is really an incredible experience and you would quite likely go mad with your camera. There is everything to see—all very beautifull and strange. Think of me occasionally.

Huncke

□ □ □

AFTER ALLEN, BARBARA, Nanao, and I were there in the fall of 1972, I returned to the farm a number of times—one in particular comes to mind. Two autumns following Barbara and Nanao, and just after a few days with Allen in the city, I took the woman I'd marry to visit East Hill.

Kathleen was struck by the beauty of the wall of forest (the state land beyond the lower meadow); it seemed to go on forever. She was no habitué of palatial abodes, but she was taken aback by the modesty and ricketyness of the house. In the pantry she noted row upon row of canned vegetables, particularly beets. Who would eat them all, she wondered, if people didn't live here fulltime? As it happened, twenty-eight years later Allen's secretary Bob Rosenthal told us they'd thrown the jars out only a year before: as time went on, everyone had grown increasingly fearful of sampling them.

Years passed and I didn't visit for decades. But I've returned three times in the course of writing this book, each visit underlining in new ways the centrality of the man behind it all. I continued working with Allen on books and photography, and was lecturing on him at James Madison University as he lay dying in April 1997, nearly three decades after we first got together in Cherry Valley. A lifetime's activity and commitment grew from our days there.

And so I'd like now to focus on what I discovered, large and small, in Allen's personality and character in those three years on East Hill:

- His profound spirituality. This is, of course, stating the most obvious: it was evident in the first photographic image I saw of him, wet with water from the

Ganges; in the informal vow of penury he took once he began drawing some income from his work; in his joining with Peter in saving a dying man from the streets of India, nursing him to health. It was at the center of virtually all he did: there was the farm itself, as a vehicle for others to escape destruction; there was his insistence that revolutionary change in America be spiritual.

- His capacity for self-correction, admission of faults. In the winter of 1969, three months after our Albany car crash and still on crutches, he told the *East Village Other*'s Jaakov Kohn (who'd suggested the Presidency be shared by a triumvirate of Leary, Dick Gregory, and Allen):

> *Concentration Camp or cancer—it is all the same. Auto crashes are the worst. They hurt. I got a whole new take on my body. Maybe sex is not so useful after all. The more fun you have with your body the harder it will be to cut off. It's like being a body junkie. If you got the body habit and then the supply of body will be cut off. . . . Why then invest all those hopes, fears, and desires in the body? I have been wrong all along in promoting meat joy. . . .*
>
> . . . .
>
> *If you insist on cultivating bodily pleasure you are also cultivating bodily pain . . . you are making a giant choice for pleasure and you are going to be pained if you don't get it. . . . car crashes instead of cock sucks. So sensational kicks of that order are not enough to build the universe on, much less a stable political society. So for that reason I wouldn't be a very good President. I was all wrong.*

Later, he reviewed himself in the 1960s in Morley Markson's 1988 film *Growing Up in America*. Appearing along with a handful of other '60s veterans including Leary, Hoffman, and Rubin, he distinguished himself by explicit and detailed apology and regret:

> *I must apologize for being mistaken in those days—I had the wrong mantra all along. My guru Chogyam Trungpa, a Tibetan lama, had suggested I try a different one—more American—the same one you hear on July 4th when fireworks go up in the air, which is "Ah!" Which is appreciation of the spaciousness around us. Chanting Om so aggressively didn't intrigue people to enter that space, but probably just simply mystified them. I didn't know*

enough then to send out any calmer vibe and a more thoughtful vibe and a more sensitive vibe. I wish I'd been more sensitive then, and I wish I'd been a little kinder to myself, actually, less outraged with myself, less guilty, carrying less white guilt, as everybody did, and I wish I had trusted my instincts more freely as I do now, which were instincts of generosity rather than paranoia.

- In speech, his frequent use of "exactly precisely" rather than just the one adverb or the other.

- His almost buoyant sense of hope or belief in the ability of people to work together, to complement each other, even on the smallest scale—as in his report to me over the phone, "Maretta lost the broom, and I found it."

- His generosity. Perhaps to a greater degree than any other individual, Allen was responsible for personally helping to keep together the lives of hundreds, possibly thousands of people. From a small emergency loan to total immersion in problems besetting others, he was willing to set aside his own interests or well-being to help someone else.

- His idiosyncratic insistences (he had his share). "Push pins! I asked for push pins! Not thumb tacks!" I'd just returned from town, brought the bags of groceries and supplies into the house, set them on the kitchen table. I'd never heard of push pins; I assumed they were the equivalent of thumb tacks. I soon became appreciative of this much finer implement.

- He was rightly disturbed by Nixon Attorney General John Mitchell's talk of "preventive detention"—holding suspects contrary to constitutional rights—and often gave it an extra syllable as he spoke of it: "preventative detention." What term might he use for the excesses of the Patriot Act?

- His ability to relate to, talk with all people—hardware store proprietor, doctor, attorney general, plumber, state trooper. . . . Once on East Hill the phone rang for Allen; it was Judy Cannon's sister-in-law Beth:

  You don't know me but we've met. You've been in the area a while, and I'm having a party on my birthday and my old [she was always ninety-three] *Aunt Bun is going to be there. I thought you might like to meet some of the old people.*

Allen came indeed, and spent much of the time sitting with Aunt Bun, listening to her, attending her. Beth told me how impressed she was by that.

It was part of his vast gift for appreciation, which got him so much out of life—from leading a volcano eruption expedition through the Mexican jungle in 1954, even though his Spanish was poor, to being crowned King of May eleven years later in Prague. Few others mixed so well and so thoroughly with their fellows, while remaining themselves: there he was getting thrown out of Havana and Prague, arrested at Rocky Flats, Miami.

- How characteristically modest he was in person: "I always thought of myself as short," he once told me, somewhat to my surprise—he was just barely shorter than I, and was surely average for his generation. How tender one friend was, he told me, a while after I'd introduced them, "for being such a big guy."

- His use of disarming humor (including some self-humor) to make a point. Once I walked into his room and he showed me a postcard he'd just written:

Dear Nixon,
Get your ass out of Vietnam.
Sincerely,
Allen Ginsberg [seal]

He looked over his shoulder at me from his seat at the desk: "Every now and then I like to send a good crank letter."

A few years later I visited Belle Carpenter, Gregory's former lady friend, in Santa Fe; one evening we were watching a late night talk show. Suddenly there was Allen, joining the host and a middle-aged woman guest. The woman—I don't remember her name—began putting down nudity; "Oh, it's just boring!" she exclaimed. "Take off your clothes and say that," Allen said, calm and good-humored.

- His sense of priorities was strong (and sometimes different from mine). Once, with him and Peter at an Albany shopping center which included a movie theater, I proposed, "Let's go to a movie." But Allen, an enthusiastic viewer of films in earlier days, returned, "I don't have two hours in my life to spend in a movie theater."

- His extraordinary intelligence, which needs no example or explanation, for it colored every aspect of his being.

- His appreciation of others. Allen could interpret what others were doing in a way that revealed sense or purpose where all had seemed formless or bizarre. Of Peter's relentlessly energetic activity early on, he remarked, "He practices karma yoga," referring to the yoga of works (as opposed to, say, bhakti yoga of devotion).

- Both Peter and Allen had slight pot bellies. "From diaphragmatic breathing," Allen explained. Even I, who could be gullible, was a little dubious.

- His refusal to be co-opted by expected social roles: toward the end of a phone conversation one afternoon he exclaimed, "No, I will *not* take care!"

  I recall his writing "Sociability's a drag," as he explained work and farm commitments in response to a John Clellon Holmes query about visiting.

  When in public encounters with strangers he'd be asked, "Are you Allen Ginsberg?" he'd sometimes answer, "That's my name."

- His empathy, his sympathy: he'd typically take into consideration the situations of others. If we were discussing someone's problems or apparent shortcomings, he'd often ask, "Well, is he [or she] in a reasonable situation" to do such-and-such a thing?

  He thought creatively, and sometimes I resented it, for it meant more complication to make one's way through. Then I saw how he was concerned with *understanding* people—and being only reasonable in expectations of them.

  To jump to 1979–1980, during the uproar in the "poetry world" over what many saw as Chogyam Trungpa's humiliating treatment of poet W. S. Merwin and his lady friend one Halloween night: Allen, in a lengthy interview, had basically supported his teacher. Especially in the Boulder, Colorado, area surrounding Naropa Institute, lines had been drawn, with a number of poets and artists (e.g., Ed Dorn, Stan Brakhage) opposing and attacking Allen. But he wouldn't let commitment to idea or ideology keep himself from human feeling. At one point as Allen and Peter and I were discussing the charged political atmosphere, trying to imagine what might come next, Allen exclaimed, "Now I know how Nixon felt!"

- His inconsistencies on cigarette smoking. In our early days on East Hill we—Allen and Peter and I—paid a brief call to the Walterses, an older couple from Florida who had a summer home across the way. It was raining but had just let up and we stood in front of the house while grey-haired Mrs. Walters spoke to us from up on their porch. After introductions and a little neighborly chitchat, she took out a cigarette. Immediately Allen asked, "May I have one?"

  This from the man who'd written in *Howl* of "the narcotic tobacco haze of Capitalism" and would later write "Put Down Your Cigarette Rag." (In 1975 poet Larry Fagin would depict him "on his hands and knees / lookin' for a smoke.") But after the Albany car wreck, Allen stayed away from True Blues or any other cigarette for a year, maybe longer: the pain of drawing breath those first days with broken ribs inspired abstinence. Eventually he resumed; few of us, including me with my Camel Filters, were particularly earnest about stopping in those days before tobacco addiction finally became a central health issue in the U.S. A little later Allen would rightly indict Senator Jesse Helms as major dope pusher, responsible for hundreds of thousands of deaths a year. But in the middle of my farm years, the best that we who were sucking our butts (to borrow from "Put Down . . .") did was to be economical about it, from time to time, and buy tobacco in bulk to roll our own.

- His love of lineage, transmission, legacy, relationship. Allen once mentioned with amusement how Neal Cassady (who'd slept with Allen) had slept with Gavin Arthur (grandson of President Chester Arthur), who'd slept with Edward Carpenter, who was Walt Whitman's young friend.

- Allen's insistent lines of demarcations between humans and pets on East Hill Farm (to his frequent exasperation, the first injunction was especially ignored):

  Cats must stay outside the house
  Bowls used by humans shouldn't be used by animals

- His promoting the works of others. His prefaces, blurbs, recommendations, and introductions are legion, from John Lennon to Herbert Huncke to Jean Genet to Robert Crumb. Who has given more, in terms of written words alone, for the sake of their contemporaries? Not only were the recognized or already mythologized among the recipients of his generosity, but many aspiring artists, writers, and poets, including myself. Composing such pieces was often an unwelcome chore, but still Allen slogged on.

- His commitment to causes—antiwar, sanity in drug legislation, candor in sexuality and in general, protection of the environment, to name but a few—was a model of bodhisattvic selflessness. Once Naropa Institute was founded, he taught there year after year without remuneration. "I loved Allen Ginsberg, man, he was the greatest of all time to me," John Sinclair told me some years back. "I hate this world without Ginsberg in it anymore."

And so now let me briefly note what I learned from Allen, who was of course the greatest teacher—directly and indirectly—I ever had. What follows are a few of the gleanings, spiritual and mundane alike, from three years on the farm with him. (Please remember I was young and slow for my age.)

- How to prepare tuna fish. Around noon one day in the kitchen I was going to make the two of us tuna fish sandwiches, when he saw me open a can of tuna and start to spread its contents onto two slices of bread. "No!" he exclaimed. "Put something in it!" He grabbed an onion, a stick of celery, and started chopping; put an egg on to boil; reached for the mayonnaise . . . and poured out the oil from the can. (In another basic home economics situation, he exclaimed, "I marvel at your occasional incredible naivete!")

- Keeping things tidy. "Would you like to consolidate your things over there?" he once asked. I got the idea.

- Doing dishes before going to bed. "Aw, we'll get them in the morning," I once said when he pointed to a pile-up in the sink. We'd been up late, talking, and were now about to go up for the night. "No, let's do them now," he returned.

- I also learned—in time—from some of Allen's errors: though I was hardly as generous as he, one should avoid indulging friends to destructive lengths (or helping them without limit—however it's to be expressed). Of course the line between help and hurt was often quite thin, and the typical human specimen would never have to worry about helping his or her fellows overly much. Nor do I mean to suggest that Allen's love, compassion, and charity for others weren't admirable (and moving) beyond expression, nor that he was without reason (or hope) for doing as he did: I know he thought that if Huncke could just stay off junk long enough, he could re-situate himself, possibly go to England, to be helped by their humane maintenance system. Years afterward, when Allen sought (and seemed to benefit from) professional help for his relationship with Peter, he told me, "I never thought of myself as an enabler."

- One of my later pleasures in life has been in discovering the similarity in things apparently dissimilar—not only as metaphor but myth: how ostensibly different entities are in certain ways the same.

  It often frustrated me at the time, but Allen had a way of pointing out such similarities—as if, I wondered then, just to push his point—even just to have something to say! One summer afternoon bespectacled Eugene was leaving in that big station wagon filled with wife and five kids, rolling out the driveway, dust rising inside through the floorboards, falling outside on all that was near. Allen and I stood watching, and as part of a larger discussion we'd been having on the nature of psychedelics he offered, "Having a family can be psychedelic." At the time I thought (but didn't say), Oh, come on, Allen, how ridiculous— Eugene has no sense of what LSD brings!

  As time has passed, with marriage and family, my doubt's diminished considerably.

- "How do you know, how can you tell if you're doing the right thing?" I asked him in March 1971.

  "Things happen," he answered, "that tell you you are. Like this encouragement or affirmation I'm getting on CIA dope." He was then meeting with journalists and others who'd been in the field. "'Coincidences.'" I thought of his dinner with Richard Helms.

- Of course, a number of teachings had to do with Hinduism and Buddhism. Early on he showed me a representation of Ganesh, the Hindu god of the home, of wisdom and good fortune. Allen seemed charmed by Ganesh, big friendly elephant supported by a mouse—the tiny supporting the enormous. And he told me that in information for *Who's Who in America* he'd identified his wife (to give Peter a little buffer) as Ganesh Orlovsky. He mentioned his having gone to the burning ghats in Benares and Calcutta, where he joined holy men sitting in meditation smoking grass as they watched the bodies burn on their pyres. "You realize," he told me of the body, "it's all furniture."

- In 1953 or 1954—I was eight or nine—I visited a Japanese mountain resort with my parents. It wasn't long after the end of the American Occupation, and the hotel where we stayed was primed to accommodate western guests. Finding myself in a sort of common living room space under a high ceiling, I beheld a large, formal full-length portrait on the wall above me. It was of an elegantly dressed woman, a sheen to her formal gown, in the style of Gainsborough or Sargent. As I looked up at it, a blond boy whom I didn't know, maybe my age or slightly younger, ran up beside me. As he too beheld this larger-than-life jewel on the wall, he exclaimed, both at me and at the object of our attention, "That's beautiful!" And in an English accent!

Such excessive (as I saw it) expression of affection for the aesthetic embarrassed me. If and when I perceived beauty in those days I would've been shy to articulate it (let alone in what seemed such giveaway tones of effete over-refinement). Though I liked to sketch and draw, and did so almost daily, I basically never actively looked at, never studied paintings. Not until, around 1970, I went to the Met—with Allen.

There, I learned, most of all, that a painting could be funny! That there could be humor in line and angle and tilt as well as human expression. I began to appreciate composition, structure. Cézanne's contradictions of perspective were odd, surprising, Allen suggested, index finger delicately pointed toward canvas.

I don't know how much I heard the word "beautiful" in that immediate context, nor a year or so later when at the Cleveland Museum of Art, we beheld one of Allen's favorites, Albert Pinkham Ryder's *Death on a Pale Horse* (which he saw as image of coming Apocalypse). But in regard to painting I was likely less afraid to use the term, at long last, after Allen's impromptu primers.

With Allen, what was funny, what was aesthetic, merged: *Howl* is not only jeremiad but invocation of laughter. His Whitmanic openness to seeming difference and even contradiction—not to mention his boldness in speaking for beauty amidst ignorant aggression's stifling of it—changed my basic view of life, from Protestant claustrophobic closed system to rich openness and possibility, to Vipassana-like sense of spaciousness (as in the mantra "Ah"). The change didn't manifest overnight, nor was it exclusive to me. But such teachings did take root, deepening the affections of all our hearts, disparate and divided as many of us were at the farm and in years to come: it was what brought Barbara back in 1972, made possible my banker father's holding hands and singing Blake with Allen shortly before his death. It was contained in the lightness and tenderness, in the face of death, of Allen's last word to Gregory, which Corso repeated at his funeral:

Toodle-oo.

PHOTO PERMISSIONS AND CREDITS

The author wishes to thank and acknowledge the following photographers and estates for the use of their photos:

My wife-to-be Kathleen, myself, Julius Orlovsky, upper front yard, November 1974. Photograph by Peter Orlovsky. Used by permission of Judy Lief, the Peter Orlovsky Trust.

Stephen Bornstein's "plaque" inscribed in ram house wall at conclusion of our work, summer 1969. Photograph by Gordon Ball. Copyright Gordon Ball.

My cartoon of a winter 1969 moment at the farm. Copyright Gordon Ball.

Allen and Gregory, summer 1970. Photographer unknown. Courtesy of the Allen Ginsberg Estate.

Attic, facing south, c. 1973. Photographer unknown. Courtesy of the Allen Ginsberg Estate.

Allen at work at dining room table, daisy print tablecloth. Photograph by Allen De Loach. Courtesy of Heather Pawlak.

Allen at the chopping block. Photograph by Allen De Loach. Courtesy of Heather Pawlak.

Peter Orlovsky at chicken house, July 1970. Photograph by Allen De Loach. Courtesy of Heather Pawlak.

Allen in Albany Memorial Hospital bed after car crash, c. November 30, 1968. News photo; photographer unknown. Courtesy of Department of Special Collections and University Archives, Stanford University Libraries.

Carl Solomon atop haystack, August 1970. From *Farm Diary*, Part Two by Gordon Ball. Copyright Gordon Ball.

Assembling windcharger, June 1970. From *Farm Diary*, Part Two by Gordon Ball. Copyright Gordon Ball.

Allen and his *New York Times*. From *Farm Diary*, Part Two by Gordon Ball. Copyright Gordon Ball.

Ed's Billy, with five foot wide horns. From *Farm Diary*, Part Two by Gordon Ball. Copyright Gordon Ball.

Stephen Bornstein and Bessie. Photograph by Ron Ropolo. Used with permission of Stephen Bornstein.

ADDITIONAL PERMISSIONS

Grateful acknowledgment is made for use of materials as follows:

To the Allen Ginsberg Estate:

Allen Ginsberg's unpublished journals and tape recordings, 1968–1971.

Unpublished letters by Allen Ginsberg:
- To Lawrence Ferlinghetti: May 26 and December 7, 1968; January 20 and January 28, 1969; July 13, 1970.
- To Charles Olson: December 7, 1968.
- To William S. Burroughs: October 15, 1968; January 25, 1969.
- To Philip Whalen: October 30 and November 17, 1968; January 31 and October 6, 1969; February 2, May 22, and December 21, 1970.
- To Louis Ginsberg: May 22 and July 3, 1970.
- To Gordon Ball: March 25, 1969; December 29, 1971.
- To Eugene Brooks: late March 1969.
- To Gary Snyder: (about) April 10, 1969.
- To Herbert Huncke: April 17, 1969.
- To Lee Crabtree: April 17 and late May 1969.
- To Louis Cartwright: February 10, 1970.
- To Timothy Leary: July 3 and November 10, 1970.
- To Dave Haselwood: January 20, 1969.

All above-mentioned materials are copyright of the Allen Ginsberg Estate. Used with permission.

To Counterpoint:

For correspondence in *The Selected Letters of Allen Ginsberg and Gary Snyder*:
- From Ginsberg to Snyder: July 8, 1968; May 30, August 24, and December 26, 1970.
- From Snyder to Ginsberg: December 28, 1968.

To Brenda Frazer (Bonnie Bremser):

Unpublished letter to Gordon Ball: March 1970.

To Penelope Creeley:

For "Love Comes Quietly" by Robert Creeley; and for an unpublished email from Robert Creeley to Gordon Ball.

To Barry Miles:

For his journals.

To Alan Brooks:

For his two letters to Gordon Ball: summer 1970.

To Stella Jane:

For correspondence from Candy O'Brien to Gordon Ball: January, February, March, April, and May 1969.

To Da Capo Press:

For correspondence in *The Letters of Allen Ginsberg*:
* From Allen Ginsberg to Mrs. La Salle: May 9, 1968; to Herbert Huncke: February 16, 1969; to David Kennedy: July 16, 1969.

To HarperCollins:

To reprint from the following poems from *Collected Poems of Allen Ginsberg 1947–1997*: "Pertussin"; "On Neal's Ashes"; "Easter Sunday,"; "Independence Day"; "Friday the Thirteenth"; "Death on All Fronts"; and "Ecologue."

To Duke University Press:

To reprint from "Book 1" in *Gunslinger*, Edward Dorn, p. 3. Copyright 1989, Edward Dorn. All rights reserved. Reprinted by permission of the publisher, Duke University Press.

To Judith Lief, the Peter Orlovsky Trust:

For "Second Poem" and "Don't Bite Please" by Peter Orlovsky; and for unpublished correspondence from Peter Orlovsky to Gordon Ball: July 1971; June 19, 1972.

To Carolyn Karcher:

For September 1970 correspondence.

To Bloomsbury USA:

For correspondence from Allen Ginsberg to Louis and Edith Ginsberg, December 7, 1968; from Allen Ginsberg to Louis Ginsberg, January 31, 1969. Copyright © 2001 by Allen Ginsberg and Louis Ginsberg. From *Family Business: Two Lives in Letters and Poetry* by Allen Ginsberg and Louis Ginsberg. Reprinted by permission of Bloomsbury USA.

Earlier versions of several chapters appeared in the chapbook "Scenes from *East Hill Farm: Seasons with Allen Ginsberg*," published in 2007 by Beat Scene Press.